Security in the Cyber Age

Cyberspace is essential for socializing, learning, shopping, and just about everything in modern life. Despite the importance of cyberspace, there is also a dark side where subnational, transnational, and international actors are challenging the ability of sovereign governments to provide a secure environment for their citizens. Criminal groups hold businesses and local governments hostage through ransomware, foreign intelligence services steal intellectual property and conduct influence operations, governments attempt to rewrite Internet Protocols to facilitate censorship, and militaries prepare to use cyberspace operations in wars. *Security in the Cyber Age* breaks down how cyberspace works, analyzes how state and nonstate actors exploit vulnerabilities in cyberspace, and provides ways to improve cybersecurity. Written by a computer scientist and a national security scholar-practitioner, the book offers technological, policy, and ethical ways to protect cyberspace. Its interdisciplinary approach and engaging style make the book accessible to the lay audience as well as computer science and political science students.

DEREK S. REVERON is Chair of the National Security Affairs Department at the US Naval War College in Newport, Rhode Island, Faculty Affiliate of the Belfer Center for Science and International Affairs, and Lecturer in Extension at Harvard University. He specializes in strategy development, national security challenges, and US defense policy. He served as a governor-appointed commissioner on the Rhode Island Cybersecurity Commission. His published work examines US foreign policy and defense strategy.

JOHN E. SAVAGE is the An Wang Professor Emeritus of Computer Science at Brown University. He is a fellow of the American Association for the Advancement of Science, the Association for Computing Machinery, and the Institute of Electrical and Electronics Engineers and a Guggenheim Fellow. He served as a Jefferson Science Fellow in the US State Department, a professorial fellow at the EastWest Institute, and a member of the Rhode Island Cybersecurity Commission. He has published over a hundred research articles and two books on theoretical computer science, has coauthored a book on computer literacy, and has coedited a book on Very Large Scale Integration (VLSI) and parallel systems. He has given more than 185 invited presentations worldwide.

Security in the Cyber Age

An Introduction to Policy and Technology

Derek S. Reveron
US Naval War College

John E. Savage
Brown University

CAMBRIDGE
UNIVERSITY PRESS

CAMBRIDGE
UNIVERSITY PRESS

Shaftesbury Road, Cambridge CB2 8EA, United Kingdom

One Liberty Plaza, 20th Floor, New York, NY 10006, USA

477 Williamstown Road, Port Melbourne, VIC 3207, Australia

314–321, 3rd Floor, Plot 3, Splendor Forum, Jasola District Centre, New Delhi – 110025, India

103 Penang Road, #05–06/07, Visioncrest Commercial, Singapore 238467

Cambridge University Press is part of Cambridge University Press & Assessment, a department of the University of Cambridge.

We share the University's mission to contribute to society through the pursuit of education, learning and research at the highest international levels of excellence.

www.cambridge.org
Information on this title: www.cambridge.org/9781009308595

DOI: 10.1017/9781009308564

First published 2024

A catalogue record for this publication is available from the British Library

A Cataloging-in-Publication data record for this book is available from the Library of Congress

ISBN 978-1-009-30859-5 Hardback
ISBN 978-1-009-30858-8 Paperback

The triumph of the industrial arts will advance the cause of civilization more rapidly than its warmest advocates could have hoped, and contribute to the permanent prosperity and strength of the country far more than the most splendid victories of successful war.

Charles Babbage, inventor of the programmable computer

Contents

Boxes

History Matters

Preface

The modern world has become more complex and less predictable over the last century. The world population doubled, radio and television emerged, and the airplane and the programmable electronic computer were invented. The transistor, which is both an amplifier and a switch, and the integrated circuit, which puts billions of transistors on a single chip, were invented, making computers and smartphones affordable and ubiquitous. Fiber-optic cables and communication satellites provided for global communications. Advances in computer science led to new ways to move data that sparked the information revolution, creating cyberspace and transforming how people lead their daily lives, corporations execute operations, and governments deliver services and function.

Cyberspace is essential for socializing, learning, shopping, and just about everything in modern life but also has become a dangerous place. Almost every day there are reports of major cyber incidents. These include businesses and local governments being held hostage through ransomware, foreign intelligence services stealing intellectual property to further national industries, governments attempting to rewrite the foundational protocol of the Internet to facilitate censorship, and militaries preparing to use cyber operations in future wars. One of the more ominous consequences of cyberspace is the possibility of undermining nuclear deterrence or of governments engaging in cyber conflict, where belligerent countries attack power grids, telecommunications networks, and banking systems, bringing conflict to individuals' devices and doorsteps.

Cyberspace is also a place of rich potential. Global communications are now commonplace, vast quantities of knowledge are at our fingertips, and enormous amounts of computational power are readily available to work on complex problems such as gene sequencing or assessing climate change. Further, artificial intelligence helps make sense of large datasets, creating new opportunities for businesses and new types of work as it displaces existing work. This is an exciting time but one with many hurdles. The challenge for humanity is to harness cyberspace's new technologies and limit its misuses so that its full potential can be realized, enabling security for every citizen, community, and country. This book starts to chart an interdisciplinary course to help students conceptualize and understand security in the modern cyber age.

One of the authors of this book is from the national security policy sphere and the other is a computer scientist with experience in the national security sector. We both served on the Rhode Island Cybersecurity Commission. Our goal is to facilitate communication across the divide that normally characterizes the technological and policy communities. *Security in the Cyber Age* considers the current and future threats in cyberspace, discusses various approaches to advance and defend national interests in cyberspace, and posits a way to improve national security in the cyber age. Fundamentally, the book establishes a coherent framework for understanding how cyberspace has become an important venue for international security by exploring the technological, policy, social, and economic dimensions of cyberspace.

The book provides a comprehensive treatment of security in the modern cyber age. Portions of the book can be used for undergraduate cybersecurity policy courses without prerequisites. To achieve this goal technical subjects are introduced with attention to concepts and terminology. The book also has enough advanced material and references for it to be useful at the advanced undergraduate and early graduate levels. The goal is to teach computer science students to appreciate the national security implications of computer science and political science students to apply national security ideas to cyberspace. The book is also written for the layperson who needs a broad understanding of these issues.

Acknowledgments

A work like this has been in the making for decades. Our students at Brown University, Harvard University, and the US Naval War College all played a small part in shaping our thinking on how to analyze the interaction between computer science and the social sciences. As we tried to highlight throughout this book, improving cybersecurity is a team sport for educators, technologists, and policy analysts; no single discipline or field can provide the solutions we need to realize the benefits of cyberspace. Faculty members need books that can explain how cyberspace works, analyze how state and nonstate actors exploit vulnerabilities in cyberspace, and provide frameworks in which to explore ways to improve security in cyberspace. We hope this book is a small contribution to this effort.

Throughout our writing process, several colleagues were generous with their time. They reviewed chapters, contributed ideas, and shared resources. While any errors or misguided ideas are our own, we thank Hank Brightman, Mary Brooks, David Cooper, Jeremy Davis, Jeremy Francis, Nick Gvosdev, Anna Hayes, Chuck Houston, Vasileios Kermelis, Steve Knott, James Kraska, Roberta Lopes da Cruz Antonio, Ryan Maness, Bruce McConnell, Michael Miner, Tyler Moore, David Polatty, Mike Rizzotti, Terry Roehrig, Jeff Rogg, David Sanger, Jacquelyn Schneider, Paul Smith, Willem Speckmann, Judith Strotz, Dana Struckman, Fred Turner, and Heidi von Stein. John is grateful to Brown University for providing him with the opportunity to spend a year in the US State Department as a Jefferson Science Fellow and to teach a course in this area. He is also very grateful to the dozens of undergraduate teaching assistants who staffed his course in this area during the 10 years that he taught it. We also thank the Cambridge University Press team and especially Katie Leach who helped us realize our goals to make these ideas widely available.

We thank Christopher Savage who created the cover image using Midjourney and are grateful to him for his permission to use it. The cover is testament to the utility of artificial intelligence and the creativity of those who can harness it.

These are our personal views and, in Derek's case, the views expressed in this publication are those of the author and do not necessarily reflect the official policy or position of the US Naval War College, the Department of the Navy, the Department of Defense, or the US government. The public release clearance of this publication by the Department of Defense does not imply Department of Defense endorsement or factual accuracy of the material.

Introduction

The Internet is for everyone – but it won't be if legislation around the
world creates a thicket of incompatible laws that hinder the growth of
electronic commerce, stymie the protection of intellectual property, and
stifle freedom of expression and the development of market economies.
Let us dedicate ourselves to the creation of a global legal framework
in which laws work across national boundaries to reinforce the upward
spiral of value that Internet is capable of creating.
Vinton Cerf (1999), one of the pioneers of the Internet

THE PROMISE AND PERILS OF CYBERSPACE

Cyberspace is woven into the fabric of modern life. It transcends boundaries,
is dynamic, offers low barriers to entry, affords a certain amount of anonymity,
enables mass surveillance by governments and corporations, and is essential
for just about everything. Within just the past few decades, people everywhere
have become as dependent on this online world for their daily activities as they
are dependent on the physical world for human activities. UN secretary general
António Guterres sees information technology as socially transforming and
as integral to human prosperity and well-being since "farmers can monitor
prices, refugees can let their families know they are safe, and health workers
can check a patient's status or respond to emergencies" (Guterres, 2017).

Guterres' point is clear and easy to see when the network is down, cell phone
calls are dropped, or a malware crashes your device. In many cases, daily routines are broken, frustrations rise, and work stops. Alternatively, reflect on how
the COVID-19 pandemic forced individuals to physically isolate, yet people
were able to find some normalcy online through remote learning, telework-
ing, shopping, streaming entertainment, and engaging through social media.[1]

---

[1] According to a Pew Research Center poll, 90 percent of Americans say the Internet has been
essential or important to them during the pandemic. Forty percent said they used digital technology or the Internet in new ways (Mcclain et al., 2021).

The forced shift online accelerated convergence between the physical and virtual worlds; these changes persisted when the pandemic ended.

From a technical perspective, cyberspace encompasses the vast network of interconnected computers that span the globe, the equipment attached to the network, the physical infrastructure of fiber-optic cables on land and below the sea, satellites in orbit, and the information that traverses and is stored in it.[2] The Internet is global, but governments can and do exert control in various ways. As former Harvard professor Joseph Nye, Jr. (2011, p. 22) sees it, cyberspace follows the "political laws of sovereign jurisdiction and control... [but] political practices ... make jurisdictional control difficult." For example, China's ban on Bitcoin did not erase Chinese citizens' digital wallets but forced them to relocate their Bitcoin to servers outside of China. Pakistan's occasional ban on YouTube requires its citizens to use a virtual private network to connect through a country where YouTube is not blocked. This inability of governments to exert absolute sovereign control is due to the open and distributed nature of the Internet as well as the prioritization of ease of access over security. Yet security matters.

Security in cyberspace, or cybersecurity, is the safeguarding of software and hardware, ensuring reliability of telecommunication pathways, and protecting information that moves in cyberspace from theft (loss of confidentiality) and manipulation (integrity) while remaining accessible (availability). Once the sole domain of information technology professionals, cybersecurity became a national security issue in response to the efforts of foreign powers to steal intellectual property, to interfere in national elections, and to compromise critical infrastructure, opening it to future attacks. Cybersecurity also means protecting equipment from damage of all kinds, including physical attack and electromagnetic disruption through naturally occurring solar flares or weaponized electromagnetic pulse weapons. Scholar James Lewis and colleagues (Lewis et al., 2012, p. 113) add internet governance to the cybersecurity list since "an outcome where the Internet becomes more secure but less free would be a setback for the U.S." Cybersecurity is now a concern for policymakers with implications for users everywhere.

Cyberspace opens apparently limitless horizons, but it is also a place of peril. Almost every day, there are major data breaches, new computer viruses, and other cyber incidents that remind us that the cyber ecosystem is fragile. Businesses and local governments are being held hostage via ransomware, intellectual property is stolen by foreign intelligence services to further

---

[2] In her important book, Janet Abbate wrote "the transcendence of geographic distance has come to seem an inherent part of computer technology" (Abbate, 1999).

national industries, governments target dissident groups and shut-off access to cyberspace, and militaries have developed cyber commands that are preparing to conduct cyber operations in future wars.

With a knowledge of adversarial intentions and US capabilities, President Biden said as much: "I think it's more than likely we're going to end up, if we end up in a war – a real shooting war with a major power – it's going to be as a consequence of a cyber breach of great consequence and it's increasing exponentially, the capabilities" (White House 2021b). Exploitations of critical infrastructure such as power, telecommunications, or banking could be such a trigger. We can see the effect during natural disasters such as hurricanes or major snowstorms that shut down electricity transmission and internet service; we do not need to wait for targeted ransomware campaigns against internet service providers or destructive malware attacks against a water treatment plant to see the effects. Organizations and governments must generate greater resilience in the systems on which we all depend.

Dave Weinstein (2021), New Jersey's first cybersecurity director, writing on the impact of cyber threats on critical infrastructure, said, "Security was no longer simply a matter of gates, guards and guns [or physical security]. It had become a matter of bits and bytes [or cybersecurity]." His observation extends thinking about the physical security of critical infrastructure to cyberspace where a security mindset needs further development to appreciate the cyber equivalent of badged access, fences, and security cameras. Then commander of US Cyber Command General Paul Nakasone (2019) saw "[c]yberspace [as] a domain in which opponents can attain strategic results without using armed force" and the Command's historian Michael Warner (2020) said that "cyberspace has itself altered the sources of strategic power that opponents can 'touch' by digital means." These ideas are shaping how governments in the United States and around the world incorporate cyberspace operations as a tool of power to defend and advance national interests. Some scholars prefer to frame the cyber challenges in the context of competition rather than conflict since operations to date are largely below the threshold of an armed attack; nevertheless, the cumulative consequences of these types of activities have important implications for cybersecurity during peacetime (Chesney & Smeets, 2020).

The perils of cyberspace are not limited to theft, disruption, and conflict; they also include the existential threat of nuclear war, as noted by the Bulletin of Atomic Scientists, an organization founded in 1945 by those who developed the first atomic weapons. It publishes the Doomsday Clock, initially designed to dramatize its concerns for nuclear war but which now includes climate change and cybersecurity. Its Science and Security Board, which includes 13 Nobel laureates, and its Board of Sponsors set the minute hand close to midnight, adjusting it annually, to reflect their perceived changes in threats to humanity. In January 2020 the boards moved the hand from 2 minutes to 100 seconds to midnight, the closest it has been since the clock was introduced in 1947, saying that the threats "are compounded by a threat multiplier, *cyber-enabled information warfare*, that undercuts society's ability to respond" (Mecklin, 2020, emphasis added).

Not all agree with an assessment of a future filled with peril. Political scientists Brandon Valeriano and Ryan Maness (2015) note that a "cyber conflict between states is rare, is restrained, and can be a tool in the domain of espionage rather than a demonstration of raw power." Others such as scholars Robert Chesney and Max Smeets posed the provocative question, "cyber war is out. But what is in?" They note that "scholars now generally recognize the limits of cyber war as a useful concept and/or framework for interpreting the strategic activity taking place in and through cyberspace" (Chesney & Smeets, 2020).

We too are wary of threat inflation, but countries such as Russia, Iran, China, and North Korea have attacked power grids, telecommunications networks, pipelines, and banking systems, thereby bringing disruptions directly to individual doorsteps. Further, the research by cyber-skeptics has largely been conducted in an era of relative peace among countries such as the United States, China, Russia, and India. If the peace breaks down and societies continue to deepen their reliance on information technology and exploit the benefits of artificial intelligence (AI), adversaries can attack their rival's critical infrastructure.

As new technologies come online, they represent significant promise for deepening society's connections in cyberspace and obviating physical presence for some activities. Improving encryption technology will continue to globalize businesses; 5G wireless communication with its potential for very high data rates will revolutionize mobile platforms, fulfilling the promises of connecting everything through an Internet of Things; autonomous vehicles will proliferate in high-speed environments; and augmented reality and virtual reality hold promise for creating the metaverse.

These are exciting times, but each new breakthrough seems to create unintended vulnerabilities that can undermine cybersecurity and produce societal-level impacts. These impacts can range from inconvenient, such as stopping payment processing systems at a major retail corporation, to serious, such as terminating power for a city in the middle of a cold winter, shutting down an airline's operations stranding travelers, or corrupting machine learning through erroneous data that undermines autonomous driving. The impacts are often temporary but can be very costly.

It is important to remember that cyberspace reflects humanity's best aspirations but is limited by humanity's fallibility and governments' malicious uses of technology. Popular science fiction portrayals of the useful AI or better-than-human robot are fiction. While algorithms can help humans make sense of large data sets to guide decision-making, their programming reflects human values and are known to exhibit human biases. For example, machine learning systems trained on historical data can exhibit racism. We will return to this point in Chapter 9 but warn the reader that all human inventions are at risk of incorporating bias, which also applies to AI. Returning to Secretary General Guterres (2019), "Artificial intelligence has the potential to accelerate progress towards a dignified life, in peace and prosperity for all people [... but] there are also serious challenges and ethical issues which must be taken into account, including cybersecurity, human rights and privacy." This serves as a good reminder that we must temper the promises of technology with actual outcomes balanced with society's goals.

It is easy to see computers as magic boxes designed to improve society, but these are human inventions constantly in need of updates to improve performance and ensure they meet human needs. These regular updates often produce new vulnerabilities that can be exploited to gain system access, resulting in data theft, system manipulation, or system capture until ransoms are paid. The challenge for humanity is to understand the limits of the technologies of cyberspace and control their misuses so that their full potential can be realized. This is the reason this book was written by a computer scientist and a national security policy analyst. We bring our combined knowledge and perspectives together in pursuit of this challenge to improve thinking about cybersecurity.

A SHARED RESPONSIBILITY FOR SECURITY

Because cyberspace is ubiquitous, cybersecurity must be a universal concern. To quote cybersecurity expert Bruce Schneier (2017), "Computer security is now everything security." Thus, to obtain local, domestic, and international security, every concerned citizen, politician, and business leader must have at least a minimal command of the elements of cybersecurity.

Computer science experts have the lead on explaining the technical aspect of cybersecurity, but humanities and social science experts understand human motivations to exploit vulnerabilities, the challenges of addressing collective action problems, and the role governments can play in either creating norms or undermining individual human rights. Those who code and design need a grounding in ethics to appreciate the impact of their work on society.

Sociologists can help explain the impact of social media, political scientists can explore the international dimensions of the cybersecurity problem, such as norms and laws, and the economists can examine the costs of cyber exploitation or barriers to cooperation to propose methods of improving cybersecurity. Those who legislate and regulate need an understanding of all these issues. When scholarship from the social sciences and the humanities informs legislators, better policies and laws are possible that impact how information and communications technology companies operate.

THE MOTIVATION FOR THIS BOOK

The challenges of cybersecurity are multidimensional, international, and hard. It is for this reason that the two us, one a political scientist and the other a computer scientist, have come together to write a book that strives to bridge the technology/policy divides characterizing this field. While the problems are hard, we humans have repeatedly shown the imagination and determination to solve hard problems. We did that quite well with the nuclear threat where, despite arms races and technological advances, the last 75 years have been free from nuclear war. We need to repeat this experience with this new challenge to ensure the next 75 years are free of major conflicts that disrupt cyberspace.

Our book is designed to help readers acquire a solid understanding of cybersecurity policy and technology issues. In addition to the main text, we include sidebars highlighting topics meant to inspire readers to explore the roles of history and policy in cybersecurity, appreciate significant cyberspace operations, and understand software exploits that have paralyzed companies, influenced electorates, and created distrust among governments. Chapters conclude with topics for discussion that offer avenues for future research. A glossary is included to provide definitions of important terms originating in computer science and political science.

We are inspired by Ted Nelson (1974, p. 2), who wrote at the dawn of cyberspace in 1974: "It is imperative for many reasons that the appalling gap between public and computer insiders be closed. As the saying goes, war is too important to be left to the generals. Guardianship of the computer can no longer be left to a priesthood." As career academics, we are both members of the "priesthood," but our message is simple and clear: Cybersecurity is more than an engineering or computer science problem; it is a team sport that requires engagement by technologists, educators, lawyers, policy analysts, policymakers, the private sector, and users. The absence of one stakeholder leads to imbalances evident in social media exploitation by violent extremist organizations, ransomware attacks by criminal groups, economic espionage by governments, and influence operations by foreign intelligence services as well as bad government policy that inhibits innovation.

CHAPTER OVERVIEWS

Chapter 1 summarizes the dramatic but unexpected societal and international security changes that have accompanied the introduction of the Internet. It also provides a quick introduction to packet-based switching that underpins the Internet as well as the World Wide Web, which transformed the Internet from a technical wonder into a very useful societal tool.

Chapter 2 introduces the reader to the hardware and software of modern computers. It begins by putting computation in a historical context, thereby showing that computation has been a concern of humanity for millennia. Surprisingly, modern computers have been foreshadowed by much older calculating devices. The chapter also examines operating systems for the efficient management of computer resources and hardware and software abstractions helpful for understanding computers, such as file systems, virtual memories, and high-level programming languages. The important topics of password security, social engineering, and malicious software are introduced, along with techniques to find and remove malware. Although one might expect that hardware would not exhibit security vulnerabilities, that is false. This is illustrated by a subtle bug introduced in the 1990s to make computers run faster by allowing some instructions to be executed out of order but only shown in 2018 to be a serious security hazard.

Chapter 3 briefly contrasts classic telephone circuit-switched communication with the more flexible packet-switched Internet. It introduces the domain name system, in effect the telephone directory for the Internet, and describes how domain names are translated into binary addresses. It explains basic internet communication protocols, that is, how computers "talk" to one another by sending packets of bits over the Internet, and describes the algorithms that route packets along different paths between sources and destinations. Packet routing helps to make packet communication robust in the face of network disruptions, which might occur because of an earthquake or during a conflict.

The chapter also introduces a variety of encryption methods, focusing on public-key cryptography, which is widely used for secure communications that enable online shopping, banking transactions, and privacy. It also introduces digital signatures, the equivalent of a human signature, for authentication of the sender of messages. Finally, it examines a major threat to secure public-key cryptography, namely, quantum computing. If large quantum computers become a reality, common methods of encryption will have to be abandoned. Research is underway to find replacement encryption methods, but the principles introduced will assist readers to make sense of next generation encryption.

Chapter 4 explores the human dimensions of cybersecurity. It describes the steps that nation-state attackers use to penetrate an organization through phishing and social engineering as well as responses that defenders can take to protect themselves. These include hardening facilities, controlling remote access, educating security personnel and users on security hazards, using reputational services, and running an effective security operations center. Because people play a central role in cybersecurity, the chapter also examines limitations on human judgment, captured in the phrase "cognitive biases," where preconceived notions and biases shape how we organize and respond to challenges. The chapter closes with discussions of applications of economics to cybersecurity and cybersecurity risk evaluation.

Over the last two decades, dozens of governments have incorporated cyberspace operations into national security thinking and developed military cyber commands. Governments are developing cyber power, which gives them a new tool to operationalize their capabilities resident in intelligence agencies.[3] We explore the impact of cyber power on strategic thinking in Chapter 5. Cybersecurity as national security will continue to grow especially considering the competition between the United States and China, where each side seeks advantage in diplomatic, economic, military, and cyber spheres. Consequently, improving cybersecurity requires a public–private partnership and a whole-of-government effort.

In Chapter 6, we explore in detail the attempts by governments to regulate cyberspace. National governments are increasingly assertive and exert control over security, privacy, and content. This is an important departure especially in democratic-capitalist countries that have been largely laissez-faire with respect to cyberspace.[4] The chapter considers these moves at the domestic regulatory level and examines how corporations, civil society, and citizens are responding. Fundamentally, the chapter addresses the role governments play in cybersecurity and foretells the beginning of more governmental intervention in cyberspace, such as mandatory data compromise reporting. Further, as certain countries promote their telecommunication companies globally, cyberspace

---

[3] Valeriano and Maness (2015, p. 28) define cyber power as "the ability to control and apply typical forms of control and domination in cyberspace."

[4] "Cyberspace has the potential to be the most fully, and extensively, regulated space that we have ever known — anywhere, at any time in our history. It has the potential to be the antithesis of a space of freedom" (Lessig, 1998).

becomes the means to increase global surveillance, which raises new policy and security issues.

Chapter 7 focuses on the impact of international cooperation in cyberspace. By design, the Internet is global, and engineering ignores traditional sovereignty concerns such as citizenship, borders, and domestic law, as discussed in Chapter 6. However, running against domestic regulation, and the consequent possible internet fragmentation, are several international efforts to cooperate in cyberspace through various stakeholder and multilateral models that include the United Nations, European Union, and the North Atlantic Treaty Organization (NATO). The latter, then composed of 30 countries from North America and Europe, issued a communique in 2021 pushing back against authoritarian uses of the Internet: "We will promote a free, open, peaceful, and secure cyberspace, and further pursue efforts to enhance stability and reduce the risk of conflict by supporting international law and voluntary norms of responsible state behaviour in cyberspace" (NATO, 2021). In 2022, 60 countries, including many NATO members, adopted "A Declaration for the Future of the Internet." Applying human rights to cyberspace was among the principles adopted (White House, 2022). To explore these issues, the chapter reviews forms of internet governance enabling technical, legal, and policy cooperation across boundaries.

Chapter 8 explores the application of international law and norms in cyberspace. It examines law that governs the use of force in international politics, the types of weapons that can be developed and used in armed conflict, how combatants engage in conflict on the battlefield, and when individuals can be held criminally accountable for violating these rules. Although a fair amount of effort has been devoted to this task, Secretary General Guterres said,

[W]e do not have clarity on legal frameworks on this. I mean, there is a general principle that international law applies in cyberspace, but it is not clear how international humanitarian law applies, and these other laws of war. The self-defense principle of the UN—how does it apply in this context? When is it war, when is it not war in these situations? (quoted in Thompson, 2020).

Some governments would classify a cyber operation as equivalent to a use of force or form of warfare only if it produces physical destruction or death, while others, such as France (2019), declare a cyber operation to be "an attack whe[n] the targeted equipment or systems no longer provide the service for which they were implemented" or functionality is lost. Finally, the chapter considers how to develop and encourage the adoption of cyberspace norms for governmental behavior and set expectations for states to regulate illicit cyber activity within their borders.

Chapter 9 takes up AI and ethics. Beginning in Ancient Greece with the first autonomous machines, this chapter presents a brief history of AI. It then examines excessively ambitious expectations in the twentieth century for the potential for AI and the adverse consequences for research funding that resulted, now dubbed the "AI Winter." New technologies, especially those with elevated expectations of AI, often draw a lot of positive speculation, some of it misplaced. The chapter further describes these technologies in realistic terms, describing their enormous potential while advising caution on deployment in situations that put valuable resources, such as human life, at risk. It also reviews technologies that were explored in developing AI, such as logic, symbol manipulation, problem-solving, expert systems, and machine learning based largely on artificial neural networks.

The chapter highlights remarkable successes of machine learning as well as its weaknesses and limitations. These include the creation of "deep fakes," which have the potential for political disruption, and the introduction of biases in decision-making when machine learning systems are trained on historical data. The chapter also examines "adversarial attacks" in which very slight changes in an input can change the classification of an image. Such attacks show that AI technologies can create life-threatening situations since algorithms can exhibit biases and/or be deceived. The chapter discusses applications of AI technologies to robots and issues caveats for their use. These include ethical issues that arise with the use of lethal autonomous weapons systems, such as armed drones. The United Nations, nongovernmental organizations (NGOs), governments, and corporations are addressing this problem. The chapter closes with a discussion of the application of AI technologies to cybersecurity.

Without a doubt, there is much uncertainty about the future of cybersecurity, a topic we explore in Chapter 10. The uncertainty is based on technological change but also on how society integrates new technologies into political, social, economic, and national security practices. Further, there is no one single way to bring security to cyberspace. Instead, we need new ways to think about cybersecurity that move beyond traditional national security paradigms that place the military and intelligence services at the forefront. As scholar Nina Kollars (2020) reminds us, "privileging states in thinking about cyber is folly. It distracts us from resolving hard policy issues by reducing social media's dysfunctional influence to Russian meddling or major systemic vulnerabilities in data management to Chinese intellectual property theft."

From its humble beginnings, the Internet has evolved through commercial activities into a global network that reflects different political systems, economic drivers, and social norms. Governments are moving past laissez-faire approaches to the information technology sector and using national and international institutions and practices to increase regulation and intervention in cyberspace. Likewise, individuals, corporations, and NGOs are active in defining cyberspace.

Chapter 11 addresses the question of leadership in the cyber age. Leadership requires many important skills, to include the ability to make good forecasts on which policy may rest. The chapter examines research by Professor Philip Tetlock of the University of Pennsylvania to identify individuals who are consistently superior in forecasting, which he calls the Good Judgment Project. In multiple competitions his teams have performed at least 30 percent better than intelligence analysts with access to classified information. Tetlock has summarized his observations in "Ten Commandments for Aspiring Superforecasters." These are important lessons for those who work in cybersecurity.

CONCLUSIONS

This book explores myriad challenges in cyberspace and ways national security professionals and computer scientists can address them. As the online and physical worlds become closer over the next 20 years, new and unforeseen challenges will emerge. But one fact is certain: Cybersecurity will remain a key feature of the national and human security landscape, and all governments will struggle to keep pace, just as all citizens will feel compelled to protect their individual activity online (Reveron & Mahoney-Norris, 2019). This overarching cyber, or informational, dimension clearly enables national security as much as it may disrupt it, which aptly reflects the realities of globalization processes that are transforming our world.

While it is easy to be pessimistic about the future of cybersecurity, we take heart in that both the national security and computer science communities have awakened to the challenge of cyber insecurity. While security is always a cat-and-mouse game, academics, governments, and corporations actively seek ways to improve cybersecurity through education, establishment of norms of behavior, and employment of best practices, both individually and collectively. This book is designed to help the interested reader by providing a solid, cogent introduction to the policies and technologies of cyberspace.

Chapter 1 provides an overview of the threats in cyberspace and presents a conceptual framework for the other chapters in this book that examine specific threats, responses to the threats, and international perspectives on cybersecurity. Fundamentally, the chapter illustrates how the convergence of the online and physical worlds make understanding cyberspace essential for all.

DISCUSSION TOPICS

1. Give and justify examples of situations when cybersecurity becomes national security.
2. Describe and justify steps that information technology professionals and policymakers can take to collaborate more effectively.
3. Analyze the statement in the chapter epigraph by Vinton Cerf, and either defend it or argue against it.

1

The Emergence of Cyberspace and Its Implications

We no longer have to debate whether we will fight wars in cyberspace, and to some, it may seem crazy that we ever had to have that discussion in the first place. Cyberspace is a recognized domain of warfare, and for better or worse, our service members and civilians are engaged with our adversaries on a daily basis.
US Representative Jim Langevin (2022), Subcommittee on Cyber, Innovative Technologies, and Information Systems

BROADLY SPEAKING, subnational, transnational, and international actors are challenging the ability of sovereign governments to provide a secure environment for their citizens, the most basic function of the state. This is true on land, air, sea, space, and cyberspace. However, in democratic states, when it comes to security in cyberspace, government is either absent or follows information and communications technology (ICT) companies that generally pursue global business models for the benefit of its owners and corporate boards, rather than national interests. The gap between threats faced by ICT companies and government responses generates security deficits, which are evidenced through regular reports of cyber insecurity. And in nondemocratic countries, governments compel ICT companies to restrict basic rights of privacy and reinforce authoritarian rule through content moderation and disclosure of encryption keys.

These dynamics illustrate that the array of cyberspace threats is broad and vast. Transnational organized criminal groups steal identities and conduct financial crimes; terrorist organizations recruit fighters and promote their destructive deeds; countries employ cyber tools for domestic repression and international espionage while laying the groundwork for military operations in cyberspace; and nations worry about disruptions to their critical infrastructure imperiling society when basic services cease and disruptions of access to vital data result from cyber blockades (Russell, 2014) (see Table 1.1). The more devices individuals use to interact in society, the more

Table 1.1 US critical infrastructure sectors

Chemical	Commercial facilities
Communications	Critical manufacturing
Dams sector	Defense industrial base
Emergency services	Energy
Financial services	Food and agriculture
Government facilities	Healthcare and public health
Information technology	Nuclear reactors, materials, and waste
Transportation systems	Water and wastewater

vulnerabilities bad actors can exploit, thus creating a cycle of dependency and vulnerability.

Cyber challenges cut across all dimensions of society and simultaneously cross into technological, political, economic, and social realms. Reinforced by intelligence assessments, public opinion polling in democratic countries places cyber insecurity as a leading national security challenge and a pressing national security concern for many governments. Facebook founder Mark Zuckerberg captured the complexity of this problem, saying, "Security isn't a problem you ever completely solve. We face sophisticated and well-funded adversaries, including nation states, that are always evolving and trying new attacks. But we're learning and improving quickly too, and we're investing heavily to keep people safe" (McMillan & Seetharaman, 2018).

Zuckerberg's comments capture the threats that exist in cyberspace yet acknowledge that ICT corporations are expected to contribute actively to improving security in cyberspace – something governments do not expect from other industries. For example, while manufacturing cars is subject to government regulation requiring seat belts and safety recalls, unless there are significant safety concerns, car manufacturers are not expected to license drivers or compel owners to perform routine maintenance of their products. In contrast, ICT corporations are expected to find and fix vulnerabilities by routinely updating their products through patches and alerting the public about vulnerabilities to improve their products after they are installed.

As the online and physical worlds continue to merge, new threats will develop that take advantage of the vulnerabilities inherent in the relatively open system we call cyberspace. When it comes to security, there is tension between the common free space that is the Internet and governments' attempts to police it or exploit it for surveillance. In the People's Republic of China, internet security is a tenet of public safety. In contrast, since 1996: "The policy of the United States [is] ... to promote the continued development of the Internet and other interactive computer services and other interactive media ... [and] preserve the vibrant and competitive free market that presently exists for the Internet and other interactive computer services, unfettered by Federal or State regulation" (Section 230 of the Communications Decency Act, n.d.-a, p. 230).

In short, hands-off or laissez-faire principles have guided the US federal government when addressing cybersecurity; Title 47 of the US Code (Telecommunications) addresses technical regulation such as the rules governing the laying of submarine cables, the granting of commercial licenses to use the electromagnetic spectrum, and the taxing of internet commerce. But there is no equivalent regulation for software standards akin to those that governments impose on auto manufacturing with fuel efficiency requirements, emissions limits, and safety features.

As think-tank scholar James Lewis and colleagues (Lewis et al., 2012, 113) wrote, "the original American view was that Internet governance should be weak and the role of government strictly proscribed, as this would empower innovation and allow an emerging global community to guide the new infrastructure. Security was largely ignored." However, there is a growing chorus within the US Congress to amend the law, but at the time of writing, outside of anti-hacking, generic anti-competitive laws, and limited breech disclosure requirements, cybersecurity regulation and law are sparse in the United States in deference to ICT companies.

There are privacy laws protecting citizens that are rooted in the US Constitution, but they are designed to protect individuals from government intrusion; constitutional protections do not apply between users and ICT companies. Yet privacy is too easily relinquished to corporations when users accept their terms of use when downloading an app or installing software, so there are some efforts to ensure users have the same basic rights in cyberspace that they enjoy in physical life.[1]

Responding to cybersecurity threats, Congress created the Office of the National Cyber Director within the Executive Office of the President in 2020.[2] This created a single voice on cybersecurity issues reporting to the president and confirmed by the Senate. Chris Inglis, who served as the deputy director of the National Security Agency, filled the post from 2021 to 2023 as the country's first national cyber director with responsibility to "coordinate the defense of civilian agencies and review agencies' budgets" (Nakashima, 2021). President Biden also appointed Anne Neuberger, formerly cybersecurity director at the

---

[1] Rising privacy concerns moved cybersecurity to the national security agenda, and presidents started to address cybersecurity in the 2000s (Obama, 2013; White House, 2018).
[2] See Section 1752 of the National Defense Authorization Act for Fiscal Year 2021 (Smith, 2021).

National Security Agency, as the deputy national security adviser for cyber and emerging technology (Riley, 2021). Finally, in 2022, the Department of Homeland Security created the Cyber Safety Board to examine significant cybersecurity incidents in a similar way to the National Transportation Safety Board, which investigates train derailments and plane crashes. These are initial signs that the US government may alter its laissez-faire approach, but there is still no national cybersecurity law comparable to the European Union's General Data Protection Regulation, adopted in 2018, or the Digital Services Act and Digital Markets Act, adopted in 2022.

We explore the ways governments around the world are active in regulating cyberspace, but suffice it to say, today the European Union protects individuals' privacy very deliberately. The European Union offers its citizens the right to be forgotten (excluded from search results) and imposes steep penalties for data loss. In contrast, China and Russia seek to isolate their networks and users from the global system and use technology as a form of authoritarian control. While there is some regulation in the United States, especially with respect to criminal uses of computers, the focus is on technical regulation. Content regulation runs against US civil liberties, such as free speech, and US foreign policy, which seeks a free and open cyberspace. Mathematician and cybersecurity scholar Susan Landau (2016a) underscores that "privacy versus surveillance in Internet communications can be viewed as a complex set of economic tradeoffs – for example, obtaining free services in exchange for a loss of privacy; and protecting communications in exchange for a more expensive, and thus less frequently used, set of government investigative techniques – and choices abound."

The absence of a comprehensive federal US cybersecurity law today relative to other democracies in Europe is striking since several US states have undertaken actions for their own residents. Traditional law applies in cyberspace, but some states have enacted new laws to reinforce applicability in cyberspace. For example, California enacted an internet privacy law in 2020, Washington State took legislative steps to protect against biases in facial recognition software, and Virginia followed California with a consumer privacy law. The new laws are grounded in the Constitution, which prohibits government from violating privacy rights, and are attempting to extend this principle to protect citizens from corporations who collect data on users with their unwitting participation when they agree to terms of use.

While this book presents general principles for cybersecurity, US actions and inactions on cybersecurity will have global effects since decisions made in Washington, DC, and the US technology sector will affect users around the world. However, the national policy gridlock as of 2023 that has forestalled a

> **Policy Matters 1.1 Internet privacy in California**
>
> The state of California has long played an important role in cyberspace. For example, several California universities were among the earliest sites to be connected to the ARPANET, an experimental packet-switched network launched by the US Department of Defense in 1969 and renamed the Internet in 1983. Silicon Valley in northern California emerged as a hotbed of innovation in cyberspace and is now home to such companies as Apple, Google, and Facebook. California passed the first US Consumer Privacy Act in 2018, which became operational in 2020. It allows individuals to request details on how companies use their individual data for commercial purposes and to opt out of a business's sale of their data.
>
> Source: California (2018)

comprehensive cybersecurity law in the United States creates a vacuum filled by other governments that will affect US users because it is more efficient for Google and other Internet-based companies to apply European privacy standards globally rather than just to those living in the European Union. We explore various ways governments are regulating companies and users in cyberspace in Chapter 6, but it is first important to review how and why the Internet was conceived as a global network.

1.1 THE EMERGENCE OF PACKET-SWITCHING

The Internet is the *network of networks* that is the backbone of cyberspace. It is a packet-switched network designed to connect computers by sending data packets between them. For intermittent computer-to-computer communications, this is more efficient than the circuit-switched telephone networks that provide dedicated channels between pairs of endpoints. Circuit-switched networks worked well for voice calls in the analog era where call volume was low and data transfer or streaming did not exist, but they do not efficiently support intermittent communication in the digital era.

In 1962, J. C. R. Licklider was hired by the Advanced Research Projects Agency (ARPA) of the Department of Defense as the first head of the ARPA's Information Processing Techniques Office (IPTO).[3] He brought with him a

---

[3] The ARPA was created by President Eisenhower in 1958 in response to the Soviet launch of Sputnik I in 1957. It is now known as the Defense Advanced Research Projects Agency.

vision that networks were needed to connect the very large and expensive computers of the day. Independently, in the very early 1960s, when Paul Baran, a RAND employee, was asked to devise a method of communication that could survive a nuclear attack, he wrote a comprehensive study for the US Air Force entitled *On Distributed Communications* (1964). At the time, the primary communication method was through circuit-switched communication systems that were highly centralized and therefore vulnerable. Baran's solution was to digitize a message, group the message bits into blocks, add source and destination addresses, and launch the blocks on a network that was capable of rerouting them in the event of a disruption and assembling them in order. In 1965, Donald Davies at the National Physical Laboratory in the United Kingdom independently developed and implemented the same concept, using the word "packet" to describe his blocks.

In 1967 Lawrence (Larry) Roberts, an electrical engineer, was hired by ARPA to be the IPTO program manager for a new computer network to be called ARPANET. He was charged with realizing the vision of Licklider. Roberts incorporated ideas from Baran and Davies into his plan for the network and contracted with Bolt, Beranek and Newman Inc. (BBN) to implement his plan for the new network by designing the interface messaging processor (IMP), a precursor to routers. Bob Kahn was one of the engineers on the BBN project.

Eventually, ARPANET became the first large-scale packet-switched network. With technical contributions from academia and the private sector, it became an important platform for experimentation on packet-based communication, bringing the ideas of Baran, Davies, BBN, and many others together. In the beginning, ARPANET was based on an open architecture where "the choice of any individual network technology was not dictated by a particular network architecture but rather could be selected freely by a provider and made to interwork with the other networks through a meta-level 'Internetworking Architecture'" (Leiner et al., 2009).

The primary ARPANET nodes were operational in 1969 when the first communication occurred between the University of California, Los Angeles, and the Stanford Research Institute. Other research nodes from California to Cambridge, Massachusetts, were later connected. Access to ARPANET had the effect of stimulating research on networking and network applications. New network protocols, that is, methods for organizing and transmitting data over networks, led to improved packet-switched networking. With the advent of personal computers in the mid-1970s, cyberspace began to grow and different networks in the United States and around the world emerged. Networks in other countries, however, did not attract the levels of funding the Department of Defense could provide. By 1980, ARPANET was widely available to

---

History Matters 1.1 Technology gap and the Cold War

At the end of World War II, the US economy accounted for a significant portion of all goods and services (gross domestic product) produced in the world. As Europe and Asia recovered, the lead slowly diminished and became evident in the Cold War. The Soviet Union shocked the world by orbiting the first satellite in space in 1957 (Sputnik I) and orbiting the first human in 1961. Both achievements, coupled with Soviet military modernization, signaled an apparent technology gap that became a major issue in the 1960 presidential election between Richard Nixon and John F. Kennedy, Jr.

When Kennedy assumed office in 1961, he pursued a national effort to revitalize US scientific and engineering activities built around the race to the moon. Kennedy told Congress on May 25, 1961, that the United States needed "to take a clearly leading role in space achievement" and "commit itself to achieving the goal, before this decade is out, of landing a man on the Moon and returning him safely to the earth" (Kennedy, 1961). While he did not see Neil Armstrong walk on the moon in 1969, Kennedy laid the groundwork with federal research and development spending that reached about 2 percent of gross domestic product in 1964 (Orszag, 2007). This had important impacts for the civilian space program led by the National Aeronautics and Space Administration, the defense industry, and ultimately the military establishment.

---

universities and research laboratories in the United States and a few other countries. The development of computers and the operation of the Internet are examined in detail in Chapters 2 and 3, but suffice it to say, the paradigm shift in the way data moved via packets rather than direct connections paved the way for the exponential growth in information technology (IT), new industries, and revolutions within old industries.

1.2 THE EXPERIMENTAL ARPANET PACKET-BASED NETWORK

The growth of cyberspace became important given the perception that the United States had fallen behind the Soviet Union in science and technology during the Cold War. As one of many efforts to revitalize US innovation, ARPA funded research on networking and time-shared computing, which is a technology that allows multiple users to use a single computer. The costs of computing were substantial, and ARPA paid to have specialized ARPANET computer equipment assembled so that the research community could join the network.[4]

As hardware developed and an interconnected network was created, new ways of communicating evolved, creating potential diverging pathways that could have led to noncompatible networks. In an example relevant today, to ensure that a file could be opened within both Microsoft Windows and macOS would require computer users to adopt a standard file format, such as .jpg or .pdf, so that users could collaborate without needing to use a common operating system or computer. In the Internet's early days, the same problem arose when US researchers on an ARPA machine wanted to connect with European researchers using machines connected to other networks. It was solved through the creation of international standards and protocols.

In 1974, electrical engineer Robert Kahn and computer scientist Vinton Cerf published the Transmission Control Protocol/Internet Protocol (TCP/IP), which forms the basic architecture of the Internet. IP is used to specify the source and destination addresses that are used for routing while TCP ensures that every packet reaches its destination. TCP/IP became critical to reliably connecting networks around the world and reinforcing the goal of a compatible network of networks; both Kahn and Cerf were later recognized with Presidential Medals of Freedom as internet pioneers since their work played a central role in the development of the interconnected network or Internet (White House, 2005). On January 1, 1983, TCP/IP was fully incorporated into ARPANET, giving rise to what now we call the Internet.

Since ARPANET was rooted in military funding, the link to the Defense Department was severed by splitting ARPANET into MILNET for defense purposes and ARPANET for civilian use. The civilian-only ARPANET also made it more palatable for networks in other countries to join since it was not associated with the US military; funding gradually shifted away from the Defense Department to the National Science Foundation (NSF). Within a few years the NSF was involved in networking, and ARPANET was formally decommissioned on February 28, 1990, with its nodes transferred to NSFNET, which became the new backbone for the network of networks.

We return to internet architecture in Chapter 3, but by the early 1990s the Internet became commercialized with internet service providers assuming

---

[4] Janet Abbate noted in her history, "individuals and organizations interested in pursuing computer networking often found it necessary to join government-sponsored projects or to present their work as responsive to contemporary political agendas" (Abbate, 1999, 40).

responsibility for the internet backbone on April 30, 1995. With the creation of a simple-to-use interface through the Web, a proliferation of personal computers, and significant investment in telecommunications, these changes marked the transition to the modern Internet that paved the way for a robust commercial space largely free of government interference.

1.2.1 Transmission Control Protocol/Internet Protocol

The TCP/IP is designed to interconnect networks using multiple technologies as well as computers with different operating systems. This was an important innovation that enabled researchers around the world to connect their networks to other networks, paving the way for the network of networks, thereby creating the Internet as we know it.

The Internet is subdivided into subnetworks called autonomous systems (ASs), each of which may have many clients. Every computer on the Internet requires a unique IP address, which is assigned to a client by an AS. Internet Protocol version 4 (IPv4) assigns 32-bit IP addresses, of which there are about 4.3 billion. Almost all the IPv4 addresses have been allocated and Internet Protocol version 6 (IPv6) now assigns 128-bit IP addresses, of which there are about 3.4×10^{38}. Each AS must have a unique AS number by which it is known to other ASs. The Internet Corporation for Assigned Names and Numbers maintains a list of AS numbers, the organizations that manage them, and the block or blocks of IP addresses that they are authorized to allocate.

The operation of the domain name system (DNS), which acts like a telephone directory for the Internet, is explained in detail in Chapter 3, but it is important to note that its operation is based on trust, which can be abused. For example, an analysis of 303 supposed government websites providing

---

Exploit 1.1 Spoofing domain names

Malicious actors have learned to trick users into visiting a domain of their choosing by sending a domain name that may look like the one a user may want to visit, such as a bank, but which is slightly different. For example, instead of sending www.jpmorganchase.com, the bad actor might send www.jpmorganchaise.com. A tired customer at the end of a busy day may not see the difference between these two domain names and the malicious actor could trick the customer into disclosing personal information that can be exploited.

Exploit 1.2 Cybersquatting

When it became apparent in the 1990s that interest in the Internet was going to explode, domain names suddenly became very valuable. That's when *cybersquatting* emerged. This is the practice of registering a domain name that might have value to a major corporation, an institution, or a well-known person.

Mike Rowe, a 17-year-old Canadian high-school student, registered the domain name MikeRoweSoft.com in August 2003, which is phonetically the same as Microsoft.com. Microsoft took legal action against him, asserting to the World Intellectual Property Organization (WIPO) that Rowe had infringed their trademark. In January 2004, it was announced that the parties had settled out of court and that Microsoft had taken control of the domain.

Recording artist and composer Bruce Springsteen filed a complaint with WIPO against Jeff Burgar, asserting that he violated Springsteen's common law rights by registering BruceSpringsteen.com. A WIPO panel evaluated the case and ruled against Springsteen in 2001.

Source: WIPO Arbitration and Mediation Center (2001)

---

information on the COVID-19 pandemic suggested that nearly 80 percent were not verified as authentic but were a combination of commercial entities selling products or others engaged in domain name spoofing (Tombs & Fournier-Tombs, 2020).

1.3 THE WORLD WIDE WEB APPEARS

For about 20 years, until the early 1990s, the Internet and its precursors around the world were largely used by universities, colleges, and research institutes. But after Tim Berners-Lee and his colleagues announced the World Wide Web in 1990, commercial and social applications exploded.[5] Berners-Lee and his colleagues at the European Organization for Nuclear Research (Conseil

---

[5] The development of the Web was not preordained, as Janet Abbate notes: "[T]he Web did not spring from the ARPA research community; it was the work of a new set of actors, including computer scientists at [the Geneva, Switzerland-based research center] CERN, the staff of an NSF supercomputer center, and a new branch of the software industry that would devote itself to providing Web servers, browsers, and content" (1999, p. 214).

Européen pour la Recherche Nucléaire, CERN) used TCP/IP for the Web, thereby demonstrating its usefulness.

The Web is a public layer of indexed content that can be found with traditional search engines and browsers, as opposed to the dark web, where content is intentionally hidden, requiring users to know specific locations and have special software to access the hidden sites. Berners-Lee built upon the work of Ted Nelson, who coined the term hypertext and believed a computer's interface should be simple and be easily understandable by a basic user (Nelson, 1974). With the simple interface that the Web offered, computer users everywhere, regardless of programming expertise, could use the Internet for email, shopping, and recreation. Within a few short years, companies such as Amazon and eBay (1995), Wikipedia (2001), Facebook (2004), Twitter (2006), and Zoom (2011) created new industries and changed the way we live and work. Social media companies enabled individuals to connect with each other and share content, while the federal government shielded companies from liability from what is expressed on their platforms.

1.4 DEFINING CYBERSPACE

The development of cyberspace and the broader information environment have been influenced by science fiction, which offers both inspiration and anxiety for thinking about technological change. Writer William Gibson coined the term "cyberspace" in a short story published in 1982 where he described cyberspace as a "consensual hallucination." Professor of English and Cinema and Media Studies Patrick Jagoda (2012) notes the etymological roots from the Greek word "kybernetes," which means steersman, seeing "cybernetics was not only a theory of communication but also one of control. Once confined to the cyberpunk literature and science fiction like the movie *The Matrix*, the information environment entered the real world in the late 1990s. Early internet providers such as AOL, CompuServe, and Prodigy gave home users easy but slow access to the Internet.

In 2003, the Bush administration described cyberspace as the "nervous system – the control system of our country. Cyberspace is composed of hundreds of thousands of interconnected computers, servers, routers, switches, and fiber optic cables that allow our critical infrastructures to work" (White House, 2003). The National Institute of Standards and Technology later defined cyberspace as "a global domain within the information environment consisting of the interdependent network of information technology infrastructures, including the Internet, telecommunications network, computer systems, and embedded processors and controllers" (National Institute of Standards and

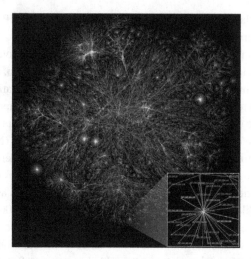

Figure 1.1   A map of internet routes by the Opte Project licensed under CC BY 4.0

Technology, 2012). A partial map of the Internet is contained within Figure 1.1. When we add people and the decisions they make to the cyberspace definition, we have the information environment.

Like the physical environment, the information environment is all-encompassing. It includes physical hardware such as routers, telecommunication lines, and servers, which are often the basis for governments to regulate cyberspace. Additionally, cyberspace includes information such as data and media, the mental or cognitive processes people use to comprehend their experiences, and the virtual world, where people connect socially through real and alternate personas. Democratic governments generally promote environments in which content (speech) is not regulated whereas authoritarian governments attempt to regulate access and content. Authoritarian governments also design content to reinforce political control. Cyberspace serves as a domain where people can adopt alternate personae on blogs, social networking sites, and virtual reality games.

Larry Johnson, chief executive officer of the New Media Consortium, predicted that we will experience the virtual world as an extension of the real one. Johnson concluded:

Virtual worlds are already bridging borders across the globe to bring people of many cultures and languages together in ways very nearly as rich as face-to-face interactions; they are already allowing the visualization of ideas and concepts in three dimensions that is leading to new insights and deeper learning; and they are already allowing people to work, learn, conduct business, shop, and interact in ways that promise to redefine how we think about these activities – and even what we regard as possible. (Johnson, 2008)

1.5 CYBERSPACE CHALLENGES

Cyberspace is powered by algorithms, which are recipes for computations, and software, or code, that is, the implementation of algorithms. Software consists of instructions in a programming language that are translated into machine-level programs executable by computers.

There is an enormous gap between the machine-level instructions of a computer and the functionality that humans need to do serious work. For example, a modern operating system may require 50 million lines of code, which may take some tens of thousands of person-years to write, test, and document. Given the enormous size of the programming task, it is easy to imagine that programmers will make mistakes and replicate mistakes when reusing previously published open-source code. When mistakes are discovered, they can be exploited as vulnerabilities, providing unauthorized users access to networks that can be exploited for gain. Consequently, software companies regularly issue patches to remove the vulnerabilities from previous versions.

Industries as diverse as water resource management and nuclear power have embraced electronic supervisory control and data acquisition (SCADA) technologies. These operational technology (OT) networks are often separated from a company's IT networks. On the one hand, this has led to developing infrastructures that would be unimaginable without technology. On the other hand, the shift from mechanical to electronic control creates new vulnerabilities that can be exploited when SCADA systems are connected to the Internet for remote access. For example, when remote access is used for nefarious purposes to target critical infrastructure, electricity can be shut off or water can be contaminated by increasing the volume of purifying chemicals to toxic levels, thereby having a widespread societal impact.

Essential Principle 1.1 Coding principles

The languages used to write programs have evolved over time. The first languages were machine-level and told machines explicitly what to do. Soon the concept of a process, a program with its data, was invented, followed by the virtual machine, which simulates a potentially infinite memory from a collection of individual memories, to today in which a program invokes an operating system to manage the memory of a computer, thereby creating a "virtual memory," and reducing the number of errors programmers make and helping them to work more quickly.

Exploit 1.3 The Aurora Generator Test

Electricity is an essential resource on which the rest of a nation's critical infrastructure depends. To determine whether or not the US electrical grid is at risk of a cyberattack, the US Department of Energy conducted an experiment, the Aurora Generator Test, to see if a cyberattack could seriously damage an electricity generator and thereby threaten the grid.

In 2007 the US government installed a new diesel generator at its Idaho National Laboratory and invited computer scientists to see if the generator could be damaged. The computer scientists repeatedly opened and closed the circuit breakers on the generator so that it was out of synchronism with the synchronous North American electricity grid. This produced great stresses on the rotor of the generator and destroyed it.

Source: Greenberg (2020)

Interdependencies across computer networks exacerbate vulnerabilities when an exploited flaw within one network sector impacts another. For example, when the 2017 WannaCry ransomware attack exploited a vulnerability in the Microsoft Windows XP operating system, which was so old that it no longer received updates, the ransomware had a disproportionate effect on the British National Health System. WannaCry also affected companies around the world using the same antiquated XP operating system (Smart, 2018).

Countries have come to realize that their infrastructure is accessible to and possibly threatened by foreign actors, challenging a government's laissez-faire approach to cybersecurity. Recognizing this, the US government has identified 16 critical infrastructure sectors and works with industry to improve their cybersecurity. President Biden gave this list to Russian president Putin in 2021 with the warning to keep Russian intelligence and Russia-based organized criminal groups out of these sectors. In addition to stepped-up defenses, this redline might explain why there were limited cyberattacks when Russia escalated its invasion of Ukraine in 2022.

Obviously, computers and networks require electricity to operate. If the electricity supply fails, there is no cybersecurity. As discussed in Exploit 1.3, the Aurora Generator Test demonstrated that a hacker could destroy a generator by briefly disconnecting and reconnecting it to the electric grid, illustrating a key US electric grid vulnerability. The risk to the grid is made worse by the fact that US electricity suppliers are heavily dependent on foreign manufacturers to replace damaged generators, transformers, and other equipment, subjecting replacement equipment both to foreign compromise at the root-level and to lengthy replacement waiting periods if global supply chains are slowed.

Very little of modern life is excluded from critical infrastructure sectors. Industries in these sectors have come together with the US government to share security information through communities of interest called Information Sharing and Analysis Organizations (ISAOs) and Information Sharing and Analysis Centers (ISACs). ISACs collect, analyze, and disseminate actionable threat information to their members to mitigate risks and enhance resiliency. ISACs were started in 1998 to facilitate information-sharing among members; ISAOs were created in 2015 to share information across sectors.

The US Department of Homeland Security through the Cybersecurity and Infrastructure Security Agency (CISA) has several information-sharing programs including Automated Indicator Sharing, the Cyber Information Sharing and Collaboration Program, and Enhanced Cybersecurity Services. CISA recognized that information-sharing with industry is paramount and launched a new program in 2021 called the Joint Cyber Defense Collaborative. Finally, the Federal Bureau of Investigation (FBI) created a partnership called InfraGard to represent businesses, academic institutions, state and local law enforcement agencies, and other participants dedicated to sharing information and intelligence to prevent hostile acts against the United States. If a company is being attacked, it can work with the FBI to stop it and possibly arrest the attacker(s). While these are important efforts, cybersecurity is very much a cat-and-mouse game; with every new product comes new vulnerabilities that get exploited until new software updates or patches are released. The limited law enforcement role in cybersecurity has resulted in a large cybersecurity industry where individuals and corporations must rely on themselves to stay ahead of attackers by bringing in third-party support.

1.6 THREATS TO THE INFORMATION ENVIRONMENT

As explored in subsequent chapters, there is a dark side of the cyber world wherein hackers, phishing scam artists, and transnational criminal groups harness technology for nefarious purposes. Through phishing, criminals and spies gain access to government and private computer networks. Through viruses and denial-of-service attacks, individuals and groups can steal intellectual property and disrupt governments and corporations with ransomware. And through spyware or government surveillance programs, the cherished civil liberty of privacy is subverted. No longer only in fiction, the personal, professional, and financial records of one's life can be exposed or stolen for malevolent purposes. Thus, for many the ultimate human security threat comes from cyberspace.

Adding cybersecurity to the national security agenda has generated some controversy. While it is common for criminal enterprises to launch ransomware attacks and for foreign intelligence services to engage in economic espionage, governments are now concerned enough to include cyber warfare in their military planning and operations. For example, a cyber operation accompanied Russia's invasion of Ukraine in 2014 and in 2022. As Russian tanks and aircraft entered Ukrainian territory, cyber warriors attacked government websites and advanced Russian interests through the information sphere. In an attack in December 2015, the nightmare scenario became real as a cyberattack shut down power for some 230,000 Ukrainians (Zetter, 2016). In 2022, a similar attempt was made to disable the power infrastructure, but Ukrainian defenders prevented exploitation (Rundle & Stupp, 2022). Although it had a temporary effect, the attack was a harbinger; future conflicts will combine physical and online operations, as militaries continue to develop ways to combine cyber and conventional operations.

Consequently, cybersecurity analyst Kenneth Geers (2014) argued that "[n]ations today use computer network operations to defend sovereignty and to project power, and cyber conflicts may soon become the rule rather than the exception. Most cyber-attacks do not rise to the level of a national security threat, but in the post-Stuxnet era, the notion of 'cyber war' has moved closer to reality." (Stuxnet was an attack on Iran's nuclear infrastructure that produced physical destruction of centrifuges used to enrich uranium gas by targeting industrial control systems through cyber means, which was revealed in 2010 [Sanger, 2010].) Political scientist Erik Gartzke (2013, p. 59), however, maintains "the need to follow virtual force with physical force to achieve lasting political consequences suggests that the application of cyberwarfare independent of conventional forms of warfare will be of tertiary importance in strategic and grand strategic terms." While the challenge for analysts remains differentiating between espionage and preparation for a future attack, analysts do believe that there is a risk of an inadvertent escalation due to cyber capabilities (Buchanan & Cunningham, 2020). As mentioned earlier, this sentiment was echoed by President Biden in 2021.

It is important to realize that governments could use cyberspace operations the same way they use drone strikes, namely, to meet immediate security needs rather than produce long-lasting results. This can lead to long campaigns of tit-for-tat operations, creating an inherent instability in cyberspace and society but may also provide de-escalatory off-ramps for governments to express displeasure with foes without causing significant harm. Because traditional definitions of war include use of violence to achieve political outcomes that produce battle deaths, Valeriano and Maness (2015, pp. 28–32) argue that cyber *conflict* is a better way than war to describe how governments interact with each other in cyberspace. War has specific meaning in law, doctrine, and academia; nevertheless, organizations that are responsible for war are developing military capabilities for cyberspace.

For its part, the United States developed US Cyber Command in 2010 with the explicit intent of defending military networks, supporting combatant commanders executing their missions around the world, and strengthening the country's ability to withstand and respond to cyberattacks. Dozens of other countries are developing similar military entities. As governments and militaries embrace technology for efficiency and effect, they also become vulnerable to cyberspace operations. And as more of society, government, and the economy move online, individuals in developed countries can no longer be isolated from the effects of conflict, which may explain why governments are largely restrained in their cyberspace operations. Former senior leaders in Defense and Homeland Security offered a sobering assessment of this situation: "Until the U.S. government makes significant strides on each of these issues, policymakers will have to accept that the offensive cyber-option isn't much of an option" since US society is so vulnerable to counterattacks through cyber means (Rosenbach et al., 2021).

As it relates to war, the Internet is both a means to support operations and a target for militaries to impose costs on their adversaries. Former US deputy defense secretary William Lynn underscored how important the information infrastructure is to national defense:

Just like our national dependence [on the Internet], there is simply no exaggerating our military dependence on our information networks: the command and control of our forces, the intelligence and logistics on which they depend, the weapons technologies we develop and field – they all depend on our computer systems and networks. Indeed, our 21st century military simply cannot function without them. (Miles, 2009)

In contrast to traditional war-fighting domains such as land, air, or sea, governments are not the only powers in cyberspace. Rather, nonstate actors can readily harness technology to compete on a global scale. And it is worth noting that virtualization will continue this trend of democratizing the Internet, giving individuals tremendous power unthinkable even 10 years ago. Satellite imagery used to be highly classified and limited by the intelligence community, but now anyone can access imagery from an iPhone using Google Earth or contract with myriad commercial satellite imaging companies. Likewise, the complexity and cost of building a nuclear weapon limit their production to governments, but the same cannot be said for malware that can destroy data and networks, undermine international credibility, and disrupt commerce. Consequently, governments are increasingly concerned with the cyber domain as a new feature within the national security landscape as individuals are exposed to the dangers of being connected.

A wired society offers many vulnerabilities. While it can take months or years to map a target's networks, speed of attack is beyond human perception, and malicious actors take advantage of human vulnerabilities through social engineering to elicit network access. Offense tends to dominate thinking in the information environment since there is an open architecture and protocols, but defense and resilient networks are important too.

While physical destruction dominates Western ways of thinking about war, it is possible cyberspace operations can be considered a use of force under international law if it is destructive, sustained, and attributed to a nation-state. Use of force through malware is rare, but since cybersecurity is occupying national security thinking, it may be better to rely on ideas of war as a bargaining model (Fearon, 1995) or use terms such as cyber conflict and cyber competition rather than war to connote disagreements among states since countries increasingly employ cyber operations as a unique tool of power (Valeriano & Maness, 2015).

As Herb Lin (2012, p. 41) wrote, "Cyber-attacks are particularly well suited for attacks on the psychology of adversary decision makers who rely on the affected computers, and in this case such effects can be regarded as indirect effects." Chamath Palihapitiya, who was a Facebook founder and a venture capitalist, sees that social media has been "used and abused in ways that we, their architects, never imagined" (Koh, 2018). Algorithms are used to amplify false or sensational messages. In other words, cyberspace operations can generate broad feelings of insecurity, which force both governments and social media companies to take users' actions more seriously and look to algorithms to identify content that is deliberately false or incendiary.

1.7 ATTRIBUTION

Attributing the source of a cyberattack, its point of origin, operator, and intent, can be difficult. Unlike a missile launch that has a discrete signature, geographic location, and obvious intent to kill, those who employ cyber tactics can easily hide their origin or conduct operations from servers inside the victim's borders, which makes attribution difficult but not impossible. The cybersecurity analyst at the prominent think tank Center for Strategic and International Studies James Lewis (2009) has argued, "Uncertainty is the most prominent aspect of cyber

Table 1.2 Malicious actors and motivations

Threat source	Motivation
Governments	Information gathering and espionage activities
Criminal groups	Monetary gain
Hackers	Thrill of the challenge
Hacktivists	Politically motivated attacks to send for monetary gain
Disgruntled insiders	Cause damage to the system or steal for monetary gain
Terrorists	Propaganda, fund-raising, recruiting, and reconnaissance

conflict – in attribution of the attackers [*sic*] identity, the scope of collateral damage, and the potential effect on the intended target from cyberattack."

Thus, when trying to analyze cyber threats, it is best to take a comprehensive approach. Accordingly, we can classify threats by the actor, such as individual and government, by the target, such as a financial sector or defense department, or by the means, such as a virus, a bot, a denial of service, or social engineering. The actors include individual hackers, organized criminal groups, intelligence services, and agencies of governments. Patterns of cyber operations among governments resemble interstate rivalries where it would be more common to observe Iran attack Israel than Iran attack China (see Table 1.2).

As the diversity of actors illustrates, the barriers to entry for cyberspace are low, which helps explain why cyberattacks have become commonplace. There are differences of opinion about the power to cause disruption or damage by various individuals, groups, or nation-states. For example, the head of the International Telecommunications Union noted, "[T]he next world war could happen in cyberspace and that would be a catastrophe. ... Loss of vital networks would quickly cripple any nation, and none is immune to cyberattack." (Hui, 2009). While a cyberspace superpower, such as China, Russia, France, Israel, and the United States, should be capable of causing massive damage to computers, networks or attached equipment, it is highly unlikely that a single individual could do it. Analyses of significant disruptions caused by NotPetya and Stuxnet illustrate that much planning and effort must go into designing malware to have a significant impact. It remains easier to order a missile strike than a cyberattack, so a future characterized by Cybergeddon is not certain (Healey, 2011).

Web-based attacks are a common source of malicious activity, which often happens by exploiting a vulnerable Web application or exploiting some vulnerability present in the underlying host operating system. A single individual or criminal enterprise can do a lot of damage through denial-of-service attacks or ransomware, but to produce a serious incident, such as turning off the electricity supply for a week or more over a large portion of a large country, requires either a lot of luck or a high level of skill in discovering vulnerabilities and designing malware that can cause failure across many subsystems. It is more likely that a nation-state would have the resources, the motivation. and the will to attempt such a serious attack.

Governments such as China, Russia, France, Israel, the United Kingdom, and the United States have significant cyber capabilities and are superpowers in cyberspace.[6] The US Defense Department predicts, "Strategic attacks will likely focus on disrupting elements of the US financial infrastructure, where trust and data integrity are paramount" (CISA, 2021a). What is important, however, is governments are not alone in using malware to further their interests. This fundamentally changes thinking about national security, which is no longer the exclusive domain of governments. To be sure, governments are still leading efforts to seek advantage in cyberspace and are the only cyber actors capable of existential operations, but now multinational companies, nongovernmental organizations, and transnational organized criminal groups are important actors in cyberspace as well. Defense is grounded in public–private partnerships where ICT companies work with governments to improve cybersecurity (see Table 1.3).

Table 1.3 Types of malware and cyberattacks

Denial of service (blockade): accomplished by flooding the targeted host or network with traffic until the target cannot respond or simply crashes, preventing access for legitimate users

Trojan: malware that, once implanted in a computer, provides remote access to an attacker

Phishing: an email or text-based social engineering attack that can trick users into providing attackers access to a targeted system

Ransomware: malware that blocks access to a computer until a ransom is paid

Virus: malware designed to replicate itself for the purpose of infecting other computers

Wiper: malware designed to corrupt or erase a significant portion of memory, usually to make a computer inoperable

Worm: malware that behaves as a standalone virus and does not need to infect an application to copy itself but does need to exploit a vulnerability in an operating system

---

[6] To measure cyber power of states, see Schwarzenbach et al. (2021).

1.8 ETHICS, NORMS, REGULATIONS, AND LAW

As with all domains in which humans operate, not all participants in cyberspace subscribe to the same moral principles (ethics) or the same rules of behavior (norms). Similarly, cyberspace has made available new violations of confidentiality, integrity, and availability of data. Thus, new laws and regulations are required to protect such data.

For example, the theft of an owner's identity can impose exorbitant costs on that owner as well as damage his/her/their reputation. Other violations, such as denial of access to information, can impose costs on users of that information. It could be as simple as having to wait to withdraw funds from a checking account to incurring costs for failure to pay bills on time.

A website that hosts a user's postings without examining the content of such postings might endanger a community by publishing inflammatory information or injure an individual's reputation by publishing defamatory information. The former might produce damaging political polarization. The latter could destroy the reputation of an innocent person. Similarly, when historical data is used to train an artificial intelligence system to be used in making decisions, if the data reflects bias, systems trained on that data will perpetuate that bias when used to make similar decisions. Novel issues arise in cyberspace that require thoughtful and informed action by individuals, organizations, and governments.

1.9 CYBERSPACE IS UNIQUE

No single entity owns the Internet, yet individuals, companies, and governments use it. Anyone with a phone, tablet, or computer with an internet connection can connect to the Internet and can operate there. And, making it more challenging for governments, most of the IT expertise resides in the commercial sector. Israeli Defense Force cyber chief of staff Brig. Gen. Yaron Rozen said, "This whole front resides in the civilian world, not in the military one. Look how long it took nations across the globe to sign the Kyoto Treaty, which deals with global warming and affects everyone. The Cyber nations are not just the superpowers, but huge international corporations like Google, Facebook, and Kaspersky" (quoted in Zitun, 2017). Likewise, international agreements can be rescinded when the political party in power changes, which further complicates trust and efforts to reach international agreement on law and norms. This may explain why corporations such as Microsoft have been promoting norms and even established an office at the United Nations Headquarters.

Cyberspace is more tightly integrated than one might expect. For example, a computer virus that infects an airline in South America can also affect a logistics company in North America since users across the world use the same software and malware can readily spread beyond the intended target. Furthermore, as Harvard Law professor Lawrence Lessig (1998) reminds us, cyberspace "architecture is inherently political. In the world of cyberspace, the selection of an architecture is as important as the choice of a constitution."

Cyberspace also reflects the culture of the locale where the code is written, hardware is designed, and rules are implemented. Thus, it matters that today's Internet is dominated by developed democracies where anonymity prevails, social spaces can be safe spaces, and users find affection with each other rather than loyalty to a particular government. While never realized, poet John Perry Barlow (1996) captured this aspiration for a cyberspace "where anyone, anywhere may express his or her beliefs, no matter how singular, without fear of being coerced into silence or conformity."

As Chapter 6 discusses, however, countries are attempting to regulate cyberspace within their borders in ways that reflect their national cultures. Consequently, China and Russia attempt to apply authoritarian principles in cyberspace, depriving users of anonymity and free speech. Alternatively, the European Union has applied human rights laws in cyberspace granting users significant privacy protections vis-a-vis ICT companies. Chapters 2 and 3 provide a foundation in thinking about computing and networking before returning to these issues and exploring ways to make cyberspace more secure for everyone.

1.10 DISCUSSION TOPICS

1. Explain the origins of the general laissez-faire approach the US government takes to the IT sector and defend the position that it is likely or unlikely to change.
2. Identify the nature of cybersecurity incidents that you believe would rise to national security incidents. Consider the possibility of cascading effects.
3. Explain why you believe that the open architecture of cyberspace is or is not a source of strength and weakness.

2

From the Abacus to the Computer

[In the Analytical Engine] a new, a vast, and a powerful language is
developed for the future use of analysis, in which to wield its truths
so that these may become of more speedy and accurate practical
application for the purposes of mankind than the means hitherto in
our possession have rendered possible.
Ada Lovelace, the first computer programmer (Manebrea, 1842)

T HE NEED FOR COMPUTATION has a long history that extends over millennia. Our ancestors developed mechanical aids to computation in support of construction projects, navigation, and general problem-solving. These
aids include the abacus (see Figure 2.1), slide rule, and the programmable
mechanical computer. Over time, these mechanical aids were replaced by
electronic computers, capable of performing enormously complex computations described using powerful languages that the nineteenth-century computer
programmer Ada Lovelace never imagined. Since cyberspace was created by

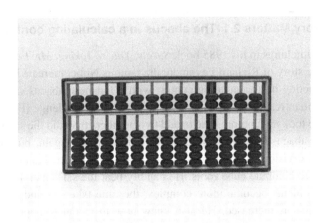

Figure 2.1   Abacus licensed under Getty Images/Vudhikul Ocharoen/EyeEm

humans, this chapter reviews the key historical drivers that led to the modern computer, explains how our devices and computers work, and begins our discussion of security vulnerabilities.

2.1 MECHANICAL AIDS TO COMPUTATION

Humans have long needed to compute. No doubt our ancestors counted using their ten fingers, providing a predilection for decimal or base-ten calculation.

As early as 500 BCE our ancestors invented the abacus as a mechanical aid for adding long decimal numbers such as 1,636 plus 3,483. The abacus is used as a device for both storing numbers in the absence of paper ledgers and performing calculations. Thus, the abacus serves as a memory tool and, with human assistance, a calculator that can be used for addition, subtraction, multiplication, division, and even square and cube roots of numbers.

The abacus is a metaphor for modern computers; the modern computer both stores information in its memory and performs calculations on the data; a computer just does it much faster for problems that are much more complex than those encountered by our ancestors who developed the abacus. In general, calculations are hidden from us but are performed in the modern computer by a central processing unit or CPU, discussed later. All computations involve the manipulation of information. The outline for such computations is now called an algorithm. One of the earliest algorithms designed to quickly multiply large numbers is based on the logarithm function.

History Matters 2.1 The abacus in a calculating contest

Edward Hutchings in his 1985 book *Surely, You're Joking, Mr. Feynman!* relates the story of Richard Feynman, the famous Nobel laureate in physics, competing in a calculating contest with a Japanese abacus salesman in a Brazilian restaurant. Feynman responded to the challenge (Feynman 1997). He took much more time to add two numbers than did the salesman using his abacus. On a multiplication problem he lost again, but not as badly. On division they both were tied. Finally, Feynman challenged the salesman to compute cube roots. He handily beat the salesman, knowing that as problems become more complex, the time taken to find answers with an abacus increased. He also knew how to calculate approximate cube roots quickly in his head!

2.1.1 The Logarithm

In 1614, John Napier of Scotland invented the logarithm to simplify multiplication and reduce the time for scientific and engineering computations. Calculation of logarithms by human computers is a tedious and complex process that introduces errors into tables of logarithms or log tables. The need for accurate log tables motivated Charles Babbage to find mechanical aids to computing and invent his Difference Engine, discussed later. (Chapter 3 examines discrete logarithms, which play a very important role in computer security.)

2.1.2 The Slide Rule

In 1620 and 1621 Edmund Gunter and William Oughtred invented the slide rule as an aid to multiplication. See Essential Principle 2.1. They wrote numbers on two pieces of wood (called Napier's Bones) such that the numbers are separated from the number 1 by distances proportional to their logarithms. ($\log_b = 1$ is 0 for every base b because $b^0 = 1$ for all numbers b.) To add logarithms of two numbers n and m, users would align the number 1 on the second bone with the number n on the first bone, as shown in Figure 2.2. Then they would align the number m on the second bone with the number p on the first bone, where p is the (approximate) product of n and m.

Essential Principle 2.1 Computing with logarithms

To reduce the time taken to multiply large numbers, logarithms were invented. They play an important role in scientific and engineering computation.

Logarithms of numbers are defined relative to a base. For example, the logarithm of the number n to the base 10, denoted $\log_{10} n$, is the exponent e such that $n = 10^e$, in which case we write $e = \log_{10} n$. Similarly, the logarithm of n to the base 2, denoted $\log_2 n$, is the exponent f such that $n = 2^f$ or $f = \log_2 n$. If $n = b^e$, then $e = \log_b n$, the logarithm of n to the base b.

Let n and m be two numbers and let $e_1 = \log_b n$ and $e_2 = \log_b m$. Thus, $n = b^{e_1}$ and $m = b^{e_2}$ The product of n and m satisfies $n * m = b^{e_1 + e_2}$ To multiply n and m, add their logarithms, $e_1 + e_2 = \log_b n + \log_b m = \log_b (nm)$, and then raise b to the exponent $e_1 + e_2$. That is, $n * m = b^{e_1 + e_2}$

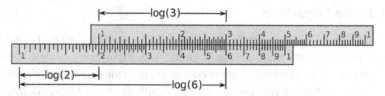

Figure 2.2   The Slide Rule licensed under CC BY-SA 3.0 by Jakob Scholbach

Until the electronic four-function calculator became widespread in the 1970s, engineering and science college students were easily identified by the slide rules that they carried around with them.

2.1.3 Mechanical Aids to Arithmetic

About 350 years earlier, Wilhelm Schickard around 1623 and Blaise Pascal in the 1640s independently constructed machines to add and subtract numbers. Their calculators, which were quite complex, did arithmetic in base 10. They used a series of gears, each with ten small spokes and one large spoke. Each gear represents one significant digit. As a digit is increased, its gear advances by one tenth of a rotation. When the least significant digit passes ten and resets to zero, the large spoke on its gear advances the gear associated with the next higher digit by one tenth of a revolution, thereby recording the carry from the previous digit. This mechanism applies to each gear.

In 1725 Basile Bouchon controlled a loom using punched holes in paper tapes. In 1746 J. M. Jacquard invented the automated Jacquard Loom (see Figure 2.3) programmed using punched cards made of a stiff material. In the figure, punched cards are on the top left and the patterned textile at the bottom center.

Herman Hollerith used punched cards in the late nineteenth century to tabulate data on such cards. His tabulating equipment was used in the 1890 US census. Punched cards were widely used during the twentieth century to record both programs and data for input to computers. A modern punched card is shown in Figure 2.4; it has 80 columns and 10 rows.

2.1.4 The Difference and Analytical Engines

In 1822, Babbage, seeking to print error-free mathematical tables, such as that of logarithms, built a small Difference Engine, a special-purpose computer, to demonstrate that one could automatically print mathematical tables

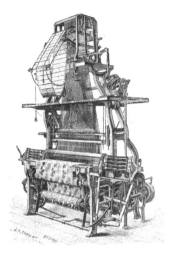

Figure 2.3   The Jacquard Loom

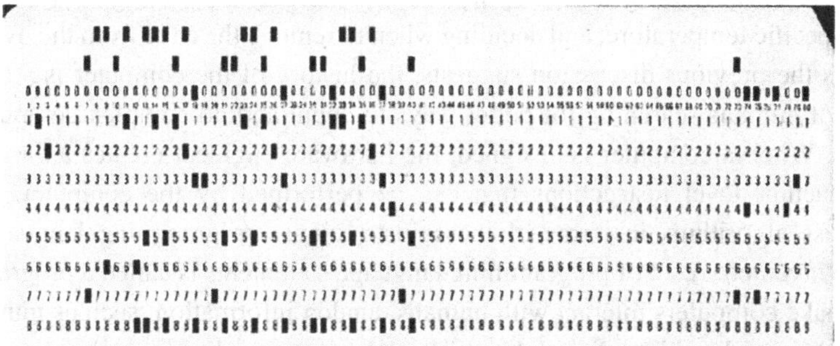

Figure 2.4   A Modern Punched Card licensed under CC 3.0 by Pete Birkinshaw

for functions that could be computed using the method of divided differences, a method of computing polynomials (Schlegel, 2017). His Difference Engine represented a major advance in automated computation.

Fifteen years later, in 1837, Babbage then set out to design a general-purpose, fully program-controlled, mechanical computer, the Analytical Engine, capable of doing any calculation set before it (Swaine & Freiberger, 2020). It was to contain a computational unit (a mill) and a memory (a store), much like the abacus and modern computers, and a printer. Babbage envisioned supplying both instructions and data on punched cards, drawing inspiration from the Jacquard Loom. Despite trying, Babbage was not able to implement his Analytical Engine and it took another 100 years before the first general-purpose computer was built in 1941 by Konrad Zuse. Called Z3, Zuse assembled his machine from electromagnetic relays, which are switches controlled by the magnetic fields of electromagnets.

The Z3 was followed by the invention of many special- and general-purpose computers using various computing technologies, such as electromagnetic relays, vacuum tubes, and transistors. Additionally, storage technologies took the form of piano wire, cathode ray tubes, magnetic cores, and transistors.

2.2 THE EMERGENCE OF PROGRAMMING

Once electronic computers were created, they could be used to perform complex calculations, such as determining the amount of fuel needed to send a satellite into space based on its weight. To do this, they implemented algorithms, procedures to direct computations. Named for al-Khwarizmi, a ninth-century Persian mathematician, an algorithm is like a recipe to bake a cake, which invokes a sequence of mixing of dry and wet ingredients, heating the mixture at a specific temperature, and deciding when to remove the cake from the oven.

As the previous discussion suggests, the history of the computer is a history of humans searching for better ways to count and do complex computations. When a computer is designed, the hardware engineer creates a variety of machine-level instructions that can be performed by the computer. To express algorithms in terms of these instructions, programming languages were invented. A set of programming language statements is called a program. To make computers interact with humans, analog information, such as music, must be translated into digital data that can be stored and processed.

The first documented attempt to write a program to use machines for more than calculations was by Ada, Countess of Lovelace, in the 1840s. She took a lively interest in Babbage's Analytical Engine and designed a computer program for it, one that computed Bernoulli numbers. She also recognized that computers could do much more than calculate, speculating that it could compose music and do algebra. For her contributions, the programming language Ada is named for her.

The modern computer stores its programs and data as binary digits or bits, that is, as zeroes and ones, rather than as decimal digits because distinguishing between two states is more reliably done than distinguishing between ten states. By using a zero or a one indicates something either isn't or is. Similarly, when data is transmitted over a noisy communication channel, distinguishing between one of two amplitudes or frequencies can be done much more reliably than distinguishing among ten.

History Matters 2.2 Lovelace's observation about the Analytical Engine

Many persons who are not conversant with mathematical studies imagine that because the business of [Babbage's Analytical Engine] is to give its results in numerical notation, the nature of its processes must consequently be arithmetical and numerical, rather than algebraical and analytical. This is an error. The engine can arrange and combine its numerical quantities exactly as if they were letters or any other general symbols; and in fact it might bring out its results in algebraical notation, were provisions made accordingly.

Source: Lovelace (1844)

Table 2.1 Examples of binary encodings of letters

Character	Binary encoding
A	0100 0001
C	0100 0011
D	0100 0100
K	0100 1011
N	0100 1110
T	0101 0100
W	0101 0111
(SPACE)	0010 0000

Shown in Table 2.1 is a fragment of a much larger table that contains the mappings from decimal numbers, upper- and lower-case letters, and punctuation symbols to eight-bit strings (bytes) that constitute the American Standard Code for Information Exchange or ASCII. This small table contains the ASCII codes used to map the message shown in Table 2.2 into a binary string. Note that a space character also has an ASCII code.

Now let's examine numbers in the binary number system. Recall that decimal numbers are represented as zero to nine multiples of powers of ten. For example, the decimal number 64 consists of six 10s and four 1s. Binary numbers are represented as zero or one multiples of powers of two. The powers of two are $1 = 2^0$, $2 = 2^1$, $4 = 2^2$, $8 = 2^3$, $16 = 2^4$, $32 = 2^5$, $64 = 2^6$, $128 = 2^7$, and so on. Thus, the decimal number 13 (one 10 and three 1s) is represented

Table 2.2   Example of a message encoded into a binary number using ASCII encodings

0100 0001	0101 0100	0101 0100	0100 0001	0100 0011	0100 1011
A	T	T	A	C	K
0010 0000	0100 0001	0101 0100	0010 0000		
(SPACE)	A	T	(SPACE)		
0100 0100	0100 0001	0101 0111	0100 1110		
D	A	W	N		

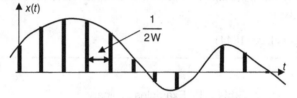

Figure 2.5   A sampled waveform

in binary as $8 + 4 + 1 = 0*2^7 + 0*2^6 + 0*2^5 + 0*2^4 + 1*2^3 + 1*2^2 + 0*2^1 + 1*2^0$. Thus, the eight-bit binary number representing the decimal number 13 is 00001101. The largest eight-bit binary number is 255 in decimal notation. Decimal numbers, letters, and punctuation symbols can also be represented with bits in ASCII.

The message in Table 2.2 is represented by a string of 14 bytes, a binary number.

Once programmers mastered the mapping of text into binary data (bits), the next challenge was to translate analog information, such as audio, images, and video, into bits.

A continuous signal, such as sound whose amplitude at time t is $x(t)$, can be sampled, as shown in Figure 2.5, and the sample values encoded with bits. Let us assume that each sample is represented approximately by one byte (eight bits). Each byte denotes 1 of 256 different amplitudes. To reconstruct an approximation to a signal from bytes, the bytes are used to generate samples that are passed through what is called a low-pass filter, a device that allows only low frequency signals to pass. This reconstructs a facsimile of the original signal. The more bits used to translate samples into bits, the more accurate is the reconstructed signal.

The last step in translating data into numbers is to ensure that the same standards are used globally to represent data. Just as everyone accepts that two plus two equals four, the same must be true for translating the letter "A" into bits. Unicode is an industry standard for encoding characters in most of the world's writing systems. The eight-bit version of the Unicode Transformation Format

(UTF-8) is the dominant digital encoding standard for the World Wide Web. It represents characters using one to four bytes. It plays an important role in the internationalization and localization of software.

2.3 COMPUTER ARCHITECTURE

A computer is a device that receives inputs and produces outputs. It is a machine that performs calculations by manipulating data, often under program control. The prototypical modern computer has two principal components, a CPU and a random-access memory (RAM). This is essentially the same as Babbage's Analytical Engine of 1837 but replaces the mill with a CPU and the store with a RAM. There are two types of computers: stateless and finite-state machines (FSMs).

2.3.1 The Logic Circuit

A logic circuit is a stateless computer, one without memory. It is given a set of input bits, each of value one (1) or zero (0), denoting the truth values True or False, respectively, and produces a set of output bits. If at two different time instants this computer is given the same inputs, it will produce the same outputs. That is not always the case with a state-based computer. Its response to inputs is generally a function of its internal state.

A stateless computer, also called a logic circuit, can be built from logical operators or logic gates, such as AND, OR, and NOT. Both AND and OR gates have two inputs and one output. The output of the AND gate is 1 or True only when both of its inputs are 1 or True. The output of the OR gate is 1 if either or both of its inputs are 1. The NOT gate has one input and one output. It flips the value of its input; its output is 1 if its input is 0 and is 0 if its input is 1. The EXCLUSIVE OR gate has two inputs and one output. Its output value is 1 exclusively when one of its inputs is 1; otherwise, its output value is 0.

History Matters 2.3 Origin of the word "computer"

Until the mid-twentieth century a computer was a person who performed calculations. The adjective "electronic" was added when electronic computers were available to distinguish them from the people who computed. Now "computer" is used only for a computing machine.

Every logic circuit can be constructed by interconnecting AND, OR, and NOT gates. For this reason, these three operations are said to form a complete basis. When the constants 0 and 1 are available, as they always are, the EXCLUSIVE OR gate alone constitutes a complete basis. Memory cells, described later, can also be constructed with these operations. That is, these operations suffice to realize all modern computers.

The logic gates of modern computers are constructed using transistors, devices that act as electronic switches. If two switches are placed in sequence in a wire, current in the wire will flow only if both switches are closed. In this fashion an AND gate can be realized. If a closed switch is denoted by 1 and an open switch by 0 and the output is said to have value 1 if current flows in the wire and value 0 if it does not, current flows in the wire only if both the first and second switches are closed, that is, each has value 1. If two switches are connected in parallel and placed in a wire, current will flow if either switch is closed, providing a realization of an OR gate. A NOT gate requires an active element, such as an electromagnetic relay.

A logic circuit is shown in Figure 2.6. It has two binary inputs labeled a and b and one binary output labeled c. We now show that it realizes the EXCLUSIVE OR gate. The output gate of the circuit is an OR gate. The other two-input gates are AND gates. The remaining two gates, each denoted by an arrow and a circle, each with one input and one output, are NOT gates. The output c is described by the following Boolean formula, the explanation of which follows.

$$c = \big(b \text{ AND NOT}(a)\big) \text{ OR } \big(\text{NOT}(b) \text{ AND } a\big)$$

The value of the output c is the OR of the outputs of the top and bottom AND gates. The value of the top gate is $\big(b \text{ AND NOT}(a)\big)$, which is 1 when $b = 1$ and $a = 0$. The value of the bottom gate is $\big(\text{NOT}(b) \text{ AND } a\big)$, which is 1 when $b = 0$ and $a = 1$. Thus, c is 1 when either a or b is 1 but not both, that is, c is the EXCLUSIVE OR of a and b, which we write as $c = a \text{ XOR } b$.

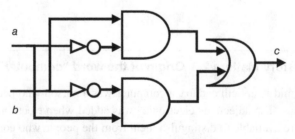

Figure 2.6 A logic circuit

A logic circuit does not explicitly specify the order in which operations are to be performed. Instead, it is assumed that gates connected to inputs must have all their input values before they can produce outputs. Once an order that respects this constraint is given to the gates, we have a *straight-line algorithm*, that is, one in which each operation is performed in sequence.

2.3.2 The Finite-State Machine

The FSM has an internal state that is recorded in a binary memory as a set of bits (see Figure 2.7). It has some initial state. On each clock tick its logic circuit receives both a fixed number of external binary inputs and the bits representing the current state of the memory. The logic circuit then computes external binary outputs and a new state that is stored in its memory. The FSM repeats this step endlessly on clock ticks until it is turned off.

The memory of an FSM consists of binary storage cells. A binary storage cell, depicted in Figure 2.8 (a), holds a 1 or a 0 and has a clock input. The clock input alternates between 1 and 0 at a steady rate. When the clock input has a value of 1, the cell acquires or "latches" the input bit. When the clock input is 0, the cell bit does not change. Its output is the value of its cell bit. A memory is a collection of binary storage cells. The three-bit memory in Figure 2.8 (b) can be in one of eight states, denoted by (000), (001), (010), (011), (100), (101), (110), and (111).

2.3.3 Moore's Law

At first, electronic computers were very large, filling entire rooms. But over time, the computer industry has benefited from the microminiaturization of logic gates and memory cells. The transistor, from which logic gates and

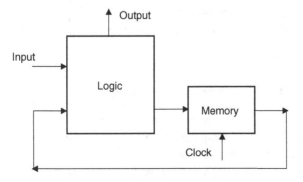

Figure 2.7   A clocked finite-state machine

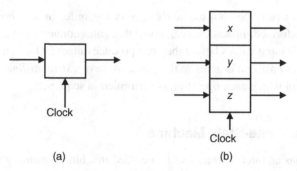

Figure 2.8   Binary memories holding (a) one bit and (b) three bits

memory cells are constructed, was invented at Bell Telephone Laboratories in 1947. Transistors are used as switches to realize gates. By 1958 semiconductor physicists learned to embed transistors into the surface of a piece of semiconductor crystal and the integrated circuit (IC) was born, leading to an explosion in the number of components in an IC.

In 1965 Gordon Moore observed that the number of transistors on an IC, a computer chip, had been doubling about every two years (see Figure 2.9). Because the doubling continued for many years, it was dubbed Moore's Law, although it is an observation, not a law.

In 1958 there was at most one transistor per chip. In 2017 IBM put 30 billion transistors on a fingernail-sized chip. This rate of growth has begun to slow and is expected to end by 2025, about 50 years after Moore identified the trend. It is ending because the dimensions of transistors have become so small that electrons jump spontaneously across gaps, creating "leakage currents" that overheat transistors and interfere with their switching properties. If no viable successor to semiconductor electronics is adopted within a few years, Moore's Law will end and increases in performance will only be possible by exploiting parallelism, which is a daunting challenge since humans find it very difficult to pay attention to more than a few activities at the same time.

2.3.4 The Random-Access Computer

The random-access computer, which is a more refined model of an FSM, is good model for modern computers. It consists of two interconnected FSMs, a CPU and a RAM, as suggested in Figure 2.10 and explained later. Programs and data are stored as b-bit words in the RAM. On most modern computers today, b is either 16, 32, or 64. Instructions are executed in the CPU. This

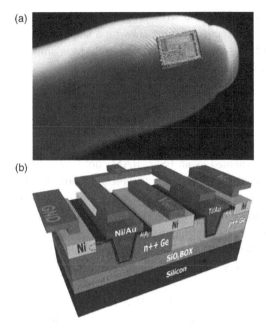

Figure 2.9 (a) A computer chip licensed under Getty Images/Corbis Documentary/ Jim Sugar and (b) a chip cutaway showing Chip Layers courtesy of Purdue University

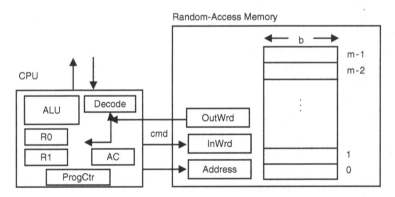

Figure 2.10 The random-access computer model

section provides a high-level treatment of this important computational model, which is useful in explaining computational security vulnerabilities.

The random-access computer model is one that programmers have in mind when writing software. They imagine that they have a very large canvas (or memory) on which they can write programs and store data. Unfortunately, it is not economical to equip computers with a single RAM memory that is as fast as the CPU. As explained later, such a RAM is simulated by an array of memories of increasing size and decreasing speed.

2.3.5 The Random-Access Memory

The RAM is a very simple storage device or memory that acts like a file cabinet but is implemented as an FSM. RAMs hold a number, say m, of words, one word per file drawer, where m is typically a power of two, that is, $m = 2^k$ for some integer k. Each word has b bits for some integer b, which is usually a power of 2. In Figure 2.10 a RAM is attached to a CPU. The CPU provides commands, addresses, and input words to the RAM and receives the output word from the RAM. It also does a variety of calculations. A RAM is given one of three commands by a CPU, cmd = Read, Write, or No-Op. It does nothing when cmd = No-Op.

When cmd = Read, the RAM is also given a b-bit word, denoted Address (see Figure 2.10). The RAM then copies the word in the file drawer at that address and places it in the RAM output register, denoted OutWrd, where it is available to be retrieved by the CPU. This register also holds a b-bit word,

When the command by the CPU is cmd = Write, the RAM is also given an address, denoted Address, and an input word, denoted InWrd, in Figure 2.10. This causes the word in the file drawer at that address to be replaced by the input word InWrd.

Each RAM word is either a b-bit data word or a b-bit instruction. An instruction is typically subdivided into an operation code (Opcode), consisting of a fixed number of bits, and an Address, which is the remainder of the bits. An instruction word is denoted [Opcode, Address].

If $b = 32$ and Opcode consists of 4 bits, Address would contain the remaining 28 bits. Because each CPU instruction is specified by 4 bits, the CPU can perform at most 2^4 or 16 instructions. The RAM holds at most 2^{28} 32-bit words. Since 32 bits constitutes 4 bytes, such a memory can hold at most $4 * 2^{28} = 2^{30}$ bytes or one gigabyte of memory.

2.3.6 The Central Processing Unit

A representative CPU has storage registers each of which holds a b-bit word. It also has an arithmetic-logic unit (ALU), a logic circuit that takes inputs from registers and the RAM, computes arithmetic and logical functions on the inputs, and deposits the results in a special register known as the accumulator (AC). Shown in Figure 2.10 are representative registers, R0 and R1. The CPU typically has other registers, not shown, that hold temporary results.

All but the simplest modern computers provide *if … then … else …* branching. Such a command has three components, (a) a predicate, call it PRED, (b) a true clause, call it TC, and (c) a false clause, call it FC. (Each clause is itself a subprogram.) This command is written as *if* PRED *then* TC *else* FC. The predicate PRED evaluates to True or False. If PRED is True, the subprogram TC is executed. If PRED is False, the subprogram FC is executed.

Typical arithmetic functions are addition and subtraction. Typical logical functions are the vector AND in which two words are combined by ANDing them bit by bit. That is, the ith bits in each of the words are ANDed together and the result deposited in the ith location of a register, such as the accumulator AC.

Another logical function, the comparison operator, compares two words bit by bit and stores a 1 in a single-bit register if they are equal and a 0 if not. The comparison operator is used in deciding program branches, that is, which of two operations to perform.

2.3.7 The Fetch–Execute Cycle

Each CPU has a program counter, a register denoted by ProgCtr in Figure 2.10. It holds the address of the next instruction. The CPU repeatedly executes the fetch–execute cycle, namely, it fetches an instruction from the RAM at the address stored in the program counter ProgCtr and then executes it. Thus, the program counter tells the CPU where to find the next instruction, which is then executed. Normally the program counter is incremented by 1, which results in the CPU executing instructions in successive memory locations. When a jump occurs, the program counter is replaced by the address to which to jump. As mentioned, No-Op instructions are executed when a computer is idle.

2.3.8 The Boot Program

The random-access computer is a rather simple device. It stores programs and data in a RAM and executes instructions from successive memory locations unless a branching step is encountered, whereupon it may branch to a new location to resume the computation.

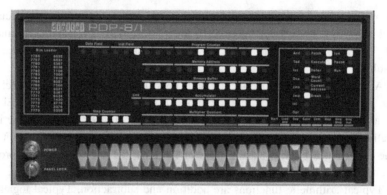

Figure 2.11 The digital equipment PDP-8 control panel licensed under MIT by Jörg Hoppe

Many of the earliest computers could not hold programs in their memories when the power was turned off. To start a computer, it had to be booted, that is, a small program had to be stored in its empty memory. This was done from the computer front panel (see Figure 2.11). The panel had one switch, shown along the bottom, for each bit of a memory word, which is set up or down to specify 1 or 0 and a button that, when pushed, loads all the bits into a first memory location, then another word is loaded into the second memory location, and so on until the boot program is loaded. This program is then used to load other programs by operating an input device, such as a paper-tape reader, to read the tape and store its contents in memory.

Today, boot programs are called firmware and are recorded in read-only memory (ROM) chips that are programmed before installation. Over time, the technology of ROM chips changed, and it is now possible to update the firmware without replacing chips, although this generally requires special steps. After a computer is booted, it loads an operating system (OS) from a storage unit, normally a disk. The first step taken is to load instructions from the first track of the disk, which holds the Master Boot Record.

Firmware is susceptible to manipulation by attackers. Because of the difficulty of modifying firmware, if an attacker manages to compromise the firmware, the compromise is likely to go undetected for a very long time. This argues for taking great care when acquiring a piece of hardware that contains firmware provided by an untrusted source. This is a supply chain problem. Such problems have gained prominence recently; if the provider of hardware can compromise the firmware residing on the hardware, the security of the system will be at risk of unauthorized access.

2.3.9 Multicore Processors

Today, chips contain multiple CPUs, called cores. The term CPU now refers to a chip with multiple cores, also called multicore processors. Today, it is common for chips to contain at least two cores as well as small fast memories, called caches, which are part of the memory management system, discussed later. These processors are capable of parallel computation, that is, the cores can compute independently of each other at the same time.

These new CPUs are very sophisticated. They use out-of-order execution to save time. When they encounter a time-consuming step, such as checking to see if a user has the authorization to access a memory location, which takes a relatively long time, they may continue to execute instructions while waiting for such checks to finish, discarding computations that failed to pass the checks. Although this technique provides very large speedups, it comes with a high price, which is explained later.

It is important to emphasize that instructions at the CPU level (machine level) are bit strings. Thus, if humans were to program a computer without the appropriate software tools, they would have to write millions of bit strings. That would present an insurmountable intellectual challenge. Consequently, software was invented to deal with this issue, as discussed later.

Policy Matters 2.1 Nationalizing semiconductor manufacturing

To date, the technology industry has largely been global with materials and components being sourced from around the world. Producers such as Intel, Nvidia, and Qualcomm manufacture semiconductors, such as memory chips and microprocessors, where it is most advantageous and sell to consumers globally regardless of nationality. Yet that may be changing. Chips have become the focus of national security concern in countries such as China and the United States. In China, the government has set a goal for all chip manufacturing to be local by 2030 to free itself from foreign dependence. In the United States, there have been various efforts to expand chip manufacturing to tighten control of the supply chain for security purposes. It is too early to say whether nationalizing chip manufacturing will be successful, but governments are crafting policies that will impact global manufacturing.

Source: Lewis (2019)

2.4 PROGRAMMING

A program consists of a set of commands, often referred to as code. A machine language program consists of instruction words and data words, each of which is a string of bits. As mentioned, instructions are typically denoted by a pair of fixed-length substrings, denoted [Opcode, Address], where Opcode specifies the type of instruction and Address denotes the memory address.

At the beginning of the modern computing era, computers were programmed in machine language. Soon Opcode mnemonics, such as ADD, AND, LDA (load a word from the RAM into the AC), STA (put the value of AC into memory), JZ (jump to a new address if all bits in AC are zero), and HLT (halt), were introduced to replace the binary sequences representing Opcodes.

Memory addresses were also given symbolic names, such as HEIGHT, AREA, PROFIT, and LOSS, instead of binary strings. The results were called assembly language programs. Such programs must be translated into bit strings before they are run on a computer. Programs that do this are called assemblers.

In the late 1950s it was recognized that assembly language programming was tedious and that an additional layer of abstraction was needed. This led to the creation of so-called high-level languages, which include ALGOL, FORTRAN, COBOL, and LISP. Programs in these languages are translated into machine language by programs called compilers.

Language development has continued. Today more than 600 programming languages have been developed, many designed to simplify programming and make it more secure. Some of these languages are very sophisticated and some are specialized, that is, providing functionality that is helpful with special tasks, such as developing web pages.

2.4.1 A Simple Programming Example

The simple multiplication program in Table 2.3, MULT(x, y, z), helps to appreciate the programming task. It is designed to multiply two integers, x and y, and produce the product $z = x * y$. It is written to show how multiplication can be done when the computer does not have a multiply operation but can add and subtract.

MULT(x, y, z) computes the product z by adding x copies of y. For example, if $x = 3$, $z = y + y + y$. This is how the algorithm used in the program multiplies two integers.

MULT(x, y, z) has six lines of instruction, or code. Instructions are executed in sequence, starting with line 1, unless a jump instruction is executed, in which case the program will resume at a new line.

Table 2.3 A simple integer multiplication program MULT(x, y, z)

Line Numbers	Command	Comment
1	Set $z = 0$, AC = x	Set register containing z to zero and AC to x.
2	JZ 6	If AC (or x) is zero, go to line 6 and exit with $z = x*y$
3	ADD y z	Add y to z
4	SUB 1 AC	Subtract 1 from AC (or x), that is, replace x with $x-1$
5	JUMP 2	Always jump to line 2
6	HALT	Here AC is zero and y copies of x have been added to z. The register z now contains the product of x and y.

The commands used here are ADD, SUB, JZ, JUMP, and HALT. ADD adds the first number to the second, SUB subtracts the first number from the second, and JZ (jump on zero AC) jumps to the specified line if all the bits in AC are zero. JUMP makes an unconditional jump to the specified line.

Each of the variables x, y, and z is stored in a CPU register. The values of x and y are obtained from the user before the program MULT(x, y, z) is run. The value of x is put into register AC. The product z is available in the register holding z when the computation is done.

On line 1 the variable z is initialized to 0 and AC is set to x. On line 2 if AC (or x) is 0 the command JZ is executed, and the program jumps to line 6 and terminates. If $x = 0$, z has value 0, which is the correct product in this case.

If AC (or x) is not 0, the code on line 3 is executed, which adds the value of y to the value of z, which is initially 0. Line 4 is then executed, which causes the value of x to be decremented by 1. On line 5, the program jumps back to line 2, where if AC is 0, the value of y has been added x times to z to obtain the correct product. If not, y is added to AC again, x is decremented again, and the test determines again if AC (or x) has been reduced to 0, in which case y has been added to AC x times and the program terminates with $z = x * y$.

2.4.2 The Programming Challenge

Programming is challenging primarily because there is a huge gap between the functionality needed by humans to perform meaningful tasks and that provided by programming languages. For example, in 2015 Google estimated that the

---

History Matters 2.4 Software development processes

Introduced in 1970, the Waterfall method was one of the earliest approaches to team-based software development. Large teams of software engineers began with a statement of user requirements, which were translated into software requirements, followed by preliminary software design, analysis of the design, final code design, coding itself, testing, and maintenance (Royce, 1987). If at any stage a modification is needed at an earlier stage, a substantial delay may occur while the change percolates through intermediate stages. This can severely delay the release of an application, making it difficult to estimate the time to completion, which can be a source of great stress for executives and software engineers alike.

In 2001, 17 software engineers, calling themselves the Agile Alliance, pursued an alternative approach to the Waterfall method. They captured their new philosophy in the Agile Manifesto is a set of values and principles that are designed to incorporate agility into the software development process:

• Individuals and interactions over processes and tools
• Working software over comprehensive documentation
• Customer collaboration over contract negotiation
• Responding to change over following a plan (Beck et al., 2001)

Their stated goals were to satisfy the customer, motivate and reward software engineers, and complete projects quickly. Agile software development supports and trusts team members and allows them to self-organize and collaborate with the end users rather than be a part of a large software development hierarchy separate from end users. The result has been rapidly produced software in line with customer preferences that can be quickly updated as needed.

---

software running its internet services, which include Google Search, Gmail, and Google Maps, consists of about two billion lines of code (Metz, 2015).

One might ask how difficult it was to produce that many lines of code. To write software one must first produce a clear and well-defined problem statement for a program. The code itself can be (a) previously written, that is, a library routine, (b) written for the program, or (c) a mixture of the two. The writing of the code must be planned. This will require assembling a team of programmers, testers, and support personnel. Finally, the code must be documented, that is, notes must be written to explain what the program is designed to do, and tested, that is, probed to determine if it meets documented objectives. Documentation serves to help the person(s) responsible for maintenance or updating the program who may not be the original author. For big programs, writing, testing, and maintaining code requires a big organization.

Although writing code itself is only a portion of the work, estimates from multiple sources report that approximately 10 to 20 lines of code can be written per day by experienced programmers, amortized over all the time spent on a programming project, which includes all the tasks described earlier. If it is assumed that a programmer works 5 days per week for 50 weeks per year, a programmer can produce between 2,500 and 5,000 lines of fully written, debugged, documented, and tested code per year.

In the case of our Google example with two billion lines of code, it took between 400,000 and 800,000 person-years of work to produce it! To simplify the task of writing code, computer scientists reuse code. Abstraction plays an important role here. When a useful piece of code is written, it is given a name and placed in a library.

Named code, variously called a procedure, routine, subroutine, method, or function, reduces the effort to write large complex programs. Once a procedure has been written, it can be used again simply by invoking its name in another program. The code itself does not have to be copied into the new program. Instead, the OS, described in the following section, retrieves the code from a software library.

While the ability to invoke procedures reduces the complexity of the coding process, it creates opportunities for a new and important security vulnerability, known as buffer overflow, discussed later. Abstraction also make reuse easier, which brings other risks.

Repeatedly programmers have used packages of open-source software, software publicly available under liberal licenses, without knowing that it contained vulnerable code, only later to be surprised and dismayed to discover that they had released software with major security vulnerabilities. To respond to such vulnerabilities discovered after code assembly, it has been proposed that software developers attach a "software bill of materials" to their code so that they can tell if they have used open-source software that later requires remediation.

2.5 OPERATING SYSTEMS

An OS is software that manages the hardware and software resources of a computer system. As suggested in Figure 2.12, an OS sits above the hardware and serves as an interface to the hardware for users and applications. It also responds

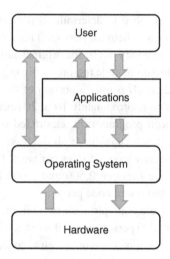

Figure 2.12   The role of the operating system

directly to user requests to start or stop an application or shut the computer down. An OS must manage multiple high-level tasks simultaneously, such as play music, run a text editor, monitor the arrival of email, and run a browser.

An OS maintains a list of active tasks and, in a round-robin fashion, gives each task a small amount of time on a single CPU core so that the user has the impression that the tasks are being executed in parallel, which is called multitasking. It also allocates tasks to separate cores so that it exhibits real parallelism. When an OS assigns tasks to a core, it does so by invoking a scheduling program that is designed to allocate computation time fairly to tasks.

When multitasking was introduced in the 1960s, it permitted a valuable resource, an expensive computer, to be shared. However, as with most innovations, it had unintended consequences. One is that a program supplied by one user could exploit coding errors to access the memory of another user, causing memory safety violations.

If a user or program with a lower security classification obtains unauthorized access to files at a higher level, it is said that the user or program has participated in an access privilege violation.

While servicing one task, a new event or activity may communicate with the OS and request its attention. The request will be signaled to the CPU with an interrupt request, a binary signal supplied by the new event to the computer. This will cause the OS to stop running the current task and add a new task to the queue of running programs. The purpose of this new task is to determine how the OS should respond to the interrupt. One very important type of interrupt is a request from a running program to either open or close a file. Such interrupts require the intervention of the OS to ensure that the calling program is privileged to access the file.

2.5.1 User Authentication

As computers became networked, there was also a need to establish individual user identities and the means to authenticate or validate an individual user in cyberspace. Authentication protects important assets, such as bank accounts, stock portfolios, personal email, corporate secrets, and national security.

In 1960 Fernando Corbató at the Massachusetts Institute of Technology introduced the password to maintain separation between individual users on a new multiuser time-sharing OS (Hafner, 2019). For a site to authenticate a user, both the site and the user must share at least one secret. The user presents a shared secret(s) and the site provides access. A breach occurs when a secret(s) is (are) revealed to a third party.

Most computers use single-factor authentication, which is based on one shared secret, namely, a user password, which, when combined with a user ID, authenticates the user. The ID and password constitute a credential. For example, if the ID is ME and the password is PSSWD, the pair [ME, MYPSSWD] constitutes a credential enabling the user to log into the system.

The OS of a computer that uses single-factor authentication maintains a password table that contains an entry for each credential. However, instead of storing pairs, such as [ME, MYPSSWD], it computes a "cryptographic hash" of the user password, denoted $H(\text{MYPSSWD})$, and stores pairs [ME, $H(\text{MYPSSWD})$)] for each user ID ME.

A cryptographic hash function H compresses a string X to another string of fixed length, namely, $H(X)$, which is called a "hash," in such a way that it is very difficult to find X or a string that compresses to the value $H(X)$. The SHA-2 family of cryptographic hash functions, defined by the National Institutes of Standards and Technology (NIST) (2023), contains the widely used SHA-256 hash function that produces a 256-bit hash.

An attacker who wants to break into a computer will supply a user ID, UNAME, and a password, SCRT, from which the OS will compute $H(\text{SCRT})$. The OS will check the password table TBL for an entry associated with UNAME, which, if it exists, will take the form [UNAME, $H(\text{PSSWD})$], where PSSWD is the password for UNAME. If $H(\text{PSSWD})$ is equal to $H(\text{SCRT})$, the OS authenticates UNAME and grants access. A security violation occurs if SCRT is not equal to PSSWD but $H(\text{SCRT}) = H(\text{PSSWD})$. This is very unlikely if H is a cryptographic hash function.

Essential Principle 2.2 Strengthening password security

There are several ways to harden a password file. First, each computer can create its own special string, which is called SALT, and, instead of storing H(PSSWD) in a password file, the OS stores H(SALT·PSSWD), where SALT·PSWWD is a new string formed by prefixing PSSWD with the string SALT. Thus, a dictionary (or rainbow table) attack requires that an attacker obtain SALT for a computer before he/she/they can construct a rainbow table, making it much harder for the attacker to break password security by constructing a rainbow table for each value of SALT.

A second method to harden password security is to employ a hash function that takes a relatively long time to compute, that is, a time that is short by human standards, say a few hundredths of a second, but long for a computer. This will make the time taken to build a large rainbow table very large. Unfortunately, reliance on a single secret, namely a password, does not provide much protection against a determined attacker. Using powerful graphics processing units (GPUs) and knowing the target's SALT string, an attacker can quickly produce a rainbow table. While a determined attacker can decipher a single password table, doing that for many targets all using different long SALT strings is very difficult.

2.5.2 Breaking Password Security

Often user IDs are known – for example, it might be firstname_lastname@ school.edu – although passwords are not known. One method of breaking password security is to try multiple passwords for a given user ID. OSs protect against this well-known technique by disabling logins when too many logins are attempted with a given ID in a short time interval. A better way to break security is to steal the password table and then analyze it at leisure.

Hash-based password management is vulnerable to a dictionary (or rainbow table) attack. Because the hash function H used by an OS is not secret, an attacker can construct a table of pairs [H(WORD)], WORD] for every word in a dictionary. If a password table has been stolen by an attacker, he/she/they can search the rainbow table to see if it contains a password hash, H(WORD). If so, WORD is a valid password, which will provide unauthorized access.

Since users do not always use dictionary words as passwords, a rainbow table should be constructed from both dictionary words and passwords known to be in common use, such as 12345 or the word "passw0rd."

Computing a rainbow table can be very time-consuming. However, once it is computed, looking up the hash of a putative password, such as PSSWD, can be done quickly. Since each hash has a corresponding input string, that string is a valid password.

2.5.3 Multifactor Authentication

It is recommended that multifactor authentication, based on multiple secrets, be deployed. A typical two-factor authentication system uses not only login credentials but also the user's phone number. When a login attempt is made by submitting a user's login credentials, the computer phones the user and requests that the user send a text response. The response confirms that the person attempting the login has possession of the user phone. Authentication security can also be strengthened by supplying biometric data, such as a fingerprint or a retinal or facial scan.

Although two-factor authentication using a smart phone is quite secure, it is somewhat tedious to reach for a phone each time authentication is needed. This can be avoided by using a hardware security key, which is typically carried on one's person and plugged into a computer.

All methods of authentication present security challenges, including two-factor authentication. For example, phones and hardware keys can be stolen and text messages can be intercepted. Since facial recognition systems must be trained, they may be tricked. However, richer authentication methods, even if flawed, do increase the work factor for the attacker. Security engineers make trade-offs between the attacker work factor and the effort required by users to authenticate themselves.

2.5.4 File System Access Privileges

An OS also provides a variety of other services such as a file system, that is, software for the creation of folders (also known as directories) in which to store files. File systems support access privileges on files. If the OS recognizes groups of individuals, a file may be given world, group, and owner privileges, which are typically different. The owner of the file decides whether to grant read (r), write (w), or execute (x) privileges to the owner, a member of a group, and every user, that is, the world. The capability to write a file includes the right to edit it. Execute privileges on file means the ability to run it.

For example, in the Unix OS the privileges $[(r,-,-), (r,w,-),(r,w,x)]$ on a file indicates that everyone can read the file but not write or execute it (the first

---

Exploit 2.1 Configuration errors

Due to a configuration error a security researcher, scanning a public Boeing Company website, found software for the Boeing 787 Dreamliner in-flight entertainment system. He analyzed the code and found vulnerabilities that he said could give a passenger a foothold to the aircraft's computer system, possibly providing access to aircraft engines and brakes. Boeing says this access is not possible but does acknowledge that critical aircraft software had been made public.

Source: Greenberg (2019a)

---

triple), thar any member of the group can read and edit the file but not execute it (the second triple), and that the owner can read, edit, and execute the file (the third triple). Similar access privileges can be assigned to a folder or directory. Sometimes, users do not manage their permissions well and private files are inadvertently made available to the public. See Exploit 2.1

A security vulnerability occurs if the owner of a file unintentionally permits everyone to read a file and then connects his/her/their computer to the Internet, thereby making it world readable, which is an example of a configuration error.

Operating systems typically have both users, whose access is limited as shown above, and administrators or superusers, whose access is unlimited; that is, they can read, modify, and execute all files and visit every folder.

2.5.5 Memory Hierarchies

Computer memory today is no longer a single large RAM that operates at the same speed as the CPU. Such a RAM would be prohibitively expensive. Thus, computer architects simulate a single large fast RAM by assembling a hierarchy of memories, ranging from very small but very fast memories (registers and caches) to larger but slower memories as well as disks and tapes, as suggested in Figure 2.13. The hierarchy has CPU registers at the top followed by caches, such as L1 and L2 caches, the dynamic RAM (DRAM), and disks. The registers are as fast as the CPU. The L1 cache has more storage than the registers but is somewhat slower than them. The L2 cache is larger than the L1 cache but slower. The DRAM is very large but today it is about 50 to more than 150 times slower than the CPU. Finally, disks and tapes are generally extremely large and very slow but still usable for long-term storage.

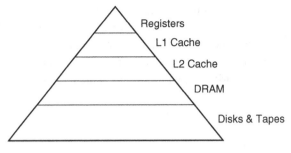

Figure 2.13   A memory hierarchy

Scheduling algorithms are used to simulate a single fast RAM from this complex by predicting when instructions and data are likely to be needed by the CPU and moving them toward the fastest cache and away from it when they are not needed soon.

Data on a disk drive is organized into circular tracks. To read or write data on a track, a head is moved to the track, which takes time and accounts for its slow speed. The physical size of the disk accounts for its high capacity. Each track is typically subdivided into hundreds of sectors of 512, 2048, or 4096 bytes each. The first sector on the first track is called the boot sector and its contents are called the Master Boot Record (MBR). It is read and executed by the CPU boot program.

If the boot sector of a disk drive is damaged or encrypted by malware, a computer will not boot. Ransomware frequently succeeds by encrypting the MBR of computers that it infects (Constantin, 2012).

2.5.6 Virtual Memory

In the early days of computing, programmers were responsible for subdividing programs stored on disks into segments of bits and then writing instructions into their programs to move segments up and down the memory hierarchy. Today, the task of breaking a program into segments and moving these segments, now called pages, up and down the memory hierarchy is handled by the OS using scheduling algorithms to position pages so that they are almost always available when needed by the CPU. The software that does this processing creates a virtual memory and it simulates a single fast RAM. It is supported by specialized hardware and software.

Virtual memory greatly simplifies the task of programmers who can now write software for computers without knowing how their memories are organized. This was a very important advance in software engineering. An extra benefit of virtual memory is that it creates a unique virtual memory for each program. This is expected to isolate the virtual memories assigned to different running programs and protect the memory of each program. However, as recently discovered, it does not always do that, which has created an extremely serious security vulnerability for which partial solutions have been found.

2.5.7 Processes

A process consists of a program P and the data that it uses during its execution. Many programs use library routines, small programs designed to be reused. Therefore, when a program is running, it is necessary for the OS to prepare for its possible interruption so that it can call upon a library routine.

To do this, as shown in Figure 2.14 (a), the OS partitions virtual memory space into space for (a) the code text for P; (b) P's static variables, whose number is known in advance; (c) P's dynamic variables, which are allocated on demand and stored in the heap whose size is unknown before P's execution; and (d) the stack, containing stack frames, which are temporary locations reserved for data used by library routines. A stack frame is illustrated in Figure 2.14 (b). The stack is like an upside-down pushdown stack (PDS) of the kind found in a cafeteria that holds trays. When a tray is put on top, the other trays move down one step. The upside-down PDS in Figure 2.14 (b) grows downward as entries are added and shrinks upward as frames are

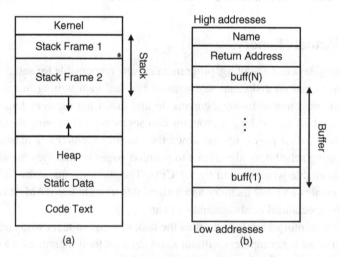

Figure 2.14   (a) Virtual memory containing the stack and (b) one stack frame

deleted. The heap grows upward as dynamic variables are added and shrinks downward as they are deleted.

When a program P invokes a library routine, LR, such as MULT(x, y, z) described earlier, it must stop its execution and start the execution of LR. When LR completes, it must return control of the computation to P. To implement this, the OS pushes a stack frame onto the stack.

The first item on the frame is the name of the library routine. (Recall that as entries are entered on the stack, they are placed at successively smaller addresses.) The second item is the return address for LR, that is, the location in P at which to resume computation when LR is finished. In this example each item occupies one memory word. These items are followed by the temporary space needed to compute LR.

As suggested in Figure 2.14 (b) we assume that LR uses one large buffer as the temporary storage space that occupies N locations, called buff(1), buff(2), ..., buff(N). We use this stack frame example to describe buffer overflow, a serious security vulnerability. buff(1) is at the top of the stack, that is, at a low address, and buff(N) is lower in the stack, that is, at a higher address. The first data entered into the buffer is buff(1) and the last is buff(N),

2.5.8 Buffer Overflow

Older programming languages, such as C and C++, allow programmers to create buffers with a fixed number of entries but allow the user to store an unlimited number of entries in them. That is, as in the example of Figure 2.14 (b), more data may be written into a buffer than there are locations reserved for it. In a typical application, data is read from a user. The first word that is read is placed in location buff(1), the second is placed in buff(2), and so on. If the programmer did not restrict his/her/their program to store at most N words and the user supplies more than N words, the OS will replace data in adjacent memory locations, such as those reserved for a return address, and a buffer overflow will occur.

A buffer overflow can produce unexpected results such as causing a computer to crash when it reads a string that is not an acceptable computer instruction.

An attacker who knows that a program is using a buffer that is susceptible to overflow can use this knowledge to change the program return address. This will cause the computer to jump to an address of the attacker's choosing, which is extremely dangerous, and a buffer overflow security exploit will occur. This might allow the attacker to run code the attacker has placed into the first N locations of the buffer, taking control of the computer.

2.5.9 Protecting against Buffer Overflow

Buffer overflow can be avoided by writing code that prevents more data to be written into a buffer than is determined by its maximal anticipated size. Modern programming languages do this automatically. Unfortunately, a lot of old code (*legacy code*) is in use today that exhibits buffer overflow vulnerabilities but is too expensive to replace.

An attacker who launches a buffer overflow attack will try to take control of a computer by either (a) running code that he/she/they place on the stack while overwriting the stack or (b) invoking a library routine or part of a routine.

To prevent the code from executing from the stack, the defender can set the data execution prevention bit that will prevent instructions on the stack from being executed. All modern OSs offer this protection.

To execute the second type of attack, invoking a library routine, the attacker must know exactly where the library routine is located in virtual memory. The defender can obtain additional protection by invoking address space layout randomization (ASLR) inside the virtual memory allocated to each process. ASLR offsets the location of the code, the stack, the heap, and libraries by a randomly chosen number of bytes.

The ASLR offsets are fixed before programs start running. Unfortunately, they often can be determined by an attacker with a limited amount of experimentation. A better solution is to use shuffling (Williams-King et al., 2016), a variant of ASLR. Here a program is analyzed, its functional pieces are identified, and links between them determined. The pieces are then periodically moved to new locations and the links updated. Shuffling can be done so quickly (in milliseconds or less) that an attacker is highly unlikely to find the code layout fast enough to launch an exploit before it changes. Even the shuffling program itself can be shuffled. Shuffling offers the possibility to protect legacy code, old code written when software engineers were not taught to avoid security vulnerabilities.

2.6 MALICIOUS SOFTWARE

As noted earlier, the purpose of cybersecurity is to ensure confidentiality, integrity, and availability (CIA) of data, resources, and systems. Malware is software designed to violate one or more of these conditions. Confidentiality is violated by obtaining access to systems without authorization. Integrity is compromised by maliciously altering or erasing data. And availability is denied either by destroying or encrypting files on a computer or by overwhelming the

---

Exploit 2.2 NotPetya, extraordinarily damaging malware

The NotPetya worm is a wiper. Released in June 2017, it had a devastating impact on companies all over the world, costing an estimated $10 billion loss. A Russian military hacking team inserted NotPetya into the update software for a widely used Ukrainian tax accounting program. One of the fastest-spreading worms ever seen, it disabled computers owned by Merck, the pharmaceutical company; Federal Express, the delivery firm; Saint-Gobain, the French construction company; and Maersk, the world's largest shipping company, among others. Each spent hundreds of millions of dollars to remediate the damage done. The cost to Merck alone was $1.3 billion.

Source: Greenberg (2018)

---

computer in some fashion, for example, by asking it to process more network traffic than it is designed to handle, which constitutes a denial of service.

Attackers often use social engineering, that is, "the use of deception to manipulate individuals into divulging confidential or personal information that may be used for fraudulent purposes" (Definition of Social Engineering, n.d.). For example, an email that seems important and looks authentic but has a slightly falsified sender email address might convince a user to open an attached document. Similarly, an urgent appeal for emergency financial help from a superior who says that he/she/they has/have been robbed in a foreign country might also work.

This type of social engineering attack is called phishing. Targeted phishing is known as spear-phishing. And an important target of a phishing attack is often called a whale. Business email compromise is the use of social engineering in email that causes harm to a business, government, or organization. For example, BlackEnergy was a Trojan launched in December 2015 against an electrical grid in Ukraine (Zetter, 2016) that resulted in the first confirmed attack against a power grid. An estimated 230,000 residents were left in the dark for one to six hours.

A more sophisticated attacker may first phish a target to determine which types of files are important to that person and encrypt those files. While ransomware is often loaded onto a computer because of a social engineering attack, it also can also be spread by a worm without user intervention by exploiting a vulnerability common to many computers, as was true of WannaCry in 2017. It affected hundreds of thousands of computers and is attributed to North Korea (Bossert, 2017).

Essential Principle 2.3 Behavioral analysis

Behavioral analysis, the identification of malware by observing its behavior, is another well-established malware identification technique. For example, a ransomware program might be detected by observing that it asks the OS to open many files in sequence, processes each file, and then writes it back. In this case the malware may be encrypting files so that it can request ransom to decrypt them. Similarly, if software attempts to communicate with a website known to be employed by attackers, that is another strong indication that a malicious or compromised program is running.

Some cyber forensics firms provide a small OS implant, a piece of code that reports such OS requests to a .website, where behavioral reports are compared with prior observations. If similar suspicious reports are generated on multiple client machines, it may be possible to identify malware even when its signature is not in the antivirus database.

2.7 ANTIVIRUS SOFTWARE

For as long as there have been malware attacks, there have been efforts to catalog and counter malware. Antivirus (AV) software attempts to identify files containing viruses using signature analysis, that is, by trying to find a malware signature, a string in a malicious file that is not generally found in a nonmalicious file. AV software is invoked when the OS is asked by an application to open a file. As the file is read from backup storage, such as a disk, the OS tries to match strings in a file with its list of virus signatures.

If a file is found to contain malware, AV software will try to remove the virus from the file or isolate the file if the virus cannot be removed. Similarly, when data is read from sources outside a computer, such as via the Internet, it too is passed through AV software. This is a way to catch some malware, such as viruses, worms, Trojans, and ransomware, before they move onto a computer and cause damage. Note, however, that malware can enter a computer via a download from a remote site or via a flash drive and will not necessarily be scanned by AV software.

Unfortunately, hackers have learned how to create polymorphic viruses that change their signatures each time they replicate. Consequently, signature analysis is losing its effectiveness. However, if a polymorphic virus has been circulating for a while, it is likely that past versions will be identified, classified, and incorporated into the list of AV signatures. If so, it will be possible to find and remove a virus if a user does a deep scan of their file system, that is, a scan of all files, looking for malware.

2.8 HARDWARE SIDE-CHANNEL ATTACKS

Although most of the attention to cybersecurity has focused on software vulnerabilities, hardware can also have security vulnerabilities and they can be more difficult to remediate than software vulnerabilities and do as much or more harm.

Many hardware attacks are side-channel attacks that reveal information that was not intended to be released by the designer of the hardware. In such an attack, information can be leaked through a variety of physical conduits, as explained shortly.

Side-channel attacks have become a severe threat to cybersecurity. For example, such attacks have been known to have broken the security of Diffie–Hellman, RSA, and other cryptosystems (Kocher, 1996; Lou et al., 2021).

The following are examples of hardware side-channel attacks categorized by the type of conduit they use.

- Acoustic Attacks

Sound emitted when keys are depressed on a computer keyboard or an ATM keypad can be recorded and analyzed to determine with high probability which keys were depressed (Guri, 2021).

Data can also be exfiltrated by generating an ultrasound oscillation on a computer that will resonate with a smartphone gyroscope. The signal is modulated with data meant to be exfiltrated. Ultrasound frequencies are above the audible range. When played through a speaker placed near a smartphone containing a gyroscope, oscillations at the right frequency will cause gyroscope vibrations, which can be analyzed by an application on the phone to extract the data that modulates the oscillation (Guri, 2021).

Acoustic attacks can be prevented by prohibiting the use of sound recording equipment and smartphones in the vicinity of a computer containing sensitive information, as would be the case for a special compartmental information facility (SCIF). If a SCIF has windows, they must also be layered so that laser reflections from vibrating glass cannot be used to recover conversations near the window.

- Electromagnetic Radiation Attacks

Bluetooth signals are a form of electromagnetic radiation (ER). Malware on a computer can collect covert information and broadcast it on Bluetooth, which then can be received by a Bluetooth-enabled computer. If the latter is outside Bluetooth's normal 30-meter range, a Bluetooth "rifle," consisting of a directional antenna attached to a Bluetooth-enabled computer, can extend the range to nearly 2 kilometers.

An ER attack on computers containing sensitive information can be prevented by operating them within a Faraday cage, a metallic enclosure that prevents ER from escaping, as would be the case for a SCIF.

• Power Consumption Attacks

In this attack an attacker measures the power consumed by a computer and, knowing the application running on the computer, uses the timing of changes in power consumption to determine which instruction has been executed. An attacker might arrange to have the target computer run a decryption algorithm whose algorithm is public. With this knowledge, an attacker may be able to deduce the bits in a secret key.

• Memory Cache Attack

This is an attack that exploits CPU innovations introduced in the 1990s to produce dramatic speedups but inadvertently allowed data to be extracted from protected memory to be recorded in the state of a local cache, only to be recovered later. The Meltdown Attack, described later, is this type of attack.

• Timing Attack

The power consumption attack and memory cache attack both use instruction timing.

Exploit 2.3 Hardware side-channel attacks

When a program P is launched, the OS creates a new virtual memory space for it and puts the OS and links to *all files on the computer* into P's virtual memory space. Although this feature should make all memory accessible to P, the OS is designed to prevent P from seeing memory locations for which it has not been granted access, such as those owned by the OS or other programs. Optimizations introduced in the 1990s allowed a program to read a byte from protected memory and treat it as an index to move a word from an array in slow memory to the fast cache. Later, P could determine how long it takes to read each word in the array. The one read most quickly has an index equal to the value of the byte read from protected memory, creating a side channel.

2.8.1 Central Processing Unit Innovations Introduced in the 1990s

The fetch–execute cycle described earlier explains how the CPU operates. The address of the next instruction, which is in the CPU program counter, is moved to the RAM and used to fetch the next instruction. The instruction is brought to the CPU, decoded, and executed. If an instruction needs data not currently available, such as a value located in a secondary memory, which may require hundreds of CPU cycles to retrieve, the CPU processor stops (or stalls) and waits until the data is available.

In the 1990s computer architects were in competition to increase processor speed. Using the fact that machine-level instructions could be broken down into small or micro-operations (μ-OPs), they observed that instead of stalling while waiting for data from slow memories to arrive, they could execute μ-OPs associated with independent instruction streams. This results in out-of-order instruction execution (O-o-OE). (The standard execution model based on the fetch-execute model is called in-order instruction execution [IOE] or program order.) Of course, the results must later be put into program order. CPUs were also equipped with multiple functional units so that several functions could be computed in parallel.

Because O-o-OE greatly increased the effective speed of CPUs, it was introduced into mainstream CPUs in the mid-1990s and subsequently incorporated in all but the least powerful CPUs.

Another CPU innovation to save time was to install branch-prediction hardware so that the history of past branch decisions could be used to predict the next branch decision. CPUs that used this feature were said to be speculating. If a CPU speculated correctly, time was saved when the processor would otherwise stall. If the CPU speculation is wrong, the other branch is computed.

If a computation done using O-o-OE and speculation had to be reversed, the CPU must undo changes that were made to its state. Unfortunately, subtle changes can be made in the local cache, which allows information to leak, creating a memory cache attack, sketched in Exploit 2.3.

2.8.2 The Meltdown and Spectre Side-Channel Attacks

In January 2018, the cybersecurity community was shocked to learn that deploying O-o-OE combined with delayed permission checks created an extremely serious security problem (Horn, 2017), affecting almost all CPUs manufactured since 1995, including smartphones, personal computers, servers, routers, tablets, and even some TVs! O-o-OE allows computation to continue while a time-consuming check for permission occurs. In this case, the check is on the authorization of a program to access an arbitrary memory location.

These CPU innovations made it possible to launch a memory cache attack and create a side channel that allows a cleverly crafted program running on a computer with one of these CPUs to read the entire computer memory, including that of the OS.

The security of the computer is completely melted down by O-o-OE. This is why it is called Meltdown. A second, similar, security violation, called Spectre, was discovered at about the same time, which also violates memory isolation using speculative execution. Once these two security vulnerabilities were found, many others were also identified. Hardware security is hard!

We now sketch a program that can implement Meltdown, that is, it can read every computer memory location. The program (a) creates an array with 256 elements, the number of different bytes (each has 8 bits), (b) tells the OS to flush the new array, that is, send it to slow secondary memory. Then, the program (c) chooses a memory address, (d) reads one byte from that address, and (e) uses that byte as an index to read one element from the new array. This moves this element of the 256-element array from slow memory to the fast cache.

The program then reads all the elements in the array, measuring the time it takes for each one. The index of the array element that arrives most quickly is the value of the byte that was read from the memory location. This violates security. The program can then repeat this operation for every memory location and completely violate security. Creating a dump of memory this way is slow, but it is effective in reading every memory location.

Moreover, O-o-OE allows memory data to be read without authorization because computer architects know that it will take hundreds of cycles for the OS to check memory access. They assumed that any changes subsequently made could be undone. However, they overlooked the possibility of a cache memory attack.

Fortunately, remediations have been found for Meltdown and Spectre. Unfortunately, once these vulnerabilities were understood, many others were also identified (Lou et al., 2021). Computer security is a hard problem, both in software and hardware.

2.9 ETHICAL ISSUES IN HARDWARE AND SOFTWARE ENGINEERING

Ethics are principles that guide behavior. The classical Greek philosopher Aristotle's discussions of ethics are concerned with questions of how people should act, emphasizing the pursuit of a balance in behavior that serves the greatest good while also pursuing a life that is personally satisfying and fulfilling (Aristotle, 2012). This classical definition persists today and each profession such as medicine, engineering, and computer science has ethical standards. The two premier professional associations that represent computer science are the IEEE Computer Society and the Association for Computing Machinery (ACM).[1] Together they have formulated the Software Engineering Code of Ethics and Professional Practice (Gotterbarn et al., 1997), which they have published in both short and long versions. The short version is summarized as Essential Principle Box 2.4. The code for software engineers is sufficiently generic to all members of IEEE and ACM.

Essential Principle 2.4 Software Engineering Code of Ethics (short version)

Software engineers shall commit themselves to making the analysis, specification, design, development, testing and maintenance of software a beneficial and respected profession. In accordance with their commitment to the health, safety and welfare of the public, software engineers shall adhere to the following Eight Principles:

1. PUBLIC – Software engineers shall act consistently with the public interest.
2. CLIENT AND EMPLOYER – Software engineers shall act in a manner that is in the best interests of their client and employer consistent with the public interest.
3. PRODUCT – Software engineers shall ensure that their products and related modifications meet the highest professional standards possible.
4. JUDGMENT – Software engineers shall maintain integrity and independence in their professional judgment.
5. MANAGEMENT – Software engineering managers and leaders shall subscribe to and promote an ethical approach to the management of software development and maintenance.
6. PROFESSION – Software engineers shall advance the integrity and reputation of the profession consistent with the public interest.
7. COLLEAGUES – Software engineers shall be fair to and supportive of their colleagues.
8. SELF – Software engineers shall participate in lifelong learning regarding the practice of their profession and shall promote an ethical approach to the practice of the profession.

Source: Gotterbarn et al. (1997)

---

[1] IEEE is the Institute of Electrical and Electronic Engineers, which describes itself as the world's largest technical professional organization for the advancement of technology.

2.10 CONCLUSIONS

Computation has played an important role since ancient times. It was needed to build the pyramids, make astrological projections, such as eclipses, put humans on the moon, create the devices we use to order food, hail a taxi, or book travel, and to navigate with ease. Skyscrapers would not be possible without it nor would the civilization that we have created. Thus, while the abacus, punch card, and slide rule look antiquated by today's standards, so too will the devices of today over the next 30 years. The common thread, however, will remain the logic of computation and the important role algorithms play. Chapter 3 explores how computers are brought together through networking in general and the Internet in particular. It also examines symmetric and asymmetric encryption technologies that provide the necessary security to ensure data remains confidential and assured.

2.11 DISCUSSION TOPICS

Note: These topics exploit analogies between cooking and computing.

1. Find one straight-line recipe in which no repetition or branching occurs and a second in which they do occur. The latter should have a loop and a test that determines subsequent steps. Comment on the parallels between these recipes and the logic circuit and the RAM.
2. Explore analogies between the roles played by equipment in a modern restaurant kitchen and OSs and virtual memory for computing.
3. To the extent that you can, compare the roles played by members of the "Brigade de Cuisine" and a software development team.
4. List four vulnerabilities that exist in and around a kitchen that if exploited, either by an insider or an outsider, such as a supplier or thief, can result in injury to clients/customers, including the loss of intellectual property in the case of a famous chef.
5. By analogy with regulation of the food processing sector (e.g., expiration dates on yogurt), formulate three major policies for regulation of the information processing sector.

3

Communicating through Cyberspace

> Over the past decade data communications has been revolutionized by
> a radically new technology called packet switching.
> > Larry Roberts (1978), an internet pioneer

3.1 COMMUNICATION NETWORKS

The Internet, a network of networks, provides the communications infrastructure on which we have all come to depend for online shopping, research, and communicating with friends and family. To be sure, the Internet is ubiquitous and "being online" and "in real life" are losing distinction. We have moved from the early days of using large mainframe computers at universities programmed with punch cards to using handheld devices wirelessly connected to the Internet and to wearables and implants that monitor vital signs. Yet, just as Chapter 2 addressed the basis for computation, which is rooted deeply in human civilization, communication also has an important and relevant history that informs ways to improve cybersecurity.

3.2 COMMUNICATION TECHNOLOGIES

Humans have used technology to communicate for centuries. This is illustrated by the simple acoustic telephone, which is a pair of tin cans connected by a taut string (see Figure 3.1). Although sound is conveyed across a line, this system was limited to the transmission of the human voice over short distances. An advance came in 1830 when Joseph Henry demonstrated the telegraph for transmitting messages using short or long pulses of electrical current over a pair of wires terminated with a buzzer. Pulses of electrical current produce short and long duration buzzing, corresponding to dots and dashes, which Samuel Morse composed into his code for telegraph transmission, now known as "Morse Code."

Figure 3.1   The Acoustic (tin can) Telephone, licensed under Getty Images/DigitalVision Vectors/Nastasic

Figure 3.2   Bell's Telephone Transmitter and Receiver licensed under Attribution 4.0 International, Museum Victoria

This enabled long-range communication, which was previously unmatched in human communication. While you might be able to find a telegraph only in a museum now, its legacy resonates, since Morse's dots and dashes correspond to the zeroes and ones of the binary system used in computers today.

Alexander Graham Bell invented the electric telephone in 1876 (see Figure 3.2). His phone transmitted speech using continuous electric currents over telegraph wires, instead of just *on* and *off* electric current. His transmitter directed sound onto a membrane fitted over a drum. The sound caused the membrane to vibrate and to vary the resistance in an electrical circuit. This in turn caused the amount of current flowing between the transmitter and the receiver to vary in proportion to the resistance and the sound. The receiver also had a membrane that was made to vibrate in response to the current and produce the sound. This great achievement allowed spoken human language to be converted to electricity and travel along a wire, which revolutionized communication.

In 1886, Heinrich Hertz proved the existence of radio waves, which are a form of electromagnetic radiation that is all around us. This was a key scientific breakthrough and triggered an effort to understand the electromagnetic spectrum, which classifies types of radiation into gamma, x-ray, ultraviolet, visible light, infrared, microwave, and radio waves. Within 10 years, Guglielmo Marconi constructed the first practical radio transmitters and receivers, which freed audio communication from connected wires. Radio came into commercial use around 1900; this had the effect of democratizing the information space since transmitted signals could cross borders and anyone with a receiver could hear the message, be it music, news, or speeches. These early discoveries are still used today; electromagnetic transmissions are now used to connect devices wirelessly via Bluetooth for local and via cables and radio for global communication, emphasizing that we are now well beyond the days of physical connections between two tin cans or telegraph stations connected by physical wires.

Once communication technologies became widely available, inventors used them to construct communication networks, which consist of communications media and protocols for data transmission. The media include copper wires that carry electric current, fiber-optic cables that carry light, and free-space electromagnetic radiation or what we know of as radio, Wi-Fi, and satellite communication. As the use of networks increased, inventors created protocols

---

Exploit 3.1 Phone phreaking

Although AT&T maintained strict control over the design of its telephone network, in the 1960s hackers discovered, partly by accident, that they could exploit a vulnerability in its design to make free long-distance calls. The same audible frequencies were used to transmit both voice and control information (tones identifying numbers).

A caller made a toll-free call during which they injected a tone from a so-called Blue Box into the phone mouthpiece telling the network to terminate the call, followed by tones for a new number to which to connect. Some famous entrepreneurs, including Steve Jobs and Steven Wozniak, were phone phreakers in their youth.

This vulnerability was fixed by redesigning switches so that data and control frequencies are separated.

(governing rules) for the efficient flow of data across the networks. These rules establish on what frequency a device or organization can operate and standards for packaging data to send and receive it over media. The object is to ensure that one user's transmission does not corrupt another user's transmission, or one television station does not occupy another station's frequency. Early telephony solved this problem by establishing appropriate protocols.

3.3 TELEPHONE NETWORKS

Traditional telephone networks are circuit-switched networks. They connect pairs of hosts. When a customer dials a number, the network connects the caller to a remote party by creating a dedicated communication path, or circuit, between them. The caller is connected via a direct connection to a local telephone exchange or switch, normally in the center of a city, whereupon a connection is made to a sequence of other exchanges until the exchange serving the called party is reached. At that point a connection is made to the called party's phone. The circuit defined by these connections persists for the duration of the telephone call and is reminiscent of the tin can telephone.

Providers of telephone networks, such as AT&T, generally maintain strict control over their network. They do not publicize its internal design, nor do they allow equipment to be attached to it unless it meets their standards. This is important to protect both the company's security and intellectual property, but it is also a good illustration of the fact that networks are corporate and proprietary rather than public. This approach led to a monopoly where only one provider existed for a large area, which stifled innovation, and to a centralized approach that was inherently vulnerable to disruption. If a particular transmission station went down, then the whole network could be disrupted.

3.4 PACKET-BASED NETWORKS

In the 1960s there was a governmental interest in ensuring communications could survive major disruptions, such as a nuclear attack or a natural disaster. As a consequence, several individuals thought beyond the centralized switching approach and conceived of a new way to communicate between two hosts, which has been dubbed *packet-based switching*.[1] Instead of sending a data

---

[1] History of the Internet (Leiner et al., 2009) describes the packet-based networks that were precursors to the Internet.

Essential Principle 3.1 Packet looping

Because routers in packet-based networks are not coordinated, a packet may enter a never-ending loop, leading to congestion. To purge such packets, a time-to-live (TTL) number is placed in a packet header that is decremented each time a packet passes through a router. A packet is discarded if its TTL reaches zero.

---

stream from a source over a single dedicated circuit, such as a telephone line, it was envisioned that data would be bundled into fixed-size blocks, or *packets*, containing the addresses of the source and destination computers and that packets would be sent to their destinations by potentially different paths. At the destination, packets would be reassembled, if necessary, in their order of transmission. Packet-based switching permits multiple data streams to share one communication path, which leads to a more efficient use of communication bandwidth and provides resiliency to disruptions.

Packet-based switching was also designed to interconnect individual networks. To achieve this goal, when a packet emerged from one network, the neighboring network into which it entered should be one that would move the packet closer to its destination. Routers, specialized computers designed to make these routing decisions, serve this purpose – they interconnect networks.

For a network to function, routers need to know to which neighbor they should send their packets, which is called the *routing problem*. The Border Gateway Protocol (BGP), described later, is designed to provide the necessary information to route packets to their destinations. The resulting structure is highly decentralized, adding to the overall stability of the system since there is no single point of failure. Packets contain the addresses (a string of bits) of the source of a packet and its destination, which are needed to route packets.

Shown in Figure 3.3 are three networks connected to each other by routers (rectangles with the lightest shading) and one domain name system (DNS) server (the rectangle with the darkest shading), discussed next. Two of these networks have three nodes (or hosts) and one has four nodes. (The nodes in the same network have the same shading.) The DNS server is accessible from the routers. The Internet is global and consists of more than 60,000 autonomous systems, that is, independently managed networks.

Once the concept of packet-based switching was introduced, several experimental packet-based networks were created in the late 1960s and early 1970s (History of the Internet, 2022). One of these was ARPANET, which was developed by the Advanced Research Projects Agency (ARPA) of the US

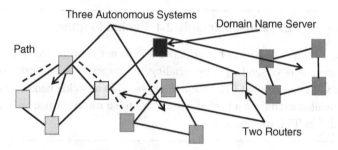

Figure 3.3   Three autonomous systems, two routers, and one domain name server

Department of Defense (DoD). ARPA was created in 1959 to develop technologies for DoD in response to the Sputnik crisis (Office of the Historian, US Department of State, n.d.). On January 1, 1983, ARPANET was renamed the Internet, which is a portmanteau of interconnected networks. It was designed to interconnect networks, regardless of what technologies are used to realize each individual network.

3.5 THE DOMAIN NAME SYSTEM

Early inventors of packet-based networks realized that nodes needed identities, whereupon they invented the *domain name system*. This system assigns binary Internet Protocol (IP) addresses (fixed-length strings of bits or numbers) to each node so that packets can be transmitted between networked devices. The inventors also realized that users could not remember long binary address strings. So, they invented domain names, text strings punctuated with periods, such as *www.papers.bostonpost.net*, so that users could remember the names of sites they wished to visit.

The DNS, which is like a telephone book for the Internet, maps domain names to IP addresses. Thus, the Internet has two namespaces, domain names and IP addresses. The publisher of this book, for example, can be accessed via the IPv4 address 104.16.55.52 or the domain name www.cambridge.org. Using either one in a browser will take you to the same site. The domain name is obviously much easier to remember than a string of four decimal numbers.

There are two types of IP addresses in use today, 32-bit addresses, *IP version 4* (IPv4), and 128-bit addresses, *IP version 6* (IPv6). IPv4 was launched in 1983 and IPv6 in 1998 when it was obvious that the IPv4 addresses would soon be exhausted, which occurred around 2011. IPv4 has 2^{32} or about 4.3 billion addresses, and IPv6, has 2^{128} or about 3.4×10^{38} addresses, which is

340,282,366,920,938,471,114,670,000,000,000,000,000 addresses, enough to satisfy any foreseeable need.

The DNS is a distributed hierarchical naming system for networked devices that translates a domain name into an IP address. Just as phone numbers need to be unique, so do domain names. The right-most label in a domain name, such as *net* in www.papers.bostonpost.net, is the name of a top-level domain (TLD). All domain names ending in .net are in this same TLD. The second-, third-, and fourth-level domains are bostonpost.net, papers.bostonpost.net, and www.papers.bostonpost.net, respectively.

The *root zone* of the DNS contains all the TLDs, of which there are about 1,500. Examples of TLDs are .com, .edu, .africa, .cn, .cymru, .earth, .fashion, .iq, .kosher, .museum, .nyc, .paris, .ru, .shop, and .vin. Internet root zone servers are located all over the globe, each containing a copy of the root zone file. The root zone file contains the IP address of a TLD server for each TLD. That server may hold the IP address for the domain, or if not, it will hold the IP address for a server of second-level domain names, and so on, as explained next.

When one host wishes to communicate with another host using a domain name, it either retrieves the IP address for the host from its local memory (a *cache*) or it submits a DNS address lookup request to a *domain name resolver*. This resolver asks a root zone DNS server for the IP address of a server for the TLD, *.net* in the example. If this server can resolve the entire domain name into an IP address, it does so. If not, it refers the resolver to a server for the subdomain ending with the remaining subdomains, *bostonpost.net* in our example. This resolution process continues until it finds the authoritative name server for the entire domain name and can return its IP address to the requesting host.

3.6 AUTONOMOUS SYSTEMS

Autonomous systems (ASs) play a central role on the Internet. Each AS is a collection of IP networks controlled by a single administrative entity, such as a business, a school, or an internet service provider (ISP). The AS plays a critical role in routing traffic.

An AS is allocated one or more prefixes, which it is authorized to assign to computers on the network that it manages. Each AS also has an *autonomous number* (AN) so that it can be identified when communicating with other ASs, as outlined in the following discussion of the BGP.

For proper functioning of the Internet, each AS should advertise to its neighbors only the prefixes it manages (See Essential Principle 3.2.) or those

---

Essential Principle 3.2 Understanding an IP prefix

An IPv4 prefix is an IPv4 address, such as 128.148.231.11, followed by a slash (/) and an integer in the range of 1 through 31. For example, 128.148.231.11/12 is a prefix. The latter is a shorthand for the set of binary strings whose first 12 bits are the first 12 bits of the IP address 128.148.231.11. Note that 128 is 10000000 in binary and 148 is 10010100, a total of 16 bits. Thus, the first 16 bits of 128.148.231.11 are 1000000010010100, and 128.148.231.11/12 denotes the 32-bit strings beginning with the 12-bit prefix 100000001001. A similar method is used to identify blocks of addresses in the IPv6 system.

---

it has received via a chain of ASs, originating with an AS that is authorized to assign it. Unfortunately, some ASs advertise prefixes that they are not authorized to assign. If this happens, a serious routing problem called *prefix hijacking* occurs. That is, packets intended for one destination are sent to another. An example of a hijacking is described in Section 3.11. Also discussed there are ways to control the hijacking problem.

3.7 ADDRESSING NETWORK DEVICES

To communicate among devices on a local network, such as Wi-Fi, Bluetooth, and Ethernet networks, each device requires a unique *hardware address*. Manufacturers cooperate in this task by assigning a globally unique, permanent, 48-bit number, called a *Media Access Control address* (MAC address), to each device designed for use on the Internet. Each networked device typically has both an IP address and a MAC address.

It is important that MAC addresses are kept confidential. Governments are concerned about their supply chains since it would be advantageous for an adversary to know all the devices a defense or intelligence agency buys by obtaining a list of MAC addresses of its users. Likewise, privacy advocates are concerned that governments target individuals through their devices. In some cases, MAC addresses can be changed temporarily under program control, but a MAC address is generally the equivalent of human DNA for a machine. This is very different from IP addresses, which do change as computers move and can be masked by using a *virtual private network* app or service.

3.8 INTERNET PACKETS

Internet packets contain a header, payload, and possibly a footer. The header has information used by the network to route packets from their source to their destination, namely, the *source* and *destination* IP addresses. It also contains a *protocol number* identifying the protocol handling the packet (discussed later), the time-to-live (TTL), the length of the header and the length of the complete packet, and checksums that can be used to determine if the packet has been corrupted and should be discarded. A *checksum* of a set of bits is their Exclusive OR (XOR). Multiple checksums of different sets of bits can reveal whether errors have occurred in transmission or a third party has altered the data. Since packets may take different paths to their destinations and need to be reassembled in order, their headers also contain a sequence number.

3.9 INTERNET PROTOCOL LAYERS

The Internet is organized into four *protocol layers*: *application*, *transport*, *internet*, and *link layers* as illustrated in Figure 3.4 and in Table 3.1. Packets are generated on a host by applications and passed down to the transport, internet, and link layers and then on to other networks until they arrive at the destination. As packets move from the application layer down to the link layer, information is appended to them, as suggested in Figure 3.5, and stripped as

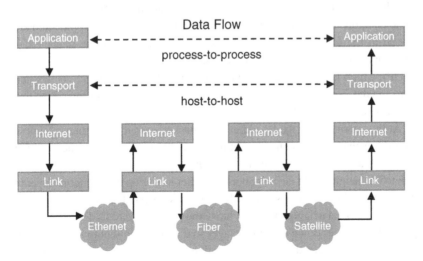

Figure 3.4 A model of internet data flow

Table 3.1 Four-layer IP model

Application Layer – Applications at this layer provide services to users. Examples of services are HTTP and HTTPS for insecure and secure web browsing, DNS for domain name resolution, SMTP and IMAP for electronic mail using TCP, and VoIP, which uses UDP for voice transmission. When an application opens a connection to an application on a host, it allocates a 16-bit port number and uses a transport layer protocol to tell the host it can respond at its IP address and the allocated port number.

Transport Layer – This layer controls the flow of packets between applications on potentially different hosts using their IP addresses and a 16-bit port number that refers to an application. Two protocols are available at this layer, the TCP, which guarantees delivery of packets in order, and the UDP, which does not guarantee packet delivery. Both are described in the text. These protocols invoke internet layer protocols.

Internet Layer – Protocols at this layer support network connections. They make a best effort to move packets between hosts on potentially different networks, each host identified by an IP address and a port number. They invoke link layer protocols.

Link Layer – Protocols, such as Ethernet, are responsible for the transfer of data between devices on a single network segment (or link) of a local area network. Device MAC addresses are used.

---

packets move up from the link layer to the application layer and the application. The link layer interfaces with the physical medium used to send packets to the next host on the path to the destination.

When an application or *process* (a running program) at one host sends packets to an application at another host, the packets created by the application are passed to the transport layer, where the flow of packets can be managed, if necessary. The two transport layer protocols are the *User Datagram Protocol* (UDP), which launches a packet without a guarantee it will reach its destination, and the *Transmission Control Protocol* (TCP), which does guarantee that each packet is delivered.

At the internet layer the IP address of a packet is used by a router to choose a neighbor that will route the packet toward its destination. Once the neighbor is chosen, a packet is prepared at the link layer for transmission over the direct link to that neighbor. At the neighbor the packet moves up to the internet layer of that computer where the destination IP address is accessed and used by the local router to choose a neighbor that will move the packet toward its destination. The packet then moves down to the link layer so that it can be sent to that neighbor. This process is repeated until the destination host is reached, at which point the packet moves up through the protocol layers until it reaches the host application.

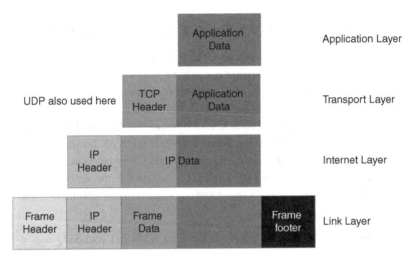

Figure 3.5   Encapsulation of application data through the four protocol layers

This standard four-layer model makes it possible for multiple vendors to offer software and hardware to support communications at each level, knowing that they will interoperate, which led to innovation and competitive pricing.[2] This contrasts with the proprietors of private circuit-switched telephone networks of the past; they only allowed approved devices to be attached to their networks, which reduced incentives for innovation. In today's world, an email sent from Microsoft Outlook on an Android phone can be read using Gmail on an Apple iPhone.

3.10 INTERNET PROTOCOLS

The Internet is used for a wide variety of purposes, such as fast and secure financial transactions or casual and unprotected email. In the former instance, the sender must be able to ascertain whether the communications reached its destination in a timely manner and speed does matter. For example, a financial services firm that engages in algorithmic high-frequency trading needs transactions to be processed in fractions of a second. In the case of email, where high speed is not essential, a crisis will not occur if an email arrives within minutes of being sent. TCP and UDP are designed to handle these two cases, respectively.

---

[2] The four-layer model is also known as the TCP/IP model. The Open Systems Interconnection (OSI) model is a conceptional model that describes the steps involved in a telecommunications system. (OSI Model, 2022)

Essential Principle 3.3 The TCP three-way handshake

The TCP engages in a three-way handshake with the destination so that the source knows that the destination is ready to accept packets. Under TCP the destination acknowledges each packet it receives from the source. The TCP packet header contains the protocol number 6 identifying the TCP, a sequence number (SEQ), an acknowledgment number (ACK), and the SYN and AK bits, each having value 1 or 0. If the SYN bit in a source packet has value 1, it signals a desire by the packet to be connected to a remote computer. If an AK bit of value 1 is returned to the sender, it signals acknowledgment of the request and a readiness to communicate. Here are the three steps:

(a) The source transmits a **SYN** packet with SYN = 1 and SEQ = x, a random integer.

(b) The destination responds with a **SYN-ACK** packet in which SYN = 1 and AK = 1, SEQ = y, a random integer, and ACK = $x + 1$.

(c) The source responds with an **ACK** packet with SYN = 0, AK = 1, SEQ = $x + 1$ and ACK = $y + 1$.

In b) the source checks that the value of ACK is equal to the value of SEQ that it sent, plus one. In c) the destination checks that the value of SEQ that it receives is equal to $x + 1$ and the value of ACK is equal to the value y that the destination sent to the source plus one. If these checks succeed, the source and destination are synchronized, and they are ready to exchange packets.

Both TCP and UDP manage traffic at the transport layer; the BGP is dynamically used to create and update routes that packets can follow to their destinations. As suggested in Figure 3.5, a header is prepended to TCP and UDP packets at the transport layer. Each header contains two 16-bit numbers to specify the ports used by the source and destination computers. Ports identify applications at the source and destination.

In addition to port numbers, the UDP packet header contains the protocol number 17, identifying the UDP protocol, the length of the packet, and a checksum. The TCP header contains the protocol number 6. A UDP packet is launched with no expectation of receiving a response. UDP is used for applications for which speed is more important and a best effort delivery are acceptable. It is suited to multicast applications, in which one message is sent to multiple sites. UDP is also used for DNS lookup, voice over IP (VoIP) to transmit sampled voice packets, IPTV to transmit sampled video, and Simple Network Management Protocol (SNMP), which is used to manage a variety of network devices.

The TCP protocol expects acknowledgment of every packet a source sends to the destination. Thus, if a packet is not acknowledged within a fixed time from its transmission (the congestion window), the source resends the packet. If an acknowledgment is delayed by congestion, multiple copies of a packet could be in the network simultaneously. If the congestion persists and too many packets are not acknowledged during the congestion window, the sender will increase the window. TCP congestion management is an important aspect · of TCP.

As noted, TCP is used for many applications that require high reliability but for which speed is less important. It sets up a virtual connection between the source and the destination. The connection is virtual because the packets do not need to travel the same path but are reassembled at the destination.

A router in one AS must decide to which neighbor AS it should direct a packet so that it moves expeditiously toward its destination, considering financial and other considerations. To do this an AS constructs a routing table that has an entry for each internet prefix. For a given prefix, the table specifies the neighboring AS to which the router will send a packet whose destination IP address is in that prefix. Routing tables are constructed using announcements of paths that a packet can take to reach the AS that is authorized to process its address combined with the AS's packet-handling policies.

Though BGP announcements play a central role in routing traffic on the Internet, they are generally transmitted without security guarantees. Thus, routers treat every announcement as valid and proceed to incorporate them into routing tables, possibly redirecting traffic from the AS that manages a prefix to an unauthorized site, resulting in BGP hijacking. In 2019, approximately 2,000 hijacking or other anomalous BGP incidents occurred per month globally.

Exploit 3.2 Pakistan BGP hijacking of YouTube

In 2008 the Pakistani government directed Pakistan Telecom to deny Pakistanis access to YouTube because of unacceptable depictions of the prophet Mohammad. Pakistan Telecom responded by issuing a BGP announcement claiming that it owned YouTube's prefixes. For up to two hours, traffic to YouTube from all over the world was sent to Pakistan, where it was discarded, disconnecting YouTube from the Internet!

Source: McCullagh (2008)

3.11 BUILDING ROUTING TABLES USING THE BORDER GATEWAY PROTOCOL

When a new prefix announcement is received by an AS, the prefix is inserted into its routing table along with the autonomous system number (ASN) of the AS that sent the prefix and the length of the path to the ASN. Because memory for routes is limited, a router will keep only one entry for each prefix. If a router gives priority to the prefix with the shortest path and if it receives an announcement of a shorter path to the prefix, it will update its routing table with the new path. A BGP withdrawal announcement of a prefix will result in the removal of the prefix from all routing tables.

An AS does not necessarily transmit every BGP announcement that it generates or receives from one neighbor to each of its other neighbors. These routing decisions may be based in part on their financial impact. For example, when two ASs are peers, that is, connected by a common gateway, neither charges the other for connectivity. However, one AS may have to pay another AS for connectivity to its remote customers.

Essential Principle 3.4 Announcements of subprefixes have priority

If a router has stored a prefix in its routing table and one of its subprefixes arrives, BGP rules dictate that the more specific subprefix is preferred.

Essential Principle 3.5 Automated mitigation of BGP hijacking

The rule of giving priority to a subprefix can be used to defend against BGP hijacking. An AS discovering that its prefix is hijacked by another AS can broadcast more specific subprefixes that cover all the IP addresses included in the hijacked prefix. Announcing these subprefixes will send traffic back to the authorized AS. These observations have been implemented in the ARTEMIS system.

Source: Sermpezis et al. (2018)

If a transit provider receives a prefix announcement from a paying customer, it is in the provider's financial interest to forward the announcement to the rest of the Internet. It is also in its interest to forward the announcements it receives to its customers. However, it is not in an AS's interest to forward announcements from one peer to another peer because it would then agree to allow traffic to travel from the former to the latter via the AS's network. This would consume the AS's bandwidth without compensation, which is not in its financial interest.

Decisions whether to enter BGP announcements into a routing table may also be determined by the available bandwidth. For example, if two routers in one AS connect by different links to one router in another AS and one of the two links has much higher bandwidth than the other, it will be given higher weight and chosen for the connection. The above rules are but a few of those that govern BGP announcements and hint at its complexity.

3.12 LOCAL AREA NETWORKS

Most of the 60,000-plus autonomous networks are *local area networks* (LANs). They provide connectivity to local hosts over a single medium. In a wired LAN, the medium consists of wires or cables. A wireless LAN uses Wi-Fi, cellular radio, or Bluetooth, each a type of electromagnetic radiation. A LAN can be subdivided into *virtual LANs* (VLANs), logical groups of hosts. Rules can be set to determine how groups may communicate with one another. A VLAN typically restricts access of a group of hosts to a common set of resources, such as printers. VLANs exist to manage traffic, improve security, and simplify network administration.

Essential Principle 3.6 Route flapping

Border Gateway Protocol is the most complex routing protocol deployed on the Internet. As a consequence, it occasionally behaves badly. For example, under pathological conditions, such as hardware or software errors, configuration errors, or unreliable connections, a router may advertise a route then quickly withdraw it only to readvertise it again or alternate between two routes to a destination. This is called route flapping, which causes instability in routing tables and increases the workload on routers.

3.12.1 Ethernet: A Wired LAN

Ethernet is the dominant wired LAN communication technology. The Ethernet protocol specifies the way that data is packaged, and devices communicate over the Ethernet LAN. The Ethernet protocol subdivides binary data streams into variable-length groups of bits, called frames. Each frame contains a source and a destination MAC address, a VLAN tag, which is used to specify the VLAN to which it belongs, a checksum so that damaged frames can be detected and discarded, a few other parameters, and a payload. The payload contains between 46 and 1,500 bytes. Source and destination MAC addresses and checksums contain approximately 200 bytes. Ethernet supports up to 4,096 VLANs. Ethernet offers transmission speeds of up to 100 gigabits per second (a gigabit is 2^{30} or $(1,024)^3$ bits).

Ethernet devices on a LAN send and receive frames on a common wire or cable. To prevent multiple devices from sending bits at the same time and garbling the communication, a device that wants to transmit a frame invokes the Carrier Sense Multiple Access with Collision Detection protocol (CSMA/CD). If the line is free, it sends the first bit of a frame, stopping if it detects a collision with another device and restarting at a random later time. Once a device successfully acquires the line, it holds it until it has finished sending its frame.

3.12.2 Wireless LANs

Wi-Fi is a family of certified radio technologies used for wireless local area networking. A Wi-Fi router is connected to the Internet via a cable and provides wireless connectivity to other devices via radio communication on the electromagnetic spectrum. A Wi-Fi router connects to devices using their unique MAC addresses. Wi-Fi equipped devices operate either in the 2.4 gigahertz UHF or the 5 gigahertz SHF radio bands. Radio signals in these bands are absorbed by intervening obstructions, which limits their range to about 20 meters inside a building and 150 meters outside, unless used with a repeater. Each radio band is subdivided into multiple half-duplex channels. A half-duplex channel permits two devices to communicate with each other but only one at a time. A full-duplex channel permits two parties to communicate simultaneously.

A channel can be shared by multiple router-device pairs consisting of the router, on the one hand, and other devices, on the other, using time-division duplexing. Here individual pairs are allocated time slots on a round-robin basis. Wi-Fi technology operates at the link layer and devices are addressed using their MAC addresses.

History Matters 3.1 The browser and the World Wide Web

In 1989 Tim Berners-Lee at CERN proposed to combine the Internet with hypertext-linked documents to provide access to important CERN materials. In 1990 he illustrated his ideas by developing the HyperText Markup Language (HTML), programming the first server to host HTML documents and a browser to view them, thereby creating the World Wide Web and the world's first website.

Both Wi-Fi and Ethernet have an important weakness: They are at risk of a man-in-the-middle (MITM) attack. For example, an observer positioned near a Wi-Fi device can eavesdrop on radio communication between it and the router and possibly interfere with it. The same applies to the Ethernet. A device on an Ethernet wire or cable can eavesdrop and interfere with traffic. End-to-end encrypted communication can help mitigate MITM attacks.

3.12.3 Firewalls

While much discussion has focused on security when operating on networks, it is equally important to protect devices, servers, and routers from unauthorized network access. A *firewall* offers a basic layer of protection to a network or a host by filtering incoming and outgoing packets. While firewalls work against known malicious senders, they can be the equivalent of the French Maginot Line of World War II, which was rendered useless by simply going around the fortified area. Nonetheless, firewalls are an important part of layered cybersecurity

A firewall can be implemented in either hardware or software. A *first-generation firewall* has a set of rules that determine whether packets with a particular set of parameters are allowed to connect to the network. For example, since Telnet at port 23 is an old and generally unmaintained text-based communications application, firewalls usually disallow connections to it because, if allowed, an attacker may be able to compromise a computer.

Each packet is treated independently by a first-generation firewall. A *second-generation firewall* is stateful, which means it can keep track of the history of a packet stream. Thus, it is better able to reject certain types of unacceptable packet streams. A *third-generation* or *application-layer firewall* can both inspect and filter packets on any protocol layer. It can recognize when certain applications and protocols, such as HTTP (Hypertext Transfer Protocol for document retrieval) and FTP (File Transfer Protocol), are misused.

3.13 SECURE COMMUNICATIONS

Given the reliance of governments, businesses, and individuals on digital communication, it is essential that it be secure. That is, senders must be able to securely authenticate themselves, communicate privately, and determine if packets are altered in transit. Cryptography provides the technology to support this type of functionality and provides users confidence in the security of the communications they receive.

3.13.1 Introduction to Cryptography

Cryptography is the science of creating secret codes (ciphertexts) from messages (plaintext). A *cryptographic system*, or *cryptosystem*, consists of an *encryption algorithm*, or *cipher*, which is used to create the ciphertext from a plaintext, and a *decryption algorithm* to obtain the plaintext from a ciphertext. A *strong cipher* is one in which two parties expend a modest amount of computational effort to encrypt and decrypt, respectively, but a third party must either be unable to decrypt a message or expend an infeasible amount of computational effort to do so. *Cryptanalysis* occurs when one party observes an encrypted communication and strives to decrypt it.

Two types of cipher exist, symmetric ciphers and asymmetric ciphers. A *symmetric cipher* has a single key that is used to both encrypt and decrypt messages. An *asymmetric cipher* has two keys, a public key to encrypt messages and a private key to decrypt them. Asymmetric encryption is also called public-key encryption.

Essential Principle 3.7 Kerckhoffs' principle

Kerckhoffs' principle asserts that a cryptographic system should be designed to be secure, even if all its details, except for the key or keys, are publicly known.

If Kerckhoffs' principle is followed, the encryption and decryption algorithms may be known but secrecy persists as long as the keys are secret. This allows the soundness of the algorithms to be tested without relying on the secrecy of the algorithms. If security relied upon the secrecy of the algorithms and they became known to adversaries, all previous communications could be deciphered. If security relies only on a key and it is discovered, only messages encrypted with that key are revealed.

3.13.2 Threats to Ciphers

Four types of cryptographic threats are listed here in which a hypothetical user, Eve, has increasing amounts of information.

- *Ciphertext-only attack* – Eve has only ciphertexts.
- *Known-plaintext attack* – Eve has plaintexts and their corresponding ciphertexts.
- *Chosen-plaintext attack* – Eve chooses plaintexts, possibly adaptively, and receives ciphertexts.
- *Chosen-ciphertext attack* – Eve chooses ciphertexts and is given the corresponding plaintexts.

The goal in each case is to decipher the message or, better still, obtain the key that was used to encipher messages.

If a cryptographic system is susceptible to a ciphertext-only attack, the weakest threat, it is completely insecure. The other threats are progressively stronger. If a system is safe against a known-plaintext attack, past encrypted messages do not have to be kept secret because knowing them and their corresponding ciphertexts will not allow the cipher to be broken.

A chosen-plaintext attack will occur if Eve is able to persuade Alice to send a specific message, perhaps by creating a crisis and knowing what message she will send in response. A chosen-ciphertext attack is best executed with help from an insider who may not know the secret keys used to encrypt plaintexts.

3.13.3 Symmetric Key Cryptosystems

In a symmetric key cryptosystem (SKC) both the sender and the receiver employ the same key to encrypt and decrypt messages. Security of an SKC requires that each pair of communicators use distinct secret keys since otherwise users would be able to decrypt messages between other pairs. If there are N parties using an SKC, they will need one key for every pair of communicators or $N(N-1)/2$ keys, which grows rapidly with N. For example, $N(N-1)/2 = 499,500$ if $N = 1,000$. This is a problem if new keys frequently need to be distributed securely to widely distributed parties.

A substitution cipher (See History Matters 3.2) is relatively easy to break because the frequency with which a letter is used in text is distinctive (see Figure 3.6). For example, within the English language, the letter "e" appears 12.7 percent of the time and the letter "a" appears 8.17 percent of the time.

History Matters 3.2 Substitution ciphers

Some of the earliest SKC systems are substitution ciphers, in which letters in alphabetical order are matched with a permutation of the alphabet. Julius Caesar's cipher, an early substitution cipher, encrypts plaintext by shifting each letter in an alphabet cyclically by a fixed number of places. For example, if the shift is by three letters, A is replaced by D, B by E, …, X by A, Y by B, and Z by C. Messages are decrypted by shifting the letters cyclically back the same number of places.

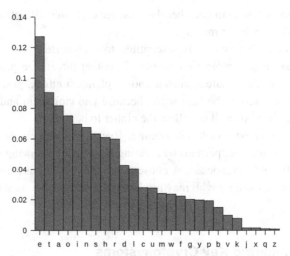

Figure 3.6   Relative frequencies of English letters

Given enough encrypted text, the frequencies of encrypted letters in a substitution cipher will be close to those of the corresponding unencrypted letters.

To decode a message encrypted with a substitution cipher, we first compute a histogram of encrypted letters from the message and compare it to the histogram of the language in question, as suggested in Figure 3.6 for English. This will provide a good first estimate of substitutions that were made to encrypt the message. Then use the spelling of words to make corrections to the estimated substitutions. This means that substitution ciphers are susceptible to ciphertext-only attacks. The ease of this approach explains why some password rules prevent use of words that appear in the dictionary and require a combination of letters, numbers, and symbols to protect against ciphertext-only attacks.

3.13.4 The One-Time Pad

Another simple but very powerful encryption method is the *one-time pad*, a substitution cipher on letters in an alphabet A. It is like the Caesar cipher except that (a) it applies to any alphabet and (b) the shift is taken from a one-time pad that contains integers in the range 0 to $|A|-1$ where $|A|$ is the size of the alphabet. $|A|=26$ for the Caesar cipher.

Each party has a copy of the same pad, which must be kept secret, containing pages of the same randomly chosen integers. To encrypt a message of length n, the next n unused integers are chosen from the pad and the *j*th letter in the message is cyclically shifted by the *j*th of these n unused integers. To decrypt, the cyclic shift is reversed.

Since the keys in one-time pad are chosen at random, Shannon (1949) has shown that it offers perfect secrecy because the ciphertext is statistically independent of the plaintext; no information about the plaintext can be inferred from the ciphertext. However, the one-time pad scheme has an Achilles Heel. If a pad is reused, portions of the message may be revealed using frequency analysis of the letters, as discussed earlier.

A second example of a one-time pad is the *binary one-time pad*. It applies to binary data, 0s and 1s. Data is converted to strings of bits and each string, say $m = (m_1, m_2, m_3, ..., m_n)$ of n bits, is encrypted by combining m with a secret n-bit string, call it $k = (k_1, k_2, k_3, ..., k_n)$, by combining the *j*th bit of m, m_j, with the *j*th bit of k, k_j, by forming their XOR, denoted $c_j = m \oplus k_j$, where c_j has the value 0 if m_j and k_j have the same values and the value 1 otherwise. To decrypt the ciphertext $c = (c_1, c_2, c_3, ..., c_n)$, encrypt it with the secret key, which restores m. This type of one-time pad is much more amenable to the computer age because all data is quantified into bits.

Two two-dimensional examples of a one-time pad are shown in Figure 3.7 (a) and (b). Each shows a black-and-white image on the left juxtaposed with the same random black-and-white bit pattern on the right. A white pixel in an image is associated with the value 1 and a black pixel is associated with the value 0. The common random pattern constitutes a secret key.

Figure 3.7 Two binary images encrypted with same 2D Random Bit Pattern by permission of Richard Smith, Cryptosmith, LLC

Figure 3.8   The result of combining encrypted images in Figure 3.7 by permission of Richard Smith, Cryptosmith, LLC

When the two patterns in (a) are XORed bitwise, the results look random. The same is true for (b). When the two results of the XORing in Figure 3.7 (a) and (b) are combined by XORing them together, the common random pattern is removed and the result is shown in Figure 3.8, which is the overlap of the two images, thereby revealing information in the two images, again showing that reusing a one-time pad may reveal information that should have been kept secret. (This example is posted on the Cryptosmith blog [Smith, 2008].)

3.13.5 Strong Practical Symmetric Key Cryptosystem Schemes

Because it is impractical to use a one-time pad, other techniques have been invented for secure symmetric key encryption. After a very robust international competition conducted by the National Institute of Standards and Technology (NIST), the *Advanced Encryption Standard* (AES) the SKC method was chosen in 2002 to protect classified US government documents. It is widely used and is supported by all mainstream operating systems.

AES is a block-structured cipher that encrypts blocks of 128 bits. There are three versions of AES, AES-128, AES-192, and AES-256, which use keys of 128, 192, and 256 bits, respectively. AES-256 has been certified by the US government for the encryption of top-secret data.

The *AES cipher* consists of ten rounds of rather simple operations such as vector XORs, substitutions, permutations, and matrix multiplications, none of which is particularly time-consuming, which explains why it is fast. Combined with the quality of the encryptions that AES provides, this explains why it is widely used by vendors of operating systems.

3.13.6 Public-Key Cryptosystems

Another method of encryption is *public-key cryptography* (PKC). In this method, each party creates two keys, a private key and a public key. They also have an encryption algorithm E_K and a decryption algorithm D_K where K is a key value. For example, let K_e and K_d be the encryption and decryption keys. If Alice wants to send a secret message M to Bob, she encrypts M with Bob's public key $K_e = P_B$ and sends him the ciphertext $C = K_e(M)$. Bob decrypts the message using his secret private key $K_d = S_B$ to produce the message $D_{K_d}(C) = M$. Bob sends messages to Alice securely in an analogous fashion.

Thus, PKC was a revolutionary solution to the *key distribution problem*, that is, the distribution of keys between parties who must engage in secure communication. As noted earlier, in an SKC between N parties, $N(N-1)/2$ keys are needed. If $N = 1,000, N(N-1)/2$ is about 500,000, which would require a huge number of couriers to transport the keys. However, PKC needs only $2N$ or 2,000 keys and they can be generated by the N parties and distributed independently unless they need to be certified by a third party. In 1976 two solutions to the key distribution problem were announced, as explained in History Matters Box 3.3.

History Matters 3.3 PKC

The PKC concept emerged independently in the United States and the United Kingdom. In work classified until 1997 it was revealed that James Ellis of the British Government Communications Headquarters (GCHQ) had sketched a method in 1970 that might be used to implement a PKC system for which Clifford Cocks, also of GCHQ, offered an implementation in 1973.

Whitfield Diffie and Martin Hellman gave a brief specification of the PKC concept in 1976, which was made fully concrete the following year by Ron Rivest, Adi Shamir, and Leonard Adelson using the same integer factorization problem proposed by Cocks in 1973.

In 1976 Diffie and Hellman also introduced the key exchange, an idea independently introduced in 1973 by Malcolm Williamson of GCHQ, also classified until 1997.

Source: Levy (1999)

3.13.6.1 The Diffie–Hellman Key Exchange Protocol

The Diffie–Hellman key exchange protocol (DH) is used to create a secret key between two parties who do not know each other over an insecure communications channel, which seems like an impossible thing to do. The method assumes that each party generates a secret integer and from it creates a public integer that it shares with the other party. Using the public integer received from the other party and their secret integer, each party computes a common secret integer, which is then used as a key in an SKC. Using an SKC such as the AES cryptosystem provides for much faster encrypted communications than is possible with the Rivest–Shamir–Adleman (RSA) public-key encryption method discussed later.

DH was conceptualized by Ralph Merkle and named for Diffie and Hellman who published it in 1976. It was independently invented by Williamson of the British GCHQ in 1973 but not made public until 1997.

3.13.6.1.1 The Diffie–Hellman Algorithm

Referring to Essential Principle Box 3.8, in DH Bob and Alice know two common public integers: p, a prime, and g, a generator, for $Z_p = \{0,1,2,...,p-1\}$. Alice creates a secret integer a, raises g to the power a to create the secret integer $I_A = g^a$ using multiplication modulo a prime p, and sends I_A to Bob. Bob creates a secret integer b, raises g to the power b to create the secret integer $I_B = g^b$ using the same modular arithmetic, and sends it to Alice. Here, a is Alice's private key and I_A is her public key. Similarly, b and I_B are Bob's private and public keys.

Alice uses I_B from Bob and her secret integer a to create the integer $C_A = (I_B)^a$ by raising I_B to the power a. Bob raises I_A to the power b to create an integer $C_B = (I_A)^b$. Because $(g^b)^a = (g^a)^b$, they both have the same integer, call it $C = (g^a)^b$, which they use for secure communication.

3.13.6.1.2 Security of the Diffie–Hellman Protocol

There are two sources of insecurity in DH. First, an observer, Eve, knowing that Alice and Bob have sent the integers $I_A = g^a$ and $I_B = g^b$ could try to determine a and b by solving the discrete logarithm problem, described in Essential Principle Box 3.8. However, as of today this is a very hard computational problem when p and g are chosen carefully for which no practical solution is known.

A second source of insecurity is an MITM attack. If the traffic between Bob and Alice passes through Eve, she can respond to Alice impersonating Bob and set up a secure communication with Alice and do the same thing to

---

Essential Principle 3.8 Discrete logarithms

Let p be a prime integer. g is a *generator* for the set $Z_p = \{0, 1, 2, \ldots, p-1\}$ of integers if each nonzero element Z_p can be obtained as a power of g modulo p. That is, g^x (g multiplied by itself x times) for integers $0 \le x \le p-1$ generates all the nonzero elements of Z_p when the multiplication is modulo p, that is, the result of the multiplication is the remainder when divided by p. Computing $z = g^x$ from g and z is easy but finding x from z is hard. x is called the *discrete logarithm* of z. Many attempts have failed to find a fast algorithm for the discrete logarithm, one that runs in time polynomial in the number of bits representing x and g.

Bob. Although the traffic between Alice and Eve is secure as is that between Bob and Eve, Eve can read and even alter the communications between Bob and Alice.

To address the MITM problem, Alice and Bob must rely on a trusted third party to certify the authenticity of the parties with whom they are communicating or have a common secret. The former method can be done by having each party register with a certificate authority in which digital signatures, discussed later, play a central role.

3.13.6.1.3 A Paint Analogy for the Diffie–Hellman Protocol
There is a paint analogy for the aforementioned technique to construct a DH secret key. Imagine that Bob and Alice both have a bucket of yellow paint (Y) as well as a bucket with their own secret paint. All the buckets are the same size. Let Bob's secret paint be red (R) and Alice's secret paint be green (G). Bob mixes R with Y and sends the mixture R+Y to Alice. Alice mixes G with Y and sends G+Y to Bob.

Neither Bob nor Alice can tell from the mixture it received what color paint the other party has. But each party can add its color to the mixture received from the other party to get a common color. To see this, Bob receives G+Y from Alice and adds a bucket of R to get R+G+Y and Alice receives R+Y from Bob and adds a bucket of G to get G+R+Y. Thus, they both have the same paint color but neither knows the other party's secret paint.

The shared DH secret key K is meant to be ephemeral; it is expected to be used for one session between Alice and Bob. If K is revealed, the security of later sessions is not jeopardized, and thus DH is said to provide perfect forward secrecy.

3.13.7 Digital Signatures

Digital signatures, which employ encryption, are used to authenticate the source of messages in digital communications. We describe how to construct them using a public-key cryptosystem.

Suppose Bob wants to send a message M to Alice, persuade her that he sent the message, and help her to assess whether the message has been modified in transit. Bob computes a *digital signature* of M, denoted $\sigma_{\text{Bob}}(M)$, and creates the new message $T = (M, \sigma_{\text{Bob}}(M))$ containing both M and its signature, which he sends to Alice. Let us see how a digital signature is used to convince Alice that Bob was the source of the message.

Bob uses a *public cryptographic hash function H*, such as SHA-256, an algorithm that takes an arbitrary string M and maps it to a fixed-length binary string $H(M)$, called the *hash* (Hash Functions, 2020). In the case of SHA-256, the hash consists of 256 bits. H is designed to make it extremely difficult to find another message M' such that $H(M') = H(M)$ (this is called a *collision*) and given a hash value h to find M such that $H(M) = h$.

Bob *decrypts* $H(M)$ using the decryption function D_K of his PKC system using his secret private key $K = S_B$ and sets his signature to $\sigma_{\text{Bob}}(M) = D_{S_B}(H(M))$. This decryption can be reversed by encrypting $\sigma_{\text{Bob}}(M)$ with Bob's public key.

Let Alice receive the message $T' = (M', \sigma')$ from Bob, where M' may differ from M and σ' may differ from $\sigma_{\text{Bob}}(M)$. Alice wants to verify that (a) Bob sent the signed document and (b) that it has been received without tampering.

Alice computes $H(M')$. If $M' = M$, she obtains $H(M)$. Alice also encrypts σ' with Bob's public key; that is, she computes $E_{P_B}(\sigma_{\text{Bob}}(M)) = E_{P_B}(D_{S_B}(H(M))) = H(M)$. Thus, if the message M and the signature $\sigma_{\text{Bob}}(M)$ are received without alteration, Alice will see that the two ways of computing $H(M)$ match. Thus, not only will the message not have been altered but it is also confirmed that the message was sent by Bob because he is the only person who has the private key that was used to compute the signature.

3.13.8 Certificate Systems

A certificate authority (CA) is a trusted entity that issues certificates, cryptographically signed data files, confirming that the CA has verified the ownership of data, such as a public key or a domain name, supplied by a third party. A CA provides certificates by signing files with its private key in a PKC system. Its public key is available so that a third party can verify that the CA has provided the certification.

Parties wanting assurance that an announced public key belongs to a particular person can use a CA to provide that assurance. The parties can also share a public-key *fingerprint*, the hash of the public key. A fingerprint, being much shorter than a public key, can be shared easily over the telephone or in person.

3.13.9 Code Signing

Code is signed in the same manner as messages are signed; that is, the executable (machine-level) code of an application, a binary string, is augmented with a signature computed with a standard cryptographic hash function, such as SHA-256, and encrypted with the private key of the originator of the code. Code signing provides security because it prevents malware masquerading as legitimate software from being executed.

Most operating systems support verification of signed code, but its application is limited. Both Windows and the MAC OS verify code signatures only the first time that code is run but not every time it is run, although code updates are verified using signatures. If code were to be verified each time it is run, infected malware could be detected.

3.13.10 Ethical Dimensions of Secure Communications

Secure communications over digital networks are essential whenever the data being transmitted is sufficiently important. If communications security is broken, confidential information may be lost, the information may be altered, or access to the information may be lost. Broken security could result in a violation of privacy, theft of identity, theft of intellectual property, or loss of national security secrets, thereby potentially imperiling the security of a nation or the life of a foreign agent. Thus, engineers in charge of creating equipment to be used for secure communication have a personal and professional responsibility to ensure that the equipment operates correctly to the best of their ability.

3.14 ISSUES INTRODUCED BY PUBLIC-KEY CRYPTOSYSTEMS

At the present time, PKC systems have two problems. First, they are computationally intensive. They require much more time to encrypt and decrypt than do SKCs. Second, if public keys are not authenticated, PKCs are susceptible to MITM attacks. For example, if Eve sends Bob her public key saying that she is Alice and Bob trusts Alice, Eve can manipulate Bob.

To address the first problem, Alice and Bob, both of whom are in a PKC, can agree in advance to use an SKC for the bulk of their communications. Let Alice begin the exchange. She uses the PKC to send Bob a secret key K for the SKC and M_1, her first message for him, encrypted with K. Bob uses the PKC to decrypt the combined message, extracts the key K, and uses it to decrypt the message M_1. Subsequent communications between them use the secret key K with the agreed-upon SKC.

If the high cost of PKC encryption and decryption are amortized over the remaining encryptions and decryptions of SKC message blocks, the cost of encrypted communication will approach that of the SKC.

To address the MITM problem, all the keys used by a PKC should be certified by a certification authority.

3.15 RIVEST–SHAMIR–ADLEMAN PUBLIC-KEY CRYPTOSYSTEM

To appreciate threats to public-key cryptosystems, we describe the widely used RSA PKC. It is not necessary to fully understand the mathematics to understand the threat. RSA is very widely used today for the applications discussed earlier, such as digital signatures, certificates, and code signing. However, as the following discussion shows, the security it provides is threatened by the advent of quantum computers.

The RSA public key is $P = (e, N)$, which consists of integers e and N, where $N = pq$ is the product of two secret prime numbers p and q. If N can be factored, a secret integer, d, can be obtained and the RSA private key $S = (d, N)$ can be used to decrypt encrypted messages.

It is believed that factoring is computationally hard with a traditional computer. Thus, RSA is believed to be computationally secure unless factoring can be done quickly, which is theoretically possible with a quantum computer. RSA can be implemented effectively by the following steps (National Institute of Standards and Technology, 2013):

- Bob chooses random primes p and q of at least 1,024 bits, each with leading bits of 1 and sets $N = pq$.
- He creates public and private keys for himself using the following guidelines. Let M be the message, viewed as an integer. It is assumed that $M < N$.
- He chooses an integer e, $1 < e < \varphi(N)$, that is relatively prime to the value of the totient $\varphi(N)$ defined in Essential Principle Box 3.9. Frequently $e = 65,537$, a prime, is used.

Essential Principle 3.9 The totient function

Two integers are *relatively prime* if they have no factors in common other than 1. Z_n^* is the set of the integers in $Z_n = \{1, 2, 3, \ldots, n-1\}$ that are relatively prime to n. Thus, $Z_{10}^* = \{1, 3, 7, 9\}$; these are the only integers in Z_{10} that are relatively prime with 10 whose factors are 1, 2, and 5. The *totient* of Z_n, denoted as $\varphi(n)$, is the size of Z_n^*, that is, $\varphi(n) = |Z_n^*|$. Thus, $\varphi(10) = 4$. If p and q are prime integers and $n = pq$, then it is known that $\varphi(n) = (p-1)(q-1)$.

Essential Principle 3.10 Integer factorization

Despite decades, if not centuries of work, all known algorithms to factor an integer n into its primes have running times that grow exponentially in $[\log_2 n]$, the number of bits needed to represent n, suggesting that this problem is computationally infeasible when n is large.

- He computes d that satisfies $(d * e) \bmod \varphi(N) = 1$, which is the remainder of $d * e$ after dividing it by the totient $\varphi(N)$.
- Bob's public key is $P_B = (e, N)$ and his private key is $S_B = (d, N)$.

It follows that N will be a binary integer of at least 2,048 bits, with the leading bit of 1, which is considered minimal for security today of RSA. As a decimal number, N will have at least 615 significant decimal digits!

The RSA algorithm uses modular arithmetic in which the numbers that result from addition and multiplication are replaced by their remainders after division by an integer called a "modulus" such as $N = pq$. Thus, if R is the result of adding or multiplying two integers, in modular arithmetic R is replaced by $R \bmod N$, which is the remainder of R after dividing it by the modulus N. For example, $3 \bmod 5 = 3$ and $7 \bmod 5 = 2$.

Alice encrypts her message M for Bob using his public key $P_B = (e, N)$ to produce the ciphertext C as follows: $C = E_{(e,N)}(M) = M^e \bmod N$. Here M^e is M multiplied by itself e times. Bob decrypts Alice's ciphertext C to produce the deciphered text $D = E_{(d,N)}(C) = (C)^d \bmod N$ using his private key $S_B = (d, N)$.

To show that the decryption algorithm produces the message M that Alice sent to Bob, we need to show that $D = M$. But $D = (C)^d \bmod N = (M^e \bmod N)^d \bmod N = (M^{de}) \bmod N = M$. The latter follows because $d * e = 1 \bmod N$, which is not hard to show but it does require some number theory.

Essential Principle 3.11 An important RSA public-key cryptosystem vulnerability

If the integer $N = pq$ in Bob's public key $P_B = (e, N)$ can be factored into p and q, the *secret integer d* in Bob's private key $S_B = (d, N)$ can be deduced and his messages can be decrypted. Although integer factorization is a computationally hard problem with a standard computer, if a quantum computer can be built with many quantum gates, the security of RSA PKC can be broken.

Technical aside: The key observation here is that if N can be factored, p and q can be deduced, and the totient $\varphi(N) = (p-1)(q-1)$ can be computed. Because e is public and d satisfies $(d * e) \bmod \varphi(N) = 1$, it is possible to solve for d using the extended version of Euclid's greatest common divisor algorithm, discovered around 300 BCE.

Policy Matters 3.1 Encryption and law enforcement

In December 2015 two terrorists attacked and killed 14 people and injured 22 at a municipal event in San Bernardino, California. They were killed after a chase. The FBI attempted to access their locked Apple iPhones as part of their investigation by appealing to federal agencies and Apple, who would not cooperate, saying that to do so would violate their commitment to customer privacy. While the FBI was able to eventually unlock the phone, the incident resulted in three senators introducing the "Lawful Access to Encrypted Data Act" to make it illegal to build systems that cannot be accessed by law enforcement. Their bill failed to become law.

Source: Judiciary Committee (2020)

It can be shown that modular exponentiation of g to exponent k, g^k, can be done with at most $2[\log_2 k]$ multiplications of g with itself, where $[\log_2 k]$ is the largest power of 2 to represent k as a binary number. Since the above decryption algorithm computes M^e with modulo N, RSA encryption involves at most 2 multiplications. This follows because to compute M^e at most $[\log_2 e]$ powers of 2 are needed to represent e and these powers need to be multiplied at most $[\log_2 e] - 1$ times. Note that if $e = 65,537 = 2^{16} + 1$, $[\log_2 e] = 17$.

Because RSA uses as many as $34 = 2[\log_2 e]$ modular multiplications of very large numbers to encode and decode, it is very time-consuming. Thus, SKC algorithms, such as AES, which use much simpler operations, are much faster.

3.16 EXCEPTIONAL ACCESS TO ENCRYPTED INFORMATION

End-to-end encryption refers to encryption of messages at the source that are only decrypted at the destination. While end-to-end encryption is considered essential for high-value commerce, it is problematic for law enforcement agencies. They see a compelling need to obtain *warranted exceptional access* to encrypted information and are frustrated when information is needed, access is authorized by a court of law, but the technology or practices prevent it. On the other hand, to many in the cryptographic community providing such access is equivalent to inserting backdoors in cryptosystems and risks violating all security, which is anathema to them.

However, a few members of the cryptographic community have explored methods of encryption that do provide exceptional access, either by requiring a large amount of computation, which it is presumed only governments can access; by attaching a silent observer (or ghost) to otherwise encrypted multi-party communication; by cooperating with device manufacturers, who store a key on a device that will unlock it but the key itself is encrypted with a key held by the manufacturer; or by replacing the manufacturer with a jury holding key shares and requiring that its members approve the aggregation of key shares to unlock a device. This issue has been studied by the US National Academies (The National Academies, 2018).

Methods for dealing with exceptional access to encrypted information are discussed in Chapter 6 on domestic regulation of cyberspace.

3.17 THE QUANTUM THREAT

The security of DH key exchange and RSA public-key cryptosystem hinge on the computational hardness of computing the discrete logarithm and integer factorization, respectively. They were thought to be secure before quantum computing was shown to be a threat to both.

Factoring and the discrete logarithm depend on integer multiplication and modular digital exponentiation, respectively, which are easy to compute but are believed to be very difficult to undo using the classical computers discussed earlier. These are called *trapdoor operations* – easy to get in, hard to get out.

Thus, imagine the shock when in 1994 Peter Shor presented a paper at a conference showing that if quantum computers could be built, both problems were solvable in practice, which was later published as a journal article (Shor, 1997). That is, the time taken to solve them on a quantum computer would grow as a polynomial in the number of bits to represent integers whereas the fastest known classical algorithms for these problems require time that grows exponentially with the number of bits.

Although no quantum computers existed in 1994, they were being imagined. Shor's result motivated many researchers, primarily physicists, to explore whether quantum computers of a reasonable size were possible.

3.17.1 Defining Quantum Computing

Quantum mechanics, the physics behind quantum computers, reflects the strange behavior of materials at very small dimensions, that is, at the scale of atoms and electrons, where objects exist in a "haze of probability" (Mann, 2022). Quantum mechanical objects behave in ways that are unfamiliar to everyday experience. For example, light, which was originally viewed as waves, was later shown to also exhibit particle behavior (photons). Similarly, particles, such as electrons, were also shown to exhibit wavelike behavior.

Individual quantum objects in isolation, such as electrons, photons, and atoms, are characterized by "wave functions" with amplitudes that are complex numbers. When objects are close enough for their wave functions to overlap, they are said to be in quantum superposition. As with sound waves, when wave functions overlap, they can interfere (cancel) or reinforce (add to) each other. If quantum objects are in superposition and are sufficiently undisturbed by external influences ("noise"), such as heat or physical vibration that may alter their quantum states, they are said to be entangled. This means that they can simultaneously occupy all the states that each quantum object could assume in isolation.

The states of quantum systems are characterized by probabilities. When a measurement is made of a quantum system, its quantum state collapses to a classical one. The classical state to which it collapses occurs with a probability that is the square of the absolute value of the wave function. Thus, the outputs that quantum computers produce are characterized by probabilities. This means that there are generally many classical states to which a quantum state can collapse when a measurement is made.

To build a quantum computer the bits of the classical computer are replaced by quantum bits (called *qubits*), quantum objects that can be in one of two states, such as the spin of an electron (up or down) or the polarization of a phonon (vertical or horizontal). If qubits are entangled, they can collectively be in all possible combinations of the states that the qubits could occupy individually. If a quantum computer has n qubits, it can assume all 2^n states for its qubits.

3.17.2 Shor's Algorithms

In 1994 Shor (1997) developed algorithms to factor an integer and to find the discrete logarithm of an element of a finite field for a quantum computer. His algorithms use the probabilistic nature of a quantum system to explore all possible states of the qubits and, with some probability, settle on a state consistent with a solution.

As with all quantum computers, to acquire information requires a measurement, which collapses the quantum state to one of many possible classical states. Shor has shown that on any run of his algorithm there is a nonzero probability that the classical state that is reached contains the prime factors of the integer to be factored. Thus, it may take many steps to find the integers whose product is the integer to be factored.

3.17.3 The State of Quantum Computers

Construction of quantum computers capable of factoring large integers is proving to be very difficult. In July 2021 it was reported that a team of researchers in China have developed a quantum computer containing 66 qubits (Wu et al., 2021) but the best so far, in November 2021, is IBM's quantum computer with 127 qubits (Sparkes, 2021). This larger number is very much smaller than 20 million qubits, the 2019 best estimate of the number needed to factor a 2048-bit integer, the recommended key length for RSA in 2019 (Gidney & Ekerå, 2021). If it could be built, it is estimated that such a quantum computer could break the security of RSA with a 2048-bit key in only eight hours! A recent report (Gouzien & Sangouard, 2021) says the number of qubits needed to factor a number of this size can be reduced to 13,436 qubits with a new architecture at the expense of increasing the factoring time to 177 days.

Quantum computing is noisy (Preskill, 2018). Thus, quantum error correction is needed to reduce the noise to a tolerable level. The number of qubits needed for this purpose is large and sensitive to the noise level. Thus, if quantum computers are noisier than expected, it may become impractical to use them to break the security of RSA.

3.18 POST-QUANTUM CRYPTOGRAPHY

The fact that it is difficult to build large quantum computers does not diminish the threat they present to security. If significant advances are made, important types of cryptosystems will be at risk. This fact has stimulated the international research community to investigate post-quantum cryptography.

The NIST, which has played a key role in standardizing cryptosystems, has identified cryptographic systems that it believes are partially or totally resistant to quantum computation (Alagic et al., 2020). The latter includes SKCs. SKCs are at risk from Grover's quantum algorithm, which can reduce the time to find a unique input among N inputs to a black box in time $\sqrt{N}$. But restoring the security of an SKC should only require using longer keys. Lattice-based encryption also appears to be quantum resistant as well as code-based cryptography (Alagic et al., 2020).

In December 2016 NIST put out the first international call for quantum resistant PKC algorithms (Federal Register, 2016). In January 2019 it announced that it had winnowed the submissions to 26 algorithms (Federal Register, 2019) and asked the international community to evaluate these submissions. Four public-key encryption algorithms and three digital signature algorithms have advanced to the final round of the competition as well as eight alternative algorithms (Alagic et al., 2020). A good description of the decision-making process used by NIST has been published (Hsu, 2019).

3.19 CONCLUSIONS

Communications have evolved from drums and smoke signals to telegraphy over wires and radio, to audio communication via radio, video over television, radar, circuit-switched telephone networks, and packet-switched data networks, giving rise to the Internet. The evolution of communication is profound for both the capabilities it provides and the vulnerabilities it brings.

The Internet was the next step in communication evolution and has been revolutionary. All traditional forms of communications are now possible on the Internet. However, the new technologies of the cyber age are not an unmitigated blessing. They have created new opportunities for malicious behavior. Anonymity is important to protect privacy, but trusted identities are important too. As we see in Chapter 4, this is a human-centered process.

3.20 DISCUSSION TOPICS

1. Today any Internet user can visit any other IP address worldwide. However, some nations have prepared their countries to disconnect from the global Internet in times of crisis. Comment on the consequences of segmenting the Internet this way so that communication is possible only between users within a segment.
2. While substitution ciphers are easy to break, they are also easy to implement. Propose a variant of such a cipher that is harder to break but not as hard as using a one-time pad.
3. Many individuals and businesses realize that it is important to have access to secure encryption technologies. However, law enforcement believes that it cannot do its job if it cannot decipher legally authorized encrypted communications. How would you resolve this dilemma?
4. Given the dependence of security on new technologies, such as quantum computing, what technology policies do you believe governments should pursue in the long term?
5. If you were responsible for national security, what governmental policies would you advise concerning staffing, research, and legislation? Justify your answers.

4

The Human Dimensions of Cyberspace

Ignorance more frequently begets confidence than does knowledge.
Charles Darwin (1981), an evolutionary theory pioneer

THE COMPUTER AGE has delivered smart phones, social media, ready access to vast amounts of knowledge, the globalization of communication, the digitization of commerce, and high-quality inexpensive goods. There have also been unanticipated consequences of these benefits by deploying technologies to benefit society. It is now much easier for nations to influence the politics of another, intelligence services to steal intellectual property, and militaries to threaten critical infrastructure, such as electricity and water systems, from afar. We have also been surprised by the invasions of our privacy, theft of our identities, disruption and defrauding of businesses, and development of military cyber commands that threaten national security.

Walt Kelly, the creator of the cartoon character Pogo, captured the problem long ago when discussing human invention. He reminds us that "we have met the enemy and he is us." That is, human nature can be dual-sided: innovative and exploitative. Applied to the cyber age, the mistakes humans make in coding can be exploited as vulnerabilities by criminals, the mistakes humans make by clicking on a phishing link can grant unauthorized access to a network by intelligence services or criminals, and the mistakes users make by trusting interlopers can compromise access privileges.

Exercising judgment is implicit in life through decisions and predictions, some of which concern security, especially that of our networks and attached equipment. Human nature makes perfect judgment impossible. To be sure, individual users cannot be expected to defend their networks against foreign intelligence services or transnational organized crime, but they do need to exercise good judgment online and develop a security mindset since cybersecurity is an all-hands responsibility.

In turn, cybersecurity professionals must anticipate threats, that is, make predictions of the ways attackers may exploit the networks they are supporting

108

and assess risk to their networks. Training users in cybersecurity is a big part of the professional's job. Often these teams operate under stress in a largely zero-mistake environment since one failure can cause massive disruptions. Thus, the structure and operation of security teams are important and require understanding the biases team members bring to their jobs as well as ways to incentivize the consumers of and producers of cyberspace.

4.1 THE SECURITY ENVIRONMENT

Chapters 2 and 3 focused on the technical aspects of cyberspace, which is complex and ubiquitous. What should be clear is that wherever there is a security problem, there often is a computer that monitors the environment being secured, and for convenience to operators, it is likely connected to a network, which creates a cybersecurity problem. In the best case, network security requires a computing facility that is well-equipped with the best technology, staffed with the best trained employees, run by the most competent managers, and guided by wise policy. This becomes more imperative as people, organizations, and governments outsource their cyber needs to the clouds, which are data centers run by a third party such as Microsoft Azure, Amazon Web Services, IBM, Google, or Oracle. In fact, the move to the cloud may be a sign that organizations simply cannot meet the challenges of cybersecurity on their own and choose to outsource to a third party.

Whether you host your own network or outsource it, humans are at the center of cybersecurity. They write the code, purchase and install computers containing billions of lines of code, develop algorithms, train and employ artificial intelligence, educate users, supervise the running of the resultant computer network, and unwittingly grant access to unauthorized users through phishing and bad cyber hygiene. Human shortcomings are responsible for cyber insecurity and "roughly 80 percent of incidents in the cyber domain can be traced to three factors: poor user practices, poor network and data management practices, and poor implementation of network architecture" (DC3I, 2015). Regarding poor user practices, technical professionals jokingly refer to this as the PICNIC problem – problem in chair, not in computer.

To reduce the PICNIC problem and maintain network security, people install firewalls and intrusion detection and data loss protection software, segment computers by functionality, and map the movement of normal data in the network so that anomalous data movement can be discovered. Individuals create and run security operations centers (SOCs) staffed by security professionals with responsibility for detecting and analyzing cyber incidents. Incidents can be anomalous communications between network segments or identified by indicators of compromise from both inside and outside their organizations.

To explore this topic, this chapter charts the human dimension of cybersecurity guided by three questions. First, what are the effective steps to be taken to protect against serious cyberattacks? Next, how do we better understand cognitive biases and their impact on cybersecurity? Finally, how can the application of economic principles incentivize producers, users, and regulators to produce better cybersecurity? By understanding biases, it is possible to appreciate risk and ways to mitigate it.

4.2 ASSESSING RISK AND MEASURING LOSS

Charles Babbage, who designed (but could not build) a programmable mechanical computer in 1837, would be amazed by the extent of computerization today. He certainly did not predict that the average person would have multiple devices with enough computing power to solve complex mathematical problems required to stream a video or mine a cryptocurrency. The same is true for the importance of cybersecurity, which has emerged as a distinct professional field given the proliferation of malicious behavior by individuals, organizations, corporations, and governments.

Predicting behavior and assessing risk are at the heart of cybersecurity. Yet, making predictions is challenging, as noted by the distinguished sociologist Robert Merton, in a 1936 paper. This assessment is captured by the famous quote "It is tough to make predictions, especially about the future," which is attributed to many individuals including the atomic scientist Niels Bohr and the baseball manager and American icon Yogi Berra (O'Toole, n.d.).

Predictions are hard, but we can say with some certainty, however, that there will be major data breaches and service disruptions in the future; countries will continue to use cyberspace operations to collect intelligence and create frameworks to integrate cyberattacks into traditional war plans. Compounding this problem is that corporations and governments are often unprepared for the inevitable compromise and are more ready with a response suitable for the last crisis rather than the current or next one. Despite knowing this, it is very difficult to predict when a major cybersecurity incident will occur or what will be exploited or what information technology (IT) or operational technology (OT) services will be denied. Cybersecurity losses include, among others, theft of valuable intellectual property and the consequent loss of business opportunities and cryptocurrencies as well as ransomware payments. Each of these losses constitutes a *risk*, which is defined as "the possibility of losing money on an investment or business venture" (Hayes, 2022).

The financial community measures risk of loss from investments by the maximum financial loss that will occur during a particular length of time, such as a day, month, or year, with a certain probability, such as 95 percent. They refer to this as the *Value at Risk model* (VaR). VaR is used to assess risk to individual portfolios, banks, regulators, and others.

While VaR has been widely used in the financial community, Max C. Y. Wong, a risk modeling specialist, said that "the credit crisis of 2008 was a tidal wave that debunked this well-established risk metric" (Wong, 2013). Others have proposed that VaR be applied to cyber risk, which they call Cyber VaR (Beckstrom, 2014). It has the same limitations as traditional VaR.

Wong identified several problems with VaR. First, VaR assumes that daily changes in a statistic, such as the price of a stock or the value of an index, are statistically independent and identically distributed. Consequently, bubbles where prices on successive days move in the same direction are not captured by VaR. Hence, Wong proposed a new variant of VaR – which he calls Bubble VaR, abbreviated buVaR (Bubble Value at Risk, 2013) – that he believes should replace VaR.

A measure of risk that considers both the probability of an event, P, and its impact, I, is needed. Here impact is defined by what is important about the event. For example, if the event is the death of a vehicle occupant, it would likely have a large legal and/or emotional impact. If the event is the loss of electricity to a large region, it would have a different but very consequential impact.

Risk, R, then, can be captured simply as the product $R = P*I$, which highlights the fact that improbable events of high impact have a large risk associated with them and, therefore, should not be ignored, as we humans are inclined to do. This issue is revisited in the Section 4.2.1.

4.2.1 Heavy-Tailed Probability Distributions and Black Swans

A probability distribution $P(L)$ is the probability of an outcome, call it the loss L, as a function of L. For example, the well-known *normal distribution* (Chen, 2022), which is used in calculating VaR, is a bell-shaped curve with a peak at the mean value, m, of L. $P(L)$ decreases very rapidly toward zero as L either increases or decreases from the mean. Thus, if the probability of a loss follows the normal distribution, it is unlikely that the loss will very far from the mean.

Normal distributions are said to have "thin tails." However, it is very common to find probability distributions that have "fat tails." Such distributions decline slowly as L moves away from the mean. Thus, for fat-tailed distributions large losses (*outliers*) will occur much more often than one would expect with the normal distribution. Ian Bremmer and Preston Keat (2009) of the Eurasia Group studied fat-tailed distributions characterizing political risks and capital market events. They were particularly interested in how rare, or outlier, events could be mitigated.

Mathematician Nassim Nicholas Taleb (2010) called outliers *black swans*. He noted that until 1967, when black swans were discovered in Australia, it was assumed by Europeans that all swans were white. Taleb introduced the black swan concept to call attention to the importance of outlier events of high impact. Examples of black swans are the financial crashes of 1929 and 2008, the Imperial Japanese attack on Pearl Harbor in 1941, the advent of the Internet in 1983, the introduction of the first web browser in 1991, the 2001 terrorist attacks by al-Qaeda against the World Trade Center, and the pandemic created by COVID-19. Taleb advised that we should not attempt to predict black swan events but rather should be prepared to respond when such events occur.

While black swan events are rare, if an incident has a potential existential impact, prudence suggests that it be incorporated into planning. For example, on January 23, 2020, the prestigious Science and Security Board of the Bulletin of Atomic Scientists advanced their Doomsday clock closer to midnight than ever before, indicating the rising danger of "the world's vulnerability to catastrophe from nuclear weapons ... *compounded by a threat multiplier, cyber-enabled information warfare*" (Mecklin, 2021; emphasis added). The board sought to highlight existential threats and raise awareness of threats to humanity. This was intended to encourage governments to undertake arms control agreements and seek ways to eliminate cyberspace operations with existential proportions.

While black swan events are rare and should be considered, we must not overlook the cumulative effects of more common but individually less impactful incidents that affect cybersecurity. These include intrusive data mining that undermines privacy, intellectual property theft that damages businesses, and influence operations that damage the internal politics of nations. The range of cybersecurity challenges extends from the least likely and most dangerous events (e.g., cyber 9/11) to the most likely events with cumulative negative effects (e.g., loss of civil liberties).

4.3 PROTECTING AGAINST NATION-STATE CYBERATTACKS

As discussed in Chapters 2 and 3, there are many places in a computer network where an attacker can break in and acquire control. Protecting a network from a nation-state attacker or one sponsored by a government, known as an advanced persistent threat (APT), can be very challenging. Countries have the motivation, talent, and resources needed for success against a talented and well-protected adversary. Unlike individuals or criminal organizations that are profit-motivated, intelligence services have the patience and funding to access hard targets. Yet individuals, organizations, state and local governments, and corporations are expected to defend against such foreign powers. Further, government-sponsored hackers recruit insiders to conduct espionage, sometimes even using social media in recruitment. As discussed in the succeeding chapters, governments are employing their cyber and intelligence forces globally in cyberspace for offense and defense.

One such nation-state organization is the US National Security Agency (NSA). According to its mission statement, NSA "leads the U.S. Government in cryptology that encompasses both signals intelligence (SIGINT) and information assurance (now referred to as cybersecurity) products and services and enables computer network operations (CNO) in order to gain a decisive advantage for the Nation and our allies under all circumstances" (National Security Agency/Central Security Service, n.d.a). To be effective at collecting SIGINT, NSA employs the most advanced collection techniques as well as large numbers of computer scientists, mathematicians, social scientists, and linguists.

Rob Joyce (2016), who served four years as head of Tailored Access Operations (TAO), NSA's top-notch cyber warfare and intelligence-gathering unit, gave public advice in 2016 at the Enigma Conference on how to improve cybersecurity to make the job of people like him harder. This public outreach was truly unprecedented; NSA is focused on issues outside of US borders and works in a highly classified environment that is opaque to the public. His talk represented a change in how the agency approached cybersecurity since Joyce explained how organizations can improve defense by explaining how a good attacker works.

In this remarkable 2016 talk, Joyce made a fundamental point, namely, to protect a network, you must first understand it thoroughly. If you do not understand your network, a persistent attacker will get to know it better than you do and find a way to get in. While zero-day-based attacks like Stuxnet that impacted Iran's nuclear program capture the imagination and is the subject of documentaries, interestingly, Joyce said that nation-state hackers generally do not need to use zero-day vulnerabilities to break into a target. They use other vulnerabilities that they discover during their analysis of the targeted system, which are often the result of human error.

The *cyberattack kill chain* defined by Lockheed Martin is useful to identify the six stages of an attack by an APT (Hutchins et al., 2011). These include:

- Reconnaissance
- Initial exploitation
- Establishment of persistence
- Installation of tools
- Lateral moves
- Collection and exfiltration of data

Before an attack begins, data on the target is collected. This includes technical information, obtained by physically scanning the network, as well as data on important personnel. Either or both sources of information will be important to the attacker. The attacker will learn what technologies you have deployed and how your system is configured, not what you have assumed, and will discover the vulnerabilities.

To protect against the reconnaissance phase, network managers should inventory all hardware and software running on their system and discard or disable any unused devices and software. They should also deploy *red teams*, who are security personnel expert at breaking into computers, to find network vulnerabilities. Red teams are paid to think in "what if" terms and can mimic the patterns of an advanced persistent threat. An APT is patient and will look for esoteric edge cases and wait for a metaphorical door to open, perhaps on a weekend, such as when a heating, ventilation, and air conditioning (HVAC) vendor is given computer access to a company.

Once a point of entry into a system is found, the attacker establishes a foothold and then creates new points of entry, or *backdoors*, so that the attack can persist if the first point of entry is blocked. Further, the attacker can acquire administrator-level accounts to facilitate access throughout the network. Because an attack typically involves exploration of a network and data collection and exfiltration, a complex toolset is installed for these tasks. Once these preparatory steps have been taken, the APT is prepared to move laterally in the network to identify and collect data, which will be organized, encrypted, and exfiltrated in a way that does not draw attention to the attacker (see Exploit Box 4.1.)

Exploit 4.1 Target data breach

Beginning on November 27, 2013, the retailer Target suffered a massive data breach. As a result, 110 million customer accounts were compromised, costing the company $162 million. Hackers accessed Target's network from its HVAC vendor, Fazio Mechanical Services. Fazio was previously penetrated by a phishing exploit.

Source: Eitan (2018)

4.3.1 Know and Protect Your Trust Zone

Network boundaries are becoming more porous as organizations encourage users to bring your own device (BYOD) or move operations to the cloud. While BYOD has its benefits, often smartphones, laptops, and other Internet devices weaken a secure network since administrators rely on individuals to keep their personal devices secure. Moving to the cloud or outsourcing a data center does not necessarily lead to better security. Cloud operators typically take responsibility for security of the infrastructure but not for the configurations that a user must choose, the applications and security software that the user deploys, or decisions that a user makes, such as to visit a website or open an email link. As we have written throughout, cybersecurity is a team sport that cannot be relegated to the IT department or outsourced to third parties such as cloud service providers.

Essential Principle 4.1 Structured Query Language injection

Structured Query Language (SQL) is a language to execute commands on relational databases, containing only tables. An SQL injection attack occurs when the person preparing database queries inadvertently allows queries to execute unwanted instructions. Depending on the information stored in the database, some very dangerous actions could result. For example, if the database is used for logins to a computer, a poorly crafted query could allow the user to login without a password or even erase the login database.

4.3.2 Modes of Attack

Three prominent modes of attack are phishing, watering holes, and SQL injection, defined in Essential Principle Box 4.1. *Phishing* is an email-based or text message-based social engineering attack, which relies on deceiving a user into divulging confidential or personal information for fraudulent purposes. A *watering hole* is a site known to be frequented by a targeted group, industry, or region. The attacker corrupts the watering hole site so that computers that visit it are infected. As mentioned in Essential Principle Box 4.1, an *SQL injection* attack occurs when an attacker exploits a failure on the part of a database manager to sanitize inputs to the database so that SQL commands cannot be supplied as inputs.

Email, websites, and removable media are the three principal intrusion vectors or means of entry into a computer. Citing one of the most infamous nation-state cyberattacks, Stuxnet, Joyce noted that an air gap between a computer network and the Internet is not necessarily a barrier to entry. Deliberate use of the electromagnetic spectrum to penetrate a network, discussed in Chapter 3, or a witting or unwitting insider can violate isolated systems to introduce malware on a supposed isolated system.

4.3.3 Protecting against Memory Corruption

Attacks that exploit memory corruption, such as buffer overflow, discussed in Chapter 2, are common. To protect against such attacks, organizations can use data executive protection (DEP) and address space layout randomization (ASLR), which are also described in Chapter 2. DEP prevents instructions from being executed from the stack, a portion of memory used to facilitate code reuse. ASLR puts software libraries at places in virtual memory that differ from computer to computer, making it difficult for an attacker to find the code that he/she/they would like to launch using a buffer overflow. Joyce also recommends protecting against return-oriented programming (ROP) attacks, a subtle variation on buffer overflow attacks (Return-oriented programming, 2022). Finally, a user can opt to deploy an operating system that is securely preconfigured and hardened by experts, that is, modified to protect against common attacks.

4.3.4 Credential Security

Since phishing is a common means to gain unauthorized network access and social engineering can produce significant outcomes for attackers, there have been major efforts to verify credentials to improve cybersecurity. With the backdrop of Edward Snowden's espionage in 2013, Joyce recommends that high-level administrator privileges be strictly limited to those who absolutely need them. Often, normal users want these privileges for convenience. With the Snowden experience in mind, access to highly sensitive files should require the approval of at least two authorized individuals.

It is especially dangerous to embed credentials in scripts (code) as a convenience for systems operators. Shortcuts for administrators make an attacker's work easier when such scripts are discovered. Finally, end-to-end encryption is an important defense against man-in-the-middle attacks where data packets can be copied or altered during transit.

4.3.5 Segmenting and Reputational Analysis

Security improves by segmenting networks into logical subsystems that are each protected with firewalls, discussed later, and antivirus and data loss protection software, also discussed later. This will make it much more difficult for attackers to move around in a network. Segmentation also makes it easier to locate intruders, who often move in uncommon ways between segments.

Joyce argues that only approved applications should be allowed on a secure network. (This is called *whitelisting*.) He also believes that every piece of code on a system should be hashed with a standard hashing function and, if the hash is not on the list of locally approved software, it should be sent to a reputation service. Software reputation services compile hashes of known safe software. If a service reports that your code has never been seen before, it should not be allowed to execute without special approval. Such a reputation service will make it very difficult for hacker tools to be activated.

A domain name reputation service can also be consulted for every domain to which a connection is requested by some application or user. Connections can be denied to sites with no or poor reputations without special permission.

Given the relatively lengthy process of breach detection, Joyce highlights the importance of maintaining logs of significant events, saying they are important in discovering intrusions. Not only should logs be maintained, they should also be analyzed to improve for cybersecurity.

4.3.6 Managing Trust

Not all data is equally valued, and an organization's most important data should be segmented and trust managed independently for each segment. Access to the most important data can be restricted to a limited number of users. Other data may be required for broad access, but it is still important to ensure only verified users have access. For outside connections to a network, Joyce recommends that communication occur via an approved application on an approved device that reports the geolocation of the device as well as the time of the day. Both the device and the user should authenticate themselves with the network since identity can be spoofed.

Geolocation and time of day can be used along with the user's internal security authorization for the dynamic allocation of access privileges. For example, if the holder of the device is attempting to connect to a computer in your network that contains sensitive information from a foreign country, the connection should probably be denied, especially if the approved user has not reported to the company that he/she/they is/are traveling.

Network penetration and data loss are inevitable, so an incident response plan is needed to manage trust within an organization. The plan should be exercised during training so that team members can get to know each other and acquire experience dealing with incidents, such as data theft, manipulation, and destruction as well as damage to attached cyber-physical systems controlled from the Internet. The latter includes supervisory control and data acquisition systems, the kind that are deployed in a nation's critical infrastructure, such as power and water systems and petrochemical plants.

Penetration testing (*pen testing*) can be used to test network security. More robust efforts involve pen testing during exercises where parts of the network can be taken down to provide insight on how operations should adapt or during simulated ransomware attacks where data become inaccessible, and the organization must practice continuity of operations during an attack. Exercises not only build experience on how to detect and respond to incidents, including restoring from backups, they also can build trust through parts of an organization that rarely interact with each other, such as the marketing department, front-line engineers, and executives who may become spokespersons during a crisis.

Another cybersecurity tool, as mentioned earlier in this chapter, is the use of *red teams*, authorized individuals who think like an adversary as opposed to *blue teams* who represent the organization. Red teams can use pen testing, social engineering, unauthorized physical entry, and other methods to test an organization's cybersecurity. The result of a red team's efforts can provide independent feedback on how effective an organization and its members are in protecting networks and data when there is no planned outage or exercise.

4.3.7 The Security Operations Center

An SOC is an essential feature of a secure computer network. A typical SOC in a large organization is run by a highly skilled team of professionals whose mission is to monitor activity in a computer system, analyze anomalous behavior,

---

Essential Principle 4.2 Security information and event management system

A security information and event management (SIEM) system collects and analyzes security information from a computer network, its servers, databases, and individual hosts. It also responds to security alerts and serves as a control point for security personnel around the clock. An SIEM system aggregates (a) logs of security events, such as repeated login attempts to a single host, (b) records of the characteristics of network traffic, such as repeated intrusion detection system (IDS) alerts from a single IP (internet protocol) address, (c) the domains to and from which data is sent, raising an alert for domains with poor reputations, (d) the network hosts on which intrusion prevention system (IPS) alerts are generated, which may indicate a compromised host, and (e) the list of active users so that correlations with logged events can be made later.

An SIEM system offers the capability of correlating events into meaningful bundles and generating alerts from them. It has a dashboard that provides visualizations of system activity as well as the controls to manage the network. Finally, an SIEM system has a database for the long-term storage of collected data for the purpose of forensic analysis of security events, such as breaches.

---

and improve system security. Operators observe changes in the levels of processor activity and monitor several types of defensive software such as firewalls, an IDS, IPSs, and breach detection systems and can issue device probes through an SIEM system.

A firewall is designed to reduce or eliminate unwanted incoming and outgoing network traffic based on user-defined rules. A simple firewall makes decisions based on the content of individual packets. A stateful firewall monitors the connection state of a packet stream. It assembles related packets until their connection state can be assessed and then applies rules. Application firewalls analyze the contents of packets to ensure that the contents meet the criteria set by an application or service. Each type of firewall can forward alerts to an SIEM system.

There are two principal types of IDS, a network-based IDS (NIDS) and a host-based IDS (HIDS). An example of a HIDS is an IDS that monitors operating system files. Thus, if a pattern of operating system accesses is suspicious, such as repeatedly opening, processing, and closing files is detected, ransomware may be encrypting files for a ransomware attack, which should raise an alert. An example of an NIDS is an IDS that looks for anomalous traffic, such as port scanning, that is, testing ports to see which ports are accessible, or sending a high rate of packets from a set of sources, indicating that a denial-of-service operation is underway. An IPS is an IDS that has a response capability, perhaps to reject a packet stream from a suspicious IP address.

According to the 2022 Mandiant M-Trends report, during the period October 1, 2020, to December 31, 2021, the medium duration of an undetected breach was about 21 days on average, down from 78 days in 2018, but it only took a few days for an attacker to obtain administrative access (M-Trends 2022, Special Report, 2022). If the gap between the start of the attack and detection can be reduced, it might be possible to kill an attack before it does serious damage. But a 21-day average gap is almost certainly too large to tolerate.

A breach detection system is a combination of tools, such as those mentioned here, plus a domain reputation service that stops a process from communicating with a domain that is known or suspected to be used for exfiltrated data. An SOC operator can also send probes, simple requests, to network devices to retrieve their status.

4.4 COGNITIVE LIMITATIONS ON JUDGMENTS AND DECISION-MAKING

Decision-making is about making choices through human judgments that concern estimation of magnitudes and probabilities. Psychologists Daniel Kahneman and Amos Tversky made profound contributions to understanding how humans make judgments and decisions, especially in the presence of uncertainty. In his book *The Undoing Project: A Friendship That Changed Our Minds*, Michael Lewis (2017) provides a biography of these two friends who revolutionized cognitive psychology and led to the creation of behavioral economics. Legal scholar Cass Sunstein and Nobel economics laureate Richard Thaler (2016) note Kahneman and Tversky "changed how people think about how people think." Because sound judgments and good decisions are central to security in the cyber age, we explore cognitive limitations on judgments and decision-making in this section.

Kahneman and Tversky demonstrated that humans do not behave as trained or intuitive statisticians, nor do they always make decisions completely rationally. But their deviations from rationality can be anticipated and specified. That is, humans err in predictable ways. The challenge for individuals is to learn how to detect their own biases and see the biases in analysis.

Kahneman (2013), in his book *Thinking, Fast and Slow*, which reflects his research with Tversky, reports that the human mind has two modes of operation, one that is fast, intuitive, and influenced by emotions, which he calls System 1, and the other, System 2, that is slow, deliberative, and rational. The latter can handle complex logic, reasoning, and calculations.

Unfortunately, System 2 requires mental work, so humans will typically opt to use a System 1 shortcut decision method, called a "heuristic," resulting in an error or "cognitive bias." For instance, people rely on heuristics when using political party identification (Democratic or Republican in the United States) to vote for an unknown candidate rather than comparing issue positions to decide for whom to vote. Or they may choose a well-known corporate brand (Apple or Samsung) to select a phone rather than doing a deep technical comparison to choose the "best" one that meets specified attributes for an individual's needs.

Using shortcuts via heuristics has been called the "cognitive miser theory," which posits that the human mind tries to be miserly and expend the minimum amount of mental effort while thinking and solving problems (Fiske & Taylor, 1991). Advertising and marketing reinforce the natural inclination for shortcuts when employing celebrities and influencers to promote brands, creating ads to portray benefits of a product, and exaggerating the impact of a purchase.

We emphasize that heuristics very often produce satisfactory decisions. When a decision-maker is tired or rushed, a heuristic or cognitive bias may be chosen for expediency when a more deliberative assessment is needed. This is especially true when the consequences of a decision are serious, such as a trauma surgeon deciding on the treatment of a seriously ill patient. In such cases structured support can be provided by a subject matter expert (SME) who is trained in cognitive psychology or a preprogrammed expert system (e.g., an artificial intelligence system) that is designed by such an SME, perhaps to help surgeons in preparing diagnoses.

Given the prominence of heuristics in decision-making, we examine the relevance of the following thirteen cognitive biases to safety and security in the cyber age. We challenge the reader to identify other security instances when these cognitive biases are likely to appear and think slowly on how to improve cybersecurity.

4.4.1 Additive Bias

"Additive bias" arises when humans are asked to improve "objects, ideas or a situation," such as how to better serve a community (Adams et al., 2021); they

---

Exploit 4.2 Social engineering in practice

Popularized by Kevin Mitnick, social engineering exploits human trust to convince someone to compromise information that can be used to gain system access. This is often achieved through phishing scams that mislead a target to believe that it received a legitimate email that requires a download but is really a Trojan providing a third party access to the user's information or system.

In 2020, hackers convinced a group of Twitter employees to disclose passwords for high-profile users that included Barack Obama, Joe Biden, Jeff Bezos, and Elon Musk. The attack started with phone phishing that resulted in one employee compromising credentials, which were then used to compromise the credentials of other employees. The hackers used the privileged access to hijack accounts and solicit an estimated $180,000 in bitcoin before being shut down when the Federal Bureau of Investigation (FBI) arrested the hackers in summer 2020 (Twitter 2020).

While there is much awareness of phishing, Karthik Raman (2008, p. 9) argues that "our susceptibility to social engineering is rooted in the design of the human brain, in the complex interplay between the centers of emotion and reason. Social engineering is the manipulation of a victim's fear, curiosity, greed, or sympathy."

---

routinely try to make improvements by adding to the current configuration rather than subtracting from it.

This bias comes into play when new features must be added to applications. Adding software to add features may result in more complex and more vulnerable software, which might be avoided by rewriting the relevant portion of the software.

4.4.2 Anchoring Bias

"Anchoring bias" is the tendency to rely too heavily on the first piece of evidence seen. This is illustrated by criminal behavior revealed by a 2016 Kaspersky security risk survey that showed that distributed denial-of-service (DDoS) attacks often served as a smokescreen for other more serious attacks. The lesson here is that SOCs should not allocate all their staff resources to responding to DDoS attacks; they should keep some staff in reserve while mitigating the DDoS attacks since these attacks can be a cover for some other intrusion.

4.4.3 Authority Bias

"Authority bias" is the tendency to comply with the requests of an authority figure even when they conflict with personal conscience. The Milgram experiment on obedience to an authority figure is the classic illustration of this bias (McLeod, 2017). In experiments conducted by Yale psychologist Stanley Milgram participants were instructed to administer electric shocks to "learners," Milgram's lab assistants. When the person running the experiment wore a lab coat and the experiment was done in a lab, a very high proportion of the participants obeyed and issued fake shocks of up to 450 volts, which, if real, would have been fatal! When the experimenter did not wear a lab coat and the experiment was done in a nonprofessional space, obedience declined markedly.

Authority bias is illustrated by business email compromise. Here a criminal, impersonating an important person, sends email to that person's subordinate requesting that he/she/they send funds because "I am stranded in London after losing my wallet and passport." The subordinate thinks the superior is in trouble, responds, and sends the funds.

In retrospect, phishing attacks that rely on authority bias are naïve but are generally effective in hierarchical organizations where there is a fear among people of upsetting the boss, a teacher, or a government agency such as the Internal Revenue Service or FBI.

4.4.4 Availability Bias

"Availability bias" is a mental shortcut that invokes an example that most immediately comes to mind when making an evaluation or judgment (Tversky & Kahneman, 1973). A recently encountered idea biases an individual to use it again if it appears relevant. It is often called the "recency bias."

Availability bias is illustrated by the influence of news reports. If ransomware attacks are prominently featured in the news because they are costly, analysts will be inclined to believe that they are much more common than phishing attacks, which is not the case (Crane, 2020).

4.4.5 Confirmation Bias

"Confirmation bias" is "[t]he tendency to test one's beliefs or conjectures by seeking evidence that might confirm or verify them and to ignore evidence that might disconfirm or refute them. This bias helps to maintain prejudices and stereotypes" (Confirmation Bias, n.d.). This bias is also related to loss aversion discussed later. A person, by choosing evidence to support a preconceived belief, does not have to admit that his/her/their belief is not correct or relevant.

A cybersecurity analyst who finds source code inside his/her/their system previously associated with nation A will typically try to confirm that A is behind the penetration. But since countries use other countries' and organizations' tools, this complicates the attribution process (Greenberg, 2019b). Previous analysis may be useful for a current problem, but we must remember that the past is not prologue.

An important criticism of social media use is that it exploits confirmation bias. People join groups and connect to like-minded people on social media. This can have positive benefits if the group is organized around a hobby or expertise, but it also has the effect of creating an echo chamber where members reinforce each other rather than challenge beliefs with new ideas. Research suggests Facebook users are highly polarized in like-minded groups, making them susceptible to misinformation (Quattrociocchi et al., 2016).

4.4.6 Dunning–Kruger Effect

"Dunning–Kruger effect" is a cognitive bias in which individuals of low ability at a task overrate their ability and those of high ability underrate theirs. The authors of this phenomenon observe that "the miscalibration of the incompetent stems from an error about the self, whereas the miscalibration of the highly competent stems from an error about others" (Kruger & Dunning, 1999). Former Naval War College professor Thomas Nichols (2017) saw this leading to the death of expertise where anyone's opinion is as good as anyone else's regardless of experience, study, or profession.

This effect biases computer users into believing that they know how to avoid infected websites and suspicious email attachments when they do not. This means that user training is going to be less successful than the trainers would like, since successful completion of a 30-minute cybersecurity training program will not be enough to ensure users do not commit errors that get exploited. Similarly, IT consultants are less likely to be as qualified as they say they are and often lack an understanding of an organization's culture, processes, and networks.

4.4.7 Endowment Effect

"Endowment effect" is the tendency for a person to assign a larger value to a person they manage or thing they own than they would be willing to pay to acquire them or it in the first place. For example, during a recruiting season a coach often will be reluctant to replace a member of his/her/their team with a recruit who is said by scouts to be more talented even though this might improve the team overall. This same behavior describes how owners value their possessions.

Once an organization has chosen a cybersecurity management philosophy, for example, choosing to adopt a self-managed versus an externally managed system or to store its data on its premises versus cloud storage, leadership will be reluctant to change the philosophy to one that its advisors consider to be more secure.

4.4.8 Framing Effect

"Framing effect" (Tversky & Kahneman, 1986) is a cognitive bias in which a decision by an individual is biased by the way it is presented or "framed."

For example, if told that 99 percent of DDoS attacks do not result in large losses to an enterprise, an IT manager may choose to tolerate them until they dissipate. However, if told that in 1 percent of the cases a major intrusion would damage the IT manager's reputation, the manager is more likely to treat DDoS attacks as a serious issue.

4.4.9 Hindsight Bias

"Hindsight bias" is also related to loss aversion. When people who have made predictions are later told of the outcomes, they often fool themselves into believing that they predicted the outcomes correctly. They do not want to admit that they were on the losing side of a prediction.

An IT manager who succumbs to hindsight bias and is unwilling to admit an error in judgment may find himself/herself/themselves confronted by more serious challenges in the future. This reminds us that after every major incident or simulated incident to test procedures, reviews should be conducted to compare expectations with results.

4.4.10 Loss Aversion

When Kahneman and Tversky applied the framing effect to economics, they found that the prospect of losing a given dollar amount, say $5, is perceived by humans as more costly than the benefit would be for winning the same amount. This is called the "loss aversion effect" (Kahneman & Tversky, 1979). This is illustrated by a stock owner who is more inclined to sell a stock that has increased in value than one that has decreased even though the former is more likely to continue to increase than the latter is likely to rebound. With respect to cybersecurity, organizations tend to underspend on cybersecurity because they can see the expense in their budget but they cannot assess the loss caused by a potential incident.

4.4.11 Planning Fallacy

"Planning fallacy" is the tendency on the part of an individual to be optimistic and underestimate the time it will take to complete a task.

Estimating the time to complete a software development project is difficult and has been the subject of many studies. The same applies to the identification of software vulnerabilities.

To reduce the risk of underestimating task completion time, it is recommended that the planner subdivide the task into a set of tasks and then use the best a priori time estimate for each subtask. Since a task may involve many parallel activities, the longest path will determine the best time estimate.

4.4.12 Representativeness Error

"Representativeness error" occurs when a person makes a judgment based on evidence that best represents a particular condition but which is insufficient to justify a decision, such as a patient who looks very robust but whose tests are judged inconclusive being declared healthy by a doctor.[1]

A representativeness error was committed by Colonial Pipeline after it was hit by a ransomware attack on May 7, 2021. The company supplied about 45 percent of the fuel consumed on the East Coast of the United States. The company's billing system was compromised, not its OT that controls the pipeline. Under an abundance of caution, the company shut down OT and the pipeline. Colonial's action led to a shortage of fuel primarily because alarmed customers began hoarding fuel.

4.4.13 Sunk Cost Fallacy

A "sunk cost" is an expenditure that has occurred and cannot be recovered. Frequently, decision-makers will justify further investment in an unprofitable

---

[1] Dr. Jerome Groopman describes a real-world event in which an emergency room doctor misdiagnosed a patient who was having a heart attack. When the tests that the doctor administered failed to definitively rule out a heart attack and being very impressed by the patient's extremely fit appearance, the doctor assessed him to be fine and sent him home. The doctor was chagrined the next day to discover his error (Groopman, 2007).

venture because of a sunk cost. A decision against further investments amounts to recognition of a loss, which, as we have seen, humans would rather not acknowledge. The sunk cost fallacy has also been called the "Concorde fallacy" because both the UK and French governments continued their investment in the Concorde fleet of supersonic aircraft knowing that it would continue to be a money loser.

When it comes to cybersecurity, sunk costs often appear as commitments to obsolete technology. For example, Microsoft ceased supporting its XP operating system in April 2014, yet XP persisted for years among large-scale users and became the vehicle for the 2017 WannaCry ransomware attack, causing significant financial losses and service shutdowns. One of the largest victims was the British National Health System (NHS). A later report noted, "All NHS organisations [sic] infected by WannaCry had unpatched or unsupported Windows operating systems so were susceptible to the ransomware" (Investigation: WannaCry Cyber-Attack and the NHS, 2018). The attack would have been thwarted had users upgraded from obsolete software, but sunk costs dissuaded them from upgrading and enabled the success of WannaCry.

4.4.14 Observations on Cognitive Biases

As the aforementioned discussion of cognitive biases illustrates, we humans are disposed by our limited decision-making apparatus to use shortcuts and thereby make errors, some of which can result in great harm. Thus, we should trust our gut less and trust evidence-based outcomes more. If we can collect data on the success and failure of diagnoses, we should use it. But we should also be aware that we are "blind to logic when it [is] embedded in a story" (Lewis, 2017), a framing error.

Traditional economic theory has been predicated on the assumption that human beings are rational (*homo economicus*) and that behavior can be explained with mathematics. When faced with a choice, it was assumed the rational actor would identify the costs and benefits of an action and choose the option that delivers the greatest net benefits. The cognitive biases discovered by Tversky and Kahneman violate this rationality assumption and led to the development of behavioral economics for which Kahneman received the Nobel Memorial Prize for Economics in 2002 (Smith, 2002).

Around 1990 medical education began to teach evidence-based medicine. That is, doctors are now taught to use the best scientific evidence available in treating patients and rely less on their experience. Likewise, the IT community should emphasize an evidence-based approach to cybersecurity by putting more emphasis on threat and impact data. This will require a new level of public–private cooperation since governments and private developers have access to unique insights to improve overall cybersecurity. The Cyberspace Solarium Commission recommended that the United States create a Bureau of Cyber Statistics (King & Gallagher, 2020).

The MITRE Corporation, a nonprofit corporation that manages US government federally funded research and development centers, is another example of an organization that could facilitate cooperation of this type. It maintains the Common Vulnerabilities and Exposures (CVE) system (CVE List Home, n.d.) and publishes MITRE ATT&CK, a widely used database of adversarial cyberattack tactics and techniques that are used "to develop a more effective cybersecurity" (MITRE ATT&CK®, 2015).

Our next subject, cyber economics, is inherently based on measurement and analysis. Before turning to this new subject, we again call attention to "black swans," highly improbable events that, if they occur, can have catastrophic consequences (Taleb, 2010). High-impact, low-frequency events are difficult to predict but very dangerous if they occur. Thus, if society is faced with an existential threat that has at least some likelihood of occurring, a very high premium should be placed on good forecasting to lower the effect a low probability event can have. Forecasting is discussed in Chapter 11.

4.5 CYBER ECONOMICS

Many cybersecurity problems are economic problems. For example, information and communications technology (ICT) companies face trade-offs between investing to produce fully tested and secure code and the opportunity costs associated with delaying a software release for this purpose. At the enterprise level, network administrators face trade-offs between user accessibility and security. Finally, users make choices based on cost while affected by the cognitive biases listed earlier. Since many cybersecurity problems are economic ones, modest incentives can significantly improve security.

Cybersecurity professor Tyler Moore's (2010) work is instructive and invaluable to thinking about the role economics plays in cybersecurity. He applied his analysis to four of the most prevalent threats, namely, online identity theft, industrial cyber espionage, critical infrastructure protection, and botnets.

Moore identified three economic challenges facing cybersecurity – misaligned incentives, information asymmetries, and externalities, discussed later – and examined regulatory options that can be taken to address them.

These include ex ante safety regulations versus ex post liability, information asymmetries, and externalities. He followed with policy recommendations concerning data breaches, industrial espionage, critical infrastructure protection, and botnets. Because cyberspace is for the most part privately owned, the principles of economics are best suited here to improve cybersecurity and serve as a guide to formulating public policy that can incentivize producers and operators of ICT to create more security for ICT users.

4.5.1 Misaligned Incentives

There is a natural tension between efficiency and resiliency in the design of information technology systems. If efficiency is prioritized, resiliency may suffer. This is not important if systems continue to operate correctly but if an unanticipated event occurs, the lack of resiliency can be very costly. This is illustrated by a scenario envisioned by the Federal Energy Regulatory Commission in which power in all of North America could be lost if a small number of grid substations are attacked on a hot summer day (see Exploit 4.3).

If security incentives are misaligned, those responsible for the security of a system may not suffer monetary losses or reputational damage for security violations and, thus, will not be incentivized to improve security. In the 2013

Exploit 4.3 The Metcalf substation incident

On January 16, 2013, the Metcalf substation in Silicon Valley was attacked just before 1 a.m. when underground fiber-optic telecommunication cables near the substation were cut. About 30 minutes later, multiple snipers using high-powered rifles over a period of 19 minutes shot holes in 17 large power transformers, causing 52,000 gallons of oil used for cooling the transformers to leak out. Within 15 minutes, a bank of transformers crashed, sending an alarm to a remote-control center that rerouted power to local customers (Smith, 2014).

In 2014, the Federal Energy Regulatory Commission concluded that "if saboteurs knocked out just nine of the country's 55,000 electric-transmission substations on a scorching summer day, … the U.S. could suffer a coast-to-coast blackout." The consequences of such an outage could be very serious. In testimony before Congress, it has been asserted that a prolonged loss of electrical power, due to an electromagnetic pulse attack, "could result in the death of up to 90% of the American population" (Pry, 2017).

Metcalf substation attack, the grid operator, PG&E, was not prepared for a physical attack that could have shut down the power to a substantial portion of Silicon Valley. PG&E did not recognize that (a) its transformers were susceptible to physical attack with guns, (b) its surveillance cameras were not positioned such that it was possible to see the perimeter from which the attack occurred, and (c) it did not realize that phone service to the facility could be disabled by cutting outside fiber-optic cables.

It is important to study events like these as the risks are significant. Given that nine substation outages nationwide could cause a power outage across the United States, incentives were clearly misaligned (Smith, 2014). They remain misaligned. The US government lacks the authority to force grid operators to adhere to high security standards. Consequently, they are largely within the purview of state regulators and corporate boards.

Misaligned incentives also arise when organizations choose to put computer systems online for the convenience of operators without adequate protection, such as a virtual private network service, or allow personal computer-based equipment to be connected to their networks without properly validating the devices or the user.

This is illustrated by a choice that bulk electric grid operators made to substitute signals from the Global Positioning System (GPS) for their atomic clocks after GPS was made available by the US government for civilian use. This reduced costs for grid operators but also put the North American grid at risk. If GPS signals are lost, say, due to a solar flare or an electromagnetic pulse produced by a nuclear explosion just outside the atmosphere, or if GPS signals are spoofed, the grid would lose synchronism and electricity would be available only if a local grid could provide it. GPS spoofing is becoming more common, having occurred thousands of times using radio equipment costing only a few hundred dollars (Korolov, 2019).

Many timing and navigation applications also rely on GPS signals. Loss of signals or spoofing of them presents a risk to cellular communication networks, smartphones, stock trading, commercial shipping, military systems, and other systems. The risk exists with all global navigation satellite systems, which includes the United States' GPS, Russia's GLONASS, China's BeiDou Navigation Satellite System, and the European Union's Galileo (GPS.Gov: Other Global Navigation Satellite Systems (GNSS), n.d.).

Misaligned incentives also arise in many cybersecurity contexts. They occur when a vendor fails to set adequate standards for writing secure software or chooses to ship vulnerable legacy software because it is less expensive. If a system is hacked because of these deficiencies, the burden for the loss is suffered by the customer, not the vendor.

Exploit 4.4 Operation Aurora

On January 12, 2010, Google revealed that it "detected a highly sophisticated and targeted attack on our corporate infrastructure originating from China that resulted in the theft of intellectual property from Google" (Google, 2010). Their confidential software repository was penetrated. At least 30 companies were also attacked in the same manner. The targeted companies were primarily engineering and tech companies that failed to properly protect their intellectual property. In the case of Google, the company said that the attackers sought intellectual property and to "access Gmail accounts of Chinese human rights activists."

According to McAfee, the attack started by exploiting zero-day vulnerabilities in Internet Explorer, which Microsoft patched the following week.

The intruders gained access to an organization by sending a tailored attack to one or a few targeted individuals... because they likely had access to valuable intellectual property. These attacks will look like they come from a trusted source, leading the target to fall for the trap and clicking a link or file. That's when the exploitation takes place, using the vulnerability in Microsoft's Internet Explorer. Once the malware is downloaded and installed, it opens a back door that allows the attacker to perform reconnaissance and gain complete control over the compromised system. (Kurtz, 2010)

4.5.2 Information Asymmetries

Good decision-making is predicated on information access. Yet, the private nature of cybersecurity leads to information asymmetries when attackers know whom they have compromised, but targets are generally reluctant to release breach incidents publicly. Companies often do not want to admit to breaches lest it hurt their reputations and, possibly, their stock prices. This complicates assessing the effectiveness of security measures since it can be difficult to obtain such data. Without good loss measurements, resources cannot be allocated properly.

When incidents have high impact, they must be published, as was the case for the Target breach or China's Operation Aurora that targeted Google and other companies. Incidents are made public if required by law. All 50 US states, the District of Columbia, Guam, Puerto Rico, and the Virgin Islands have laws that require private or governmental entities to notify individuals of loss of personally identifiable information, but that may be too narrow to affect cybersecurity. When reports are too narrow, government can act, as in the case of Uber's technology officer who was indicted. David Anderson, a

US attorney in San Francisco, said, "When a company like Uber gets hacked, we expect good corporate citizenship, we expect prompt disclosure to the employee and consumer victims in that hack. In this case, what we saw was the exact opposite" (Conger, 2020). In 2022, the Cyber Incident Reporting for Critical Infrastructure Act of 2022 (CIRCIA) was passed by the US Congress and signed by President Biden.

Information asymmetries can disrupt markets, as illustrated by automobile lemon laws. They protect consumers when they purchase a car that is under warranty, suffer a defect protected under the warranty, but multiple attempts to remediate the defect are unsuccessful. Such cars are called "lemons." Because there was a period when lemons were common in the US auto market, all 50 US states have passed lemon laws to ensure consumers are not duped into buying bad cars.

In a 1970 paper for which he shared the 2001 Nobel Memorial Prize for Economics, George Akerlof (1970) explained how markets degrade when they

---

History Matters 4.1 Perfect code: The story of NASA software engineers

Software used on earth can be readily updated through patches. But there was a time when software going into orbit had to be flawless since over-the-air updates were not possible to patch software operating the Space Shuttle's engines. The National Aeronautics and Space Administration (NASA) had to guarantee its software was perfect with zero bugs. Its 420,000-line code had just one error compared to commercial software that would have about 5,000 errors. Charles Fishman, who investigated how NASA programmers created such flawless software, attributed it to the NASA culture. Relative to Silicon Valley workplaces, Fishman found the NASA culture to be quite boring, with 40-hour work weeks and simple offices occupied by "programmers [who] are intense, but low-key" (Fishman, 1996).

The coding process consisted of four simple ideas:

1. The product is only as good as the plan for the product, with no deviations without significantly new planning.
2. The best teamwork is healthy rivalry with subgroups and subcultures.
3. Software is written based on a history of the coding and a history of errors.
4. Do not just fix the mistakes but fix whatever allowed the mistake to occur.

contain both lemons and "peaches," high-quality cars, but there is asymmetric information between buyers and sellers. A seller knows whether his/her/their car is a lemon or a peach, but if a buyer does not, the buyer will not pay a premium for quality that cannot be measured. This has the effect of driving peach sellers out of the market and can lead to a market collapse since consumers will gradually lose faith in the used car market if it supplies only lemons.

The software market is a market for lemons. Because buyers cannot tell which software is more secure, they have no incentive to spend more for one product or another. The more secure software is, the more expensive it is to produce. Thus, information asymmetry discourages vendors from investing in making their products more secure since there is no penalty for producing inferior products. Further, consumers simply cannot differentiate between good and bad software, though ratings can help. Yet, the sunk cost fallacy described earlier often prevents migration from platforms once they have been adopted.

4.5.3 Externalities

An externality in economics is a "side effect or consequence of an industrial or commercial activity that affects other parties without this being reflected in the cost of the goods or services involved" (EXTERNALITY English Definition and Meaning | Lexico.com, n.d.).

There are positive and negative externalities. The pollination of local crops by a honeybee hive is a positive externality. Another is the early mover or first-mover advantage gained by being among the first to market a particular product or service (Suarez & Lanzolla, 2005). Microsoft Windows is an example of an early mover but it was not the first to introduce graphical user interface.

A negative externality is one in which the provider of a product or service passes on costs to the market. A firm that ignores security to be a first mover and achieves market dominance creates a negative externality. Its customers live with less secure products that are more easily compromised and then potentially used in botnets.

Free riding is another negative externality that occurs when a party enjoys an increased security benefit from the investment made by others in security while it does not invest in its own security. A consequence of free riding is that it generates dependence on a third party for security and can result in overall spending reductions.

The Border Gateway Protocol (BGP) discussed in Chapter 3 is based on trust, which can be violated when an autonomous system (AS) announces a block of addresses that it has not been assigned by the Internet Corporation

---

Exploit 4.5 Mirai botnet-based DDoS attack:
2016 Internet outage

In 2016, a Mirai botnet-based DDoS attack affected internet service on the East Coast by targeting Dyn, a New Hampshire-based company, which offered domain name system (DNS) services. (Dyn was acquired by Oracle in 2017.)

The DDoS attack targeted the DNS registrar by overwhelming it with malicious traffic, making major sites unreachable. The botnet was largely composed of compromised Internet of Things devices such as cameras, home routers, and baby monitors, devices that are not normally protected by security software. The Mirai malware used a table of common factory default usernames and passwords to log into the vulnerable devices and infect with its malware to gain control.

The FBI arrested three individuals who pled guilty to crimes related to the Mirai botnet. This is a good illustration of a negative externality.

Source: Stahl (2017)

---

for Assigned Names and Numbers so it can steal traffic from the legitimate custodian of the block. Methods that are somewhat costly to deploy have been proposed to provide guarantees that an AS making a BGP announcement of a prefix is its custodian. If some, but not all, ASs deploy these methods, others will be free riding.

4.5.4 Responses to Economic Barriers

We now explore five possible methods to address misaligned incentives, information asymmetries, and negative externalities. They are ex ante regulation versus ex post liability, information disclosure and sharing, risk management, cyber insurance, and indirect intermediary liability.

4.5.4.1 Ex Ante Regulation versus Ex Post Regulation

The goal of ex ante regulation is to prevent incidents in advance. The goal of ex post regulation is to threaten organizations that violate regulations with monetary damages. Regulation of either kind is thought to have a negative externality, namely, to reduce the pace of innovation. This view is reflected in Section 230 of the US Communications Decency Act of 1996, which protects intermediaries from legal responsibility for what others say or do using their platforms.

The Glass–Steagall Act of 1933 was a type of ex ante regulation. It created a wall between banks that engaged in "risky investing from those that did basic lending." It was introduced during the Great Depression to prevent future failures of overleveraged banks with the effect of separating commercial banking from investment banking. Subsequently in the 1930s, President Franklin D. Roosevelt's New Deal ushered in unprecedented federal programs that brought the national government down to the community level through public works, electrification, and supplemental income through Social Security.

While there were subsequent attempts to increase federal activity at the local level in the 1960s through President Lyndon B. Johnson's Great Society programs, the 1980s were marked by deregulation or the reduction of government's role in the economy. The deregulatory spirit is encapsulated in President Ronald Reagan's assertion that the most terrifying words in the English language were "I'm from the government, and I'm here to help" (Reagan, 1986). The spirit continued during the 1990s under President Bill Clinton, who worked to reform government programs and respect the technology sector's independence. The 1999 Gramm–Leach–Bliley Act "swept away" the remnants of the Glass–Steagall Act, freeing business from regulation (Leonhardt, 2008).

Changes in law and politics resulted in a favorable climate for business. In some sectors it might be best to use both ex ante and ex post regulation. Ex ante regulation is not very effective if the regulator lacks information about harms or is uncertain about minimum standards. But ex post regulation does not work well when firms are not always held responsible or they cannot afford to pay. Interestingly, both conditions often hold in cybersecurity.

4.5.4.2 Information Disclosure and Sharing

Since information asymmetries are a barrier to cybersecurity, information disclosure may be the answer. As Justice Louis Brandeis (1914) famously said, "Sunlight is said to be the best of disinfectant; electric light the most efficient policeman." By sharing vulnerabilities and lessons from attacks, cybersecurity can improve. Yet, there are economic reasons companies do not share information with competitors or law enforcement.

Legislation can help. For example, the Cyberspace Solarium Commission, established by the 2019 John S. McCain National Defense Authorization Act to "develop a consensus on a strategic approach to defending the United States in cyberspace against cyber-attacks of significant consequences," recommended the creation of a Bureau of Cyber Statistics to address the need for data on the types of cyberattacks that occur and their frequency and cost (King & Gallagher, 2020). This resulted in the passage of the Cyber Incident Reporting for Critical Infrastructure Act of 2022 mentioned earlier.

Policy Matters 4.1 Promoting information-sharing

There are major benefits of information-sharing to improve cybersecurity, but the competitive marketplace creates disincentives for one company to share information with another company, who is like a competitor. This is where government can step in to remove disincentives.

In 1998, largely in response to significant terrorist attacks against physical targets, the Clinton White House issued Presidential Decision Directive 63 (PPD-63) with the goal to "take all necessary measures to swiftly eliminate any significant vulnerability to both physical and cyber-attacks on our critical infrastructures, including especially our cyber systems." The policy prioritized this effort through vulnerability analyses, remediation plans, warning capability for significant attacks, response system to significant attacks, capability to reconstitute after an attack, education and awareness programs, and federally sponsored research and development to support infrastructure protection.

Source: White House (1998)

There have been important US government executive branch actions that benefited cybersecurity such as Information Sharing and Analysis Centers (ISACs), which are nonprofit organizations designed to help operators of the US critical infrastructure sectors protect their facilities, staffs, and customers. Created within the context of protecting physical infrastructure against terrorist attacks, ISACs came into existence through a Presidential Policy Directive by President Bill Clinton "to serve as the mechanism for gathering, analyzing, appropriately sanitizing, and disseminating private sector information to both industry and the NIPC [National Infrastructure Protection Council]" (White House, 1998). There are now dozens of ISACs in the United States and other countries. They share data on a confidential basis by sector since attackers tend to target the same industry.

President Obama expanded the federal government's role in promoting information-sharing through a 2015 Executive Order: "[T]he Secretary of Homeland Security ... shall strongly encourage the development and formation of Information Sharing and Analysis Organizations (ISAOs)" (White House 2015).

In both cases, ISACs and ISAOs provide companies voluntary ways to cooperate and interface with the federal government. There is anecdotal evidence that companies attach more value to targeted threat data, which they

---

Essential Principle 4.3 Risk management

When an organization confronts a risk, there are four choices available:

* Accept it – pay for the loss through fees.
* Mitigate it – install better technology, which increases costs.
* Avoid it – impose customer requirements, which may result in loss of business.
* Transfer it – buy cyber insurance or let others absorb the cost.

---

obtain through ISACs, than to generalized threat data they can obtain from government sources. One study noted: "They [ISACs] create an ecosystem in which trust is being built among critical operators and experience can be shared" (ENISA, 2018).

4.5.4.3 Cyber Insurance

Cyber insurance policies can provide coverage for a variety of losses, such as data breaches, malware infection, ransomware costs, damaged computer systems, liability for loss of private information, legal fees, business email compromise, and business interruption.

Insurance can provide incentives to take precautions and reward security investments by lowering premiums. This is an important form of private sector regulation where an insurance company can establish thresholds of security to limit its liability but also encourage better cybersecurity practices among its customers. Insurance companies can collect incident data, anonymize it, and pass it on to actuaries to better calibrate expected loss. This information helps insurance companies to price insurance policies. Insurance also encourages data collection, which helps to ameliorate information asymmetries.

The cyber insurance field is growing. In 2022, there were more than 500 insurers offering some type of protection. Of these approximately 140 insurers offered stand-alone policies with $1.11 billion in coverage. Cyber insurance coverage that was issued as part of a package policy amounted to $915 million in 2019 (Grones, 2019).

4.5.4.4 Indirect Intermediary Liability

There are many situations in which legal responsibility, that is, liability for stopping an illegal or harmful act, can be assigned to a third party. In such incidents there is usually a bad actor, a victim, and a third party. For example, when it is in the public interest to eliminate a botnet, a collection of compromised computers (bots) or victims, a third party could be the internet service provider (ISP) that provides connectivity to the victim. In such a case a state could assign legal responsibility to the ISP to find and help disinfect compromised computers and thereby stop the illegal activity in return for legal protection for the ISP.

Using indirect intermediaries works when (a) the bad actor is inaccessible or cannot pay if caught, (b) it is too costly to assign blame fairly, or (c) the third party can detect and prevent the harm and can benefit from elimination of the harm or illegal activity. For example, the ISP benefits from identifying and helping disinfect the bot because it reduces the excess ISP bandwidth consumed by the bot.

4.6 DESIGNING AN ETHICAL ORGANIZATION

As Epley and Kumar (2019) observe in their *Harvard Business Review* article, "Creating an ethical culture … requires thinking about ethics not simply as a *belief* problem but also as a *design* problem." It is a design problem because it requires not only the articulation of values, incentives, and norms but also shaping the way members use this information to make decisions and mold an organization's culture, recalling one of the famous lines of management guru Peter Drucker, "culture eats strategy for breakfast" (Engel, 2018). Put simply, individuals through their own practices drive an organization's behavior, so it is essential to establish and follow principles to have an ethical organization.

Epley and Kumar (2019) identify four essential features of an ethical organization: "*explicit values, thoughts during judgment, incentives* and *cultural norms.*" They say ethical values should be articulated in clearly stated principles and incorporated into a "simple, short, actionable, and emotionally resonant" mission statement. Employees need to see how ethical principles influence organizational practices. The mission statement must be reflected in hiring, firing, promotions, and operations so that the ethical principles are "deeply embedded throughout the organization."

When people make judgments, they are often influenced by their peer group and issues that are top of mind, which include cognitive biases. To nudge them to make ethical judgments, it is important that the organization create an incentive system that should appeal to the employee's better nature rather through compensation or punishment. Signs hanging in appropriate places, such as over a sink when handwashing, are important, and remarks by the convener of meetings can be helpful. For example, one of us is fond of saying at faculty hiring meetings that organizations that tend to hire the best candidates improve over time whereas those that do not tend to weaken. This encourages colleagues to put aside concerns about competition from new hires and focus on mentoring them.

The last feature, cultural norms, refers to the tone set by the leadership and by the "tone in the middle." If the both the top and the middle adhere to cultural norms, it encourages all employees to do the same. This requires senior leaders in an organization to lead by example, change rules for everyone if the system is not meeting the organization's needs, and create channels where employees can express concerns without fear of retribution.

These principles were on display in 2018 when 3,000 Google employees wrote to the CEO Sundar Pichai a letter condemning Google's work on a US Defense Department program called Project Maven. In the letter, employees contrasted Google's vision of "don't be evil" with helping design artificial intelligence (AI) to assist with pattern recognition in full motion video that could be used to target individuals through missile strikes (Shane & Wakabayashi, 2018). Pichai responded by ending Google's involvement in Project Maven and subsequently issued its own set of ethical principles that included it will not support the use of AI for weaponized systems (AI at Google, n.d.). These issues are discussed further in Chapter 9.

4.7 CONCLUSIONS: MANAGING CYBERSECURITY RISKS

Live-streaming events from around the world, tapping a screen to connect with friends, or gaining fuel efficiency through a software upgrade can give the impression that technology is both magical and independent of society. Robotics and artificial intelligence will further enhance this impression, but we must remember that humans are involved in all aspects of technology. Humans create the hardware and software to solve problems we face as a society or provide capabilities to translate imagination into reality. We design the systems, purchase and install the hardware and software, train employees to use them, and then manage them. Our most inspired thinking and fundamental flaws are reflected in the technology we use; technology does not exist independent of human beings.

With each new tool, cybersecurity challenges are created. These challenges require serious attention from humans, but as this chapter illustrates, human limitations are real. Once recognized, however, it is possible to deploy procedures to compensate for these limitations and help improve the security of these systems. The next chapters consider how governments exploit technological vulnerabilities inherent to cyberspace and the ways to improve cybersecurity through regulation, norms, and international law.

4.8 DISCUSSION TOPICS

1. Identify three new ways that cognitive biases undermine cybersecurity. Justify your decisions.
2. Provide examples in which the sunk cost fallacy limits the effectiveness of cybersecurity and explain your reasoning.
3. Cyber insurance is a nonregulatory method for improving cybersecurity. Give examples of other mechanisms that might achieve the same objective.
4. Give illustrations of ways that information-sharing can improve cybersecurity.
5. Is it fair to put the onus on users to ensure that computation is secure? If not, how should the responsibility be allocated?

5

Strategy and Cyberspace

Rarely has something been so important and so talked about with less clarity and less apparent understanding [than cyberspace capabilities] .... I have sat in very small group meetings in Washington ... unable (along with my colleagues) to decide on a course of action because we lacked a clear picture of the long-term legal and policy implications of any decision we might make.

General Michael Hayden (2011), USAF (retired), former head of the Central Intelligence Agency and the National Security Agency

GENERAL MICHAEL HAYDEN'S comments should be startling; he was a senior leader in the US intelligence community and a regular participant in White House national security discussions with his contemporaries at the forefront of cybersecurity decision-making. Over the last decade, government struggled as leaders often lacked the frame of reference to assess massive Chinese intellectual property theft and their censoring of US companies, Russian influence operations and the use of malware in its regional wars, North Korean malicious evasion of economic sanctions and coercion of Sony Pictures Entertainment through doxing and disrupting its business, and Iranian cyberspace operations against the commercial banking sector and US allies. Policymakers lacked the ability to know when a cybersecurity incident becomes a national security incident warranting White House involvement.

The confusion among US policymakers and national security professionals is illustrative of the challenges in cyber-related decision-making. In short, there is too little experience with cyber incidents to assess the likelihood that cyberattacks are impactful and would be escalatory nor to formulate a playbook to guide action when an adversary employs cyberspace operations. Also, there are no clear indicators to establish whether a cyber incident rises to the level of a use of armed force. The ambiguity inherent in cyberspace operations and challenges of military escalation in the physical world complicates policy formulation and challenges the ability to think strategically about cyberspace.[1]

Even something as seemingly simple as attributing an event in cyberspace can be fraught with uncertainty. For example, how does one tell whether an individual who gains access to a computer is doing so for criminal purposes or on behalf of a nation-state? If the individual acts on behalf of a nation-state, how can a government tell if the access is for espionage – which is unregulated under international law – or an influence operation – which could be a violation of sovereignty – or is designed to cause serious damage to a country's critical infrastructure – which might constitute a use of force? In all these cases, it matters if the individual is acting alone, for a criminal syndicate, or for a nation-state, which is difficult to assess.

These determinations are complicated by the views that governments hold about their own roles in cyberspace, relationships with information and communications technology (ICT) corporations, and views of civil liberties. To provide context for addressing these questions, which parallel traditional national security discussions, this chapter examines ways in which strategy guides governmental behavior, how cyber can be used as a tool of national power, and how cyber operations are deployed in conflict.

5.1 STRATEGY AND NATIONAL POWER

Derived from the Greek word *strategos*, meaning a general officer in the military, strategy is the art of planning. The term is widely used in government, business, and society to describe an organization's overall goals, the ways the goals could be achieved, and the resources necessary for success. A classic definition derives from the work of nineteenth-century thinker Carl von Clausewitz (1976), who saw strategy as a plan to meet objectives during war. He placed war on a continuum of politics, writing, "war is not merely a political act, but also a real political instrument, a continuation of political commerce, a carrying out of the same by other means." Wars are waged not solely to destroy but to advance national interests and pursue national objectives through coercion. Implicit in this definition of war is the use of violence by a government that, in the case of cyberspace operations, should be distinguished from intelligence operations designed to collect information without destruction. In other words, governments

---

[1] A consequence of this cyber-confusion as scholar Michael Poznansky (2021) has written, "is a high risk of tactics driving strategy."

use cyberspace operations for some larger purpose connected to that government's national objectives.

Modern interpretations of strategy tend to be broader in scope and view strategy as relevant not only in military campaigns but during peacetime as well (Freedman, 2013). From this perspective, strategy concerns the use by leaders of the power available to the state to exercise control over people, places, things, and events to achieve objectives that accord with national interests (Reveron & Cook, 2013). Today, governments write national security strategies and other strategies that outline major initiatives to guide governmental behavior and rationalize government spending. To be effective, strategy should be forward-looking – offering some vision of the future – and chart a course to reaching objectives.

There are important differences around the world regarding how policymakers view their roles in cyberspace. In market-oriented democracies such as the United States and Canada, governmental roles are largely limited, and corporations dominate cyberspace. Software is largely produced free of government regulation, telecommunication companies operate within a government's technical guidelines but are profit-driven, and the market for hardware and their ICT supply chains are largely open and global. Cyberspace is mainly a private space, which highlights the importance of public–private partnerships to improve cybersecurity.

There are calls to regulate the ICT industry from within democratic governments and from industry, but we must remember that these calls are tempered by democratic political culture in which users have the right to privacy and can remain anonymous, content is minimally regulated, and laissez-faire prevails. This can create the impression of a lawless "wild west" where government is largely absent, with no national organization providing cybersecurity and no national sheriff to police cyberspace; but this can also be characterized as a preserve where individuals are free to cooperate, innovate, and win or lose in a competitive marketplace benefitting consumers and investors. To be sure, there has always been internet governance, as we discuss in Chapter 7, but most governance issues have been technical in nature and mirror democratic practices. It is only since the early 2010s that governments became more directly involved in cyberspace.

Market-oriented democratic culture limits the degree to which the US government can use cyberspace to advance and defend its national interests. US Cyber Command and the National Security Agency (NSA), within the Department of Defense, the Federal Bureau of Investigation (FBI), within the Department of Justice, and the Cybersecurity and Infrastructure Security Agency (CISA), within the Department of Homeland Security (DHS), have very narrow roles and largely coordinate with the private sector or cyber-security companies hired to mitigate a significant cyberspace incident. Cybersecurity in the United States is largely the domain of hardware and software vendors, and corporations rather than the government. Reflecting a democratic commons or a free market, cyberspace is largely a self-help system for individuals, local governments, or corporations who must protect and defend their data and networks. The US government can provide guidance, but there is no national cybersecurity law imposing standards. For example, after much public discussion and input in the United States, the National Institute for Standards and Technology developed a *voluntary* Cybersecurity Framework (NIST, 2018) that consists of standards, guidelines, and practices to promote the protection of critical infrastructure. Clearly the standards are helpful for companies who willingly comply since their reputations and revenue are at stake, but regular data breach disclosures illustrate attackers can still be successful.

In authoritarian countries, such as the People's Republic of China, cyberspace is not free and is highly regulated for the benefit of the government rather than society or corporations. For example, the Chinese Communist Party regulates content and limits free speech, denies anonymity, does not protect freedom of association (virtual private networks [VPNs] are banned), and actively directs Chinese information technology companies to support the state and the Chinese Communist Party to further its political aims. China's citizens do not experience a global Internet as its Western designers envisioned. Official state media even says, "shutting down the internet in a state of emergency should be standard practice for sovereign countries" (Qiu, 2019), which is anathema in the United States. And China's president states that his government "will provide more and better online content and put in place a system for integrated internet *management* to ensure a clean cyberspace" (Xi, 2017; italics added).

The *People's Daily* newspaper, the online arm of China's Communist Party, offers services that screen for objectionable content and anticipates that content management will become a $70 billion industry within China, employing one million people (Li, 2020). As China's internet companies go global, they will offer these services to other authoritarian states – and in fact already are – effectively exporting tools to strengthen state control of societies. This reality enables China to promote its national agenda of development through economic espionage, to counter dissident movements through surveillance and arrest, and to promote its national image through influence operations and penalizing multinational corporations that violate the Chinese Communist Party's priorities. Since preserving the Chinese Communist Party rule of China is a desirable political end-state for the party, the government bans access to international media such as the *New York Times*, has developed tools to block its citizens' access to the global internet, and attacks websites it deems run counter to its political goals through distributed denial-of-service attacks.[2] When these tools are combined with a domestic social credit system that evaluates citizens' behavior as a form of control, the way a citizen of China experiences the Internet runs counter to what users in the United States experience.

Based on their political cultures and national laws, other countries tend to fall somewhere between these two poles as it relates to levels of regulation of actors and content. Regulation can be technical (e.g., mandating that a Wi-Fi router operate on 5 GHz), user-centric (e.g., verified identity required to connect to a network or banning VPN use to enable surveillance), and content-based (e.g., banning certain ideas or histories). When governments let laissez-faire prevail, users assume much risk in cyberspace and are largely responsible for securing their own devices and networks. Governments that are authoritarian and more activist in cyberspace use international institutions and pressure corporations to reflect their national priorities by attempting to manage cyberspace. This is mirrored in the current rivalry between China and the United States. China is often identified as a likely adversary and could exploit US vulnerabilities through cyberspace. This has as much to do with scholars' predictions about the inevitability of war among great powers as it does with Chinese government behavior in cyberspace (Inkster, 2018).

As the Chinese military *PLA Daily* stated, "Internet warfare is of equal significance to land, sea, and air power and requires its own military branch," and "it is essential to have an all-conquering offensive technology and to develop software and technology for net offensives ... able to launch attacks and countermeasures" (Alexander, 2007, p. 59). Ming Zhou, a China specialist, noted that "information warfare is not just a theology, they can integrate it into nation-state interests" (Nakashima & Pomfret, 2009). Around the world, other militaries are wrestling over the meaning of this as it relates to warfare and national interests.

---

[2] Euphemistically, the tools are known as the Great Firewall and the Great Cannon. The Great Firewall blocks Internet Protocol addresses that the government views as undesirable. Citizens can circumvent using it via a VPN to connect through a different country, but there are tools in place to identify these individuals if the government wants to arrest them since VPN use is banned. The Great Cannon is a tool to conduct distributed denial-of-service attacks against sites the government cannot block or wants to disrupt service for users outside of China. The Great Canon can also be used to monitor web traffic, divert traffic to other sites, and inject malware by hiding it in traffic. See Marczak et al. (2015).

5.2 ROLE OF NATIONAL INTERESTS IN FORMULATING CYBERSECURITY STRATEGY

National interests are often used to justify a government's role in national security and feature prominently in strategy formulation. National interests can be written down in strategic documents, such as a national security strategy, to serve as a form of communication for both the people they are intended to protect and potential adversaries. They communicate the values for which a country stands to prevent conflict by signaling to potential adversaries the triggers for conflict. By comparing a list of strategic documents issued by a variety of countries, we can easily grasp the centrality of national interests to strategy-making. All countries share fundamental national interests such as survival and economic prosperity and can use national interests to guide policies to avoid catastrophe in war or promote peace through diplomacy and economic integration through trade. The following excerpts from the five permanent members of the UN Security Council identify a common frame of reference to consider cybersecurity at the national level.

- United States: "[O]nly a foreign policy grounded in America's national interests can identify priorities for American engagement in the world. Only such a policy will allow America's leaders to explain persuasively how and why American citizens should support expenditures of American treasure or blood" (The Commission on America's National Interests, 2000).
- People's Republic of China: "China resolutely safeguards its national sovereignty and territorial integrity [and] safeguard[s] China's security interests in outer space, electromagnetic space, and cyberspace" (McClintock et al., 2021).
- Russia: [prioritizes] regime preservation and national defense from internal and external threats, influence in the "near abroad", an increase in "the competitiveness and international prestige of the Russian Federation," and increase in Russian economic output (McClintock et al., 2021).
- United Kingdom: "[T]he primary duty of the Government is to defend the country from attacks by other states, to protect citizens and the economy from harm, and to set the domestic and international framework to protect our interests, safeguard fundamental rights, and bring criminals to justice" (Hammond, 2017).
- France: "any cyberattack against French digital systems, or any effects produced on French territory by digital means … constitutes a breach of sovereignty. Interference by digital means in the internal or external affairs of France, i.e., interference which causes or may cause harm to France's political, economic, social, and cultural system, may constitute a violation of the principle of non-intervention" (France, 2019).

Essential Principle 5.1 Sovereignty

Established after the Treaty of Westphalia in 1648, sovereignty is a fundamental concept in international relations. Conceptualized in seventeenth-century Europe, its purpose is to protect governments from foreign interference; a country that is sovereign has recognized borders, a monopoly on organized violence and taxation, and recognition within international institutions.

National interests are the starting point for thinking through when cybersecurity becomes national security. How one frames a cyber incident can determine whether the issue is addressed as a criminal matter (e.g., hacking), an intelligence problem (e.g., stealing defense secrets), or a national security matter (e.g., shutting down a power plant).

There is some universality of defined and published national interests, many of which are on display in the selected statements given earlier. Of utmost importance are fundamental national interests, such as ensuring survival of the state, maintaining integrity of a country's borders, and preserving sovereignty. Threats against the government and its citizens or the integrity of the state can be viewed as threats to survival, sometimes triggering a military response (Reveron & Gvosdev, 2015).

A second type of national interest is economic. Prosperity is considered essential to the modern state, seeing as the economy produces both goods and services required for society and a tax base to generate revenue to fund other government services, including for defense. Thus, threats to prosperity – such as a maritime blockade – are considered by some to be an act of war (Russell, 2014). On the other hand, intellectual property infringement is more often considered to be a trade violation rather than an existential threat. However, it can have long-term effects on the health of an economy and society, in which case this too can be viewed as an existential problem.

A third type of national interest is encompassed in the term "values." Values can include civil liberties such as freedom of expression, the integrity of democratic processes, social and economic stability, preservation of a single-party monopoly of government, or open access to economic markets. Values are often an outgrowth of historical and cultural experiences of a particular society that can be captured in terms like "the international liberal order" (Mazarr et al., 2017). As it relates to cyberspace, there are important differences in how governments treat privacy online and whether it is viewed as a right – in the

> ### History Matters 5.1 The Thucydides Trap
>
> In his fifth-century BCE *History of the Peloponnesian War*, describing the war between Athens and Sparta, Thucydides, the Greek general, politician, and historian, sought to understand why the city-states went to war in the first place. His conclusion was that when a dominant state, such as Sparta, is challenged by a rising state, such as Athens, tensions are created, which can lead to military conflict that neither wants. Graham Allison, seizing on this observation, has argued that "China and the United States are heading toward war neither wants" (Allison and Simes, 2016). This instability has also been recognized by the Bulletin of Atomic Scientists who advanced their Doomsday Clock from 2 minutes to 100 seconds to midnight on January 20, 2020 (Mechlin, 2020).

case of the European Union – or as a threat to the government – as in the case of Russia, China, and some democracies like India that "turn off" the Internet during social protests.

Cybersecurity is relevant in all three dimensions of national interests: Government survival is dependent on command and control of the military and nuclear forces, economic prosperity is inextricably linked to the information economy and cybersecurity that protects intellectual property and commercial transactions, and society's values can be promoted online by governments – or undercut by adversaries.

Policymakers also use national interests to set priorities, anchor budgets, and explain actions. Finally, national interests can be used to explain why one thing is more important than another in setting a government's policies. The latter is extremely important when a cybersecurity incident reaches the highest levels of a government and there is pressure to respond to some actions by a foreign power. Taking a cue from Harvard political scientist Joseph Nye, Jr., national interests can guide governments' uses of cyber power, which is "the ability to obtain preferred outcomes through use of the electronically interconnected information resources of the cyber domain" (Mazarr et al., 2017).

External observers can use national interests as a lens through which to interpret and anticipate actions by a state within the international system – a system in which norms, laws, and international institutions are designed to mitigate interstate rivalry and create a forum to address transnational issues.

5.3 GRAND STRATEGY

Grand strategy is a term of art in academia that refers to the plans and policies that guide the full use of national power to secure a nation. There is a robust literature within political science and history that examines grand strategy and theories of statecraft. But implementing a grand strategy largely proves elusive since national security policymaking encompasses governmental, domestic, and international influences, many of which include competing interests or are otherwise difficult to achieve or secure (Gvosdev et al., 2019). Nonetheless, policymakers do find value in articulating a strategy to provide guidance to the government's bureaucracy and to signal to international friends and foes. Strategy need not be a strictly followed blueprint but can be a broader narrative that explains how a government attempts to advance its interests and when a government will defend itself.

Governments around the world routinely engage in strategy development processes that generate national strategies or white papers on how a government views the international system and how the government intends to approach its foreign policy. The process that produces a written strategy document is often as important as, if not more important than, the document itself since the process brings together stakeholders from around the government and the private sector to discuss challenges and identify roles and missions to meet them. In a novel crisis – when an unrehearsed scenario occurs and response playbooks are no longer valid – team members will know each other well and be better prepared to address the crisis.

The process of strategy development illustrates that modern government is large and is not immune from internal and external influences, making it difficult to develop a blueprint that will promote the general welfare and national security. Internally, bureaucratic preferences, media, partisan differences, and public opinion affect strategy development. Externally, allies' demands and adversaries' actions shape national objectives as well. When adding democratic politics into the mix, there can be substantial policy differences concerning strategy depending on the political party in power, the relationship between the executive and legislative branches, and the impact of organized interests on strategy development.[3] Political scientists Simon Reich and Peter Dombrowski

---

[3] As Reich and Dombrowski (2017, p. 5) note, "Bureaucratic and organizational impediments—and the occasionally tendentious relationship between civilian and military leaders—complicate the nation's ability to respond to the plethora of threats, differing actors, and various forms of conflict. The cumulative effect obstructs the nation's ability to implement any single grand strategy, no matter how sound its overarching principles or how carefully it prioritizes particular threats and allocates resources."

(2017, p. 9) summarize succinctly thinking about strategy implementation: "[M]ilitary personnel generally lack faith in the virtues of any grand strategy. They are pragmatic problem solvers, more comfortable with a response to specific problems than a recourse to abstract principles."

Despite what political commentary suggests, there tends to be long-term consistency concerning basic ideas on foreign policy. For example, the United States is largely committed to regulated capitalist principles, the movement of goods, people, and ideas across borders, and collective security organizations (Reveron et al., 2014). Compare this to Russia, where the government sees itself as a great country projecting influence globally and has long sought strategic autonomy from the West and ways to undermine the liberal international order.

When developing strategy, strategists must answer four fundamental questions:

(a) Where do we want to go or what are the desired ends?
(b) How do we achieve our ends or what are the ways?
(c) What resources are available or what are the means?
(d) What type of risk is the country willing to assume?

These questions illustrate that strategy is a choice often along a continuum of coercion; governments can threaten with force or induce change through incentives. In a competitive environment, any good strategy should endeavor to define national objectives that attempt to shape the international environment, ensure survival while promoting prosperity, and seek opportunities to promote national interests. The questions can also expose gaps between grandiose aims such as preserving a free and open cyberspace (ends) with limited legal authorities (means) and in the face of competing ideas in the international system.

A good strategy considers both short-term and long-term implications of action (or inaction). Further, it should use more than one tool of power. Governments do have choices on how to intervene or act by using diplomacy or political inducements, information or cyber means, economic and financial leverage, and military force or law enforcement actions.

Finally, a good strategy should heed the words of former US secretary of state George C. Marshall, who said in a 1947 radio address, "Problems which bear directly on the future of our civilization cannot be disposed of by general talk or vague formulae – by what Lincoln called 'pernicious abstractions.' They require concrete solutions for definite and extremely complicated questions" (Zelikow, 1997). Consequently, strategy also predisposes a government to identify challenges and to seek to advance and defend national interests. The Trump-era 2017 US National Security Strategy encapsulates the proactive nature of strategy, noting, "there is no arc of history that ensures that America's free political and economic system will automatically prevail. Success or failure depends upon our actions" (White House, 2017). The Biden administration's 2021 interim national strategic guidance carries the idea forward: "This moment calls upon us to lean forward, not shrink back – to boldly engage the world to keep Americans safe, prosperous, and free" (White House, 2021a). As both statements – one from a Republican president and one from a Democratic president – illustrate, strategy must be forward-looking and proactive and should improve the situation for the country.

As General Hayden noted in the epigraph at the start of this chapter, the United States (and many governments) have not been able to address cyber insecurity in any meaningful way in part due to the nature of the medium – cyber does not have a border to protect, territorial waters to monitor, or an airspace to patrol. Many governments feel not only some level of threat in cyberspace from their external rivals (e.g., India and China or Israel and Iran) but also from the domestic deployment of the technology itself – encryption can deny government access to its own citizens' communication by keeping them private, while cryptocurrencies can undermine a government's monopoly of currency and enable illegal financial transactions.

Chapters 6–8 explore governments' efforts to regulate cyberspace through domestic means, international means, and norms. The remainder of this chapter addresses cyberspace operations as a tool of national power.

5.4 DETERRENCE IN THE CYBER AGE

Deterrence is an effort to dissuade an adversary from taking an action – either by bolstering its own defenses to such a level that the adversary's efforts are rendered moot or by retaining the ability to retaliate so profoundly that it outweighs the benefit to the adversary of the initial attack. Within modern defense strategy, deterrence draws from thinking by Nobel Prize laureate Thomas Schelling, who captured the essence of the psychological nature of deterrence as addressing intentions. Political scientist Patrick Morgan (2003) formulated deterrence as simply "the use of threats of harm to prevent someone from doing something you do not want him to do." The Defense Department expands this definition of deterrence to include "the prevention of action by the existence of a credible threat of unacceptable counteraction and/or belief that the cost of action outweighs the perceived benefits" (Scott, 2018).

Deterrence does not work if the adversary is able to identify a bluff and call it. Former secretary of state Henry Kissinger (1957) notes that to be effective, "deterrence requires a combination of power, the will to use it, and the assessment of these by the potential aggressor. Moreover, deterrence is the product of those factors and not the sum. If any part is zero, deterrence fails." In other words, governments must have both the capability to threaten an adversary *and* the political will to use that capability to prevent an adversary from acting, as indicated earlier.

Deterrence is successful when rational opponents identify what each other values and then holds that at risk. In other words, if both parties can simultaneously and credibly threaten each other, no action is taken. For this to work, each side must preemptively signal or indicate what it values, thereby establishing redlines that cannot be crossed without producing retribution.

Deterrence worked well in the age of empire when impregnable castles were built to deny an adversary's advances – dissuading would-be attackers by raising the difficulty of pillaging – at least until innovation produced new weapons such as the trebuchet and cannons to launch projectiles at castle walls. Even then, defenders could launch their own attacks against invaders, decimating the oncoming forces and increasing the costs of an attack. The approach was deepened by developing capacity through large armies that could be raised or, most famously, in the nuclear age, when the Soviet Union and United States had sufficient second-strike nuclear capabilities to prevent a first strike by either side by threatening annihilation of the other side if a nuclear attack were launched in so-called mutually assured destruction.

As explained, deterrence is operationalized in two ways: by denial and by punishment. In a cyber context, denial can be achieved through good network security and good user practices (e.g., two-factor authentication and secure operational procedures, as discussed in Chapter 4). In addition to reducing vulnerabilities, promoting resilience to attack is another way to deny an adversary the benefits of a cyberattack. Through backups and network redundancy, an attack can be muted through resilience, minimizing the benefit to the attacker. Punishment can occur either through cyberspace (e.g., hacking back) or outside of cyberspace (e.g., criminal indictment, sanctions, or physical attack). Through both denial and punishment, deterrence is designed to change an adversary's calculus and to prevent an attack by persuading the adversary that an attack would likely result in greater harm to it than the target, creating an incentive for restraint.[4]

---

[4] The congressionally chartered Cyberspace Solarium Commission advocates that "the United States must pro-actively observe, pursue, and counter adversaries' operations and impose costs short of armed conflict" (King & Gallagher, 2020).

Of course, all of that is theoretical. In fact, the applicability and effectiveness of deterrence for cyberspace remain hotly contested.[5] There are several reasons why. The first is that cyber activity frequently takes place in a secret or even covert environment, making it difficult to accurately identify an adversary's abilities. Professor Jon Lindsay (2020) has written that "actors deliberately conceal or obfuscate their cyber capabilities and operations because compromise would enable the target to patch or take countermeasures that mitigates the capability. This cyber commitment problem is one reason why cyber is ill suited for coercive bargaining."

Similarly, it can be difficult to determine cause and effect in cyberspace. When a government conducts offensive operations in cyberspace, it seeks to change a rival's behavior or achieve some national interest.[6] Unlike hackers who conduct activities for the thrill of the challenge or criminals that seek profit, governments generally conduct cyber activities for some larger purpose.[7] If one can identify why an adversary pursues action in cyberspace, one can develop a counterstrategy. But since cyberspace operations are often kept hidden, those that do get discussed publicly making it difficult to discern if a cyberspace operation was in response to another action in cyberspace or another domain. For example, did Iran conduct distributed denial-of-service attacks against US banks as a provocation or a response to US sanctions or a military build-up in the Middle East?

Another reason for concern over the effectiveness of deterrence in cyberspace is that cyber activities often fall short of a crisis threshold and are "short-of-war." As senior vice president at the think tank Center for Strategic and International Studies James Lewis (2021) says, "In the absence of an existential threat or even the risk of the significant damage that armed conflict brings, there is little incentive for opponents to make concessions on the use of coercive cyber actions or to stop using them." However, as countries mature their cyberspace capabilities and test their weaponized code, they

---

[5] While not adopted, the Cyberspace Solarium Commission promotes a layered cyber deterrence strategy: shaping behavior through norms and nonmilitary instruments of power, denying benefits to adversaries by promoting national resilience and promoting public–private collaboration, and raising security standards across the cyber ecosystem.

[6] As cyberspace operations relate to power balances in the international system, retired Harvard political scientist Joseph Nye, Jr. (2010) finds, "The characteristics of cyberspace reduce some of the power differentials among actors, and thus provide a good example of the diffusion of power that typifies global politics in this century. The largest powers are unlikely to be able to dominate this domain as much as they have other domains like sea or air."

[7] Political scientists Richard Harknett and Max Smeets (2020, pp. 1–34) argue that "cyberspace has opened a new dimension of power politics in which cyber campaigns could potentially become a salient means, alternative to war, for achieving strategic advantage."

may engage in active conflict with each other and, consequently, this calculus may change.

The perpetual dilemma of deterrence is that there is no way to prove that it works. Herb Lin, an expert on cyber policy and strategy at the Center for International Security and Cooperation and Stanford University's Hoover Institution, as quoted by Williams (2021), said, "The problem with deterrence is that you can never tell when you've been successful because what you're measuring is non-events. You don't know why something doesn't happen" To be sure, deterrence has not prevented large-scale intellectual property theft, massive losses of national security data, and outright foreign intelligence activity on social media. These limitations again challenge the relevancy of deterrence to cyberspace or at least create an unfair expectation that deterrence can prevent data theft and other events popularly called cyberattacks.

Nonetheless, while cyber capabilities cannot be easily demonstrated like nuclear or conventional capabilities, governments have still endeavored to signal to other governments what are clearly unacceptable targets that, if incapacitated by a cyberattack, could trigger a shooting war (Gartzke & Lindsay, 2017). These include attacks against nuclear command and control and critical infrastructure, such as energy production, telecommunications, and the financial sector.[8] If countries engage in war, then their most dangerous cyber capabilities could be used.[9]

It is important to ensure cyberattacks are always viewed in a larger strategic context and within an assessment of political will to respond. Just because

---

Policy Matters 5.1 Bombing hackers

In June 2019, Israel used military force to destroy a building in Gaza, Palestine, where Hamas cyber operatives worked. Although the attack was part of a larger conflict between Israel and Hamas, the fact that Israel claimed credit for the bombing marked the first known attack of this kind.

Source: Newman (2018)

---

[8] In fact, James Lewis (2021) notes this when diagnosing why escalation due to cyberspace operations has not occurred; he says governments "maintain careful control of their most dangerous cyber capabilities and have devoted their own strategies to reduce risk."

[9] Valeriano and Maness (2015, p. 210) reinforce the point in that governments have strong incentives to avoid triggering war and "cyber conflicts are not disconnected from the normal international relations policy sphere…and are directly connected to the long history of interactions between states."

something starts in cyberspace does not mean conflict will be confined only to cyberspace. Cyber power alone may have limited effectiveness – although it has significant utility when coupled with other elements of national power (Borghard & Lonergan, 2017). Thus, retaliation for an attack in cyberspace is not necessarily limited to cyberspace but can produce criminal indictments and arrests, financial sanctions, and diplomatic expulsions.[10] This is important also because a counterattack via cyber means could have the effect of infecting friendly systems or generating blowback when these systems are on the open Internet.

5.5 CYBER AND WAR

As noted at the start of the chapter, war has specific meaning in international law as an armed attack and strategy as a use of violence for a political purpose to advance national interests. As US Cyber Command strategist Emily Goldman (2021) has written, "Cyberspace has emerged as a major arena of conflict between liberal and illiberal forces across the globe." Since great powers are in relative peace and limiting actions through a competitive framework, Goldman uses the word "conflict" rather than "war" to illustrate that governments are using cyberspace operations to destroy, degrade, or seriously disrupt the information technology infrastructure or data therein. All this aggression is taking place outside of any named zone of conflict, yet the pace of this conflict is rapid and, in the future, could create severe and lasting damage.

A very serious cyberattack is one that rises to the threshold of "use of force," a term that is recognized in the UN Charter and customary international law. Any kinetic or physical attack that does very significant damage to a nation's military or critical infrastructure would rise to the level of a use of force regardless of whether it was caused by a missile or malware.

There have been just a few instances of cyberspace operations that rise to the definition of a use of force where a cyber-penetration caused physical damage to attached critical infrastructure. Examples of this are cyber-physical attacks – so called because a cyberattack generates a real-world consequence. These include the 2010 Stuxnet attack on Iran's nuclear program that resulted

---

[10] Former director of National Intelligence James Clapper testified,

> we should use all the tools potentially available to us, diplomacy, economic sanctions, and other forms of military power, when we consider responses to cyber threats. Just because someone attacks us using cyber should not automatically mean that we should respond the same way. In fact, if the adversary chose cyber because it asymmetrically favored them, responding in kind means we are sort of letting them define the terms of the engagement and fighting on their terms (U.S. Senate Armed Services Committee, 2017).

Exploit 5.1 BlackEnergy compromise of a Ukrainian power station

In December 2015 attackers used the BlackEnergy malware to compromise a Ukrainian power station, which left about 230,000 people without electricity for up to six hours. Introduced through phishing, the malware was launched when compromised Microsoft Office documents were opened about six months before the power outage. The attackers gained control of industrial control systems and remotely switched off electricity substations, conducted a denial-of-service attack on a call center, and destroyed files. The power station was able to revert to manual operation to restore power. This is the first publicly recognized attack that resulted in a power outage.

Source: Zetter (2016)

---

in the physical destruction of centrifuges used to enrich uranium and the 2015 BlackEnergy attack that shut down electricity in a part of Ukraine. Additionally, there have been instances of cyber "blockades" – such as Estonia in 2007 or Georgia in 2008 – during which the free flow of data was interrupted by a third party (Russell, 2014). During Russia's 2022 invasion of Ukraine, there were attempts to disrupt critical infrastructure, but the defenders largely prevailed.

Identifying a cyberattack is still subject to legal interpretation and the vicissitudes of the policymaking process, which helps explain why such attacks are rarely classified as armed attacks under the Geneva Convention as "acts of violence against the adversary, whether in offence or in defence" (Protocol Additional to the Geneva Conventions of 12 August 1949, and Relating to the Protection of Victims of International Armed Conflicts, Art. 49, 1, 1977). This threshold for interpretation often results in referring to cyberattacks as subversion, espionage, or sabotage (Rid, 2013).

Stuxnet could be defined as a *use of force* since there was physical damage to Iranian centrifuges, but it did not rise to the level of an *armed attack* since it was not severe and Iran never claimed it was the subject of an armed attack (Foltz, 2012; Lindsay, 2013). Likewise as political scientist Alison Lawlor Russell (2014) concluded, the cyber blockades in Estonia in 2007 and Georgia in 2008 "can be considered an act of war (although it is ultimately up to the targeted state whether or not it *wants* to consider it an act of war and potentially escalate the situation)." International legal scholar Michael

---

Exploit 5.2 Stuxnet and zero-day vulnerabilities

Stuxnet, the first serious cyber weapon, is a worm, discovered in 2010, designed to degrade and destroy about 1,000 centrifuges separating U235 from U238 in the Iran nuclear refinement facility at Natanz. U235 is a fissionable material that is used to manufacture nuclear weapons. Stuxnet was designed to give the impression that the centrifuges were self-destructing due to faulty manufacture. Interestingly, the computer system driving the centrifuges was not connected to the Internet but was hacked, nonetheless. Using four zero-day vulnerabilities, Stuxnet was designed to launch only on the computers known to be in use at Natanz, which clearly required thorough reconnaissance. Stuxnet is thought to have been developed jointly by the United States and Israel.

A team of legal experts assessed that Stuxnet was a use of force as defined by the UN Charter and a likely violation of international law but was not clear if it constituted an "armed attack," which would have justified use of counterforce by Iran.

Source: Zetter (2013)

Schmitt (2012) underscores, "an 'armed attack' is an action that gives States the right to a response rising to the level of a 'use of force.'" Thus, sabotage may be a better term to describe what happened in Iran after Stuxnet rather than an armed attack, but this is subject to legal debate within a country's domestic political context and how the country chooses to engage internationally through institutions such as the United Nations. We will elaborate on this in Chapter 8 but note here that there are competing definitions of the use of force in cyberspace and what constitutes a cyber-penetration of national security consequence.

Predictions of escalating cyber violence and even cyber war have fascinated policymakers and the public. As early as 1993 political scientists John Arquilla and David Ronfeldt (1993) forecast that cyber war in the twenty-first century would be the equivalent of Nazi Germany's blitzkrieg operations in the twentieth century, which were characterized by speed, surprise, and overwhelming force. Later, General Keith Alexander (2007, p. 60), former NSA director and Cyber Command commander, predicted that militaries would use "cyberspace (by operating within or through it) to attack personnel, facilities, or equipment with the intent of degrading, neutralizing, or destroying enemy combat capability, while protecting our own." Many analysts, like General Alexander, have framed these violations as representing an era of ever more sophisticated and dangerous cyber conflict.

Yet as of 2023, the most dangerous cyberattacks – rising to the level of a cyber 9/11 – have not occurred. However, we know many militaries continue to experiment with integrating cyberattacks into traditional war plans and we can observe governments' uses of cyberspace operations in other ways. These include Russian influence operations in US elections, Iranian wiper attacks that deleted data from US and Saudi businesses, and China's targeting of dissidents and decades-long espionage campaign against the United States (Sanger, 2018). Current analysis suggests the use of cyberspace operations hews more toward traditional state behavior consistent with intelligence operations than to combat operations. Generally, what we call cyberattacks have produced limited damage and little political coercion. Aside from Stuxnet or BlackEnergy, more common uses of malicious cyber activities are defacements of government websites, denial-of-service attacks, influence operations, and data theft.

Nevertheless, even minor cyber incidents can be escalated, rapidly. Once a system is penetrated, it is relatively easy to pivot from stealing data to altering data or causing effects that are either physically or functionally destructive. For example, in 2021, a Russia-based criminal organization successfully conducted a ransomware attack against a US-based energy company, Colonial Pipeline. While only the information technology networks were "held hostage," and the operational side of the business was not attacked (operations technology was safe), out of prudence it was decided to stop delivery of fuels. The effect was the shutdown of a major pipeline in the southeastern United States for about five days, which resulted in economic disruptions and civil disturbances caused by fuel shortages (Chesney & Smeets, 2020; Sanger & Perlroth, 2021). The attack illustrated the importance of maintaining a high level of security between information technology and operations technology networks.

There is an open debate on whether "cyberwar" is even a feasible scenario. Other known state-sanctioned cyberspace operations have generated a robust scholarly debate on the value of fighting in the information environment and even whether cyberspace operations can rise to the level of armed attack. Scholars generally discount what the media often portray as cyberattacks – even if they generate a feeling of insecurity – unless the effects meet traditional definitions of use of force that are violent, destructive, and attributable to a nation-state.[11] For example, Thomas Rid (2013) has declared "cyber war will

[11] Herb Lin (2010) makes an important distinction between attack and exploitation; for it to be an attack, the payload must be destructive, while an exploitation acquires information nondestructively.

not take place." Data collected by Ryan Maness, Brandon Valeriano, and Ben Jensen found that most successful cyber incidents could be classified as cyber espionage (but not war) (Dyadic Cyber Incident and Campaign Dataset [DCD] Version 1.5 in Valeriano et al., 2018). These exploits sought information or served to spread disinformation; on the other hand, coercive actions that lead to physical destruction are much rarer (Maness & Valeriano, 2016).

Further, cyber effects are often temporary given the ability to back up data and restore systems, the ability to create security patches to close attack vectors, and the existence of redundant networks to restore services. The limited effects may also reflect how adversaries can limit the damage through code. Zeros and ones are not as sensational as, for example, a missile attack that would rouse nationalist feelings and compel policymakers to take decisive actions. Finally, countries with significant cyber commands certainly face normal friction with each other but are not in a state of war where destructive physical attacks would occur.

Despite the limits of cyber power, senior military leaders worry about vulnerabilities and the potential for a cyberattack that rises to the level of war with the use of force. "Like strategic airpower before it, state-based cyber advocates will develop strategies that attempt to 'leap over' traditional military forces and directly influence the decision calculations of political and military leadership" (Joint Chiefs of Staff, 2016). In fact, the air power analogy is instructive. The first flight by the Wright Brothers occurred in 1903, but aircraft played only a minimal role in World War I (1914–18) and was used mostly for surveillance, with some air-to-air combat. During the succeeding decades, countries experimented and refined aircraft to play significant attack roles, which saw the rise of aerial bombardment in World War II (1939–45). Today, bombers and aircraft carriers are strategic weapons and a hallmark of military powers such as the United States, Russia, and China.

The use of cyberspace operations need not parallel the development of aircraft and war, but the analogy reminds us that it is simply too early to tell how countries will use cyberspace operations. Empirical studies of cyberspace operations in peacetime paint a picture of largely restrained actions among major cyber actors and we should not easily fall victim to the cyber-hype created by speculation. There are many incentives for the United States, Russia, China, India, Pakistan, Israel, Iran, and North Korea to avoid escalation that leads to war.

At the same time, we cannot readily dismiss thinkers like Herb Lin (2019), who writes, "Cyber-enabled information warfare provides the tactics, tools, and procedures – in short, the means – to replace the pillars of logic, truth, and reality with fantasy, rage, and fear... [leading] to the end of civilization as we know it." Or, Glenn Gerstell, then general counsel for NSA, who wrote in 2019 that soon "we will be in a world of ceaseless and pervasive cyber-insecurity and cyberconflict against nation-states, businesses and individuals." This view is shared across the Atlantic, as noted in the British Cybersecurity Strategy: "We regularly see attempts by states and state-sponsored groups to penetrate UK networks for political, diplomatic, technological, commercial and strategic advantage, with a principal focus on the government, defence, finance, energy and telecommunications sectors" (Hammond, 2017). Indeed, past and present cyberspace operations largely fall short of war, but governments around the world have been developing cyber commands in case interstate rivalry and strategic competition does escalate to war.

5.5.1 Organizing the Military for Cyberspace

With long-recognized vulnerabilities and threats to cyberspace, there are clear gaps in the way that policy and law address these concerns. International law and national security policy offer no clear answers on important issues such as how to respond to cyber intrusions, whether offensive cyberspace operations constitute a form of warfare, and whether the UN conception of self-defense applies in cyberspace. The North Atlantic Treaty Organization (NATO) has identified cyberspace as a domain of operations and has stated that offensive cyberspace operations could be interpreted in the context of collective self-defense through Article 5. Dozens of countries have created cyber commands to integrate cyberspace operations in support of tactical, operational, and strategic objectives.

In the United States, the military services have recognized the importance of cyberspace both in peace and in war (Slayton, 2021; White, 2019). Each of the services now have a cyber capability, having converted tens of thousands of service positions to cyberspace support positions – the US Air Force claimed cyberspace as one of its operating domains (Reveron & Mahoney-Norris, 2019); the Navy created the Fleet Cyber Command (Tenth Fleet), while the director of National Intelligence created the Joint Interagency Cyber Task Force; and US Army Cyber Command "integrates and conducts cyberspace, electronic warfare, and information operations" (Army Cyber Fact Sheet, 2019). At the same time, service capabilities are aggregated under a joint US Cyber Command, which is responsible for developing and implementing integrated operations for defense and attack in the cyber domain through the National Cyber Mission Force. In 2022, this force was composed of 133 teams of about 6,000 individuals with responsibilities for defending defense networks, preparing for offensive operations, and sharing threat data (see Figure 5.1).

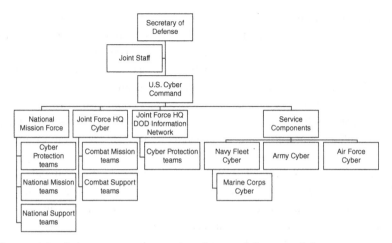

Figure 5.1 Cyberspace command and control Source: Cyberspace operations (2018)

The Cyber Mission Force organizes and resources organizations to conduct cyberspace operations of offense, defense, and assurance. The National Mission Force counters significant threats to the Department of Defense Information Network (DODIN) and, when ordered, protects the nation. The Joint Force Headquarters provides cyber combat mission teams and support teams to combatant commands. The Joint Force Headquarters-Cyber protects DODIN and local Department of Defense networks. The military services (Army, Air Force, Navy, and Space Force) organize, train, and equip teams to enable these missions that are focused at the national, combatant command, or military service levels (Cyberspace operations, 2018).

Despite this force structure, the US military sees itself as uncomfortably vulnerable in the cyber domain. The often-heard phrase is, while the United States has big cyber rocks, it also has the "glassiest house," meaning its national capabilities are significant, but society is highly vulnerable to cyber disruptions.[12] The attack surface is simply too large for the federal government to monitor cyberspace like it would airspace. This upends the traditional US strategy of deploying military forces abroad to conduct combat operations or presence missions to deter conflict, seeing that adversaries thousands of miles away can attack the United States on its own soil via a cyberspace operation.

---

[12] Former NATO supreme allied commander of Europe General (retired) Wesley Clark and Peter Levin (2009) argue: "Everything about the subtlety, complexity, and effectiveness of the assaults already inflicted on the United States' electronic defense indicates that other nations have thought carefully about this form of combat."

Cyberspace military operations are more likely to be used at the start of a conventional conflict involving bombs and missiles rather than be used primarily for stand-alone cyber conflict. Russia operated this way in Georgia in 2008 and Ukraine in 2022. Such cyberspace operations could suppress an enemy's air defense network or cause aircraft to drop their weapons on their territory rather than that of their adversary. They could also disrupt military communications between civilian leaders and deployed forces or undermine public confidence in a government, undercutting its resolve for war. Countries can hold another country's power grid hostage to de-escalate a military confrontation. As Vice Admiral T. J. White, who commanded the National Cyber Mission Force, has written, "I am certain the opening rounds of a 21st century great power conflict, particularly one impacting the maritime domain, will be launched in the electromagnetic, space, or cyber domains" (US Fleet Cyber Command/US Tenth Fleet, 2020). There are already examples of governments spoofing Global Positioning System signals that interfere with maritime navigation, and electronic warfare has denied communications in many military campaigns. Cyberspace operations offer another tool where malware can be used to disrupt satellite operations or cause widespread communication outages that enable an adversary to conduct surprise physical attacks.

At this stage the global security implications of developing cyber capabilities for militaries are profound. In recognition of this, as noted earlier, Hamadoun Touré, former secretary general of the United Nations International Telecommunications Union, pessimistically warned more than a decade ago: "The next world war could happen in cyberspace and that would be a catastrophe. We have to make sure that all countries understand that in that war, there is no such thing as a superpower. ... The best way to win a war is to avoid it in the first place." (Hui, 2009)

With these concerns in mind, Stanford researcher Jacquelyn Schneider (2020) argues the United States should declare a no-first-use policy in cyberspace. The United Nations may be one such venue to pursue international agreements since it is organized around the nation-state concept and has a track record of supporting arms control (UN Press Bureau, 2014, 2018).

5.6 US APPROACH TO CYBERSECURITY

There has been a steady evolution of US strategic thinking on cyberspace over the past quarter century. The US government's main early priorities centered on the defense of key infrastructure. Cybersecurity first emerged as a distinct national security policy area in 1998 when President Clinton signed

Presidential Decision Directive 63, which established a White House structure to coordinate government and private action to "eliminate any significant vulnerability to both physical and cyberattacks on our critical infrastructures, including especially our cyber systems" (White House, 1998). In an effort to deter such attacks by establishing red lines, President George W. Bush declared in 2003 that it would be "the policy of the United States to protect against the debilitating disruption of the operation of information systems for critical infrastructures and, thereby, help to protect the people, economy, and national security of the United States" (White House, 2003).

The March 2005 National Defense Strategy identified cyberspace as a new theater of operations for the first time and assessed that cyberspace operations could be a potentially disruptive challenge. It concluded that in "rare instances, revolutionary technology and associated military innovation can fundamentally alter long-established concepts of warfare" (Rumsfeld, 2005). The 2008 National Defense Strategy explored these implications further, assessing small groups or individuals "can attack vulnerable points in cyberspace and disrupt commerce and daily life in the United States, causing economic damage,

---

Exploit 5.3 Denial-of-service attacks against the US financial sector

Cyberspace operations provide governments opportunities to retaliate against the United States when they would otherwise not have the opportunity. In the case of the United States and Iran, the two countries have been rivals since 1979. A key rationale for US military presence in the Middle East is to contain and counter Iranian influence. Additionally, the United States has imposed economic sanctions on Iran in an attempt to isolate the country from the international economic system.

For its part, Iran has supported proxy forces against US forces in the Middle East and even conducted a missile strike against Iraq-based US forces in 2020. Given its distance from the United States, cyber provides Iran a way to "attack" the US. Over a two-year period, Iranian nationals conducted a coordinated campaign of distributed denial-of-service attacks against the US financial sector and other US companies. A grand jury indicted seven of these nationals. While they are unlikely to see a US courtroom, the exploit illustrates how a country can use cyberspace operations as a tool of power.

Source: FBI (2016)

compromising sensitive information and materials, and interrupting critical services such as power and information networks" (Gates, 2008).

Many of the US government's early efforts in cyberspace focused on criminal elements. In 2008, the National Cyber Investigative Joint Task Force was formed as a multiagency center with a mandate to pursue those who violate US cybersecurity laws. Their work enables the Department of Justice to indict individuals accused of violating US hacking or espionage laws.

The pace and evolution of US cybersecurity policy has been driven by necessity. Deputy Defense Secretary William Lynn warned back in 2009 that the Defense Department's culture regarding cybersecurity issues had to change because "we're seeing assaults come at an astonishing speed—not hours, minutes or even seconds—but in milliseconds at network speed" (Garamone, 2009). As early as 2010, Defense Department officials admitted that their systems were being probed by unknown users some 250,000 times an hour, a staggering 6 million times a day (Bain, 2010). (This was the same year US Cyber Command was created.) In some respects, this was familiar in form to the military and government because it resembled more traditional intelligence collection. But it differed significantly in scale. Furthermore, while the probes themselves appeared nonthreatening, there is always the potential to convert an intelligence-collection operation into a destructive attack. These attributes have meant that the rising rate of cyber penetrations is not so easily dismissed in national security circles.

Yet here we return to the ambiguity and unique challenges posed by cyberspace upon which Hayden opined in our opening epigraph. Whereas the Pentagon has long had a plan to stop an air attack against the United States or to shoot down enemy satellites, reducing malicious activity in cyberspace has been elusive. After wading through the meaning of Iran's distributed denial-of-service attacks on the US financial sector beginning in 2011 (FBI, 2016), North Korea's attack on Sony Entertainment in 2014, China's decades-long economic espionage against US corporations and the US government, including stealing millions of security clearance files, and Russia's influence operations beginning in 2014, strategic thinking looked beyond deterrence. *New York Times* national security correspondent David Sanger (2018) captured the feeling of the Obama administration in 2016: "[I]n the cyber age, we have not found that balance [of power] and probably never will…it amounts to an admission that our defenses at home are wildly insufficient and that the only way to win is to respond to every perceived threat."

Part of this challenge is a technical one: Even after an adversary is detected on a network, it is difficult to discern its intent, even as defenders try to remove it from the targeted systems. Hayden, as a former director of

NSA, agreed: "[I]n the cyber domain the technical and operational aspects of defense, espionage, and cyberattack are frankly indistinguishable — they are all the same things" (Hayden, 2017) Analyzing tactical uses of cyber operations complicates how governments attempt to protect citizens in the information environment.

The 2018 National Cyber Strategy emphasized that "[e]conomic security is inherently tied to our national security," so close public–private collaboration is a cornerstone of US cyber strategy (White House, 2018). Also in 2018, Congress created CISA overseen by DHS. CISA grew out of the National Protection and Programs Directorate at DHS and today serves as an important coordinating function within the national government and between the government and private sector. DHS's distance from NSA helps promote space between applications of cyberspace at the military and the civilian level to promote public–private cooperation. As Figure 5.2 illustrates, the US government gradually created new cyber organizations shown on the left often influenced by significant cyber incidents shown on the right.

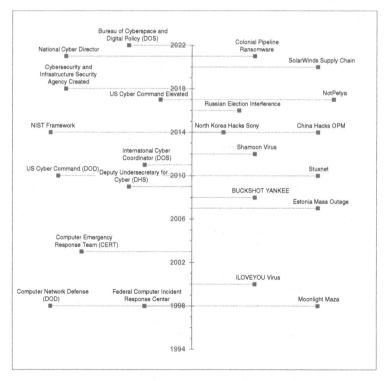

Figure 5.2   Select US cyber organizations and significant cyber incidents

5.6.1 Persistent Engagement and Defend Forward

Beginning in 2019, US Cyber Command announced that it would pursue a strategy of persistent engagement. This should be understood as a substantial shift in thinking and in legal authorities, because "persistent engagement" and its sister concept "defending forward" mean that Cyber Command will try to establish a presence overseas, at the invitation of friendly governments, to help fend off attacks before they ever reach US shores. According to the head of US Cyber Command, General Paul Nakasone (2019), "this persistence force will contest our adversaries' efforts in cyberspace to harm Americans and American interests. It will degrade the infrastructure and other resources that enable our adversaries to fight in cyberspace." Nakasone later wrote in *Foreign Affairs*, "We learned that we cannot afford to wait for cyberattacks to affect our military networks. We learned that defending our military networks requires executing operations outside our military networks" (Nakasone & Sulmeyer, 2021). Scholar Erica Lonergan (2020) explains defend forward as "the proactive observing, pursuing, and countering of adversary operations and imposing costs in day-to-day competition to disrupt and defeat ongoing malicious adversary cyber campaigns, deter future campaigns, and reinforce favorable international norms of behavior, using all instruments of national power."

A concept like "defend forward" means working with other countries to hunt for malware on their own networks and increase information-sharing to improve defense. This was evident in 2022 after Russia invaded Ukraine. General Nakasone explained to Congress how the US helped Ukraine.

U.S. Cyber Command (with NSA) has been integral to the nation's response to this crisis since Russian forces began deploying on Ukraine's borders last fall. We have provided intelligence on the building threat, helped to warn U.S. government and industry to tighten security within critical infrastructure sectors, enhanced resilience on the DODIN [Department of Defense Information Network] (especially in Europe), accelerated efforts against criminal cyber enterprises and, together with interagency members [e.g., CISA], Allies, and partners, planned for a range of contingencies. Coordinating with the Ukrainians in an effort to help them harden their networks, we deployed a hunt team who sat side-by-side with our partners to gain critical insights that have increased homeland defense for both the United State and Ukraine. In addition, USCYBERCOM is proactively ensuring the security and availability of strategic command and control and other systems across the Department [of Defense]. We have also crafted options for national decision makers and are conducting operations as directed. (Posture Statement of General Paul M. Nakasone, Commander, United States Cyber Command before the 117th Congress, 2022)

This was made possible by a change to law where Congress granted the secretary of defense the authority "to conduct, military cyber activities or operations in cyberspace, including clandestine military activities or operations in cyberspace, to defend the United States and its allies, including in response to malicious cyber activity carried out against the United States or a United States person by a foreign power" (Title 10 USC 394: Authorities Concerning Military Cyber Operations, n.d., p. 10). This legal authority provides the functional equivalent of an authorization of use of military force. Whereas previously the president had to approve a cyber strike, now the secretary of defense can do it on his/her/their own authority without congressional notifications under the War Powers Resolution Act.

While persistent engagement and defend forward were hailed in some quarters as freeing up the military and enabling the executive branch to be more proactive in defending the United States, they also coincided with a period of increased scrutiny by Congress. Congress had long deferred to the executive branch on cyberspace but in recent years has expressed an increasing desire to exercise its oversight function more acutely. Partly because of this, a new authority was created in the 2021 National Defense Authorization Act, establishing an "Office of the National Cyber Director" to coordinate across the government on cyber issues.

In his 2021 confirmation hearing, the first national cyber director, Chris Inglis, summarized the enormity of the role Congress created for him: "forging a coherent and unified federal effort; developing and overseeing the implementation of the National Cyber Strategy, ensuring the coordination of appropriate federal budgets, policy, plans, and procedures; fostering mutually beneficial public-private collaboration; and demonstrable improvements in the resilience, robustness and defense of the cyber ecosystem" (Statement for the Record, Nominee for the National Cyber Director, 2021). For the Office of the National Cyber Director to be successful, its leaders will have to successfully navigate the policy process.

5.7 CYBERSPACE OPERATIONS AND THE POLICY PROCESS IN THE UNITED STATES

Using offensive cyberspace capabilities as a tool of power does pose several challenges for the national security process. While cyber is a relatively new tool of national power, former State Department official Philip Zelikow (2019) has written that the US response to cyber issues already has "a record of policy failures: the tendency to react to events rather than drive them, poorly specified objectives, confusing guidance, reliance on weakly evidenced suppositions, little grasp of organizational capacities, inability to adapt organizations to new problems, overreliance on ill-managed contractors. These are all symptoms. They are symptoms of policies that are badly designed."

Essential Principle 5.2 Defense support of civil authorities

Based on law and tradition, US military and intelligence services are allowed to operate only outside of US borders. Since cyberspace can render international borders meaningless, this has the effect of sidelining capable organizations from cybersecurity. For example, NSA has unique capabilities and is at the forefront of communications and information technology yet is generally barred from operating inside the United States. (NSA is a member of the Department of Defense and the Intelligence Community.) However, there are cases when the military can provide direct support to civil authorities such as CISA and the FBI in accordance with the law. When this is deemed necessary by civil authorities for domestic emergencies, the military exercises defense support of civil authorities. When this occurs, there is strict oversight by both the executive branch and Congress through its intelligence committees to ensure that US values are not compromised under the aegis of national security.

Underpinning Zelikow's diagnosis is the fact that cyberspace upends the entire frame of reference for policymakers. Threats to cyberspace challenge the notion of domestic and foreign boundaries that the US government uses to address national security – because it is borderless – our traditional framework for defining the use of force and what constitutes an act of war – and where cyberspace operations fit in national tools of power. As conceived, the Internet is a technologically borderless network, so cybersecurity is a global issue even if governments attempt to regulate within their sovereign territory through data localization laws or content moderation. The Department of State, which created the Cyber Affairs Office in the Bureau of Intelligence and Research in 2009, has elevated the office in 2022 to the Bureau of Cyberspace and Digital Policy "to encourage responsible state behavior in cyberspace and advance policies that protect the integrity and security of the infrastructure of the Internet" (Fick, n.d.).

The open nature of cyberspace creates legal and organizational challenges for countries that have sharp divisions between domestic and international security, such as the United States. Currently, the United States has a complex and at times overlapping system of responsible agencies and authorities. To ensure that nothing falls through the gaps, there is generally a lead authority with jurisdiction. For example, CISA, within the DHS, coordinates with the private sector to protect critical infrastructure. The FBI, located within the

Department of Justice, has jurisdiction over domestic surveillance and cyber-security. NSA sits within the Department of Defense – which views cyber as a domain of warfare where offense and defense are as important as intelligence collection – and has jurisdiction over external surveillance and cyber offense. NSA shares its leadership with the military lead for cyberspace, US Cyber Command, and works closely with the military on international cyberspace issues. However, only the military, not NSA, has the authority to launch an offensive cyber strike on another country. Notably, the president's cyber policy decision-making is vested in the National Security Council, and the Department of Defense can be directed to support civilian agencies such as CISA or the FBI in accordance with legal authorities.

While these are some of the preeminent drivers of cybersecurity and cyber operations in the United States, there are also other agencies or departments that operate in cyberspace, shape cyber policy, endeavor to constrain offensive actions and establish norms, coordinate domestically and internationally, and prevent criminal action. The Department of Justice investigates cybercrimes, leads domestic national security operations, and coordinates cyber threat investigations. The Department of State represents the United States at international bodies for discussion of cyberspace norms and treaties and works with lawyers at NSA and the Department of Defense to ensure actions respect international laws. The Department of Commerce promotes technology exports of American companies. The Treasury Department supervises foreign investment in the US technology sector under the Committee on Foreign Investment in the United States process. Finally, it is important to note that the existing national security system divides responsibilities further, muting the federal government's role in domestic cybersecurity (and security more broadly), leaving it largely in the hands of state governments. This is illustrated, for example, by the fact that New York City operates its own cyber command (NYC Cyber Command, n.d.).

Of course, geographically defined jurisdictions quickly get complicated in cyberspace. Therefore, information-sharing across the government, private sector, and society at large is very important. This is one of the reasons why NSA, Cyber Command, and CISA regularly publish common vulnerabilities and exposures (CVE) in the form of CVE alerts. Cyber power also challenges distinctions among federal agencies that rely on thematically defined jurisdictions or authorities to guide action. The traditional "DIME" construct (diplomacy, information, military, and economic) – which has long served as a useful mnemonic to identify roles and missions within the federal government – needs adjustment when cyber capabilities are considered.

For example, it is the responsibility of the Defense Department to defend the nation from attack and to support national efforts to recover from a major incident. The Defense Department conducts limited operations within the United States – it has an international orientation and is focused on identifying and mitigating threats before they come to US borders. What this means for cyberspace is that NSA and Cyber Command are not scanning systems or monitoring networks inside the United States. Unfortunately, this division of geographical authority was exploited by US adversaries to launch two major cyber exploitations against the United States (Tavakoli, 2021), SolarWinds and the 2021 Hafnium attack against Microsoft Exchange servers, by operating from servers located inside US borders. In 2021, Microsoft executive Tom Burt acknowledged this, explaining that adversaries took advantage of the international orientation of NSA and Cyber Command: "The Chinese actor [Hafnium] apparently spent the time to research the legal authorities and recognized that if they could operate from inside the United States, it takes some of the government's best threat-hunters [widely considered to be NSA and Cyber Command] off the field" (quoted in Sanger et al., 2021).

Burt has publicly acknowledged what may be a fundamental challenge for the US government as it attempts to defend US networks. Put simply, in cyberspace there is no "water's edge," seeing as adversaries can conduct attacks from servers inside US borders. As such, traditional legal authorities based on boundaries may need to be reconsidered when considering civil liberties.

The fact that each of these diverse authorities all have a stake in cyber policymaking may make it difficult to quickly achieve a unified decision or course of action. In the Obama administration, for example, an enduring sense of caution and a desire to make sure all stakeholders were represented were reported to slow down decision-making and mute more aggressive action in cyberspace by issuing Presidential Policy Directive 41 (PPD-41, 2016). The Trump administration and, thus far, the Biden administration have reportedly issued and utilized policies that enable more aggressive and streamlined decision-making. Yet different organizational perspectives and legal authorities prevent singular solutions in cyber policy discussions. As the famous adage by American government administrator Rufus Miles (1978) goes: "Where you stand, depends on where you sit." In other words, policymakers' incentives are shaped and influenced by their authorities, responsibilities, concerns, constituencies, and interests.

The enduring debate over encryption offers us an illustrative example. For over a decade, stakeholders have argued over whether strong encryption services should remain impenetrable to everyone alike or if they should be weakened or include a so-called "backdoor" to allow law enforcement to monitor and prevent criminal or malicious activity. NSA collects foreign intelligence, so it wants to limit encryption capabilities to ensure it can read intercepted communications. The Department of State has an internet freedom agenda, so it generally thinks strong encryption is essential for civil society and dissidents to organize and communicate in authoritarian countries. The Department of Commerce wants to promote US standards as global ones. The FBI would prefer a backdoor to track domestic criminal elements online. Although the public is often split (Olmstead & Smith, 2017), the academic cryptographic community is clear: They do not want backdoors in encryption. Obviously, this is a complicated issue that the US government has not been able to resolve and there are strong arguments by the various sides, which illustrates why policy is so difficult to figure out, leading us back to the start of the chapter with Hayden's comments about cyber-confusion.

Cybersecurity also challenges public–private responsibility for defense. Unlike traditional domains such as airspace, land borders, and maritime boundaries that are generally controlled and monitored by a national government, cyberspace is often created and monitored by private companies. Key infrastructure, including operating systems, hardware, and telecommunications lines in the United States, is owned by corporations and not the government.

While both US corporations and the US government have an incentive to secure infrastructure and protect US citizens, there are important differences in their incentives and missions. Private companies, for example, are generally for-profit and endeavor to protect their bottom line, with every dollar spent on cybersecurity evaluated for its effectiveness. The government may be drawn into partisan or international battles that corporations want no part of. Furthermore, corporations are global and not national. Thus, while the United States may not wish a US-based company to operate in China or to share proprietary information or intellectual property with Chinese counterparts, the company may do so unless prohibited by law to expand their market share in ways the executive branch might not like.

This is not to say that corporations do not appreciate their central role in cybersecurity. As will be explored in Chapter 8, Microsoft is taking a lead from the corporate side on promoting international norms for all government use of cyber, Facebook is countering misinformation and inauthentic posts globally, and Twitter is closing terrorists' feeds. In other words, cyberspace, unlike missile defense or nuclear strike capacity, is not the exclusive domain of government. Corporations create and maintain cyberspace, making them essential leaders in cybersecurity. Many are lobbying government on questions of privacy, encryption, and vulnerability disclosure. At the same time, governments' own intelligence agencies and cyber commands exploit vulnerabilities in private sector products to identify threats and to disrupt terrorist plots – and may enact security laws compelling companies to turn over private data for security reasons, such as the US Foreign Intelligence Surveillance Court or China's national security laws. This creates multiple dilemmas related to civil liberties, regulation, and free enterprise. And this is a dynamic challenge that is constantly evolving: For example, while the private sector has a responsibility for patching the software and hardware vulnerabilities that create cyber insecurity, governments are becoming more active through regulation, as will be explored in Chapter 6.

5.8 THE INTERNATIONAL AGENDA AND THE CYBER POLICY SPACE

Cybersecurity challenges international relations, and policymakers must consider the broader geopolitical context when making decisions. Cybersecurity issues are often just one piece of a larger relationship. For example, the United States and China are negotiating over trade, foreign direct investment, debt, Korean security issues, climate change, excessive maritime claims, and intellectual property theft. In cases such as this, the US government may be challenged to isolate malicious cyber activity from broader bilateral issues; the international affairs agenda is full, and progress in one area might be to the detriment of progress in another area.

Furthermore, as discussed previously, various countries interpret the rights, risks, and opportunities posed by cyberspace in very different ways. Privacy and online access are rights in the United States but are much more sharply defined in Europe, which gives its citizens the right to be forgotten in cyberspace by legally mandating that companies delete data upon request. Russia and China see internet freedom as a national security threat and block access of their citizens to companies such as Google, Twitter, and international news sources; they also make VPN use illegal.

Different histories, cultures, laws, and political systems are good signposts for the ways that governments use domestic law to regulate cyberspace. They also serve to make sense of the reasons that governments interject sovereign control into internet use within and across their borders, which we explore next.

5.9 DISCUSSION TOPICS

1. Characterize and analyze the threats to peace arising from cyberspace operations. Propose steps to reduce the risk of conflict. Base your analysis on a recent cyber incident that impacted national security.

2. Describe and justify the issues on which a nation must confront to formulate a new strategic approach to cyberspace management.
3. List and justify the ways that governments might incorporate their cyberspace operations into their national security systems.
4. Examine the extent to which nations can rely on deterrence to improve cybersecurity.
5. Describe and analyze the potential consequences of governments developing capabilities for cyberspace operations during peacetime.

6

Domestic Regulation of Cyberspace

We need to work together – with our Allies and partners, with the private sector, with academic researchers and with civil society – to uphold and strengthen a global framework for how nations behave in cyberspace in order to promote lasting peace, and prevent further conflict.

Wendy R. Sherman, US Deputy Secretary of State 2022

6.1 EMERGENCE OF THE INTERNET

In 1964 American engineer Paul Baran at the RAND Corporation proposed what is now called a packet-switched communications network as an alternative to the then prevailing circuit-switched network model so that it would be more likely to survive a nuclear attack. The new network would transmit blocks of digital data, each containing source and destination addresses. If some communication links were damaged in an attack, other links were expected to be available so that messages could reach their destinations. The new network was resliant by design.

Donald Davies at the British National Physical Laboratory, after visiting the Massachusetts Institute of Technology's (MIT) Project MAC time-sharing team, proposed in late 1965 that the use of communication bandwidth would improve if messages were decomposed into packets that would allow multiple packet streams to share the same communication link. His proposal was almost identical to that proposed by Baran (Campbell-Kelly, 1987).

In 1969, universities in Los Angeles, Stanford, Santa Barbara, and Salt Lake City linked their networks for the first time, using the nascent ARPANET, which was just launched by the Advanced Research Projects Agency (ARPA). ARPANET borrowed ideas developed by Baran and Davies but were fleshed out over many years by electrical engineers and computer scientists in both academia and private research labs.

To be sure, there were other networks around the same time that ARPANET developed, but through significant US government funding and dedicated efforts to improving collaboration, ARPANET thrived in a democratic, science-driven environment where networks could be easily connected from anywhere in the world. The early designers such as Baran and Davies (packets), Robert Kahn and Vinton Cerf (Transmission Control Protocol/Internet Protocol, or TCP/IP), Ted Nelson and Doug Engelbart (hypertext and links), and Tim Berners-Lee (World Wide Web) were guided by sound engineering principles rather than political considerations (Abbate, 1999; Kahn et al., 1997, pp. 129–51; Leiner et al., 2009).

While guided by science, we cannot overlook the important fact that the Internet's early developers were also living in the United States and Europe in a particular historical time. Nelson, who is credited with early work on hypertext, published his manifesto *Computer Lib* in 1974 to compel readers to understand computers and promote "personal freedom, and against restriction and coercion." The HTML (HyperText Markup Language) approach to publishing data would be recognizable by democratic political theorists since the web was designed to be a collaborative workspace where ideas would be easily accessible regardless of platform or language. The World Wide Web would be the ultimate public square reinforcing the US constitution's principal writer James Madison's sentiment: "The people shall not be deprived or abridged of their right to speak, to write, or to publish their sentiments...the people shall not be restrained from peaceably assembling and consulting for their common good" (James Madison's Proposed Amendments to the Constitution, 1789). The British enshrined this concept in an 1872 Act of parliament setting aside a "Speakers' Corner" in Hyde Park in London to be a site for public speeches and debates. This helps explain why privacy and free speech have become central to the value of the Internet for many people around the world. Brazil updated these principles for the twenty-first century by amending its constitution to make data protection a fundamental right where "it is ensured, under the terms of law, the right to protection of personal data, including in digital media" (Mari, 2022).

By 1995, US government funding of the Internet ceased, and the Internet benefited from commercial investment and the spirit of economic and political liberalism at the same time communism disappeared in Central and Eastern Europe (Greenemeier, 2009). Within this social, economic, and political context, the Internet retained its decentralized character to create an open space where the best ideas could prevail, individuals could freely associate (anonymously if they wanted), commerce could flourish, and the private sector rather than government would be the source of innovation. As the relevance of cyberspace grew, stakeholders expanded beyond engineers and scientists to include governments, corporations, civil society, and international organizations. This

---

History Matters 6.1 The right to privacy

Written more than 200 years ago, the Fourth Amendment to the US Constitution articulates an important principle that underlies Americans' views of government and echoes through privacy advocates today. It states: "The right of the people to be secure in their persons, houses, papers, and effects, against unreasonable searches and seizures, shall not be violated, and no Warrants shall issue, but upon probable cause, supported by Oath or affirmation, and particularly describing the place to be searched, and the persons or things to be seized."

---

had the effect of broadening the meaning of Internet governance from technical considerations to include cybersecurity, privacy, and norms for governments' behavior.

Driven by high-profile data breaches and creation of cyber military commands, governments are reasserting their authority in cyberspace in ways that will shape it for the next generation. As think tank analyst James Lewis (2012, p. 113) wrote, "The extension of sovereign control into cyberspace is the single most important trend shaping governance and security." At the user level, governments are denying anonymity and controlling what individuals can do in cyberspace. Notably, countries as diverse as Russia, China, Ethiopia, Vietnam, Sudan, and Algeria have imposed restrictions on cyberspace that are reflections of their political strategies to dominate their societies. Despite accepting universal human rights enshrined in the United Nations Universal Declaration of Human Rights, authoritarian governments are attempting to control their citizens' free speech, free expression, free association, and media. In contrast to the importance of individuality, privacy, and decentralization prized in democratic states, authoritarian governments attempt to monitor content and use the Internet as a means of social control.[1]

Governments try to limit access and privacy by declaring that VPNs themselves are illegal. Denying VPN use exposes a user to monitoring of his/her/their location and activity on the Internet, negating any sort of privacy and protection of their online activities ranging from banking to socializing. Niels ten Oever, a former Dutch delegate at the International Telecommunications Union, captured the change: "[T]he internet was supposed to be a neutral

---

[1] These actions are leading to what Chris Demchak and Peter Dombrowski (2013) term "Cyber Westphalia" and "most states will delineate defensible borders in some measure across the formerly ungoverned, even chaotic cyberspace."

Essential Principle 6.1 Virtual private network

A virtual private network (VPN) is software that securely extends a private network across the public Internet and grants to a remote user access that would normally require being physically inside the private network. VPNs, which were created to allow workers to gain remote users access to branch offices, are often used to provide access to proscribed sites.

---

infrastructure, but it has become a politicised (sic) arm of control. Increasingly internet infrastructure is being used for policy goals – to repress people economically, and physically – we saw it in Kashmir, Myanmar and in the Snowden revelations" (quoted in Murgia & Gross, 2020). This has raised various concerns, for instance among LGBTQI+ groups that rely on online privacy in countries where it is illegal to be LGBTQI+. In this case, internet regulation and government intervention jeopardize identities and lives. Thus, some internet pioneers' aspirations for creating a global network unfettered by politics are under stress because of domestic regulatory efforts around the world that impact supply chains, encryption, internet speech, and data storage.

6.2 SUPPLY CHAIN REGULATION

If you were to crack open your most used internet-connected device and lay out the primary components on a table, you could see what the global supply chain looks like. The overall computer design and architecture are likely American, the screen is likely made in South Korea, the main processing chip is likely an American design made in Taiwan, the circuit content may be Dutch, the battery may be Chinese, the memory may be made in Japan or South Korea, and various other components may be made in Europe, North America, or Southeast Asia. The primary materials were mined in Latin America, Central Asia, or Sub-Saharan Africa. The device runs on software produced by a US-based multinational corporation with developers in North America, Europe, and Asia. And all of this was likely assembled in a Taiwanese company's factory located in the People's Republic of China.

The story of your now broken device is a story of globalization where companies outsource components and intellectual property from around the world to assemble in China. The device is neither American nor Chinese but is an illustration of how modern manufacturing seeks out the best components and services at the lowest price. The most successful corporations have been able to scale their production to the point of virtual monopolies, with certain corporations dominating. Intel, for example, is the leading global manufacturer of chips, with about 80 percent of the CPU market (Team, 2019). Cisco is a leading global manufacturer of routers, representing about 40 percent of routers on the planet (Medberry, 2019). And Microsoft is ubiquitous, running on 80 percent of desktop computers (Statista, n.d.). Cloud storage providers such as Amazon Web Services, Oracle, Google Cloud, and Microsoft Azure are US-based giants with a global presence.

The dominance of US-based multinational corporations would suggest the US government would be comfortable with its supply chain, yet there has been a growing concern about how the global supply chain affects national security.[2] At least since 1997, the US Government Accountability Office (GAO) has been raising concerns about supply chain risks that include installation of harmful software or hardware, reliance on malicious vendors, and deliberate installation of defective code. GAO notes that "supply chain threats are present during the various phases of an information system's development life cycle and could create an unacceptable risk to federal agencies" (Wilshusen, 2018). High-profile intrusions of US government systems reinforce this insecurity.

From the White House perspective, the president issued Executive Order 13873 on May 15, 2019. The order establishes the authorities to prohibit certain transactions that involve the supply chain for information and communications technology or services designed, developed, manufactured, or supplied by persons owned by, controlled by, or subjected to the jurisdiction or direction of a foreign adversary that pose an undue or unacceptable risk to the national security of the United States. While running up against the nature of the global supply chain, the US government is attempting to protect its supply chain. The semiconductor chip shortage that began in 2019 reinforced the effort to reshore or support relocating production within the United States to protect the integrity of IT components from foreign powers. This culminated in the passage of the 2022 Creating Helpful Incentives to Produce Semiconductors (CHIPS) Act, which will provide hundreds of billions of dollars to bolster semiconductor production in the United States. Similar efforts are underway in Europe and Japan.

A key concern driving nationalization of semiconductor production is the potential for harmful code to be inserted in firmware, as discussed in Chapter 2, which makes discovery extremely unlikely. In the worst-case scenario, during

---

[2] A report by the Foreign Policy Research Institute declares that "the U.S. semiconductor industry faces an existential competitive threat. China's efforts to catch up and eventually overtake the U.S. in semiconductor technology is not only an economic challenge—it is also a security threat" (Crichton et al., 2021).

wartime, an adversary could activate a logic bomb, rendering a ship's weapon systems unusable or disrupting aircraft navigation and thus causing national shutdown of air traffic. Subsequently, federal acquisition rules were tightened to include cybersecurity threat evaluations and the National Institute for Standards and Technology released guidelines for risk management (NIST, 2018). However, the challenge of safeguarding the supply chain down to the processor level may be insurmountable, propelling the need to promote norms discussed in Chapter 8. Such norms would encourage governments to work together to restrain from using tactics that would jeopardize the foundational role for semiconductors.

The US concerns for security of its supply chain, reflected in the president's Executive Order 13873 and the passage of the CHIPS Act, are echoed in Beijing given US corporate dominance of the information and communications technology (Lindsay et al., 2015). The Chinese government expressed similar concerns about its supply chain, making it a national priority to disconnect from equipment made by US companies. In 2015, China's national security law limited foreign access to the information and communications technology market, and the "made in China" plan was announced to reduce its dependence on foreign-supplied technology; its 2017 cybersecurity law promoted development of indigenous technologies; in 2019, the Central Office of the Chinese Communist Party (CCP) ordered all government and public institutions to replace all foreign equipment by 2022 (DoD, 2019; Yang & Liu, 2019).

Exploit 6.1 A supply chain attack

In 2018, *Bloomberg Businessweek* published an alarming story: Operatives working for China's People's Liberation Army had secretly implanted microchips into motherboards made in China and sold by US-based Supermicro (Robertson & Riley, 2018). The implants allegedly gave Chinese spies clandestine access to servers belonging to over 30 American companies, including Apple, Amazon, and various government suppliers, in an operation known as a "supply chain attack," in which malicious hardware or software is inserted into products either before or after they are shipped to surveillance targets. While this report was challenged by many of the companies cited in the article, a February 2021 report by the same authors confirmed the 2018 report and provided additional detail about supply chain compromises of Supermicro motherboards. This report was based on interviews with "50 people from law enforcement, the military, Congress, intelligence agencies and the private sector" (Robertson & Riley, 2021).

By 2025, the CCP expects Chinese firms to dominate in its domestic market so that Huawei and ZTE routers can replace the ones made by Cisco. By 2030, it expects China to be the world's primary artificial intelligence innovation center, and by 2050 to be a technological and internet superpower. If these goals are achieved, the decades-long pace envisioned by the CCP may lead to major changes in the supply chain and fundamental changes in the internet landscape.

In 2020 Huawei proposed replacing the protocols at the heart of the Internet with new protocols, dubbed "New IP" (ETNO Position Paper on the New IP Proposal, 2020). Jointly with Russia it took its proposal to the International Telecommunications Union (ITU), a UN standards body for telecommunications and information technology (Bertuzzi, 2022), rather than the multistakeholder Internet Engineering Task Force (IETF, n.d.), which has been standardizing IPs since the 1980s. As such it would constitute a major change in internet governance discussed in Chapter 7.

At the ITU only states have a vote on major issues, unlike the IETF, where any stakeholder can participate. The new protocols would give governments control of the Internet. The protocols would also be incompatible with current protocols and would require new hardware and software. If the ITU endorses the new IPs and China and other autocratic countries adopt it and Western nations do not, a true Splinternet may become a reality, putting an end to aspirations for a free, open, and global internet.

To complement China's global cyber infrastructure program, its Belt and Road Initiative (Freymann, 2020) is designed to promote the Digital Silk Road program, which extends its influence throughout the developing world, as well as to incentivize the adoption of its technology globally, particularly 5G wireless telecommunication equipment. It is assumed that Chinese telecommunications equipment, when deployed, provides Chinese intelligence services a global surveillance capability (Allen-Ebrahimian, 2021; Fidler, 2018). This has prompted the United States to ban the federal use of Huawei products for fear that they will be used for espionage and, in times of conflict, disable domestic telecommunications, including internet traffic.

This behavior is greater than normal tit-for-tat trade politics and is playing out globally since there are significant national security issues at stake for those who "own" encryption technology. Senator Richard Burr (Republican – North Carolina), as a member of the Senate Select Committee on Intelligence, said:

When it comes to 5G technology, the decisions we make today will be felt for decades to come. The widespread adoption of 5G has the potential to transform the way we do business, but also carries significant national security risks. Those risks could prove disastrous if Huawei, a company that operates at the behest of the Chinese government, military, and intelligence services, is allowed to take over the 5G market unchecked. This legislation will help maintain America's competitive advantage and protect our national security by encouraging Western competitors to develop innovative, affordable, and secure 5G alternatives. (Quoted in Warner, 2020)

And Senator Mark R. Warner (Democrat – Virginia), of the same committee, sees that "widespread adoption of 5G technology has the potential to unleash sweeping effects for the future of internet-connected devices, individual data security, and national security. It is imperative that Congress address the complex security and competitiveness challenges that Chinese-directed telecommunication companies pose" (quoted in Warner, 2020).

The Department of State sees Huawei not simply as a technological challenge to US corporations' products but as "a political and geopolitical challenge" (Ford, 2019). The United States waged a campaign to prevent its allies from allowing Huawei and ZTE to upgrade their networks. The efforts were bolstered given disappointment in China's lack of information-sharing related to the global health pandemic that began in 2019. For example, the North Atlantic Treaty Organization (NATO) secretary general Jens Stoltenberg (2020) concluded that China was "multiplying the threats to open societies and individual freedoms and increasing the competition over our values and our way of life." In 2021, this was reinforced by broad condemnation by NATO, the European Union, Australia, Britain, Canada, Japan, and New Zealand of Chinese intelligence compromise of Microsoft Exchange email servers. Finally, while there are other well-known cases of Chinese intelligence infiltrating the telecommunications infrastructure (Inkster, 2018), much of the debate centers on security and privacy, which places encryption front and center in ways governments want to intervene in cyberspace.

6.3 ENCRYPTION

As discussed in Chapter 3, encryption can provide secure communications, identify the sender of data, and promote privacy. Encryption is a basis for cybersecurity and its role in information security is unassailable since encryption is involved in individuals' bank transactions, online purchases, and select communications. But the privacy and security that are essential for users to freely exchange ideas, goods, and money pose a challenge to governments that have a public security responsibility. In short, encryption provides terrorists and criminals with the same level of security that students and stock traders have, complicating law enforcement's efforts to conduct authorized surveillance. This is the modern version of the age-old dilemma that pits security and liberty against each other.

Essential Principle 6.2 Data confidentiality, integrity, and availability

The goals of cybersecurity are confidentiality, integrity, and availability (CIA), which require that information be protected from theft and alteration and be available, respectively.

Although governments can compel their domestic firms to cooperate with intelligence and law enforcement, many international phone and computer vendors, concerned about the security of user information, have designed products that provide end-to-end encryption in which transmitted data is encrypted at the source and decrypted at the destination, thereby preventing companies from complying with court-authorized requests. End-to-end encryption, which is found in products such as Signal, WhatsApp, iMessage, and Facebook Messenger, complicates court-authorized law enforcement surveillance; the Federal Bureau of Investigation (FBI) refers to this phenomenon as "going dark," challenging law enforcement's ability to provide public security in the information age.

Former FBI director James Comey (2014) remarked, "Those charged with protecting our people aren't always able to access the evidence we need to prosecute crime and prevent terrorism even with lawful authority. We have the legal authority to intercept and access communications and information pursuant to court order, but we often lack the technical ability to do so." Comey's successor, Christopher Wray (2017), in testimony to Congress, also identified encryption as a challenge to public safety. He said,

"The exploitation of encrypted platforms presents serious challenges to law enforcement's ability to identify, investigate, and disrupt threats that range from counterterrorism to child exploitation, gangs, drug traffickers and white-collar crimes. We respect the right of people to engage in private communications, regardless of the medium or technology. Whether it is instant messages, texts, or old-fashioned letters, citizens have the right to communicate with one another in private without unauthorized government surveillance, because the free flow of information is vital to a thriving democracy. Our aim is not to expand the Government's surveillance authority, but rather to ensure that we can obtain electronic information and evidence pursuant to the legal authority that Congress has provided to us to keep America safe. The benefits of our increasingly digital lives, however, have been accompanied by new dangers, and we have seen how criminals and terrorists use advances in technology to their advantage."

6.3.1 Exceptional Access to Encrypted Information

To cope with "going dark," governments are requesting that phone and computer vendors provide "backdoors" or "keys left under the doormat" (Landau,

2015b) for court-ordered access to these products. This is called *exceptional access* or *targeted lawful access* to subvert encryption.

For example, in 2018 Australia passed a telecommunications law that requires companies provide access to encrypted communication. Proposed under the guise of promoting public safety, Australia's attorney general Christian Porter explained, "This ensures that our national security and law enforcement agencies have the modern tools they need, with appropriate authority and oversight, to access the encrypted conversations of those who seek to do us harm" (quoted in Tarabay, 2018).

In the United Kingdom, two employees of Government Communications Headquarters, the British signals intelligence and information assurance agency, have proposed that telecommunications services insert the capability to add a third party, a "ghost user," to two-party calls at the request of legal authorities (Levy & Robinson, 2018). They assert that their proposal does not require modification to encryption algorithms, a claim that has been disputed (Schulman, 2019).

Australian legislators and UK cryptographers could point to larger global efforts as noted in this communique from the G20 (2017), which represents the world's 20 largest economies:

We will work with the private sector, in particular communication service providers and administrators of relevant applications, to fight exploitation of the internet and social media for terrorist purposes such as propaganda, funding and planning of terrorist acts, inciting terrorism, radicalizing and recruiting to commit acts of terrorism, while fully respecting human rights. Appropriate filtering, detecting and removing of content that incites terrorist acts is crucial in this respect. We encourage industry to continue investing in technology and human capital to aid in the detection as well as swift and permanent removal of terrorist content. In line with the expectations of our peoples we also encourage collaboration with industry to provide lawful and non-arbitrary access to available information where access is necessary for the protection of national security against terrorist threats. We affirm that the rule of law applies online as well as it does offline.

On the surface, a global effort to combat terrorists' use of the Internet is important. However, there is no internationally agreed definition of terrorism and governments do label their opponents as terrorists to stifle dissent and repress those who challenge single-party rule (Reveron & Murer, 2006). Because of this, civil society and corporations are resisting efforts to undermine essential principles of internet freedom and cybersecurity. Cindy Cohn, executive director of the Electronic Frontier Foundation, wrote, "I don't think it's appropriate for the government to decide that they get security, and we don't" (quoted in Evans, 2020). In addition to civil liberties activists, social media companies challenge government's intentions to regulate. For example, Twitter founder Jack Dorsey (2021) testified before Congress, "Twitter grapples with complex considerations on how to address extremism and misinformation. How do we prevent harm, while also safeguarding free expression and the right of diverse individuals to express a range of views?" Susan Landau (2016b), a computer scientist and mathematician, says that the "latest battle [over encryption] is actually a collision over differing notions of security in a digital age." A backdoor is simply a planned security weakening of a product, possibly exposing users to unauthorized actors. There is simply no way to guarantee that governments are the only ones that would use exceptional access tools.[3]

6.3.2 Assessing the Need for Exceptional Access to Content

Given the claims by leading policymakers, it is prudent to ask whether something other than access to encrypted content is essential in pursuing criminal prosecutions. For example, would the metadata associated with communications suffice? Metadata consists of subscriber and traffic information. The former includes a subscriber's name, possibly a phone number, and an email address. Traffic information includes IP addresses, connection logs, and other data. Normally when encrypted data is sent over the Internet, its source and destination addresses are not encrypted so that a packet can reach its destination and a response can be sent.

There is highly credible anecdotal evidence that metadata is at least as important as access to encrypted content. In a 2015 *Wired* article Stewart Baker, former National Security Agency (NSA) general counsel, is quoted as saying, "If you have enough metadata, you don't really need content," and Michael Hayden, former director of both NSA and the Central Intelligence Agency (CIA), is cited as having said that "We kill people based on metadata" (Schneier, 2015). Through analysis of metadata, it is possible to conduct

---

[3] A report published by MIT examined the costs and benefits of planned vulnerabilities so that governments can have exceptional access to encrypted content. The report noted:

"We have found that the damage that could be caused by law enforcement exceptional access requirements would be even greater today than it would have been 20 years ago. In the wake of the growing economic and social cost of the fundamental insecurity of today's Internet environment, any proposals that alter the security dynamics online should be approached with caution. Exceptional access would force Internet system developers to reverse forward secrecy design practices that seek to minimize the impact on user privacy when systems are breached. The complexity of today's Internet environment, with millions of apps and globally connected services, means that new law enforcement requirements are likely to introduce unanticipated, hard to detect security flaws. Beyond these and other technical vulnerabilities, the prospect of globally deployed exceptional access systems raises difficult problems about how such an environment would be governed and how to ensure that such systems would respect human rights and the rule of law" (Abelson et al., 2015).

network analysis and identify associates of known criminals, intelligence operatives, or terrorists. Therefore, one does not need to know the content of the messages but needs to know who is connected to whom, know the depth of the connection as measured by the frequency of contacts, and have a preexisting understanding of an individual's connections to illegal behavior.

There is also statistical evidence supporting the importance of metadata. In 2019 Europol surveyed the frequency and nature of requests by "European Union authorities ... (for) electronic evidence from foreign based [American] Online Service Providers (OSPs), in the context of criminal investigations." Europol found that 81 percent of the requests were for noncontent data, a synonym for metadata, 15 percent were for content, and 4 percent were unknown (EUROPOL, 2019).

In many contexts revealing metadata does not reveal compromising information. For example, the fact that a subsidiary of a major corporation was in communication with its headquarters is not sensitive information although the content of the communication itself may be sensitive. In other contexts, metadata is sensitive, such as when a journalist wants to correspond with a confidential source but does not want to inadvertently reveal the name or location of the source. While journalists in the United States have constitutional protections of freedom of the press, the same is not true for the source, who may be prosecutable for unauthorized disclosure of classified information (Stone & Bollinger, 2018). Additionally, journalists in other democracies such as the United Kingdom, let alone journalists in authoritarian countries, lack the legal protections afforded to US journalists. If law enforcement organizations were to acknowledge the value of metadata, they may be able to reconcile the needs of public safety with those of privacy rights so that legislation could be crafted that more accurately targets activity that needs regulation without weakening the encryption that is essential for the operation of digital economies. Since it is now known how to obfuscate metadata as well as content (Gilad, 2019), governments may want to consider outlawing the former.while allowing the latter.

6.3.3 Backdoors to Secure Computers and Phones

In February 2016 the US Department of Justice sued Apple Computer to provide it with access to an iPhone that was recovered in a December 2015 domestic terrorist attack in San Bernardino, California. Apple CEO Tim Cook (2016) refused saying, "While we believe the FBI's intentions are good, it would be wrong for the government to force us to build a backdoor into our products. And ultimately, we fear that this demand would undermine the very freedoms and liberty our government is meant to protect." Microsoft CEO Satya Nadella extends the idea and charges us "to think about data and privacy rights as a human right" (Nusca, 2020). And three former senior national security leaders agree: "We believe that the greater public good is a secure communications infrastructure protected by ubiquitous encryption at the device, server and enterprise level without building in means for government monitoring" (McConnell et al., 2015).

In authoritarian countries such as Russia and China, the problem is less ambiguous. These governments have imposed strict requirements for access, outlawed the use of VPNs, and forced companies that operate in their country to enable privileged access. Companies and individuals simply lack a choice and must comply with governments' regulations even if it undermines their corporate values for fear of being shut out of the marketplace.

In 2019, Russia passed the Sovereign Internet Law, requiring preinstallation of Russian-made software on all internet-accessible devices (Sherman, 2020). This is an effort to both promote the Russian software industry and ensure government regulation gets to the user level through software developers. For example, when a new iPhone is set up in Russia, an additional screen enables users to download (or ignore) a list of Russian government-approved apps (Owen, 2021).

Additional Russian laws require companies to share encryption keys with intelligence and law enforcement services, and all internet traffic on RuNet (Russian Internet) must be encrypted with government-controlled encryption tools. Under SORM (*Wikiwand – SORM*, n.d.), telecommunication providers are required to install monitoring equipment to enable the Federal Security Service (FSB, the successor of the KGB) to monitor all telephone calls, email traffic, and web-browsing activity. The Russian government has resisted calls to rollback internet restrictions and rejected the 2015 European Court for Human Rights opinion in Roman Zakharov v. Russia (2015), which found that Russia's surveillance practices violated the right to privacy.

The situation is similar in China, with its 2020 encryption law noting that "the scientific research, production, sales, service and import and export of it [encryption] must not harm the state security and public interests or other people's rights and interests" (China Focus: China adopts law on cryptography, 2019). The overall goal is to "make networks opaque to bad actors but transparent to the government and the CCP" (Dickinson, 2019). More than other countries, China rejects the notion that the Internet is borderless and the World Wide Web is global. The CCP sees that once data crosses its borders, it must be accessible by China's government. Article 7 of the Chinese National Intelligence Law states, "[A]n organization or citizen shall support, assist in and cooperate in national intelligence work in accordance with the law and

Table 6.1 Internet freedom in the world

Top 5 "most free"	Bottom 5 "least free"
Iceland	Cuba
Estonia	Vietnam
Canada	Syria
Germany	Iran
United Kingdom	China

Source: Shahbaz, A., Funk, A., & Vesteinsson, K. (2022).

keep confidential the national intelligence work that it or he knows" (Peking University School of Law, 2018). This is part of the general movement for governments to regulate content, resulting in declines of internet freedom (see Table 6.1).

As this chapter suggests, internet freedom is imperiled throughout the world. Examples include Algeria using its state-controlled telecommunications company to turn off the Internet during the 2011 Arab Spring, inhibiting protestors' abilities to organize, India periodically disabling telephone and internet service in Jammu and Kashmir in response to political protests, Bangladesh blocking news sites while restricting mobile networks, and Ethiopia using localized network shutdowns. Content moderation tools provide governments the means to monitor (and punish) those who criticize the government or simply censor through aggressive content regulation curtailing freedom of speech.

6.4 CONTENT REGULATION

The increasing use by governments of regulation navigates a difficult balance between freedom of speech and incitement to violence, deliberate spreading of false information, and hate speech that can generate social unrest. Democracies are not immune from the challenges of algorithmic enhancement of hate speech; domestic and foreign groups have been able to use social media to amplify falsehoods and undermine dialogue and compromise, which are essential for democracy. During the January 6, 2021, insurrection in Washington, DC, which included storming the US Capitol building, social media played an important role (U.S. House Committee on Energy & Commerce, 2021).

The case of the United States is instructive and is rooted in the original telephone circuit-switched networks that operated under principles grounded in the

1934 US Communications Act.[4] This law requires that service providers create the means for law enforcement to physically tap phone lines for monitoring. In 1967, the Supreme Court ruled in *Katz* v. *United States* that citizens' expectation of privacy extended to telecommunications, negating unauthorized content monitoring. Thus, for the US government to monitor communications it must obtain a court-authorized warrant and conform to the Fourth Amendment of the Constitution, which prohibits illegal searches. In 1979, the court adjusted this law via *Smith* v. *Maryland*, which allows law enforcement to use a pen register that records all numbers called to a particular phone number to track with whom an individual communicates, that is metadata, but still preserves privacy protections on the content of conversations. The 1986 Electronic Communications Privacy Act reinforced this concept, and law enforcement was further restricted from using surveillance without a court order.

The communication laws were significantly updated in 1996 with the passage of the Telecommunications Act, which deregulated the broadcast and telecommunications markets and explicitly recognized the Internet with the goal of reducing regulation and promoting competition among private enterprises. The Act includes allocation of the electromagnetic spectrum and physical location of fiber-optic cables that are the principal carriers of high-speed internet traffic.

The AT&T Corporation was the dominant provider of telephone service in the United States until 1984, when it was broken up in response to an antitrust lawsuit. Shortly thereafter, the Internet became dominated by commercial entities. This occurred around the time the Cold War ended in 1991, when ideological divides collapsed and the Internet came to be viewed as a global common, like the oceans. US government policymakers, fearing that too much regulation would stifle innovation, added Section 230 to the Communications Decency Act, which grants legal protection from publishing third-party content (Section 230 of the Communications Decency Act, n.d.-b). Developers also prioritized ease of access over security, thereby reducing barriers to entry. Further, they turned to private capital to fuel large investments in the infrastructure of cyberspace. Consequently, telecommunications lines shifted from copper wire to fiber-optic cables, computing transitioned from mainframes to desktops, and software usage expanded from scientific research to commercial activities.

The Federal Communications Commission (FCC), which was created in 1934, retained the right to regulate interstate and international communications

---

[4] To trace the roots of privacy law in the US since colonial times, see Solove (2006).

Exploit 6.2 SolarWinds supply chain attack

Brad Smith, president of Microsoft, described the Russian compromise of the SolarWinds Orion product as "the largest and most sophisticated attack the world has ever seen" (Reuters Staff, 2021). It was a supply chain attack done by corrupting the Orion update procedure. It persisted for at least ten months before its discovery in December 2020 by FireEye. Thousands of companies and organizations were hacked along with many federal agencies, including Treasury, Justice, and Energy Departments and the Pentagon (Temple-Raston, 2021).

---

by radio, television, wire, satellite, and cable in all 50 American states, the District of Columbia, and US territories. The FCC is the primary authority for communications law, regulation, and technological innovation. The regulation is primarily technical, however, governing where on the electromagnetic spectrum companies can operate.

The 1998 Digital Millennium Copyright Act criminalized efforts to circumvent copyright control but exempted internet service providers from liability. These laws had the effect of keeping a separation between data flow and data content. This effectively shields companies from responsibility for hate speech and extremism disseminated through their platforms.

When it comes to content monitoring or surveillance in the United States, the 2001 terrorist attacks on the United States resulted in a series of laws and amendments that thrust US intelligence into cyberspace with a focus on data content. The US government's surveillance authorities are rooted in the Foreign Intelligence Surveillance Act (FISA) of 1978. Since the United States is a very open society that is widely targeted by foreign intelligence services operating inside US borders (NCSC, 2020), FISA provides the means to collect intelligence inside US borders. The Foreign Intelligence Surveillance Court (FISC) reviews such requests, thereby honoring the separation of powers between the executive branch and the judicial branch of government (U.S., 1978).

The 2001 USA PATRIOT Act expanded law enforcement's surveillance powers, which were viewed as too limiting in the age of terrorism and modern communications. The urgency for domestic surveillance coincided with the shift from circuit-switched networks to packet-switched networks, with voice over internet largely replacing telephone service over circuit-switched networks. Technological changes undercut traditional methods of surveillance.

Essential Principle 6.3 Intelligence collection process

1. The National Security Agency identifies foreign entities (persons or organizations) that have information responsive to an identified foreign intelligence requirement (e.g., terrorist).
2. It develops the "network" with which that person's or organization's information is shared or the command and control structure through which it flows. In other words, if NSA is tracking a specific terrorist, it will endeavor to determine who that person is in contact with and who the person is taking direction from.
3. It identifies how the foreign entities communicate (radio, email, telephony, etc.)
4. It then identifies the telecommunications infrastructure used to transmit those communications.
5. It identifies vulnerabilities in the methods of communication used to transmit them.
6. It matches its collection to those vulnerabilities or develops new capabilities to acquire communications of interest if needed.

Source: National Security Agency/Central Security Service (n.d.b)

In the early 2000s, with significant controversy the Bush administration undertook mass collection of metadata to identify terrorist networks. Metadata was collected with the expectation that it would help identify terrorist networks.

Various government surveillance programs became public when government contractor Edward Snowden illegally disclosed classified programs before fleeing to Hong Kong, China, and later settling in Russia. Among the disclosures Snowden made was a program, called PRISM, that allowed the government to obtain communications related to specific identifiers, such as an email address or a telephone number with a connection to a foreign source, as determined under the supervision of the FISC, a court created by FISA (Litt, 2016). FISA and the FISC were designed to ensure the executive branch was balanced against the judicial branch. Then director of National Intelligence James Clapper (2013) said, "Their purpose is to obtain foreign intelligence information, including information necessary to thwart terrorist and cyber-attacks against the United States and its allies."

According to *New York Times* reporter David Sanger,

THE SNOWDEN AFFAIR [sic] kicked off a remarkable era in which American firms, for the first time in post-World War II history, broadly refused to cooperate with the American government. They wrapped some of that refusal in Silicon Valley's typical libertarian ideology. But their real fear was that any open association with the NSA would prompt customers to wonder whether Washington had bored holes into their products. (Davis & Sanger, 2015, p. 85; emphasis in original)

President Obama (2013) largely continued the Bush-era programs but noted that "we will have to keep working hard to strike the appropriate balance between our need for security and preserving those freedoms that make us who we are. That means reviewing the authorities of law enforcement, so we can intercept new types of communication, but also build in privacy protections to prevent abuse."

The program changed with the passage of the 2015 USA Freedom Act; instead of US government entities retaining the metadata, telecommunication companies were required to retain it subject to release via court order. Five years after the program changed, an appeals court ruled on the former program: "We conclude that the government may have violated the Fourth Amendment and did violate the Foreign Intelligence Surveillance Act ('FISA') when it collected the telephony metadata of millions of Americans" (USA v. Basaaly Faeed Moalin, USA v. Mohamed Mohamed Mohamud, USA v. Issa Doreh, USA v. Ahmed Nasir Taalil Mohamud, US Court of Appeals, Ninth Circuit, 2020).

While this controversy was generated by government counterterrorism efforts, the history of surveillance is illustrative of the larger dynamic at play among government, industry, and citizens as it relates to intercepting communications. Simply, what should be collected? Who shall collect and retain the data? And what is the process for government to analyze the collected data? This is an important set of questions since US regulation has largely been technical up to this point, with significant challenges to warrantless content surveillance related to counterterrorism efforts.

While Snowden's espionage seemed to shift the balance away from government and back to industry, Russian interference in US elections brought the issue back to the forefront of national security discussions. Facebook founder Mark Zuckerberg (2018) said in a post. "We face sophisticated and well-funded adversaries, including nation states, that are always evolving and trying new attacks. But we're learning and improving quickly too, and we're investing heavily to keep people safe."

Recent efforts to regulate content in the United States are rooted in the Communications Decency Act of 1996. The law made it a crime for anyone to engage in online speech that is indecent or patently offensive if the speech could be viewed by a minor. The provisions were struck down by the Supreme Court in *Reno* v. *ACLU* in 1997 and the judges affirmed the dangers of censorship by citing District Judge Dalzell's earlier opinion that we must protect "the most participatory form of mass speech yet developed" (Reno, Attorney General of the United States, et al. v. American Civil Liberties Union et al., 1997).

The indecency speech regulatory part of the law never went into effect, but as mentioned earlier, Section 230 of the Act remains and the Electronic Freedom Foundation considers it "the most influential law to protect the kind of innovation that has allowed the Internet to thrive" (Section 230 of the Communications Decency Act, n.d.-b, p. 230). Section 230 says that *"no provider or user of an interactive computer service shall be treated as the publisher or speaker of any information provided by another information content provider"* (47 U.S. Code § 230 – Protection for Private Blocking and Screening of Offensive Material, n.d.; emphasis added). In an important case, *Zeran* v. *America Online, Inc.*, "Chief Judge Wilkinson held that Section 230 protected America Online from a defamation claim based on messages posted on its bulletin boards" (Section 230 as First Amendment Rule, 2018, p. 230), that is, the company was not liable for users' posts, giving corporations a liability shield. The Supreme Court reaffirmed corporate immunity in 2023 when it refused to address a lower court decision in *Gonzalez v. Google LLC* (US Supreme Court, 2023).

This body of law became important when foreign intelligence services commenced influence operations in the United States. Twitter, Facebook, and other social media companies were not liable for foreign intelligence activities using their platforms. Each corporation took voluntary action by labeling posts, removing accounts exhibiting inauthentic behavior such as posing as a neutral account or using multiple Facebook accounts, but were not compelled by the government to do so. How the US government approaches content regulation is important and will have global implications since the United States commits to a global leadership role for a free and open internet and US-based corporations have global influence.

The United States does not have a true domestic intelligence agency such as Canada's Canadian Security Intelligence Service, France's Directorate of Territorial Security (DST), and the United Kingdom's MI5. Thus, cooperation is required among the FBI, the Department of Homeland Security, and US intelligence agencies to investigate foreign intelligence activity on US-based networks. However, NSA and CIA are strictly prohibited from engaging in domestic surveillance. Nation-state attackers have exploited these domestic prohibitions by launching attacks from US-based servers, as was done by Russian intelligence with the SolarWinds exploit (Vavra, 2021). With this as

---

Exploit 6.3 Russian intelligence hacks the Democratic Party

Early in 2016 Russian military intelligence (GRU) gained access to the Democratic Congressional Campaign Committee (DCCC) servers and engaged in influence operations by releasing documents damaging to Hilary Clinton's presidential campaign. Ironically, the Russians warned that such game-changing exploits were possible in their report to the UN (GGE, 2000).

The GRU personnel gained access through simple spear-phishing and spoofing a malicious link that resembled Google security. Once on the DCCC network, the GRU personnel installed the X-Agent malware to monitor employees' activity, steal passwords, and maintain network access through a GRU-leased server in Arizona, later moving the data to a computer in Illinois. Using the false identity "Guccifer 2.0" they released the documents to the websites DCLeaks and Wikileaks; the GRU claimed these were American hacktivists in order to obfuscate a Russian intelligence operation. Two years later, 12 GRU personnel were indicted for this activity under computer hacking laws, and the issue of government monitoring content reemerged (*USA* v. *Viktor Borisovich Netyksho [and 11 others]*, defendants: Case 1:18-cr-00215-ABJ, 2018).

---

a backdrop, the US national government launched a new program through the Cybersecurity and Infrastructure Security Agency called Joint Cyber Defense Collaborative. The program leverages authorities provided by the National Defense Authorization Act 2021 to bring together public and private sector entities (CISA, 2021a).

6.4.1 The Case of the People's Republic of China

In contrast to the United States government, writes scholar Jon Lindsay et al. (2015, p. 11), "a distinguishing characteristic of the Chinese concept of information security (xinxi anquan) is that it emphasizes Internet content as much as, if not more than, technical network security (wangluo anquan)." This reflects China's political culture, which promotes the interests of the CCP over those of individuals. The CCP relies on this cultural representation to reinforce its political monopoly in China.

The Chinese government uses aggressive content moderation (censorship) not only to eliminate objectionable political speech but also to promote a particular political agenda. For example, in the wake of the COVID-19 pandemic that originated in China, the main messaging app WeChat removed blacklisted keywords from the content of messages (e.g., coronavirus and Wuhan seafood market) between senders and receivers (Ruan et al., 2020). This ability is an authoritarian's dream in that a government can now change text messages while in transit to limit information flow among individuals, thereby enabling the government to control the narrative. Further, the Cyberspace Administration of China told technology companies that it would punish "websites, platforms, and accounts" for publishing "harmful" content and "spreading fear" related to COVID-19 (Ruan et al., 2020).

The CCP also uses content moderation and cyber means to target political opponents inside China and around the world. Cyber legal advisor Sarah McKune (2015) states, "efforts to control Tibetans have ramped up in the digital realm, which is perceived as a primary conduit for hostile foreign influence." Similar efforts are made against religious groups such as Falun Gong, pro-Taiwan independence groups, and ethnic minorities such as Uyghurs. Australian scholar Anna Hayes (2020) has argued that "Xi [Jinping] has overseen a hardline approach towards Xinjiang and the Uyghurs, increasing surveillance and policing to unprecedented levels." By transforming Xinjiang into a surveillance state, Beijing seeks to control Uyghurs in both cyberspace and physical space. The CCP's approach to censorship is similar: both companies inside China and outside China are intimidated if they reference any of the three T's, Tiananmen, Taiwan, and Tibet (Spector & Ma, 2018).

6.5 DATA LOCALIZATION

Aggressive content moderation and speech censorship are complicated when data moves along global routes or when citizens in authoritarian countries use VPNs to navigate around a government's attempt to control their behavior. Consequently, several countries are regulating the location of data of their citizens both to enable surveillance and to promote economic development. For example, Vietnam's cybersecurity law states:

Domestic and foreign service providers on telecom networks and on the Internet and other value added services in cyberspace in Vietnam [cyberspace service providers] carrying out activities of collecting, exploiting [using], analysing and processing data [being] personal information, data about service users' relationships and data generated by service users in Vietnam *must store such data in Vietnam* for a [specified] period [to be] stipulated by the Government. (Vietnamese Law 24 on Cybersecurity, 2018; emphasis added)

There has been a backlash against data localization laws that pit democracies and corporations against authoritarian governments. The European Union banned data localization for its members. Concerning its members, the EU regulation states: "Data localisation requirements represent a clear barrier to the free provision of data processing services across the Union and to the internal market. As such, they should be banned unless they are justified on grounds of public security" (European Union, 2018). While data should move freely in Europe, preventing localization within a European country, the European Union has ruled that it must localize data of European citizens within EU borders due to "the limitations on the protection of personal data arising from the domestic law of the United States... [which] are not circumscribed in a way that satisfies requirements that are essentially equivalent to those required under EU law" (Court of Justice of the EU, 2020).

Corporations that rely on large data centers to service the world rather than a country's population are resisting data localization efforts. Google's director of law enforcement and information security testified before Congress: "If data localization and other efforts are successful, then what we will face is the effective Balkanization of the Internet and the creation of a 'splinternet' broken up into smaller national and regional pieces, with barriers around each of the splintered Internets to replace the global Internet we know today" (Miller, 2014).

As companies start to shift to space-based networks (Meyer, 2019) data localization laws may be redundant, literally putting data out of government's reach. Governments will continue to regulate where on the electromagnetic spectrum they can transmit data as well as satellites' orbits. At the time of writing, companies have plans to create constellations of tens of thousands of internet satellites in low earth orbit creating a mesh network with ground stations around the planet. In the United States, three federal agencies regulate in this area: (a) the Federal Aviation Administration regulates space launch or reentry by US citizens anywhere in the world or by any individual or entity within the United States, (b) the Federal Communications Commission approves the licenses to operate communications satellites, and (c) the National Oceanic and Atmospheric Administration licenses commercial remote-sensing satellites, which include imaging the earth. If data centers follow and are truly above the clouds someday, data localization efforts will become obsolete as users can connect to satellites holding their stored data in privacy-friendly locations. Just as some countries have favorable privacy banking laws, the same may be true some day for favorable privacy data laws.

6.6 MALWARE AS CRIME

While domestic law varies across countries, there are basic principles that identify the use of malware as a crime. Most often, cybercrimes are those that draw from existing laws such as child exploitation, fraud, breaking and entering, and theft. In these cases, existing legal principles are applied to cyberspace. For example, the Computer Fraud and Abuse Act, which prohibits access to a computer without authorization, covers cyberattacks and intrusions against computers that are used in or affect interstate or foreign commerce and communications, even when the targeted computers are outside the United States. This law has the effect of making "hack-back" attacks by individuals or companies illegal.

Hacking has enabled unprecedented levels of data theft. To reduce it, economic espionage laws seek to prevent intellectual property theft. Individuals can also be prosecuted under economic espionage laws. These laws were initially

---

Policy Matters 6.1 Defining economic espionage

- (a) In General.—Whoever, intending or knowing that the offense will benefit any foreign government, foreign instrumentality, or foreign agent, knowingly—
- (1) steals, or without authorization appropriates, takes, carries away, or conceals, or by fraud, artifice, or deception obtains a trade secret;
- (2) without authorization copies, duplicates, sketches, draws, photographs, downloads, uploads, alters, destroys, photocopies, replicates, transmits, delivers, sends, mails, communicates, or conveys a trade secret;
- (3) receives, buys, or possesses a trade secret, knowing the same to have been stolen or appropriated, obtained, or converted without authorization;
- (4) attempts to commit any offense described in any of paragraphs (1) through (3); or
- (5) conspires with one or more other persons to commit any offense described in any of paragraphs (1) through (3), and one or more of such persons do any act to effect the object of the conspiracy,
- shall, except as provided in subsection (b), be fined not more than $500,000 or imprisoned not more than 15 years, or both.

Source: U.S. Government Publishing Office (2011)

designed to promote cybersecurity but have also been applied in an extraterritorial fashion against foreign actors committing crimes inside the United States.

In the United States, the use of malware outpaced law enforcement efforts to provide for public safety online. FBI director Christopher Wray (2019) testified to Congress that malware had caused billions of dollars in damages and that the number of victims was growing rapidly:

Botnets used by cyber criminals have been responsible for billions of dollars in damages over the past several years. The widespread availability of malicious software that can create botnets allows individuals to leverage the combined bandwidth of thousands, if not millions, of compromised computers, servers, or network-ready devices to disrupt the day-to-day activities of governments, businesses, and individual Americans. Cyber threat actors have also increasingly conducted ransomware attacks against U.S. systems, encrypting data and rendering systems unusable — thereby victimizing individuals, businesses, and even emergency service and public health providers.

6.7 PRIVATE BUT PUBLIC NETWORK

Although the Internet is publicly available, it consists of privately owned computers and networks. Thus, a key challenge is to understand who oversees making the network secure and who is responsible if it is not secure. The private sector primarily designs, builds, owns, and operates the Internet, but there is a growing expectation that governments will protect it. In the United States, the Defense Department is responsible for ensuring the .mil domain remains safe, while the Department of Homeland Security oversees security of the .gov domain and provides support to critical infrastructure, most of which is in private hands. But the .com and other nongovernmental domains are entrusted to the organizations that operate them.

In recognition of this reality, Richard Harknett and James Stever (2009) call for cybersecurity to rest on a balanced triad of intergovernmental relations, private corporate involvement, and active cyber citizenship as a model. Yet it is unclear how the government, information technology companies, and individual users would manage this complicated relationship. National computer security incident response teams (CSIRTs) and computer emergency response teams (CERTs) are one possibility. The first CERT was a government-sponsored entity formed in 1988 at Carnegie Mellon University. National CSIRTs and local security operations centers have been deployed around the world to provide a limited degree of coordination in response to cyber threats.

Relatively unsophisticated phishing attacks continue to generate cyber insecurity for which users are largely responsible today, although the private sector can help to minimize their impact. These ideas are discussed in Chapter 4. Then vice chairman of the Joint Chiefs of Staff, who is the second-highest ranking military officer in the United States, emphasized the human factor: "One key lesson of the military's experience is that while technical upgrades are important, minimizing human error is even more crucial. Mistakes by network administrators and users – failures to patch vulnerabilities in legacy systems, misconfigured settings, violations of standard procedures—open the door to the overwhelming majority of successful attacks" (Winnefeld Jr. et al., 2015).

6.8 CONCLUSIONS: FROM INTERNET TO INTERNETS

At the heart of the domestic regulation of cyberspace is finding the balance between public security and private use of the Internet that is largely defined by openness. With its American roots and US-based information technology corporate dominance of cyberspace, the democratic characteristics of the Internet appear threatening to authoritarian regimes. Scholar Adam Segal (2017) noted that openness poses "a threat to their [Beijing and Moscow] national security and as inordinately benefiting Washington strategically, economically, and politically." Increasingly, governments are asserting sovereignty in cyberspace by creating alternative Internets and imposing technical and content restrictions for users within their borders.

Content regulation may seem foreign to those living in societies where the Internet is largely free, but it is important to note that technology companies already use content moderation systems to screen out child exploitation, pornography, hate speech, and extreme violence online (Li, 2020). Authoritarian countries simply extend this principle to protect their political monopolies or cultural values.

In the extreme case, Russia has created its .ru network and required all internet traffic to be monitored as an attempt to isolate Russian users from the global internet architecture. A variation of this isolation occurs through site blocking, isolating a country's top-level domain through firewalls, hosting a copy of the domain name system root zone file, and demanding users stay within a national version of the Internet.

China seems well positioned to offer its own unique Internet apart from the one born in the United States, especially if it implements and deploys its proposed New IP model (Hoffmann et al., 2020). Its domestic programs that prioritize "made in China" software and hardware, when coupled with an aggressive export program, have the potential to change the open-natured

Internet around the world in the coming decades as China promotes its technology through the Digital Silk Road program.

In a pro-privacy way, the European Union has imposed its own laws on corporations for the benefit of its citizens. The General Data Protection Regulation went into effect in 2018 and is a real government effort to protect individual users rather than corporations, who are shielded in the United States, or a political party's notion of internet security, as practiced in China. Additionally, the European Union adopted in 2022 the Digital Services Act and the Digital Markets Act, which are intended to deepen privacy protections and hold corporations to high standards for protecting its citizens' data when the laws go into effect by 2024. The consequence, however, is the European Union is isolating its citizens' data from the rest of the world. Concerns about foreign intelligence operations inside democracies can lead to more governmental intervention, but it is important to heed the advice of former US national security leaders who cautioned, "Cyberspace is fundamentally a civilian space—a neighborhood, a library, a marketplace, a school yard, a workshop…the vast majority of cyberspace is a civilian space" (Holl Lute & McConnell, 2011).

If the US government can find a balance between an aggressive surveillance approach to cyberspace and the existing laissez-faire regulatory approach, then the future may side with the vision that cyberspace pioneers had where the Internet is global, governed by good engineering principles, and embraced by individuals. However, if protectionism and national security concerns come to dominate US government actions, then the country may follow a path that leads to isolation, running contrary to the Internet's pioneers' expectations of a globally interconnected set of networks to promote collaboration. These issues will be addressed in Chapter 7 by exploring Internet governance.

6.9 DISCUSSION TOPICS

1. How does a country's political culture affect a government's approach to regulating cyberspace within its borders?
2. What are the implications of global supply chains for information technology on national security?
3. What are the principal ways governments attempt to regulate cyberspace?
4. How are information and communications technology companies responding to governments' efforts to intervene in cyberspace?

7

Internet Governance and International Institutions

[I]n order both to capture the upsides of technology but also to deal with the downsides there is a number one imperative in working together. No single country – whether it's the United States, whether it's Germany – can actually effectively meet these challenges alone. There's a premium, more than at any time since I've been engaged in these issues – and it's now coming on 30 years – for finding ways to cooperate, to coordinate. And that is no more true than when it comes to technology, when it comes to the digital world we're living in.

Secretary of State Blinken (2022)

WHILE THE INTERNET is decentralized by design, Chapter 6 highlighted how governments' traditional sovereignty concerns and regulation are hindering unfettered access to cyberspace. This is unfortunate since global fiber-optic networks have enabled communication in an unprecedented manner, connecting people in unique ways, propelling global supply chains, and giving consumers access to a variety of data from around the planet. As of 2022, about two-thirds of the world's population used the Internet on a regular basis (Internet World Stats, 2022).

The internetworking of networks that connect the world's population within and across societies holds tremendous implications for economic growth and development, particularly for impoverished areas as Secretary Blinken told leaders of the 20 richest countries in the world (G20), as reflected in this chapter's epigraph. The Internet gives countries the potential to overcome the challenges of being landlocked or geographically isolated from the developed core countries in North America, Europe, and East Asia. Starlink (Mann et al., 2022), and other space-based internet service providers, will further connect the disconnected; interconnecting societies at the individual level has important benefits for every person, organization, commercial enterprise, and government. Despite the real and future value of the Internet, no central authority or organization manages the Internet or directs its benefits.

Early internet governance was highly decentralized, and technologists were the main contributors. They focused on technical rules for packet switching and naming conventions to ensure the efficient flow of data discussed in Chapter 3. The Internet Engineering Task Force (IETF) continues to be a vehicle to improve the Internet through shared governance to address technical issues. But as Chapter 6 suggests, a country's political system and regime type are driving domestic regulation that may limit users' privacy and speech and assert sovereignty through data localization laws or accessible encryption. These measures have been a reaction to the Internet's capacity to empower individuals that caused many governments to become alarmed by activists seeking democratic change or criminals evading laws.

If they have the chance, many governments will prefer to limit the free flow of information and ideas in the name of social stability or economic protectionism. This would have negative consequences for individuals, businesses, and the scientific community. Researcher Jason Healey offered a caricature of this possible future, evoking the historic analogy of the Balkan Peninsula in southeastern Europe where multiple empires bordered and later gave rise to the multiethnic state of Yugoslavia in 1918 that later fragmented through civil war in 1991. For Healey (2011), "In the Balkanization future, different actors in cyberspace – predominantly, nations – would build sovereignty and borders so that there would no longer be a single Internet, but a collection of smaller Internets."

Balkanization or fragmentation is in part driven by a new era of internet governance since the set of stakeholders expanded beyond technologists to include information and communications technology (ICT) companies, civil society, governments, and intergovernmental organizations. At the same time, internet governance issues expanded beyond domain name services, email server protocols, and exchangeable file formats. Regulation by governments described in Chapter 6 is leading to a splintered internet. This is a reaction both to the malicious activity on the Internet and to governments' desires for technical and content control. Since the Internet is intertwined with society, it is unsurprising that governments are engaging in internet governance under the guise of public security and online safety. Governments' increasing roles in cyberspace create the need to move internet governance beyond technical agreements and find policy solutions through international institutions, as one of the Internet's pioneers Vinton Cerf asserted.

With few exceptions, most of the public policy issues associated with the Internet lie outside the purview of ICANN [Internet Corporation for Assigned Names and Numbers] and can and should be addressed in different venues. For example, spam, and its instant messaging and Internet telephony relatives ... are pernicious practices that may only be successfully addressed through legal means, although there are some technical measures that can be undertaken by Internet Service Providers (ISPs) and end users to filter out the unwanted messages. Similarly, fraudulent practices such as 'phishing' and 'pharming' may best be addressed through legal means. Intellectual property protection may, in part, be addressed through the World Intellectual Property Organization (WIPO) and business disputes through the World Trade Organization (WTO) or through alternative dispute resolution methods such as mediation and arbitration. (Quoted in Kapur & United Nations Development Programme, 2005)

Domestic regulation or nontechnical internet governance policies fuel internet fragmentation, but as Cerf notes, existing international organizations can address the gap between technology and policy. Governments, organizations, companies, and individuals are working together to reduce cyber insecurity through multilateral and multistakeholder ways. (Multistakeholder governance is discussed later.) In fact, 60 countries came together in 2022 with "A Declaration for the Future of the Internet." The countries specifically underscored the importance of a global Internet that is a "single interconnected communications system for all of humanity" and advocated a "multistakeholder approach to avoid Internet fragmentation" (White House, 2022).

Additionally, there tends to be global agreement on combatting criminal activity in cyberspace. Further, countries within the European Union have embraced the open nature of cyberspace and passed several laws preventing data localization and empowering users relative to corporations to protect its citizens' privacy. Finally, the North Atlantic Treaty Organization (NATO) took up the question of when cyberattacks constitute a use of force and justify the use of force in self-defense under Article 51 of the UN Charter (Charter of the United Nations, n.d.). These ideas arise in the context of internet governance, which is no longer solely focused on technical questions related to protocols but also on cybersecurity, civil liberties, and international cooperation or conflict.

Policy Matters 7.1 Internet governance levels

Internet governance exists on many levels.

- Infrastructure level: to address interconnections among telecommunication companies, internet service providers, and governments
- Logical level: to address the domain name system, Internet Protocol allocation and numbers, and protocol standards
- Content level: to address pollution control (spam), cybercrime, intellectual property rights, and data movement

7.1 EVOLUTION OF INTERNET GOVERNANCE

In 1986 the IETF began as "a forum for technical coordination by [DARPA] contractors for ... working on the ARPANET... and the Internet core gateway system" (Internet Engineering Task Force, n.d.). Today "[t]he IETF is a loosely self-organized group of people who contribute to the engineering and evolution of Internet technologies. It is the principal body engaged in the development of new Internet standard specifications." These standards are defined in documents that are called Request for Comments, a name that was first used in 1969 by Steve Crocker, a graduate student at the University of California, Los Angeles, at the time for unofficial notes on ARPANET.

The nonprofit Corporation for National Research Initiatives (CNRI), founded by Robert Kahn in 1986, operated the Secretariat for the IETF after its creation. CNRI also led the formation and early funding of the Internet Society (ISOC), whose mission is to work for "an open, globally-connected, secure, and trustworthy Internet for everyone" (The Internet Society, n.d.). Today ISOC is the corporate home of the IETF LLC.

The IETF welcomes all interested parties and functions in a multistakeholder fashion but does not have members. It publishes *The Tao of the IETF: A Novice's Guide to the Internet Engineering Task Force* (n.d.), which cites the IETF Guidelines for Conduct that explain the IETF informal governance system. The guidelines are summarized as follows:

1. IETF participants always extend respect and courtesy to their colleagues.
2. They have impersonal discussions.
3. They devise solutions for the global Internet that meet the needs of diverse technical and operational environments.
4. Individuals are prepared to contribute to the ongoing work of the group.

The World Wide Web Consortium (W3C, 2022) operates in a similar manner but differs in three ways. First, its focus is on technology that supports building web pages and the production of web technology. Second, it does have a membership of individuals, nonprofits, corporations, governmental entities, and universities. Finally, membership is fee-based. W3C is jointly administered by MIT Computer Science and Artificial Intelligence Laboratory in the United States, the European Research Consortium for Informatics and Mathematics in France, Keio University in Japan, and Beihang University in China.

As discussed in Chapter 3, the Internet is composed of independently run networks (autonomous systems) linked through standard protocols (e.g., Transmission Control Protocol/Internet Protocol, or TCP/IP) so that, for example, a user in Shanghai can access a website in Boston. To make this possible, early decisions on internet governance focused on assigning IP addresses to devices as well as IDs for the autonomous systems. This facilitated internetworking. Computer scientist Jon Postel originally managed the Internet Assigned Numbers Authority (IANA), which is now part of the ICANN – a global multistakeholder organization that coordinates the internet domain name system and the IANA process.

While the Internet matured globally in the 1990s, the United States and mostly US-based computer scientists and engineers still dominated decision-making; web protocols and standards created in the United States became universalized as the Internet spread. From its beginning, the Internet flourished in this manner, but as it became internationalized, there was a growing demand to broaden who was involved in internet governance. This parallels discussions in traditional diplomatic circles in part to reactions to the 1999 NATO war for Kosovo and the 2003 US-led coalition of the invasion of Iraq. Countries such as Brazil, Russia, India, China, and South Africa argued that the United States played too large a role in global affairs (irresponsibly) and sought various ways to throttle US foreign policy activism; Internet governance became one way to dilute US hegemony.

At the 2005 World Summit on the Information Society (WSIS), held in Tunisia, discussions broadened beyond technical considerations and the narrow group involved in internet governance. WSIS defined internet governance as "the development and application by governments, the private sector and civil society, in their respective roles, of shared principles, norms, rules, decision-making procedures, and programmes that shape the evolution and use of the Internet" (WSIS, 2005). Harvard political scientist Joseph Nye, Jr. (2014) observed that some of the issues concerning internet governance include: domain name system/standards, crime, war/sabotage, espionage, privacy, content control, and human rights. Science and technology think tank analyst Daniel Castro and think tank president Robert Atkinson added equity, access, and architecture-based IP rights enforcement to Nye's list (Castro & Atkinson, 2014).

International security think tank scholar James Lewis sees an uncertain evolution for internet governance. Lewis (2013) wrote,

[T]he source of legitimacy in the existing governance model was technical expertise. This is now being displaced by political processes. While the current, informal multi-stakeholder model must be transformed ... [w]hat will replace these processes remain(s) unclear ... [T]here is real risk that any transition could lead to an Internet that is less free ... innovative and ... valuable to the nations of the world.

Castro and Atkinson (2014) remind that national efforts that undermine global internet governance come from different national priorities and countries

---

History Matters 7.1 IANA

On March 26, 1972, Vint Cerf and Jon Postel called for establishing a socket number catalog, which became a registry of assignments of port numbers to network services. In December 1988, Postel and Joyce K. Reynolds referred to this registry as the IANA. Funded by DARPA, IANA managed a key part of the Internet's infrastructure overseeing global IP address assignments to regional internet registries, autonomous system number allocation and top-level domain allocation, and the root zone management of the domain name system. During 1999–2000, IANA became an operating unit of the ICANN, which contracted with the Department of Commerce, illustrating an important shift from national security to commercial value.

Responding to the Snowden disclosures in 2013, internet technical infrastructure leaders met in Montevideo and "called for accelerating the globalization of ICANN and IANA functions, towards an environment in which all stakeholders, including all governments, participate on an equal footing" (ICANN, 2013). In 2016, ICANN became a not-for-profit corporation, no longer bound by a contract with the Department of Commerce but dedicated to "keeping the Internet secure, stable, and interoperable" (*ICANN History Project – ICANN*, n.d.).

---

projecting national values internationally. It is largely Western scientific principles and laissez-faire economic principles that underlie internet standards and protocols, but countries such as China, Russia, India, and others described in Chapter 6 seek greater government control of both traffic and content. Scholar Shoshana Zuboff observed, "Right now we have two versions of the Internet — a market-led capitalist version based on surveillance, which is exploitative [for commercial purposes]; and an authoritarian version also based on surveillance [for political purposes]" (quoted in Murgia & Gross, 2020). Both versions stray from the ideal of the Internet's founders that wanted cyberspace to to be a place where researchers can collaborate and the best ideas can flourish for the benefit of humanity.

As outlined in History Matters Box 7.1, after US intelligence contractor Edward Snowden's disclosures of surveillance activities by US and British intelligence, these concerns came to a head when leading internet organizations met in Montevideo, Uruguay, in 2013 to explore multistakeholder internet governance and move beyond a US-centric model. They "identified the need for (an) ongoing effort to address Internet governance challenges and agreed to catalyze community-wide efforts towards the evolution of global multi-stakeholder Internet cooperation" (ICANN, 2013). This was a clear assault on the US-dominated Internet in part reaction to frustration with US foreign policy and China's goal to counter US hegemony.

The governance debate largely separated into two camps. The first camp, dominated by the United States and other advanced democratic-capitalist societies, endorsed a multistakeholder model – one in which internet policy is set collectively by representatives from technology, business, and public policy sectors. The second camp, dominated by China, Russia, and other governments skeptical of US foreign policy, favored a nation-state grounded approach, turning control of internet governance over to the United Nations under the auspices of the International Telecommunications Union (ITU). The situation has largely stabilized and there is now an implicit agreement that a multistakeholder governance model is essential, but the two tracks largely continue in parallel since the discussion of internet governance is shaped by strategic rivalry between the United States and its allies on the one hand and China on the other, illustrated by China's floating of a replacement for the TCP/IP protocols, dubbed New IP (Hoffmann et al., 2020), discussed in Chapter 6.

7.1.1 Multistakeholder Model

In general, multistakeholder governance offers a framework for engagement on policies that affect the architecture and users of cyberspace. ICANN (2019) enshrined this approach in its bylaws where the organization is guided by "multistakeholder policy development processes that are led by the private sector (including business stakeholders, civil society, the technical community, academia, and end users), while duly taking into account the public policy advice of governments and public authorities." This multistakeholder approach enshrined the principle of decentralization of the Internet with no single individual or organization responsible for internet governance but created processes where stakeholders can put forth proposals that a community can address.[1] A stakeholder can be a person, group, organization, or government with an interest in a specific subject.

---

[1] Lawrence E. Strickling (2013), then administrator of the National Telecommunications & Information Administration in the US Department of Commerce, saw the importance of the multistakeholder governance:

> The Internet has flourished because of the approach taken from its infancy to resolve technical and policy questions. Known as the multi-stakeholder process, it involves the full involvement of all stakeholders, consensus-based decision-making and operating in

Through a multistakeholder model and Request for Comments process, differences among users, corporations, and governments have often been bridged. This led to recommendations that became de facto standards only after enough companies adopted them and began to ship hardware and software that met these standards, and customers bought them.

While, in principle, all stakeholders may participate in the multistakeholder model on equal footing in open, transparent, and accountable ways, many multistakeholder groups rely on informal rules. Thus, although the goal may be consensus, a multistakeholder process may lead to either failure or undesirable outcomes, which may adversely affect the reputation of an organization. Without formal rules, binding decisions may be difficult to reach, and decisions may not be made in an orderly fashion. Also, when rules for the conduct of meetings are not explicit the chair of a meeting has much more authority than may be prudent. Thus, it is not advisable for the important matter of internet governance to be managed in a multistakeholder fashion unless rules for the conduct of business are explicit and approved by participants in advance (Savage & McConnell, 2015).

7.2 ROLE OF UNITED NATIONS

The United Nations was conceived by European and American leaders during World War II as a means to prevent World War III. It was intended to be the backbone of international politics where the victors of World War II (the United States, the Union of Soviet Socialist Republics, the United Kingdom, France, Nationalist China, and other allies) would cooperate to protect international security (Weiss et al., 2019). US president Franklin D. Roosevelt was the driving force behind the United Nations and coined its name, hoping that the world's powers could set aside national differences and approaches to governance for the sake of peace. Early in World War II, allied governments captured the role of insecurity in uniting nations: "The only true basis of enduring peace is the willing cooperation of free peoples in a world in which, relieved of the menace of aggression, all may enjoy economic and social security; It is our intention to work together, and with other free peoples, both in war and peace, to this end" (Allied Powers, 1941). Yet, the organization quickly fell victim to divisions created by competing political systems that produced gridlock,

an open, transparent and accountable manner. The multi-stakeholder model has promoted freedom of expression, both online and off. It has ensured the Internet is a robust, open platform for innovation, investment, economic growth and the creation of wealth throughout the world, including in developing countries.

endemic to the Cold War, between the United States and the Union of Soviet Socialist Republics (Boutros-Ghali, 1992).

Nevertheless, the UN organizations and committees have made important contributions to international cooperation. These include organizations such as the World Health Organization and the International Atomic Energy Agency, which make substantive contributions to global health and arms control. There are specialized agencies that coordinate through the UN Economic and Social Council, which facilitates global transactions such as the Universal Postal Union, the International Civil Aviation Organization, and the International Maritime Organization. The ITU has emerged as an important multistakeholder forum for cybersecurity.

7.2.1 International Telecommunications Union

Headquartered in Geneva, Switzerland, the ITU was founded in 1865, a century before the Internet was created, to promote cooperation in international telegraphy after Samuel Morse and others proved that it is possible to use electricity to communicate. It standardized the use of Morse code for communication, regulated radiotelegraph (wireless) communications, and established country codes for international phone calling (e.g., 1 for the United States, 33 for France, and 86 for the People's Republic of China). In 2019, the ITU consolidated its texts and constitution considering the widespread use of digital communications. ITU secretary general Houlin Zhao wrote, "As industries and technologies converge, new market structures, business models, investment strategies and revenue streams emerge, there is a need to strengthen the role of ITU as the leading global platform for transformative technologies" (Foreword in ITU, 2019). This view generally reflects the policy of the Chinese Communist Party, which sees itself in an important role in shaping cyberspace through regulation and promoting the nation-state as the central authority for internet governance. In 2023, an American succeeded Zhao and this will be a good area to analyze on how the agenda and approach to internet governance changes.

Russia first put information security on the UN agenda in 1998, but this call was largely ignored by countries in Europe, North America, and East Asia who opted for a laissez-faire approach to the growing internet industries. At the time, those governments saw the Internet as a nascent commercial and economic space, with little consideration for its national security implications, and did not want government regulation to stifle innovation. Russia, with its history of state-owned enterprises and public surveillance, had different ideas. Its UN resolution "[c]all[ed] upon Member States to promote at multilateral levels the consideration of existing and potential threats in the field of information security" (Brunner, 2020, p. 70).

In 2002, the UN General Assembly called for a world summit on the information society. Meetings were convened in 2003 in Geneva, in 2005 in Tunis, and subsequently on an annual basis in Geneva. The group linked its activities to the UN sustainable development goals to help "people achieve their potential, promote sustainable economic and social development, and improve the quality of life" (Utsumi, 2002). The United States does see value in multilateralism in cyberspace and seeks to strengthen core internet principles, as reflected in a statement by Deputy Secretary of State John J. Sullivan (2019): "We as an international community must come together to mainstream and make universal well-established standards for state behavior in cyberspace and hold accountable those who transgress them."

The key challenge facing the United States and other democratic governments is preventing authoritarian governments from using international organizations to subvert the free and open Internet in favor of an Internet dominated by political control of content. Scholar Adam Segal (2020), in testimony before the US–China Economic Security Review Commission, said, "China envisions a world of national internets, with government control justified by the sovereign rights. Beijing also wants to weaken the bottom-up, private-sector-led model of internet governance, known as the multi-stakeholder approach, championed by the United States and its allies." Annual meetings in Geneva provide one venue to promote these ideas.

Additionally, there are two ongoing processes examining the issue of cybersecurity through the United Nations. The Group of Governmental Experts (GGE) has been meeting regularly since 2004; the second process began in 2019 as the Open-Ended Working Group (OEWG), with the goal "to further develop the rules, norms and principles of responsible behaviour of States," a mission similar to that of the GGEs (United Nations, 2018, p. 27). The OEWG differs from the GGEs in that it is open to every UN member whereas the first six GGE committees had between 15 and 25 member states, and the seventh, also launched in 2019, has 25 members. The GGE and OEWG are explored in greater depth in Chapter 8.

While the mission statements of the OEWG and the GGEs are similar, the OEWG is a bit broader. Because the OEWG was proposed by the Russian Federation whereas the seventh GGE was proposed by the United States, there is a risk that their recommendations may diverge, particularly on the "applicability of the principles of international humanitarian law, ... [which was absent] in the establishment of the OEWG" (Ruhl et al., 2020). As legal scholar Michael Schmitt (2020) wrote, "Clearly, the BRICS [Brazil, Russia, India,

China, and South Africa] countries see international law as a shield against interference by other States, an approach that some other countries view as an effort to avoid condemnation of their compliance with human rights norms." The concerns were well-founded since international humanitarian law was largely missing from the OEWG report released in 2021 (O'Sullivan, 2021).

While the United Nations is a multilateral organization made up of sovereign governments, the ITU sees itself as a multistakeholder governance organization and advocates for a central role in the Internet's future. The ITU argues that its membership is globally representative by virtue of its member states, regional seats that are occupied by governments, and its approximately 1,000 sector members and associates. Bilel Jamoussi, the Tunisian-born head of the ITU's study groups department, captured the diversification of internet governance discussions: "The pendulum has swung to the east, and now we see more participation from China, Japan, Korea," he says. "Twenty years ago, it was Europe and North America that were dominating the products, solutions and standards development, now we have a swing to the east" (quoted in Murgia & Gross, 2020). In many respects, this discussion parallels decades-old discussions on individual rights versus community stability. What is different this time, however, is that there has been a steady decline in democracy around the world and individuals steadily lose privacy and individual rights while online.

Although the United Nations and the ITU operate in democratically organizational ways, countries such as the United States see the United Nations and its bodies dominated (even contaminated) by nondemocratic countries, which dilutes US power and influence. A Department of State official told a UN audience,

It is fair to say that the model of an open and interoperable internet, driven by the multistakeholder approach, is facing challenges by those that are threatened by the benefits it can bring. ... We must work with other countries to find interoperable solutions, because a fragmented Internet with unpredictable rules will frustrate innovation, limit the reach of its benefits, and result in unnecessarily bureaucratic processes and regulations. (Strayer, 2019)

As an illustration of this point, the People's Republic of China blocks Taiwan from membership in the United Nations even though Taiwan is a major producer of ICT. Beijing views Taiwan as a renegade province that should be excluded from international bodies and actively undermines any claims that Taipei is a sovereign entity.

Other differences on international security have generally led to the United States being outvoted in the UN General Assembly and its bodies, in addition to frequently needing to rely on its veto through the Security Council. Consequently, countries such as the United States, the United Kingdom, and

> ### Exploit 7.1 International cybercriminal ring's use of botnets
>
> "Between December 2015 and October 2018," several individuals operated a purported advertising network … and carried out [a] … digital ad fraud scheme. … [T]he defendants developed an intricate infrastructure of command-and-control servers to direct and monitor … infected computers and check whether a particular infected computer had been flagged by cybersecurity companies as associated with fraud. By using this infrastructure, the defendants accessed more than 1.7 million infected computers … and used hidden browsers on those infected computers to download fabricated webpages and load ads onto those fabricated webpages. Meanwhile, the owners of the infected computers were unaware that this process was running in the background on their computers. As a result of this scheme, … [they] falsified billions of ad views and caused businesses to pay more than $29 million for ads that were never actually viewed by real human internet users. (U.S. Attorney's Office, Eastern District of New York, 2018)
>
> "The charges [by the US Department of Justice] include wire fraud, computer intrusion, aggravated identity theft and money laundering." Arrests were made in Malaysia, Bulgaria, and Estonia "pursuant to provisional arrest warrants issued at the request of the United States" (U.S. Attorney's Office, Eastern District of New York, 2018).

Japan advocate a different approach that is inclusive but protects the free flow of data, rule of law, intellectual property protections, and civil liberties in cyberspace. While leaders want to deny creating a new Cold War between authoritarian and democratic states, the competition that has emerged within internet governance clearly resembles the ideological rivalry between the United States and Soviet Union from 1945 to 1991.

7.3 OTHER INTERNATIONAL AGREEMENTS

While there are concerted efforts to create broad agreements on internet governance, there have been several successes beyond technical standards. There has been significant cooperation fighting cybercrime to include data breaches leading to fraud and intellectual property theft, which undercuts innovation. While open globally, these treaties originated at a regional level through the Council of Europe to address cybercrime, racism and xenophobia, and child exploitation in cyberspace. Consequently, nations that did not participate in crafting these treaties are less interested in signing them. Although, there is interest in arms control agreements in cyberspace, negotiations have not yet yielded the equivalent requirements that exist for biological, chemical, conventional, and nuclear weapons to limit development, use, and stockpiling of those weapons.

7.3.1 Cybercrime

The Convention on Cybercrime or the Budapest Convention on Cybercrime was a milestone in international cooperation. Signed in 2001, it is the first international treaty addressing cybercrime. It was drafted by the Council of Europe with the active participation of Canada, Japan, the Philippines, South Africa, and the United States. When he transmitted the treaty to the US Senate for ratification, President George W. Bush wrote:

By providing for broad international cooperation in the form of extradition and mutual legal assistance, the Cybercrime Convention would remove or minimize legal obstacles to international cooperation that delay or endanger U.S. investigations and prosecutions of computer-related crime. As such, it would help deny "safe havens" to criminals, including terrorists, who can cause damage to U.S. interests from abroad using computer systems. At the same time, the Convention contains safeguards that protect civil liberties and other legitimate interests. (White House, 2003)

The convention recognizes that nation-states are the first line of defense concerning the control of undesirable content, such as spam or child exploitation. Consequently, governments that ratify the treaty should align their domestic laws

to deter action directed against the confidentiality, integrity and availability of computer systems, networks and computer data as well as the misuse of such systems, networks and data by providing for the criminalisation of such conduct, as described in this Convention, and the adoption of powers sufficient for effectively combating such criminal offences, by facilitating their detection, investigation and prosecution at both the domestic and international levels and by providing arrangements for fast and reliable international co-operation. (CoE, 2001)

The treaty's intent is to harmonize domestic laws to facilitate international cooperation against fraud, copyright infringement, and other crimes using digital devices. As a matter of policy, the United States encourages countries to accede to the treaty. President Obama's secretary of state John Kerry said, "There is no better legal framework for working across borders to define what cybercrime is and how breaches of the law should be prevented and prosecuted" (Office of the Coordinator for Cyber Issues (S/CCI), 2015). Australia "considers it to be the best practice model in framing domestic and international responses to cybercrime" (UN Office on Drugs and Crime, 2018). Despite these favorable remarks, others have expressed reservations about the treaties, as indicated in Policy Matters 7.2.

Policy Matters 7.2 Objections to the Cybercrime Treaty

While the United States ratified the Cybercrime Treaty in 2006, there was significant domestic opposition from those who feared the treaty would undermine civil liberties. In particular, the American Civil Liberties Union articulated seven reasons to reject the treaty.

1. The treaty lacks privacy and civil liberties protections.
2. The treaty is far too broad since it would address any crime that can be computerized.
3. The treaty lacks a "dual criminality" requirement for US cooperation with foreign police.
4. Protection for political activities is too weak.
5. The treaty threatens to further unbalance US intellectual property law.
6. The treaty would give police invasive new surveillance powers.
7. The treaty was drafted in a closed and secretive manner.

Source: American Civil Liberties Union (2003)

Russia opposed the treaty in large part because it views the treaty's transborder Article 32b to permit a violation of sovereignty. The article allows a party to the treaty (a state authority) in one country to obtain "stored computer data" from a person in another country if that person has "lawful authority to disclose the data to that Party through that computer system (CoE, 2001)."

While it is the first treaty of its kind, Harvard law professor Jack Goldsmith (2011) thinks it "is widely viewed as unsuccessful… with vague definitions… that [were] further diluted [at the national level] making the treaty's obligations…less demanding." As of 2023, 68 countries have ratified this treaty and there continues to be a diplomatic effort to promote acceding to it despite the treaty's flaws.

7.3.2 Racism and Xenophobia in Cyberspace

While the Convention on Cybercrime was adopted, it was considered incomplete. Initial discussion of the agreement included efforts to combat racism and xenophobia on the Internet. However, the United States objected on its own constitutional grounds:

The United States deplores racism and xenophobia, and the violence and other harmful conduct that racist and xenophobic groups often seek to foster. The United States also supports dialogue among Internet users, providers, and others regarding racist and xenophobic content. However, as the Report suggests, there are a number of factors – legal, as well as political, ethical, and technological – that would impose significant constraints on the implementation of any provision restricting racist and xenophobic content on the Internet. Foremost among these factors for the United States is our Constitution's protection of freedom of speech and expression.[2]

The 2003 Protocol to the Cybercrime Treaty defined *racist and xenophobic material* as "any written material, any image or any other representation of ideas or theories, which advocates, promotes or incites hatred, discrimination or violence, against any individual or group of individuals, based on race, colour, descent or national or ethnic origin, as well as religion if used as a pretext for any of these factors" (Council of Europe, 2003). Like the Budapest Convention, this protocol requires each government to adopt the necessary domestic laws to enforce this treaty and establish criminal penalties for its citizens who intentionally violate this law. Only about one-half of the parties that ratified the Budapest Convention ratified this additional protocol, but it was considered an important step by the Council of Europe to expand these prohibitions from society to cyberspace.

7.3.3 Convention on the Protection of Children against Sexual Exploitation and Sexual Abuse

In 2007, the Council of Europe came together to enhance protections for children, who are defined as under 18 years of age. Known as the Lanzarote Convention, this treaty is comprehensive and larger than that for cybercrime, the treaty does prohibit the use of ICT to access child pornography, to distribute child pornography, or to solicit children for sexual purposes over the Internet. All 46 Member States of the Council of Europe have ratified it. The treaty is open to non-European states; Tunisia became the first non-European State to accede to it.

7.3.4 Calls for Arms Control Treaty

Chapter 8 examines the application of existing international law in cyberspace and the growth of international norms to restrict governments' behaviors in cyberspace, but there currently is neither a cyber weapon ban nor a cyber weapon treaty. However, there is a growing chorus to adopt an agreement

---

[2] Letter from US Department of Justice assistant attorney generals Ralph F. Boyd, Jr., and Michael Chertoff to the chairman of the Council of Europe. Published in Murphy (2002).

to restrict military uses of cyberspace operations and destructive malware (Schneider, 2020).

Former White House advisor Richard Clarke and researcher Robert Knake (2011) called for a cyber war limitation treaty to ban first use of cyber weapons. British academic Rex Hughes (2010) argues that "the complete absence of any meaningful regulation or treaty infrastructure leaves the way open for a digital 'war against all.'" US Air Force officer Benjamin Hatch (2018) states, "While the greater issue of cyber is vast and complex, limiting it at present to the destructive potential of specific cyber weapons affords the opportunity to focus on the most dangerous malicious code." Law professor Ido Kilovaty (2015) extends the concern to economic cyber warfare as it "can represent a new form of warfare, with suffering of innocents involved and potential substantial harm to physical objects, it is time to rethink the dated distinction between physical, economic and political harms, and redraw the boundaries of the use of force framework." According to political scientist Joseph Nye, Jr. (2015), "Whenever countries confront a disruptive new technology that they cannot control, they eventually seek arms-control agreements."

The Russian government in fact did this at the United Nations in 1999 when it called for restraint in cyberspace as the country was significantly behind other countries and had well-developed doctrine on information warfare from its Soviet past. Among its proposed principles are the following:

The United Nations and ... agencies ... shall promote international cooperation for the purpose of limiting threats in the ... field of international information security and creating, for that purpose, an international legal basis to:
(a) Identify the defining features of information wars and to classify them; (b) Identify the characteristic features of information weapons, and of tools that may be regarded as information weapons, and to classify them; (c) Restrict traffic in information weapons; (d) Prohibit the development, dissemination or use of information weapons; (e) Prevent the threat of the outbreak of information wars; (f) Recognize the danger of using information weapons against vital structures as being comparable to the threat of use of weapons of mass destruction; (g) Create conditions for the equitable and safe international exchange of information based on the generally recognized rules and principles of international law; (h) Prevent the use of information technologies and tools for terrorist or other criminal purposes; (i) Prevent the use of information technologies and tools to influence social consciousness in order to destabilize society and the State; (j) Develop a procedure for the exchange of information on and the prevention of unauthorized transboundary influence through information; (k) Create an international monitoring system for tracking threats that may arise in the information field; (l) Create a mechanism for monitoring compliance with the conditions of the international information security regime; (m) Create a mechanism to resolve conflict situations in the area of information security; (n) Create an international system for the certification of information and telecommunications technologies and tools (including software and hardware) with a view to guaranteeing

their information security; (o) Develop a system of international cooperation among law enforcement agencies with a view to preventing and suppressing crime in the information area; (p) Harmonize, on a voluntary basis, national legislation in order to ensure information security. (GGE, 1999)

The Russian Federation made a similar proposal a decade later, seeking to "ban a country from secretly embedding malicious codes or circuitry that could be later activated from afar in the event of war" and "would prohibit deception operations in cyberspace" (Gvosdev, 2012).

Russia's actions through its intelligence services clearly illustrate it intends to exploit cyberspace while promoting a diplomatic smokescreen in international institutions, which might explain why its proposal was largely ignored during the Bush administration.

During the Obama administration, however, General Keith Alexander, who was the first commander of US Cyber Command, said,

I do think that we have to establish the rules and I think what Russia's put forward is, perhaps, the starting point for international debate – not at my level, but at levels above me. And I think when they put that on the table, I think the secretary of defense, the secretary of state, the administration would take those, carefully consider those and say: Now, what's the counterproposal from the United States, from China, from Russia, from Europe, from the Middle East? How do we put that on the table? And I think we do have to establish that in the lanes of the road. (Center for Strategic and International Studies (CSIS), 2010)

These ideas certainly penetrated international discussions, but as of 2023, there is no such cyber weapons ban or treaty. Further, Russia's active use of cyberspace for influence operations, cyberspace operations during wars with its neighbors Georgia and Ukraine, and espionage undercut the credibility of its original proposals and the confidence NATO countries would have with any agreements with Russia.

Proponents of a treaty to reduce use of cyber weapons draw from previous and existing arms control agreements that regulate relations among governments; there has been a steady effort to use treaties to preserve peace and reduce human suffering during war. Among these are treaties that ban the use of chemical weapons and biological weapons, limit the size of conventional military and nuclear forces, ban placing weapons on the moon, and commit countries to avoid developing nuclear weapons.

In all cases, good treaties have verification mechanisms to ensure the parties meet their commitments. Former arms control negotiator David Cooper (2021) has argued that in the case of nuclear arms control those treaties with intrusive verification mechanisms (e.g., START-1) are more effective than nonintrusive treaties (SALT-1). For arms control agreements to be effective, the object of verification (OOV) must be large and tangible enough to verify and control. For example, under the 97-page Open Skies Treaty, Russian surveillance aircraft could fly over US territory to facilitate the monitoring of arms control agreements; the same is true for the other signatories who could overfly Russian territory (Organization for Security and Co-operation in Europe, 1992). While the intelligence gained through the overflights have some use, retired Air Force nuclear and missile operations officer Dana Struckman (2022) has argued the agreement is more of a commitment about trust, transparency, and predictability. US withdrawal from the treaty in 2020 will give future researchers an opportunity to test this proposition, but needless to say, arms control agreements have been in steady decline (DoD, 2020b).

When it comes to cyber weapons, there does not appear to be anything comparable to a territorial overflight to surveil military capabilities or to count nuclear warheads or missiles. There is simply no good way to track stored zero-day vulnerabilities let alone peer into highly classified cyberspace operations programs of other countries. This suggests that cyber weapons cannot be effectively controlled through traditional arms control measures. However, the US position on biological weapons control is instructive in that the United States identified these weapons as inherently unverifiable due to their small size, the ubiquity of facilities to make them, and the difficulty in distinguishing defensive and offense biological weapons research. While the biological weapons treaty was signed in 1972, there is a clear historical record of violations (Vestergaard & Roul, 2011). Consequently, the UN Security Council called for restraint at the national level and "decided that all States shall refrain from providing any form of support to non-State actors that attempt to develop, acquire, manufacture, possess, transport, transfer or use nuclear, chemical or biological weapons and their means of delivery" (UN, 2004).

Just like biological weapons, information technology exploits are inherently dual use; penetration testing is a simple example of the use of offensive code to improve cyber defense. If cyber weapons cannot be counted without intrusive disk scans for reputational analyses, an alternative would be confidence-building measures (CBMs) to regulate use. For example, analogies might include the OSCE Vienna Documents (On confidence- and security-building measures, 2011) that regulated things such as prenotification of unusual military activities or the Incidents at Sea Agreement (Incidents at Sea Agreement, 1972) between the US and Soviet navies that established rules to manage dangerously confrontational naval encounters. The Russian Federation noted during the UN OEWG discussions that "confidence-building measures (CBMs) can contribute to preventing conflicts, avoiding misperception and misunderstandings, and providing a 'safety valve' for the reduction of tensions" (OEWG, 2021d). The Organization for Security and Co-operation in Europe issued in 2016 a set of CBMs to reduce the risks of conflict stemming from the use of ICT (OSCE, 2016). Further, if CBMs are used, cyber weapons would likely be analyzed by civilian security researchers who could provide insight into such weapons as well as that of government activities. While such comprehensive agreements may not be obtainable, there are other regional cases that are instructive for international cooperation.

7.4 UNITING SOVEREIGNTY: CASE OF THE NORTH ATLANTIC TREATY ORGANIZATION

With renewed focus on Russia as a threat to Europe since its annexation of Ukrainian territory in 2014 and full-scale war in 2022, its influence operations that interfered with democratic processes around the world, and its assassination operations in Europe, NATO countries have focused their attention on territorial defense. The allies are increasing defense spending to rebuild conventional forces, but they are also addressing critical threats in cyberspace that undermine economic integration and democratic institutions. NATO's approach to addressing cyber insecurity reflects varying members' national security interests and political cultures, yet the alliance provides a unifying vector for countries when it comes to defense, promoting international cooperation, and establishing norms.

Essential Principle 7.1 Collective defense

In 1949, several European and North American countries came together to establish the NATO as a collective defense organization. The collective defense pillar is enshrined in Article 5 of NATO's founding treaty – that the

Parties agree that an armed attack against one or more of them in Europe or North America shall be considered an attack against them all and consequently they agree that, if such an armed attack occurs, each of them, in exercise of the right of individual or collective self-defence recognised by Article 51 of the Charter of the United Nations, will assist the Party or Parties so attacked by taking forthwith, individually and in concert with the other Parties, such action as it deems necessary, including the use of armed force, to restore and maintain the security of the North Atlantic area (NATO, 1949).

7.4.1 The North Atlantic Treaty Organization Policy on Use of Force

An important role of NATO is deterrence through collective defense. Put simply, an adversary like Russia would not attack a NATO member for fear that the NATO alliance would counterattack. This idea has been apparent since NATO's founding in 1949 and there is a relatively clear understanding of how a conventional or nuclear attack against a NATO member could trigger Article 5, which states an attack against one ally is considered an attack against all allies (NATO, 2022). Yet, invocation of Article 5 is exceptional, having occurred just once in history – after the United States suffered attacks from al-Qa'ida in 2001.

The rarity of Article 5 usage and the ambiguity of cyberspace operations posed a challenge when NATO member Estonia requested assistance during a 22-day-long distributed denial-of-service attack in 2007. The attack brought Estonia to a standstill, but there was no consensus on whether it was attacked in a way that would trigger Article 5 (Ottis, 2008). Estonia attributed the attack to Russia, but then Estonian president Toomas Ilves later reflected, "[W]e were met by incredulity on the part of even NATO, saying 'No, no, how do you know [it was Russia]? Can we really be sure? And what does it all mean?'" (quoted in Schultz, 2017), but the event generated a concerted effort to understand if Estonia had been attacked in a legal sense and how the alliance should treat cyber-enabled attacks. The event was a watershed event since it illustrated the intersection of cyberspace operations and interstate rivalry (Valeriano et al., 2018).

Seven years after the Estonia denial-of-service attack, the alliance did recognize a cyberattack *could* be considered a use of force (not necessarily an armed attack) in 2014, echoing Ilves. He said, "Ultimately [it's] the same law if someone shoots a missile at your electrical power plant and destroys it and if someone directs malware there and destroys it. The effect in the context of international law is the same. An aggressor has destroyed something on your territory that is of vital importance to the civilian population" (quoted in Schultz, 2017). We explore this point more deeply in Chapter 8.

To summarize, the focus of discussion should be on the *effect of an action* rather than the way the action was carried out, cyber or otherwise. This shifts the focus from the means of an attack to the consequences. This conclusion has an important effect on internet governance since NATO's interpretation of an attack through cyber means establishes a baseline to interpret future cyberspace operations outside of NATO.

Since the strength of NATO is collective defense, the 2014 Wales Summit Declaration raised the question of when an attack on one could be considered an attack on all. The Allies noted that the "impact [of a cyberattack] could be as harmful to modern societies as a conventional attack...a decision as to when a cyberattack would lead to the invocation of Article 5 would be taken by the North Atlantic Council on a case-by-case basis" (NATO, 2014). NATO secretary general Jens Stoltenberg clarified where cyberattacks fit in NATO defense thinking. He said, "Cyber is now a central part of virtually all crises and conflicts. NATO has made it clear that cyber-attacks can potentially trigger an Article 5 response. We need to detect and counter cyber-attacks early; improve our resilience; and be able to recover quickly" (NATO Secretary General Jens Stoltenberg, 2015). Attribution remains critical as the cyberattack must be attributable to a foreign power.

When considering whether a cyberattack should invoke Article 5, researchers Jason Healey and Klara Jordan offer four compelling questions. First, is the attack widespread geographically or by sector? Is it a single event or of long-term duration? Has the incident caused physical destruction or death? Can it be attributed to a foreign power? In response to an attack, either conventional or cyber, Article 5 invocation is not automatic. Instead, answers to these questions would inform debate and thinking at the North Atlantic Council and national capitals prior to reaching a decision on whether a cyberattack rises to the level of an armed attack worthy of a collective defense response (Healey & Jodan, 2014).

Two years later, at the Warsaw Summit, NATO declared cyberspace a domain of operations like land, air, and sea. Then, in 2017, it established a policy that cyber defense is a core task of collective defense but eschewed incorporating offensive operations into its plans.

While information-sharing is the hallmark of NATO, each ally is responsible for its own cyber defense. But the organization does serve to promote international cooperation. In 2016, NATO countries, as a signal of international cooperation, took this Cyber Defence Pledge:

We reaffirm our national responsibility, in line with Article 3 of the Washington Treaty, to enhance the cyber defences of national infrastructures and networks, and our commitment to the indivisibility of Allied security and collective defence, in accordance with the Enhanced NATO Policy on Cyber Defence adopted in Wales. We will ensure that strong and resilient cyber defences enable the Alliance to fulfil its core tasks. Our interconnectedness means that we are only as strong as our weakest link. We will work together to better protect our networks and thereby contribute to the success of Allied operations. (NATO, 2016)

Additionally, under Article 4 of the North Atlantic Treaty, "The Parties will consult together whenever, in the opinion of any of them, the territorial integrity, political independence or security of any of the Parties is threatened"

(NATO, 1949). In support of this, NATO created a Computer Incident Response Capability to protect NATO's networks and provide 24/7 cyber defense support. It is also promoting information-sharing and best practices, so that every country has better national capabilities. Finally, there are many training and education initiatives. Among these are the NATO Cyber Range and the Cooperative Cyber Defence Centre of Excellence in Estonia, which sponsored the Tallinn Manual on international law discussed in Chapter 8 (Schmitt, 2017a).

7.4.2 Role of the North Atlantic Treaty Organization in Military Operations

In addition to NATO embracing cyber defense as a core function of the alliance, the organization is mirroring its members' national decisions by building cyber capabilities of the alliance. Under NATO's Comprehensive Cyber Policy, the alliance will "employ the full range of capabilities at all times to actively deter, defend against, and counter the full spectrum of cyber threats, including those conducted as part of hybrid campaigns, in accordance with international law" (NATO, 2021). By 2023, NATO plans to operate a Cyber Operations Center in Belgium at the Supreme Headquarters Allied Powers Europe. The new center will provide situational awareness, support cyberspace operational planning for all aspects of allied operations, and promote freedom of maneuver in all domains affected by cyberspace activities. The center is intended to coordinate NATO's cyber activities but has no plans to develop offensive capabilities. This reflects the defensive orientation of the alliance and key members' national policies. However, the allies can contribute their own cyber offensive capabilities for NATO operations and missions or undertake them concurrently with NATO operations (Lewis, 2019).

7.5 OVERCOMING SOVEREIGNTY: CASE OF THE EUROPEAN UNION

In the case of NATO, countries retain sovereignty and pool resources for collective defense. In the case of the European Union, countries share sovereignty through an intergovernmental organization that can dictate national laws. The European Union has been developing since France and Germany agreed on economic cooperation in 1951 when they formed the European Coal and Steel Cooperative. The goal of creating a more integrated Europe is illustrative of states relinquishing some sovereignty to an intergovernmental organization. Over the last 70 years, the organization has evolved to create a single economic market, with some countries replacing national currencies with a single common currency, removing borders to ease the flow of people and goods across the continent, and coordinating foreign policy (Pagden & Hamilton, 2002).

The 27 countries of the European Union represent some of the richest countries in the world and are required by the Union to have stable political institutions to guarantee democracy, the rule of law, human rights, and a functioning market economy (EU, n.d.). In contrast to the US government, which is largely laissez-faire when it comes to the private sector and cybersecurity, the EU has been at the forefront on international cooperation for the benefit of individual citizens who reside in EU countries. Europe draws its strength from the European Commission on Human Rights that is applied in cyberspace with some of the most robust privacy protections in the world.

On May 25, 2018, the General Data Protection Regulation (GDPR) went into effect in EU countries (Bensoussan, 2018). The three guiding principles are: the protection of fundamental privacy rights for individuals, promoting transparency in the way companies process data, and enabling the free movement of data. The first two principles reflect European human rights laws where individuals retain ownership of their data, whereas the third principle is a rebuttal of data localization attempts discussed in Chapter 6. These objectives reflect the European Union as a single economic and political space that transcends sovereignty.

Among the many GDPR provisions, the "right to be forgotten" is one of the most salient. Under Article 17, individuals have the right to direct "the erasure of personal data concerning him or her without undue delay... [where] the personal data are no longer necessary in relation to the purposes for which they were collected or otherwise processed; the data subject withdraws consent ... and there are no overriding legitimate grounds for the processing" (Bensoussan, 2018). Effectively, European users can request a search engine company to delist results that are "no longer relevant" or otherwise outdated. While the individual's data may still reside in a database or on a server somewhere, search companies' removal of the results would give individuals more privacy since the data would not be easily discoverable.

More broadly, the GDPR law is intended to promote transparency and ensure corporations do not unfairly take advantage of users. This is a stark contrast to the United States. As scholar James Joyner (2012) has written:

The United States and United Kingdom conceive of cyber primarily as a national security problem to be handled by the military—which in turn sees the Internet as a fifth domain of war to be dominated. The European Union, by contrast, sees cyber threats mostly as a nuisance for commerce and individual privacy that should be dealt with by civilian authorities in conjunction with private enterprise.

Since it is one of the largest information technology companies in the world, it is unsurprising that Google has been scrutinized under GDPR. France's data protection regulator issued Google a 50 million euro fine for failing to provide users enough information on its data consent policies or failure to give users enough control on how their information is used. Irish regulators accused Google of sharing data with Google's business partners without users' consent. Swedish regulators fined Google for alleged violations of the right to be forgotten. And privacy groups filed complaints alleging Google lacked the legal basis for creating targeted ads. For its part, Google has appealed the alleged violations but noted the seriousness of the law:

Ensuring compliance with the GDPR is an ongoing commitment that involves substantial costs, and despite our efforts, governmental authorities or others have asserted and may continue to assert that our business practices fail to comply with its requirements. If our operations are found to violate GDPR requirements, we may incur substantial fines, have to change our business practices, and face reputational harm, any of which could have a material adverse effect on our business. In particular, serious breaches of the GDPR can result in administrative fines of up to 4% of annual worldwide revenues. (Alphabet Inc, 2020)

Even though GDPR applies to EU citizens and companies doing business in "European cyberspace," Microsoft president Brad Smith was optimistic that the EU privacy standard would become global: "The integrated nature of the global economy and the long reach of Europe's privacy rules will create pressure even on countries like China to adopt strong privacy measures. In other words, Europe is not just the birthplace of democracy and the cradle of privacy protection. It's quite possibly the world's best hope for privacy's future" (Smith & Browne, 2019). The regulation became a model for many national laws and foreshadowed the California Consumer Privacy Act, which went into effect in 2020.

7.6 CONCLUSIONS

The blurring divide between what is an online problem and what is a physical problem, and between what is a human rights issue and what is a technical issue, suggests that internet governance benefits from the participation of governments and intergovernmental organizations, civil society, and the corporate world. For example, intellectual property theft could be addressed through the

World Trade Organization, cybercrime could be addressed through international legal conventions, and privacy could be addressed through the Human Rights Commission. There is still an important need for technical internet governance addressed through organizations such as ICANN and IETF, but internet governance is too important to be left to the internet designers, operators, and telecommunications companies alone.

Technologists have provided societies with unique gifts that connect individuals around the world, expand commercial activities internationally, and improve academic collaboration globally. However, the technical decisions that dominated early internet governance often had social, economic, and political implications and they had unwittingly created gaps in policymaking that fail to address nefarious activities in cyberspace. Thus, technologists, economists, social scientists, politicians, academics, and civil society need to understand that if these categories of stakeholders act independently when making decisions, their actions may have serious unintended consequences for other communities. This chapter offers several models of international cooperation as individuals, companies, nongovernmental organizations, governments, and intergovernmental organizations work together to improve cybersecurity, reinforcing the point that cybersecurity is a team effort.

Cybersecurity, like other contemporary security challenges, such as pandemic diseases, water scarcity, or terrorism, is transnational and requires international cooperation. This reality necessitates internet governance share best security practices, develop acceptable norms of behavior, protect intellectual property and critical infrastructure, cooperate to reduce cybercrime, and ensure continued expansion of access and content. As the chapter makes clear, multistakeholder discussions are important, but they must be organized and executed according to acceptable transparent rules and reconciled with national policies and political culture without undermining basic principles of internet governance and internationally accepted definitions of human rights. Chapter 8 considers how international law and norms can improve cybersecurity.

7.7 DISCUSSION TOPICS

1. Describe the strengths and weaknesses of multistakeholder and multilateral forms of internet governance.
2. Russia submitted United Nations Resolution 53/70 in 1999. Explain what might have been the consequences if the United States had taken the proposal more seriously.

3. What approaches would you propose to arrive at international agreements between the United States, Russia, China, and the European Union? Justify your proposals.
4. Explain and analyze the differences in approach to internet governance taken by the IETF and the United Nations.
5. Explain how you think the rivalry between the United States and China will play out with respect to internet governance issues.

8

International Law and Norms in Cyberspace

We have seen individuals, groups inside critical U.S. infrastructure.
That suggests to us that this vulnerability is an area others want to
exploit," the admiral said. "All of that leads me to believe it is only a
matter of time when, not if, we are going to see something traumatic."
Admiral Michael S. Rogers, Commander, US Cyber Command,
and Director of the National Security Agency
(quoted in Pellerin, 2014)

WITH PERSISTENT VULNERABILITIES in software and the relative impunity with which states, groups, and individuals operate in cyberspace, data breaches will continue resulting in fraud, intellectual property theft, and other disruptions in our information technology-reliant society. Additionally, governments are incorporating cyberspace activities into their national strategies and using cyberspace capabilities as instruments of power in peacetime and prepared to use them in wartime. International law and norms of behavior guide these activities.

If violent and destructive cyberspace operations can be the equivalent of air and missile attacks, it is essential to understand how international law applies in cyberspace. To date, cyberspace operations against the US financial sector and elections, Ukraine's critical infrastructure, Iran's nuclear sector, and Saudi Arabia's energy sector provide ready examples of malware uses that have national and international repercussions. While these are serious illustrations of governments' use of cyberspace operations as tools of power, they did not rise to the level of armed attack and, so far, have been classified as espionage, sabotage, or influence operations. International law and norms play important roles defining these activities as such; they establish thresholds for when they would rise to the level of a use of force and armed attack; law and norms also can limit state behavior if strategic competition gives way to war among major powers.

Harvard Law School professor Lawrence Lessig (1998) reminds us that there are various mechanisms at our disposal to reduce cyber insecurity,

226

such as law that regulates by sanction, social norms that regulate by expectations, economic markets that regulate by cost, and information technology architecture that governs by code and hardware design. Given the low costs associated with cyberspace operations, law and norms are important ways to address when and how governments use cyberspace operations. Likewise, analysis of cyberspace incidents should be done with an understanding that there is a relative state of peace at the international level reinforced by law and norms.

While Chapter 5 discussed the ways that governments are developing cyber commands to incorporate cyber tools and techniques into conventional military planning, international law and norms are guiding governments to harmonize relations bilaterally and multilaterally through regional and intergovernmental organizations. For example, in September 2015, the United States and China agreed not to target commercial entities for economic value to slow down intellectual property theft (Davis & Sanger, 2015). (Note that they did not agree to refrain from targeting military or political entities for national security purposes.) The impact of the US–China agreement was short-lived but illustrated that cooperation and restraint are possible through bilateral negotiation that leads to norms of behavior (Reuters, 2018). And in January 2020, China committed to the United States that it would strengthen domestic criminal law to reduce intellectual property theft through electronic intrusion or improper use of a computer system (G7, 2016). As discussed in Chapter 7, a goal like this can be inspired by international treaties that have the force of law such as the Budapest Convention or a North Atlantic Treaty Organization (NATO) summit, where the allies agreed to improve cyber defense capabilities and offer assistance beyond the military realm (Brent, 2019). These types of actions set expectations, that is, norms, for governments on matters such as information-sharing, assistance in recovery, and improvement in cyberspace security.

There are also other intergovernmental efforts to promote norms that develop through multilateral gatherings. For example, at a G7 summit in 2015, participating governments recognized that cybersecurity is a key component of the global economy through trade, development, and quality infrastructure investment. This group of seven advanced economies declared, "We will take decisive and robust measures in close cooperation against malicious use of cyberspace, both by states and non-state actors, including terrorists" (G7, 2016). Expanding beyond the seven countries, at a G20 summit in 2015 that included China, Russia, and India, governments agreed that nation-state conduct in cyberspace should conform to international law and the UN charter (G20, 2015).

This is significant considering that the G20 organization represents the 19 wealthiest countries in the world, along with the European Union. These efforts parallel the work of the UN Group of Governmental Experts (GGE), which is a set of cyber security experts from a small number of nation-states. The UN group has agreed that no country should intentionally damage the critical infrastructure of another state or impair infrastructure that serves the public and would undermine the human rights guaranteed by the UN Declaration (CCDCOE, 2015). In addition to the GGE, there is also the UN Open-Ended Working Group (OEWG), which concluded in 2021 that malicious activity in cyberspace targeting critical infrastructure "undermines international peace and security, trust and stability between States, and may increase the likelihood of future conflicts between States" (OEWG, 2021b). In other words, the threats to international peace and security are the same whether an attack occurs through land invasion or through cyberspace, thus requiring intergovernmental organizations such as the United Nations to promote cooperation among countries to preserve international peace through law and norms.

In addition to governments' efforts to promote international peace and security, corporations that develop information technology hardware and software are promoting norms, too. These corporations have articulated norms designed to limit destabilizing cyberspace operations by governments and other global information and communications technology (ICT) corporations. The executive chairman of Google's parent company, Alphabet, Eric Schmidt "think[s] getting the governments to agree that we are better off collectively by having a more open internet with less attacking – especially at nation state level – would be a clear improvement for everybody" (Edwards, 2017). Microsoft has promulgated a set of norms "to detect, contain, respond to, and recover from events in cyberspace" (McKay et al., 2014). Furthermore, Microsoft's president and chief legal officer Brad Smith thinks the world actually needs "a Digital Geneva Convention that will commit governments to protecting civilians from nation-state attacks in times of peace...[and the tech sector] should commit ourselves to collective action that will make the internet a safer place, affirming a role as a neutral Digital Switzerland that assists customers everywhere and retains the world's trust" (Smith, 2017) And Germany-based Siemens advocated for a Charter of Trust; the company's global head for industrial cyber and digital security Leo Simonovich said there is a growing need for "a new approach to digital safety and security" (quoted in Buntz, 2019).

We explore these points building on Chapter 7, which made clear that internet governance has moved beyond technical decisions and the base of stakeholders has broadened beyond technologists. To make sense of how this larger group of stakeholders is attempting to promote cybersecurity through international law and norms, this chapter first considers how governments attempt to prevent conflict and control behavior through existing international law. This is important since what occurs in cyberspace is largely a mirror of what occurs in physical space, yet the application of international law is not uncomplicated when governments balance military necessity with international humanitarian law. The chapter then examines norms as ways to restrict behavior through commonly accepted practices rather than law (Finnemore and Sikkink, 1998). Since international institutions such as the United Nations are instrumental in international affairs, we examine past and ongoing efforts to preserve peace by promoting expectations of behavior in cyberspace through two separate UN groups that have been developing norms. Finally, the chapter takes up corporate and nongovernmental efforts to develop and promote norms in cyberspace.

8.1 INTERNATIONAL LAW AND ETHICS

The modern concept of international law is defined as "rules and principles of general application dealing with the conduct of States and of international organizations and with their relations *inter se*, as well as some of their relations with persons, whether natural or juridical."[1] Fundamentally, public international law seeks to promote harmony and reduce conflict through shared ideas on rules of behavior that is legally binding and "governs when an international obligation is breached, the consequences that flow from a breach, and who is able to invoke those consequences" (Borelli, 2017). Implicit in this understanding of international law is that governments are bound by treaties and customs (Wallace & Visger, 2017).

8.1.1 The Evolution of Sovereignty

International law emerged when empires created trade agreements, but its relevance for the modern international system begins with the Treaty of Westphalia in 1648. Concluded among warring European states divided along religious lines, the treaty enshrined the important concepts of sovereignty and nonintervention, where a state had the ultimate authority to rule within its borders free from external interference; it requires that states not interfere in other states' internal affairs.

---

[1] Restatement (Third) of Foreign Relations Law of the United States, § 101 (1987)

The 1933 Montevideo Convention, Article 1 specifies: "The state as a person of international law should possess the following qualifications: (a) a permanent population; (b) a defined territory; (c) a government; and (d) capacity to enter into relations with other states" (Pan American Union, 1933). Thus, sovereignty is understood in international law as one of the benefits of statehood. This is the basis for the ways governments regulate cyberspace within their borders as discussed in Chapter 6 but is also the basis for intergovernmental organizations such as the United Nations to determine membership requirements and responsibilities members have to each other.

International law grew in importance as empires dissolved into nation-states that sought ways to reduce tensions with neighbors and rivals (Janis, 1984). When the United Nations was founded in 1945, for example, there were just 51 member countries. Through decolonization, independence movements, and wars, the number of UN members grew to 193 in 2011 (United Nations, n.d.-c).

While the United Nations is an important intergovernmental organization, it is not an international legislature. Article 38 of the Statute of the International Court of Justice (IJC) identifies the sources of international law as international conventions (treaties), general principles of law recognized by civilized nations, and established customs practiced by states over time (Statute of the International Court of Justice, 1945). The latter is called customary international law. Today, there are more widely accepted sources of international law such as judicial decisions by the IJC and other international tribunals, acts of international organizations such as UN Security Council resolutions, transnational public regulations also known as global administrative law, and other sources (Damrosch, 2019).

An important customary law that became enshrined in a treaty is freedom of the seas. Dutch philosopher Hugo Grotius argued in his early seventeenth-century book *Mare liberum* that governments would benefit from unfettered trade by treating the oceans as a passage instead of a place. Since he published his book in 1609, governments have embraced the concept of freedom of the seas enshrining the principle "every nation is free to travel to every other nation, and to trade with it" (Grotius, 1916). Instead of sovereign control of the oceans, governments are responsible for removing obstructions to its use (e.g., pirates or excessive maritime claims by states). The idea was enshrined in the 1982 UN Convention of the Law of the Sea and created distinct areas known as territorial seas, contiguous zone, exclusive economic zone, and continental shelf over which coastal states have different rights, while leaving the high seas open to all states (United Nations, 1994). Some have argued that a similar idea should be applied to cyberspace, seeing it not as a place that has territoriality that can be regulated but as a passage or trade route and thus viewing cyberspace as a global common preserved by states (Hildebrandt, 2013; Hoffman & Levite, 2017; Thumfart, 2020). This view simultaneously recognizes cyberspace as everywhere and sees an important role for governments to ensure cyberspace functions well by restraining from disruptive behavior, controlling malicious actors that operate within their borders, and working together to keep the common of cyberspace open and safe.

The United Nations can play an important role in coordinating states' actions and in developing international law, as noted in the preamble to its charter: The organization exists to "establish conditions under which justice and respect for the obligations arising from treaties and other sources of international law can be maintained." Further, in 1947, the UN General Assembly established the International Law Commission "to promote the progressive development of international law and its codification" (United Nations, n.d.-a). Formalized agreements such as the Geneva Conventions (1949) and the Additional Protocols play important roles determining when states can legally go to war (*jus ad bellum*) and how states should behave in armed conflicts (*jus in bello*) (International Committee of the Red Cross, 2016). In the event of hostilities among countries with cyber commands, these principles would undoubtedly come into play.

The UN Security Council is particularly important in discussions of international law and war. It is composed of five permanent members (People's Republic of China, France, Russian Federation, the United Kingdom, and the United States) and ten nonpermanent members elected on a rotating basis. Article 24 of the United Nation's charter states that its members "confer on the Security Council primary responsibility for the maintenance of international peace and security," and in Article 25, members "agree to accept and carry out the decisions of the Security Council in accordance with the present Charter" (United Nations, n.d.-b). As discussed in Chapters 6 and 7, the regime-type diversity (e.g., democratic or authoritarian) on the Security Council highlights divergent perspectives on governance, and consensus can be difficult to achieve. Regardless, the Security Council can draw from a body of law collectively known as the law of war or law of armed conflict, which is also known as International Humanitarian Law (International Committee of the Red Cross, 2002), to guide decision-making. But it is useful to remember that countries do not forgo their national interests when engaged in international institutions. In fact, governments often use their roles in international institutions to further their national interests (Abbott & Snidal, 1998). Thus, international law can be used by member states either in support of justification for action or as an argument for inaction.

8.1.2 Law of Armed Conflict

When World War II ended in 1945, there was a concerted effort to prevent World War III through international law and institutions. Headquartered in New York City, the United Nations was created in part "to save succeeding generations from the scourge of war" by members settling disputes through peaceful means and refraining from the use of force (Abbott & Snidal, 1998). Specifically, Article 2 (4) states, "All Members shall refrain in their international relations from the threat or use of force against the territorial integrity or political independence of any state, or in any other manner inconsistent with the Purposes of the United Nations" (United Nations, n.d.-a). If a state is attacked, then Article 51 of the UN Charter recognizes that states have

the inherent right of individual or collective self-defence if an armed attack occurs against a Member of the United Nations, until the Security Council has taken measures necessary to maintain international peace and security. Measures taken by Members in the exercise of this right of self-defence shall be immediately reported to the Security Council and shall not in any way affect the authority and responsibility of the Security Council under the present Charter to take at any time such action as it deems necessary in order to maintain or restore international peace and security. (United Nations, n.d.-a)

We should note that the word "war" was eschewed in favor of the term "armed conflict."[2]

Except for self-defense, there was an effort to renounce war beginning with the 1928 Kellogg–Briand Pact and enshrined in the 1945 UN Charter. Article I of the Kellogg–Briand Pact indicates that states party to the treaty would "condemn recourse to war for the solution of international controversies, and renounce it, as an instrument of national policy in their relations with one another" (Congressional Document, 1928). Of course, there have been many armed conflicts since 1928. Some of these such as US involvement in the Korean War in 1950–3 and in Afghanistan in 2001–21 or the European engagement in Bosnia in 1992 and in Libya in 2011 began with UN Security Council support. Other wars such as the 2003 US invasion of Iraq or the 2014 and 2022 Russian invasions of Ukraine occurred without UN sanction. The legality of the latter conflicts has certainly been questioned, but the wars ensued, nonetheless.

---

[2] This is important and was noted after the Geneva Conventions were written: "The substitution of [armed conflict] for the word 'war' was deliberate. One may argue almost endlessly about the legal definition of 'war'... The expression 'armed conflict' makes such arguments less easy. Any difference arising between two States and leading to the intervention of armed forces is an armed conflict ... [i]t makes no difference how long the conflict lasts, or how much slaughter takes place" (ICRC, 1950).

8.1.3 When War Begins

Under international law, there are two principles that attempt to regulate armed conflict. *Jus ad bellum* sets the criteria for going to war, while *jus in bello* serves to regulate conduct within war.

As noted earlier, engaging in armed conflict should be rare, undertaken in self-defense, and supported by the UN Security Council. It is important to note that a state does not need to suffer an armed attack to defend itself. A state may undertake self-defense to protect its sovereignty, people, and institutions in advance of an attack. For example, if intelligence indicates an adversary is preparing to launch missiles and an attack is imminent, a government can attack the adversary to neutralize the missile threat prior to launch. In such a case, a country is legally justified to act first to neutralize the threat.

This principle of self-defense was established in international law long before the missile (and cyber) age through the Caroline Case of 1837, where the circumstances leading to the use of force were "instant[aneous], overwhelming, and leaving no choice of means and no moment for deliberation." More recently, legal scholar Michael Schmitt (2002) argued that for states to be legally able to employ force in advance of an attack, evidence must show that an aggressor has committed itself to an imminent armed attack and delaying a response would hinder the defender's ability to mount a meaningful defense. Self-defense is valid if the attack (a) is imminent; (b) is currently in progress; or (c) has begun and is merely paused (i.e., attack has occurred, but another is shortly to begin).

When countries go to war, including during cases of self-defense, their behavior should be restricted by international law through what is collectively known as the law of armed conflict, which encapsulates the Hague and Geneva Conventions and their Additional Protocols and customary international law.

Essential Principle 8.1 Principles on legality of war

Jus ad bellum and *jus in bello* are two fundamental principles related to the legal basis of war. *Jus ad bellum*, or the right to go to war, is a set of criteria to determine whether war is permissible under international law. The thirteenth-century theologian St. Thomas Aquinas explored this notion termed "just war" where the purpose of war is morally justifiable. *Jus in bello*, or the right conduct in war, guides the behavior of combatants during war. The concept has been developed through various treaties that seek to protect civilians and ensure the fair treatment of captured combatants.

Military operations should be defined by actions that protect civilians and cultural property, while using minimal amounts of violence to return to peace. This body of law guides state behavior and is the outgrowth of centuries of legal and policy decisions.

There are three fundamental principles that govern the use of force to meet this standard.[3] First, the principle of *necessity* says a country may use force necessary to secure prompt submission of the enemy with a *minimum* expenditure of time, life, and physical resources; it regulates the level of force employed. Second, the principle of *distinction* requires countries to ensure respect for and protection of the civilian population and civil objects; it regulates how force should be directed at military objectives. The principle of *proportionality* requires countries to ensure action does not cause excessive suffering, injury, or destruction to civilians or civil objects relative to achieving military objectives to end hostilities; it requires countries to measure the anticipated incidental damage and death against the "direct and concrete military advantage expected" (Gardam, 1993).

8.1.4 Application of the Law of Armed Conflict to Cyberspace

Applying these principles in cyberspace is not clear-cut. International legal scholar Julia Hörnle (2021) says the Internet creates challenges for the concept of jurisdiction and sovereignty. Researchers Daniel Castro and Robert D. Atkinson (2014) wrote,

[C]onflicts over jurisdiction can be difficult to resolve. For example, if a hacker in China breaks into a French company's server located in Brazil and steals data from the company's Canadian users, which country's laws apply? And what recourses do nations have if other nations do not take action to prevent a crime or disagree that a crime has taken place?

The scenario certainly points to a role for intergovernmental organizations such as the United Nations to play to help define what sovereignty in cyberspace looks like.

As it relates to military operations, interpretation of the law is not clear. The *Department of Defense Law of War Manual* notes, "Precisely how the law of war applies to cyber operations is not well-settled, and aspects of the law in this area are likely to continue to develop, especially as new cyber capabilities are developed and States determine their views in response to such developments"

---

[3] For a detailed description of these principles, see DoD (2016).

(DoD, 2016, p. 1011). UN secretary general António Guterres notes that since "there is no regulatory scheme for … [cyber] warfare, it is not clear how the Geneva Convention or international humanitarian law applies to it [cyberspace]" (quoted in Khalip, 2018). Legal scholar David Fidler (2012) sees four problems with applying existing international law in cyberspace: (a) appropriate legal category (e.g., espionage or armed attack), (b) attribution of the attacker (e.g., state or nonstate actor), (c) the assessment problem (e.g., scope of self-defense required in response to the cyberattack), and (d) the accountability problem (e.g., assigning responsibility for the action). However, the rules of armed attack do not depend on the type of weapon used (cyber or otherwise). The US Department of Defense's *Law of War Manual* is instructive.

Cyber operations may in certain circumstances constitute uses of force within the meaning of Article 2(4) of the Charter of the United Nations and customary international law. For example, if cyber operations cause effects that, if caused by traditional physical means, would be regarded as a use of force under *jus ad bellum*, then such cyber operations would likely also be regarded as a use of force. Such operations may include cyber operations that: (1) trigger a nuclear plant meltdown; (2) open a dam above a populated area, causing destruction; or (3) disable air traffic control services, resulting in airplane crashes. (DoD, 2016, p. 1015)

The French Ministry of the Armed Forces' interpretation is similar and focuses on the impact of a cyberspace operation that reduces the functionality (not necessarily physical destruction) of the targeted network:

France reaffirms that a cyberattack may constitute an armed attack within the meaning of Article 51 of the United Nations Charter, if it is of a scale and severity comparable to those resulting from the use of physical force. In the light of these criteria, the question of whether a cyberattack constitutes armed aggression will be examined on a case-by-case basis having regard to the specific circumstances… Contrary to the *Tallinn Manual*, France considers that an attack within the meaning of Article 49 of AP [Additional Protocol] I may occur even if there is no human injury or loss of life, or physical damage to goods. Thus, *a cyberoperation constitutes an attack if the targeted equipment or systems can no longer provide the service for which they were implemented, including temporarily or reversibly, where action by the adversary is required to restore the infrastructure or the system.* (France, 2019, pp. 8, 13; italics added)

To clarify the application of international law in cyberspace, the NATO Cooperative Cyber Defence Centre of Excellence convened a group of legal scholars and practitioners who crafted two books to serve as guidelines (Schmitt, 2012, 2017a). The first, published in 2013, examined how international law applies in cyberspace during armed conflict. The second, published in 2017, incorporated a revised first book and expanded thinking on how international law applies in cyberspace during peace and war. As an illustration that the application of law in cyberspace is still unsettled, the author offered a humbling caveat to their work: "[I]t is not a 'best practices' guide, does not represent 'progressive development of the law', and is policy and politics neutral. In other words, *Tallinn Manual 2.0* is intended as an objective restatement of the *lex lata* [the law as it exists]" (Schmitt, 2017a).[4] Yet, *Tallinn Manual 2.0* still provides a useful starting point to think about how international law applies in cyberspace and shapes national and international discussions on interpreting a cyberattack as a use of force or violation of sovereignty. With a Tallinn Manual 3.0 being developed and a projected release of 2025, the effects of major exploits will likely clarify remaining legal questions since there are more publicly known cases of cyberspace operations than existed a decade ago.

8.1.5 Role of Domestic Law

Whereas war can be illegal under international standards, the decision to use armed force should also be consistent with a country's national interests and its own domestic laws. For example, in the United States, the 1973 War Powers Resolution Act is an attempt to provide Congress a greater check on the president's authority as commander-in-chief to deploy military forces. And, as discussed in Chapter 5, domestic national security decisions can drive countries to war without UN approval when deemed in the national interest. For example, the Obama administration maintained that "the United States must reserve the right to act unilaterally if necessary to defend our nation, yet we will also seek to adhere to standards that govern the use of force" (White House, 2010). The Trump administration did not articulate a specific use of force policy but relied on existing US law such as the 2001 and 2002 Authorization for Use of Military Force (AUMF) to conduct counterterrorism strikes. The Biden administration declared, "The United States will never hesitate to use force when required to defend our vital national interests." And "we will hold actors accountable for destructive, disruptive, or otherwise destabilizing malicious cyber activity, and respond swiftly and proportionately to cyberattacks by imposing substantial costs through cyber and non-cyber means" (White House, 2021a). Nevertheless, when it comes to a cyberattack, application of domestic law is less clear. A former US Cyber Command leader testified before Congress:

[W]ith regard to what is legal, what fits policy, the problem is we do not have any case law. We do not have any generalized recognition of what constitutes accepted international practice. One way to create accepted international practice is to practice.

---

[4] Supra note 14, at 2–3.

We actually have the opportunity to establish case law. We have the opportunity to begin to set out what is accepted international practice. And I would suggest a country like ours with checks and balances and transparency would be doing the world a service by creating an accepted regime in this domain by prudently using some of the capacities we have. (Hayden, 2017)

8.1.6 Interpretation of Domestic and International Laws

While these principles of international and domestic laws are known and international legal institutions exist, they are subject to interpretation. Under the UN system, the International Court of Justice exists to address legal disputes submitted by states and to provide advisory opinions (not legal rulings) referred to it by other UN organs and agencies. Additionally, the International Chamber of Commerce operates the International Court of Arbitration that offers individuals, corporations, and states a forum to administer the resolution of disputes but does not make formal judgments on legal matters. Countries can also redress grievances through other intergovernmental organizations such as the World Trade Organization or regional organizations such as the European Union. These institutions exist so that diplomatic and economic differences can be resolved peacefully.

History Matters 8.1 Legal basis for restraint in domestic cybersecurity

The United States government largely exhibits a laissez-faire attitude to cybersecurity, deferring to the private sector that creates and maintains cyberspace. This approach is based not only on fundamental views of economic market principles and corporate lobbying of Congress but also on American political culture that rejects the military in civilian affairs, which is rooted in nineteenth-century post-Civil War reconstruction activities. When the Civil War ended in 1865, federal troops enforced the law in former Confederate states. After a decade, Southerners were ready to reinstate local rule and evict federal troops. In 1878 in an effort to move past the war, Congress passed the Posse Comitatus law that outlawed the use of the armed forces to enforce the law, deferring to state and local government for security. While the president has ordered the military to perform domestic missions throughout history, objections persist to use intelligence agencies, such as the National Security Agency and U.S. Cyber Command, playing a role in domestic cybersecurity.

If international law is violated and a country receives a favorable ruling in the International Court of Justice, there is no mechanism to enforce the ruling, there is no international police force to make arrests, and there is no international organization to disrupt the illegal behavior. Instead, states must individually and collectively enforce decisions and seek to impose the settlement if a state fails to adhere to international law or a ruling. This enforcement can be carried out by individual countries or regional organizations penalizing governments found guilty through various tools such as sanctions or the indictment of the other country's citizens. In the extreme case, the UN Security Council can suspend sovereign recognition of a government and authorize a military intervention that results in regime change by invoking the Responsibility to Protect doctrine to protect a civilian population (United Nations Office on Genocide Prevention and the Responsibility to Protect, n.d.).

8.2 DEFINING AN ARMED ATTACK IN CYBERSPACE

The well-established law of armed conflict predominately addresses use of force that causes physical damage or violence against people. When it comes to defining an armed attack in cyberspace, proposed criteria require attribution to another country's government and an assessment that the cyberattack resulted in severe harm, that is, the attack is widespread, sustained, and damaging (Healey & Jordan 2014). Destruction of data is generally not considered an armed attack since it is both temporary and not the equivalent of an attack on a single physical location. In general, legal scholars agree that the determination of an armed attack will be based more on the consequences of an attack rather than on the means used to conduct the attack, cyber or otherwise (Fidler, 2012).

During the development of the Tallinn Manuals, a group of legal "experts did concur that a cyber operation interfering with or usurping another state's inherently governmental function, such as law enforcement, is a sovereignty violation irrespective of whether damage or injury results" (Schmitt, 2017a, para 15–18). In short, sovereignty violations are not the same as a use of force that can be interpreted as an armed attack. While the Stuxnet attack did produce physical destruction and satisfied criteria to be a use of force, Iran did not charge any country in the wake of Stuxnet or say it was the victim of an armed attack. As it relates to cybersecurity, legal scholar Fred Cate (2015) notes there is a "'tragedy of the commons' phenomenon by which many key players assume someone else is providing for security, combined with a sense of despair about the size and complexity of the challenge that often frustrates significant investment."

Exploit 8.1 Espionage at the Office of Personnel Management

In April 2015, the federal agency that manages the civilian workforce, Office of Personnel Management (OPM), lost millions of personnel records of workers granted top-secret clearances. (The attackers gained access through stolen credentials and had been on the network about a year before being discovered.) At the time, discussions centered on whether the United States was attacked. The attackers used an active directory privilege escalation technique to obtain root access. Through a remote access tool, the attackers navigated OPM's networks, compressed, and exfiltrated data. The agency discovered the hack when large, encrypted files moved across their networks; the alarm was triggered when an OPM security engineer noticed the security software the hackers used was not one OPM used. While there was considerable debate at the national level, ultimately the attack was deemed espionage.

Policy Matters 8.1 Cyber's Most Wanted

How governments respond to cyberspace operations by foreign agents is an important policy matter. While legal experts can differentiate between a use of force and an armed attack, policymakers are concerned with their impact of their responses on international affairs and domestic politics. This makes determining "what to do?" the challenge for policymaking.

The US government has frequently turned to indicting foreign actors in the domestic court system. Since it is the lead federal agency for investigating cyberattacks, the Federal Bureau of Investigation maintains a cyber most wanted list. The list includes members of China's Ministry of State Security, China's People's Liberation Army, and Russia's military intelligence, as well as foreign nationals who are alleged to have committed cybercrimes in the United States.

As of this writing, no cyberattack has been ruled as an armed attack and the International Court of Justice has yet to consider state-driven cyberspace operations (Shackelford et al., 2016). Instead, what we observe as cyberattacks have largely been characterized as criminal violations or intelligence operations where states seek remedy through their own domestic court systems

(Zetter, 2013). In fact, the United States has often applied US domestic law to address international intrusions. These violations can include computer intrusion, wire fraud, identity theft, and intellectual proprietary data theft. The Federal Bureau of Investigation maintains a cyber most wanted list and the Department of Justice has indicted these individuals through the US justice system even though they are unlikely to appear in a US court and the legality is uncertain (Balzano, 2012). High-profile indictments have been issued against Russian intelligence officers for their role in interfering in US elections and Chinese military personnel for intellectual property theft.

8.3 NORMS DEVELOPMENT PROCESS

While international law could be the standard for setting behavior among governments in the international system, norms usually come first. Norms are the collective expectation for proper behavior that is based on shared beliefs within a community (Katzenstein, 1996). Michelle Jurkovich (2020) contends norms have three components: a moral sense of "oughtness," a defined actor, and expected behavior by that actor. When any of these parts is missing, a norm does not exist. As indicated by the Venn diagram (Jurkovich, 2020) of Figure 8.1, if the actor is not specified, the combination of "oughtness" and action defines a moral principle. The specification of actor and "oughtness" define character. Finally, when the actor and action are specified, routine or normal behavior is identified.

A norm involves all three components; it establishes expectations for actors with respect to actions. Norms frequently start as best practices and can often become precursors to law, but once widely accepted, norms have the potential to be more universal than law but do not require enforcement mechanisms.

Given how rapidly the information environment and cyberspace change, norms may be preferable to keep up with the pace of technological change rather than to pursue international laws and treaties that may be stymied within domestic legislatures before reconciling with international institutions. The diversity of actors in cyberspace complicates this dynamic. Political scientist Martha Finnemore (2017) further argues that "many professional norms in cyberspace began as best practices (or norms) but have, over time, been written into law in various ways. Not all norms have become legalized, however." Nevertheless, when legalized norms are violated, governments can seek remedy through bilateral meetings or through the extraterritorial application of domestic law as previously discussed regarding indictments in domestic courts.

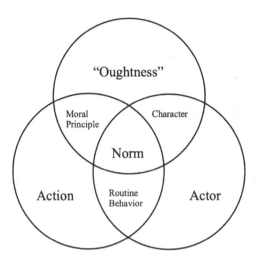

Figure 8.1 Redefining conceptual boundaries of norms. © Michelle Jurkovich. Michelle Jurkovich, What Isn't a Norm? Redefining the Conceptual Boundaries of "Norms" in the Human Rights Literature, *International Studies Review*, Volume 22, Issue 3, September 2020, Pages 693–711, by permission of Oxford University Press

Chapter 6 offered perspectives on how different countries view what is acceptable behavior in cyberspace. Whereas one country discourages intellectual property theft, another might simply see it as a shortcut to promote innovation and reduce poverty. Patents and copyright are old concepts in advanced market democracies such as the United States and the United Kingdom, but there is no universal acceptance of protecting or paying for the use of someone else's work. International organizations such as the World Trade Organization and the World Intellectual Property Organization or bilateral and multilateral trade agreements are attempting to promote stricter respect for copyrights and patents, but the norms to restrain bootlegging of movies, stealing intellectual property, or counterfeiting goods are not universally accepted.

Jason Healey and Tim Maurer (2017) identify three phases of norm development: contestation, translation, and emergence. During the contestation phase, scholars and practitioners recognize that existing laws and norms do not apply to particular behavior and something new is needed. The second phase focuses on the translation of existing law to address new problems. For example, how could the law of armed conflict be applied in cyberspace? New norms emerge when governments start behaving in an internationally acceptable way that is consistent over time. Bearing in mind the rapid pace of change in cyberspace and increased attention by a variety of domestic and international actors, cybersecurity is increasingly perceived as essential to national security. We next explore the various actors developing norms, including corporations, the United Nations, and nongovernmental organizations (NGOs).

8.4 ROLE OF CORPORATIONS

Unlike other sectors within national security, corporations fulfill important roles in cybersecurity. This is unsurprising since about 90 percent of cyberspace is produced and operated by the private sector. For a company like Boeing that produces aircraft, there is no expectation that Boeing fly or maintain the aircraft once sold to a military or an airline. In contrast, when Microsoft sells an operating system, there is an expectation for Microsoft to maintain its software by providing security patches free directly to users.

When thinking about cyberspace, it is useful to remember that telecommunication companies operate the pathways for data flow, hardware companies develop the machinery of cyberspace, and software developers create the tools to operate within cyberspace. Microsoft's president and chief legal officer Brad Smith (2017) captured the breadth of the cybersecurity ecosystem when he wrote, "[T]he targets in this new battle – from submarine cables to datacenters, servers, laptops and smartphones – ... are private property owned by civilians." Within this context, there are two innovative cybersecurity norm-building efforts underway, led separately by Siemens and Microsoft.

Launched at the 2018 Munich Security Conference by the Germany-based multinational corporation Siemens, the Charter of Trust Initiative has a key goal of "ensuring cybersecurity throughout the networked environment" (Buntz, 2019). Considering Siemens is an industry leader in supplying supervisory control and data acquisition equipment used in industrial controls such as power, water, and manufacturing, the initiative is important to overall social and economic safety. The chairman of the Munich Security Conference, Wolfgang Ischinger, recognized how cybersecurity is different than other aspects of national security. He said, "Governments must take a leadership role when it comes to the transaction rules in cyberspace" (quoted in Schmid, 2018).

The Charter of Trust is based on a core set of ten principles. First, the problem of cybersecurity should be addressed at the highest level. Second, there should be responsibility throughout the supply chain with continuous protection from chip to box. Third, security (rather than openness) should be the default for all manufacturers. Too many hacks began by exploiting a default password, such as "password." Next, the user should be a trusted partner throughout the life cycle. Fifth, firms and policymakers must cooperate, innovate, and adapt to new threats. Next, cybersecurity should be incorporated into school curricula to broaden the base from which to produce cyber professionals. Seventh, it is important to develop certifications for protecting critical infrastructure. Eighth, information should be shared to improve insights on ways to protect data and systems. Ninth, the global nature of cyberspace requires multilateral collaboration on regulation and standardization. Finally, joint initiatives are needed to implement these principles (Charter of Trust Principles, n.d.).

Executives from Microsoft are also leading the way to promote norms, drawing inspiration from existing international law. Specifically focused on the government level, Microsoft calls for "a Digital Geneva Convention [that] would create a legally binding framework to govern states' behavior in cyberspace" (MSFT, 2017). This is important since governments are likely to develop the most sophisticated malware used specifically as a tool of power to advance national interests through activities more far reaching than attacks by criminal groups using malware for profit. The fact that technology companies are engaging in international politics is significant as Microsoft founder Bill Gates explained that in the early days of the tech industry he "prided himself on how little time we spent talking to people in the federal government" (Bill Gates foreword to B. Smith & Browne, 2019). That view evolved and was given energy under Microsoft's president Smith, who thought "just as governments had pledged to protect civilians in times of war, perhaps a Digital Geneva Convention could capture people's imagination about the need for governments to protect civilians on the internet in times of peace" (Smith & Browne, 2019).

Eventually expanding beyond Microsoft to encompass other technology companies, the proposed norms would impose restraints on governments' cyber efforts to protect (a) critical national infrastructures, (b) the global economy, including financial transactions, and (c) personal accounts of journalists and those involved with electoral systems. Additionally, the proposal calls on governments to (d) refrain from intellectual property theft for commercial gain, (e) refrain from inserting backdoors into commercial products, and (f) act responsibly with respect to the discovery of security vulnerabilities. With many countries developing cyber commands as a part of their military establishments, the norms would (g) promote restraint in developing cyber weapons so that they are limited, precise, and not reusable, (h) promote nonproliferation efforts in cyberspace, (i) ensure cyberattacks are localized to prevent mass damage. Finally, Microsoft recommends that (j) governments assist the private sector in detecting, containing, responding to, and recovering from cyberattacks.

To advance norms at the international level, Microsoft established an office at the United Nations, illustrating how a multinational corporation can be involved in promoting peace and security. Smith championed this view: "As technology creates more opportunities and challenges for the world, tech companies need do more to work with governments in a supportive and collaborative way" (MSFT, 2020). Having an office at the United Nations can promote this goal and potentially shape norms beyond traditional corporate borders.

8.5 ROLE OF THE UNITED NATIONS

By 1999 the information age had begun to rewire global thinking on cybersecurity and internet governance. Around the same time Google was founded in California, as mentioned in Chapter 7, the Russian Federation submitted a draft resolution on information security to the New York-based UN General Assembly which, when adopted, "[c]all[ed] upon Member States to promote at multilateral levels the consideration of existing and potential threats in the field of information security" (GGE, 1999). As the most important global intergovernmental organization, the United Nations has been a key forum discussing norms for cyberspace for decades. Since 2004, five GGEs were convened by the United Nations to study threats posed by ICTs; a sixth GGE said international humanitarian law (IHL) applies to cyber operations in armed conflict. (Schmitt, 2021). Separately, the General Assembly established an OEWG, with broader participation than the GGE.

8.5.1 Groups of Governmental Experts

The UN GGEs produced unanimous recommendations in 2010, 2013, and 2015, which recommended eleven voluntary, nonbinding norms of behavior (see Table 8.1) (UNODA, 2022). In 2010, governments agreed on the importance of dialogue among states to mitigate risk and protect critical infrastructure, the importance of confidence-building measures, and simply agreeing on common definitions of terms. In 2013, the group recognized that international law, including the UN Charter, applies in cyberspace, that state sovereignty applies in cyberspace, and that states should not intentionally engage in harmful acts in cyberspace. In 2015, they outlined additional confidence-building measures, identified efforts to promote cooperation and assistance on cybersecurity, and further examined how international law applies in cyberspace. As mentioned earlier, the latter built on work by a separate group of legal experts convened under the auspices of NATO that produced the Tallinn Manual. UN GGE discussions are open-ended and will continue to shape international discussions of cyberspace into the next decade and beyond.

Table 8.1 Norms to promote international peace and security in cyberspace

(a) Consistent with the purposes of the United Nations, including to maintain international peace and security, States should cooperate in developing and applying measures to increase stability and security in the use of ICTs and to prevent ICT practices that are acknowledged to be harmful or that may pose threats to international peace and security;

(b) In case of ICT incidents, States should consider all relevant information, including the larger context of the event, the challenges of attribution in the ICT environment and the nature and extent of the consequences;

(c) States should not knowingly allow their territory to be used for internationally wrongful acts using ICTs;

(d) States should consider how best to cooperate to exchange information, assist each other, prosecute terrorist and criminal use of ICTs and implement other cooperative measures to address such threats. States may need to consider whether new measures need to be developed in this respect;

(e) States, in ensuring the secure use of ICTs, should respect Human Rights Council resolutions 20/8 and 26/13 on the promotion, protection and enjoyment of human rights on the Internet, as well as General Assembly resolutions 68/167 and 69/166 on the right to privacy in the digital age, to guarantee full respect for human rights, including the right to freedom of expression;

(f) A State should not conduct or knowingly support ICT activity contrary to its obligations under international law that intentionally damages critical infrastructure or otherwise impairs the use and operation of critical infrastructure to provide services to the public;

(g) States should take appropriate measures to protect their critical infrastructure from ICT threats, taking into account General Assembly resolution 58/199 on the creation of a global culture of cybersecurity and the protection of critical information infrastructures, and other relevant resolutions;

(h) States should respond to appropriate requests for assistance by another State whose critical infrastructure is subject to malicious ICT acts. States should also respond to appropriate requests to mitigate malicious ICT activity aimed at the critical infrastructure of another State emanating from their territory, taking into account due regard for sovereignty;

(i) States should take reasonable steps to ensure the integrity of the supply chain so that end users can have confidence in the security of ICT products. States should seek to prevent the proliferation of malicious ICT tools and techniques and the use of harmful hidden functions;

(j) States should encourage responsible reporting of ICT vulnerabilities and share associated information on available remedies to such vulnerabilities to limit and possibly eliminate potential threats to ICTs and ICT-dependent infrastructure;

(k) States should not conduct or knowingly support activity to harm the information systems of the authorized emergency response teams (sometimes known as computer emergency response teams or cybersecurity incident response teams) of another State. A State should not use authorized emergency response teams to engage in malicious international activity.

Source: Report of the Group of Governmental Experts on Developments in the Field of Information and Telecommunications in the Context of International Security, © 2015 United Nations. Reprinted with permission of the United Nations.

The 2017 UN GGE meeting did not produce unanimous agreement as experts seemed to differ on responses to cyberattacks. Two legal scholars saw disagreement based on politicization rather than international law. In particular, they highlighted "1) the right to respond to internationally wrongful acts (a veiled reference to countermeasures); 2) the right to self-defense; and 3) international humanitarian law" (Schmitt & Vihul, 2017). Cuba was among those states that objected and declared: "I must register our serious concern over the pretension of some, reflected in paragraph 34 of the draft final report, to convert cyberspace into a theater of military operations and to legitimize, in that context, unilateral punitive force actions, including the application of sanctions and even military action by States claiming to be victims of illicit uses of ICTs" (Rodríguez, 2017). Cuba's objections are representative of the larger split among governments such as the United States, which sees an open and global Internet where individuals can be free, and governments such as China, which sees an important role for state regulation and imposing borders in cyberspace as discussed in Chapter 6.

In 2019, the General Assembly once again called on the secretary general to convene a GGE on advancing responsible state behavior in cyberspace. General Assembly resolution 73/266 called on a GGE to explore "cooperative measures to address existing and potential threats in the sphere of information security, including norms, rules and principles of responsible behaviour of States, confidence-building measures and capacity-building, as well as how international law applies to the use of information and communications technologies by States" (UNGA, 2018). Chaired by Ambassador Guilherme de Aguiar Patriota of Brazil, the GGE also consulted with regional organizations such as the African Union, Association of Southeast Asian Nation, the European Union, the Organization of American States, and the Organization for Security and Cooperation in Europe.

A group of experts from 25 countries added new voluntary norms of behavior in May 2021.[5] Among these norms are: acknowledging the complexity of attribution, discouraging states from knowingly allowing their territory to be used for internationally wrongful acts, promoting information-sharing, applying human rights laws in cyberspace, admonishing states not to damage critical infrastructure, preventing proliferation of malware, valuing application of international norms, and supporting confidence-building

---

[5] The 25 states were: Australia, Brazil, China, Estonia, France, Germany, India, Indonesia, Japan, Jordan, Kazakhstan, Kenya, Mauritius, Mexico, Morocco, the Netherlands, Norway, Romania, the Russian Federation, Singapore, South Africa, Switzerland, the United Kingdom of Great Britain and Northern Ireland, the United States of America, and Uruguay.

measures (OEWG, 2021c). The final report came close on the heels of US condemnation of Russia for the SolarWinds hack and China for its compromise of Microsoft Exchange Server (Robertson et al., 2021). Since Russian intelligence conducted the SolarWinds supply chain exploit and Chinese intelligence conducted the Microsoft Exchange Server exploit, the value of these norms did not meet the Jurkovich standard of key actors behaving in accordance with the agreement reached.

8.5.2 Open-Ended Working Group

The OEWG developed from UN General Assembly resolution 73/27, which called upon member states to engage multilaterally to consider threats in cyberspace and strategies to preserve the free flow of information. The resolution explicitly acknowledged the value of the GGE's work and the relevance of international law to cyberspace and sought measures to strengthen cybersecurity at the global level. Ambassador Jürg Lauber of Switzerland chaired the OEWG and noted member states agreed that "international law governs actions and relations between States and voluntary, non-binding norms provide additional guidance on what constitutes responsible State behaviour" (OEWG, 2021a).

By design, the OEWG was broader and more inclusive than the GGE, which included 25 countries during the 2019 GGE compared with 44 countries that submitted comments on the draft OEWG report in 2021. The OEWG also included some countries left out of GGE discussions such as Iran and smaller regional groups such as the Caribbean Community (CARICOM-*Caribbean Community*, 2023) to pursue their concerns about cybersecurity. There was considerable overlap between the two groups; Australia, Brazil, China, Estonia, France, Germany, India, Indonesia, Japan, Kenya, Netherlands, Romania, Russia, Singapore, South Africa, Switzerland, United Kingdom, and United States participated in both.[6] Of note, Russia objected to the zero draft report published in May 2020 seeing it as biased and too long and suggested the final draft be five to seven pages and argued the draft report did "not reflect fundamental elements of Russia's approach."[7]

---

[6] For a list of participating countries, see Group of Governmental Experts (GGE 2019) and Open-Ended Working Group (OEWG, 2021c).

[7] See Statements by Dr. Vladimir Shin, Deputy Director, Department of International Information Security, Ministry of Foreign Affairs of the Russian Federation and Ambassador Andrey Krutskikh, Special Representative of the President of the Russian Federation for International Cooperation in the Field of Information Security and Director of the Department of International Information Security of the Ministry of Foreign Affairs of the Russian Federation at OEWG (2021c).

After two years of discussions and reconciling many national positions as diverse as those of Russia and the United Kingdom, the OEWG produced an 11-page report and offered important principles for states to pursue (in a voluntary way). These include narrowing digital divides and promoting "universal, inclusive and non-discriminatory access to ICTs and connectivity" (OEWG, 2021c). This was of particular concern to South Africa, which noted technology is essential to economic development (South Africa, 2021). There was widespread agreement that state behavior in cyberspace should be consistent with international law. The OEWG (2021c) also recommended "deepening common understandings on how international law applies to State use of ICTs [which] can be developed by exchanging views on the issue among States and by identifying specific topics of international law for further in-depth discussion within the United Nations."

8.6 ROLE OF NONGOVERNMENTAL ORGANIZATIONS

As in other policy spaces, NGOs are active in the cybersecurity field, promoting dialogue, offering expertise to governments and international institutions, and proposing norms. NGOs contribute to the UN groups discussed earlier and draw from their expertise in computer science, electrical engineering, international affairs, government, ethics, and the ICT sector. Shared goals focus on developing expertise to inform national, international, and corporate projects to improve cybersecurity. Examples of NGOs include regional groups such as the Atlantic Council and the Council on Foreign Relations in the United States and the International Institute for Strategic Studies in London and international groups such as the Global Commission on the Stability of Cyberspace (GCSC) based in The Hague, the Netherlands.

Cochaired by former US secretary of homeland security Michael Chertoff and former deputy national security adviser of India Latha Reddy, the GCSC sought to promote norms for the public and private sector (GCSC, 2017). The commission's initial work included representatives from 16 countries and was guided by four principles. First, the stability of cyberspace is not the responsibility of any single entity or government but a shared responsibility of everyone. Second, no one should take actions that impair the stability of cyberspace. Third, state or nonstate actors should take reasonable and appropriate steps to ensure the stability of cyberspace. Finally, everyone must respect human rights and the rule of law in cyberspace (GCSC, 2019). After three years of work, the commission released its own set of norms in November 2019. They are summarized in Table 8.2.

Table 8.2 Norms developed by the GCSC

1. State and non-state actors should neither conduct nor knowingly allow activity that intentionally and substantially damages the general availability or integrity of the public core of the Internet, and therefore the stability of cyberspace.
2. State and non-state actors must not pursue, support or allow cyber operations intended to disrupt the technical infrastructure essential to elections, referenda or plebiscites.
3. State and non-state actors should not tamper with products and services in development and production, nor allow them to be tampered with, if doing so may substantially impair the stability of cyberspace.
4. State and non-state actors should not commandeer the general public's ICT resources for use as botnets or for similar purposes.
5. States should create procedurally transparent frameworks to assess whether and when to disclose not publicly known vulnerabilities or flaws they are aware of in information systems and technologies. The default presumption should be in favor of disclosure.
6. Developers and producers of products and services on which the stability of cyberspace depends should (1) prioritize security and stability, (2) take reasonable steps to ensure that their products or services are free from significant vulnerabilities, and (3) take measures to timely mitigate vulnerabilities that are later discovered and to be transparent about their process. All actors have a duty to share information on vulnerabilities in order to help prevent or mitigate malicious cyber activity.
7. States should enact appropriate measures, including laws and regulations, to ensure basic cyber hygiene.
8. Non-state actors should not engage in offensive cyber operations and state actors should prevent such activities and respond if they occur.

The GCSC was created by The Hague Centre for Strategic Studies, the Netherlands. Source: GCSC (2019)

8.7 NORMS FOR THE NEXT DECADE

As the preceding sections make clear, there is no shortage of public and private or national and international efforts to produce norms. As Bruce McConnell, the president of the East West Institute, said, "I think it's a very confusing environment. More frameworks could make it even more confusing…Nobody has the right answer yet and I think it's good to have a lot of different discussions" (quoted in Johnson, 2019). The proliferation of norms is significant, and the NGO Carnegie Endowment for International Peace collected and documented over 150 accords, declarations, and joint statements in support of norms for cyberspace (Carnegie, n.d.).

The proposed norms do not all meet the standard Jurkovich offers of a moral sense of "oughtness," a defined actor, and expected behavior by that actor, but they illustrate a broad commitment of a variety of actors attempting to improve cybersecurity. Most thinking about norms is focused on how governments interact with each other and corporations, but we must not overlook how citizens and users are included in norm development. After all, the nature of cyberspace puts the individual user at the epicenter of cybersecurity. Thus, as norms develop in the future, however, we see four important norm categories: (a) norms for governments with governments, (b) norms for governments with corporations, (c) norms for governments with their own citizens, and (d) norms for the information technology sector with its users.

The modern international order that emerged in the aftermath of World War II, which includes the UN system, the international economic system, and regional organizations, has largely driven the development of norms around the world. While consensus is limited, emerging norms suggest governments should not use cyber means to disrupt international economic flows, target another country's critical infrastructure, undermine nuclear command and control, or attempt to influence the politics of other governments. They should also support and assist allies to recover and respond to a major cyberattack. Additionally, there is general agreement that existing international law and norms should apply in cyberspace.

Corporations are regulated where they are physically located and where they virtually operate, but they also seek more universal norms considering how information technology applications and hardware have become global. Corporations prefer fewer standards rather than attempting to operate in accordance with 190+ separate and distinct national laws. Norms between governments and corporations might address financial penalties for negligence, particular standards for security, sharing of threat data, establishing an open dialogue between government and industry, and privacy enforcement. Mathematician Susan Landau (2015a) wrote that privacy protections are inadequate today and "user control sits at the heart of the FIPs [fair information practices]." Likewise, industry should expect government not to hoard cyber vulnerabilities but to share them with industry to deploy software patches to improve cybersecurity.

Just as citizens expect civil and criminal laws to protect them as individuals, norms between governments and citizens should play a similar role in cyberspace. Although diverse political cultures across the world may make universal norms difficult to reconcile, as demonstrated by the 2017 UN GGE meetings, the Universal Declaration of Human Rights can be the starting point to apply them in cyberspace. Article 3 of the rights resonates with a universal audience in practice and aspiration: "[E]veryone has the right to life, liberty and security of person" (UN, 1948). Article 12 is also relevant: "No one shall be subjected to arbitrary interference with his privacy, family, home or correspondence, nor to attacks upon his honour and reputation. Everyone has the right to the protection of the law against such interference or attacks" (UN, 1948). Additional rights articulated in the document and agreed upon by all UN members include free expression, privacy, and freedom of association. When it comes to cyber policy, this would mean governments should ensure citizens' privacy is protected from government, corporations, and other groups.

Finally, a set of norms between the information technology sector and users can be developed. These include a reasonable expectation that users' privacy is protected, terms of service are understandable, users' data is not shared without users' consent, and data breaches are transparent. Users do have a reasonable expectation that their data is secure and accessible, yet very few companies' policies are explained in terms that most can understand. To improve privacy, Landau (2016a) thinks users can pay for services rather than obtain them without charge from ICT companies in return for allowing them to monetize their personal data. When corporations fail to protect individual users, this can result in governments stepping in, such as the European Union did with its General Data Protection Regulation and US state legislatures did with new privacy protection laws.

Increasingly, users are expressing a preference for companies that prioritize these expectations of greater privacy. Higher levels of connectivity in the workplace and at home will mature as the private sector integrates previously disparate user connections within familiar technological ecosystems in new ways. For example, as Google enters the healthcare industry, a user might be entrusting a single company with data on their personal health, communications, location, consumer preferences, web traffic, and finances. How the private sector meets increasing user expectations has the potential to strengthen or weaken a company and user relationships that are now measured in decades. Such dynamics will have a profound effect on shaping norms in the present and the future.

8.8 CONCLUSIONS

As the various efforts discussed in the chapter illustrate, it is possible to articulate a set of norms, but it is also important to recognize there are incentives to cheat and not necessarily follow international law and norms. As Law professors Jack Goldsmith and Eric Posner (1998) argued, "Because they lack a centralized judicial and enforcement regime, and because violations often go unpunished, both treaties and CIL (customary international law) have long been plagued by doubts about whether they establish genuine legal obligations." Consequently, we should not exclusively look to norms for providing greater cybersecurity, noting that norms that do not align with states' interests or common goals are unlikely to be successful. However, governments can use law and norms as important lenses to interpret significant cyberspace operations and to guide their own policy processes in responses in what is perceived as a cyberattack.

Likewise, corporations are driven by the profit motive, which may undercut the collective good of cybersecurity. Software companies do not always prioritize clean code but tolerate coding errors that can be exploited for malicious purposes until the company discovers and patches them. The ideas of government regulation from Chapter 6 might compel corporations to spend more resources on code testing prior to release to squelch regulatory efforts. Similarly, large-scale exploitation of their products may compel corporations to adopt norms to reduce vulnerabilities. With the forever promise of better technology and prospects for artificial intelligence addressed in Chapter 9, there may be new technical ways to improve cybersecurity.

8.9 DISCUSSION TOPICS

1. Explain how international law applies in cyberspace during peace and during war and give and justify a cyber incident not in the book that violates international law.
2. Give a plausible explanation why Iran did not choose to declare Stuxnet an armed attack.
3. Under what conditions is self-defense against a cyberspace operation justified under international law?
4. Why do you think multinational corporations are promoting norms for cyberspace?
5. How do state-sponsored exploits undermine the norms agreed to through UN processes?

9

Artificial Intelligence and Ethics

The development of full artificial intelligence could spell the end of the human race. ... It would take off on its own, and re-design itself at an ever-increasing rate. ... Humans, who are limited by slow biological evolution, couldn't compete and would be superseded.

Stephen Hawking, theoretical physicist
(quoted in Cellan-Jones, 2014)

9.1 ARTIFICIAL INTELLIGENCE

Artificial intelligence (AI) is the name John McCarthy coined in 1955 for research designed to give computers abilities that are associated with human intelligence. In fact, he conjectured that "every aspect of learning or any other feature of intelligence [could] in principle be so precisely described that a machine could be made to simulate it" (McCarthy et al., 2006). The latter statement was used in a request to the Rockefeller Foundation for a grant to support a two-month summer workshop that was held in 1956 at Dartmouth College. It was the AI founding event.

The proposal was coauthored by Marvin Minsky, Nathaniel Rochester, and Claude Shannon, three distinguished scientists and engineers. Their goal was to learn "how to make machines use language, form abstractions and concepts, solve kinds of problems now reserved for humans, and improve themselves" (McCarthy et al., 2006). Their goals continue to motivate AI engineers and scientists today.

Movie franchises such as the Terminator and Star Wars conjure up expectations for AI that are often inflated and sometimes frightening, as suggested by the opening quotation. The introduction of ChatGPT and other generative AI tools in 2022 resulted in significant public interest and further speculation on the power of algorithms. Reality is much more modest, however.

As the name "artificial intelligence" suggests, the early development of AI was predicated on the assumption that human thought can be formalized and machines can be programmed as intelligent agents. Today the primary focus of AI is to solve well-defined specialized problems rapidly with great accuracy. For example, the AI community understands how to train neural networks to do facial recognition with high reliability and to identify objects such as airplanes, cars, trucks, or humans. The AI community also knows how to program computers to play rule-based games so well using reinforcement learning, in which two computer programs play against each other, that AI systems can defeat all human players. They are also excellent at translating text from one language to another, although it is possible for experts to detect subtle translation errors since language often has exceptions to rules. As the New England poet Robert Frost once said, poetry is what is lost in translation.

Some tasks, such as facial recognition and natural-language understanding, are easy for humans but hard to implement through programming. Others, such as playing chess or Go at the level of a master, are hard for humans but, with sophisticated AI techniques, are easy for computers. Games have fewer rules whereas grammars for human languages typically have many exceptions and regional variations. However, one area in which AI technologies will always outdo humans is in their ability to store and process vast quantities of information rapidly, so it is important to identify the right problems for AI systems.

Despite remarkable advancements it is widely recognized that AI systems do not (yet) replicate human intelligence. Today, many AI systems based on machine learning (ML) with neural networks are more like idiot savants; they exhibit outstanding ability in narrowly defined areas. Fortunately, the AI community understands and appreciates the limitations of AI technologies and is working hard to address them. If they succeed, they will have created what is called *artificial general intelligence* (AGI), that is, an intelligence equal to human intelligence. Today what they have created is called *weak AI* or *narrow AI* although recent dramatic advances illustrated by ChatGPT have alarmed some to be concerned that AGI is close to being realized.

The chapter lays out the history of modern AI technologies, describes how AI is realized, and illustrates the challenges of reproducing human thinking in machines. While the goal of completely emulating human intelligence, sensing, and action may be out of reach now, AI research is making computers more "intelligent," helping to automate many important and challenging problems and showing remarkable ability to win at board games with extremely complex rule sets.

As Google CEO Sundar Pichai noted, "AI is one of the most important things that humanity is working on. It's more profound than, I don't know, electricity or fire" (quoted in Schleifer, 2018). It remains to be seen if Pichai is correct. There is no question as to the importance of AI. The big question is whether it will be possible to realize the full potential of AGI. If so, then Stephen Hawking's warning at the start of this chapter will be prescient.

9.2 THE DEVELOPMENT OF INTELLIGENT MECHANICAL MACHINES

Artificial intelligence is the latest attempt to emulate human behavior. For millennia humans have constructed machines that appear intelligent. Called *automata*, a word derived from the Greek word that means "acting of one's own will," early machines entertained and amazed 2,000 years ago (Mechanical Art & Design Museum, n.d.). Since then, there have been many efforts to re-create human behavior in form and in thought.

9.2.1 2,000-Year-Old Programmable Robots

Among the most famous of the ancient inventors of automata was Hero of Alexandria, a Greek mathematician and engineer who lived from about 10 CE to 70 CE. While millennia old, his inventions are still impressive today (Shuttleworth, n.d.). Around 60 CE he built one of the world's first robots, a self-propelled cart that used a weight and ropes wound around orthogonal axles that moved the cart around a stage. When the weight was released, it pulled on the ropes causing the axles to turn and the cart to move; pegs on the axles controlled how the cart moved.

Shown in Figure 9.1 is a small contemporary implementation of Hero's concept described in an article by Noel Sharkey of Sheffield University (New Scientist, 2007).

The cart has two axles each connected to an independent wheel. As a weight falls inside a tube mounted on the platform, ropes on each axle unwind, causing both wheels to spin. If a rope reaches a peg, the axle to which it is connected reverses the direction of its spin, causing a change in the direction in which the robot moves. Because the positions of the pegs on the axles can change, the machine was indeed programmable! Hero used similar concepts to create a 10-minute mechanical play showing sailors working on a ship with dolphins swimming nearby. His machine even dropped metal balls on a metal sheet to simulate thunder.

Figure 9.1 Model of Hero's programmable robot, by permission of *New Scientist*

Hero also built an organ powered by a windmill. A piston moved up and down as the windmill turned and forced air through a set of pipes, creating sounds. And 2,000 years ago, he also designed the first vending machine. When a coin was dropped through a slot at the top of a box, it fell on an arm that tilted downward for a few seconds under the weight of the coin and released a bit of holy water. After the coin slipped off the arm, the arm reverted to its initial position, turning off the water (Shuttleworth, n.d.). Undoubtedly a novelty in Ancient Greece, Hero's vending machine concept is ubiquitous today.

9.2.2 Golden Age of Automata

The golden period for automata was from the mid-eighteenth to the early twentieth century in Europe. Many ingenious automata were produced, some of which are on display in the Morris Museum in New Jersey (Guinness, n.d.).

In Paris in 1740 Jacques de Vaucanson demonstrated his Digesting Duck to French King Louis XV, philosopher Voltaire, and the public. At his command it "flapped its wings, and, stretching out its long neck, pecked, nibbled, then swallowed a handful of grain. The duck took water, splashing with its beak. ... It sat. It settled itself, then, with a quack, rose again and — miracle upon miracles! — defecated onto a silver dish" (Pearson, n.d.). All were amazed; humans had re-created nature!

One of the most famous automata was Von Kempelen's chess-playing Turk. Sitting on top of the machine was a life-sized figure in an Ottoman costume. The automaton was presented in 1770 to the court of Empress Maria Theresa of Austria. It beat Napoleon Bonaparte, Benjamin Franklin, and others at chess. European, British, and American audiences were dumbfounded by this invention. The device was not an automaton. Instead, it was operated by a human chess master hidden inside the contraption. Mathematician and mechanical engineer Charles Babbage, who saw it in London, knew it was a hoax but was motivated by it to invent his Difference Engine, the precursor to his Analytical Engine, a programmable mechanical computer discussed in Chapter 2 (Pearson, n.d.).

Although many of the early automata did emulate human action, it is doubtful that they were seen as intelligent; they were considered novelties. But the attempts did whet the appetite to understand and create machines in human form that exhibit intelligence. While the science at the time posed real limits on translating concepts offered by Babbage and others into practice, writers were not constrained by physics nor by the limits of the yet-to-be-created field of computer science. For example, novelist Mary Shelley (1922) envisioned the creation of a sapient creature by Dr. Victor Frankenstein in her 1818 novel *Frankenstein; or the Modern Prometheus*. Shelley's character reanimated the corpse of an adult man, but it had to be taught to become human, which is recognizable in ML today.

9.3 A BRIEF HISTORY OF ARTIFICIAL INTELLIGENCE

After the invention of Babbage's general-purpose Analytical Engine in the middle to late 1800s, creating artificial life was no longer confined to novelists. Rather, it could be imagined that a computer could simulate human intelligence. This is an issue that interested Alan Turing, the famous British mathematician who played a key role in helping to break the encryption of the German Enigma cipher that was vital to Allied success in World War II. He also helped to lay the mathematical foundations of computer science with his 1938 PhD thesis.

When electronic general-purpose computers first became known to the public, beginning with the Electronic Numerical Integrator and Computer (ENIAC) at the University of Pennsylvania in the 1940s, the press took to calling them electronic brains. About the same time far-sighted individuals were exploring the possibility of emulating human intelligence using such machines. Thus, the modern concept of AI was born. The ENIAC used vacuum tubes, was programmed by plugging in cables, and was massive (see Figure 9.2).

Figure 9.2 US Army photo of the ENIAC at the Moore School of Electrical Engineering

9.3.1 The Turing Test of Intelligence

In 1950, Alan Turing (1996) published a paper entitled "Computing Machinery and Intelligence" in which he entertained the question "Can machines think?" Rather than address this amorphous question, his approach was to formulate the "Imitation Game," now known as the "Turing Test," in which a game is played with a person, a computer, and an interrogator.

In the Imitation Game, the computer and person are hidden behind screens and communicate with a human interrogator via text so that the mode of communication does not identify the human. The interrogator is free to ask probing questions of the person and the computer. The computer is said to be intelligent if the interrogator cannot distinguish between the two. Reflecting on this test, in 1950 Turing made the following unrealized prediction:

I believe that in about fifty years' time it will be possible to programme [sic] computers, with a storage capacity of about 10^9, to make them play the imitation game so well that an average interrogator will not have more than 70 percent chance of making the right identification after five minutes of questioning. ... I believe that at the end of the century the use of words and general educated opinion will have altered so much that one will be able to speak of machines thinking without expecting to be contradicted. (Turing, 1996)

9.3.1.1 The Turing Machine
The computational model that Turing had in mind in formulating the Imitation Game is now called the Turing machine (TM). Recall the stateless logic circuit

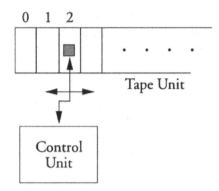

Figure 9.3 The TM with a control unit (an FSM) and tape

and the finite-state machine (FSM) introduced in Chapter 2. The TM is an FSM supplemented with a potentially infinite roll of tape, as suggested in Figure 9.3. Turing envisioned a limited-memory human, in effect an FSM, using paper tape both as a potentially unbounded storage space to hold inputs, written initially on the tape as well as temporary data generated during a computation.

A TM has an FSM "control unit" and a tape of unbounded length ruled into cells, each of which contains a letter from a tape alphabet. The tape has a head that moves back and forth on the tape under control of the FSM.[1] When the FSM is turned on, it reads the symbol in the cell under the head and uses it as an input. The FSM makes a state transition and generates two outputs. One output replaces the contents of the cell, possibly with the previous value. The second output directs the head to stay put or move one cell left or right but not left from the first cell. It repeats these operations endlessly unless it halts. On some inputs a TM may enter a loop and never halt.

Turing invented his model of computation to address a question in mathematical logic posed by David Hilbert early in the twentieth century, which is whether every statement in a formal logical system can be proved or disproved, that is, decided.

9.3.1.2 The Church–Turing Thesis
The TM is postulated to be the most general computational model. That is, it is believed that every computational problem that can be solved by some real-world model of computation, including the quantum computer introduced

---

[1] Initially the head is over the leftmost cell and each tape cell of the TM contains the blank symbol. Beginning with the leftmost cell, the user provides an input string to the TM by replacing blanks with input string characters. The head cannot move left from the leftmost tape cell.

in Chapter 2, can be solved by a TM. This is known as the Church–Turing Thesis, named for Alonzo Church and Turing. Church and Turing independently proposed equivalent methods of computing. It has been shown that any computation done by Church's method could be done by a TM and vice versa (Rowland, n.d.).

Some problems can be solved faster with real-world computers than with a TM, but so far, no computer has been shown to solve problems that cannot be solved with a TM. Since the TM uses a tape as its principal means of storage, a TM can be much slower in solving problems than the random-access machine of Chapter 2.

9.3.2 AlphaGo Beats Go Master

There have been significant advances in AI systems that play board games since Von Kempelen's chess-playing Turk inspired Babbage to develop real thinking machines. The tests have moved beyond playing chess to more complex games such as Go, which was invented in China at least 4,000 years ago. Go plays a central role in Chinese culture and strategic thinking. In fact, "in ancient China one of the four arts any cultivated scholar and gentleman was expected to master was the game of Go" (Koch, 2016).

Go is played with 181 black and 180 white pebbles on a square board with 19 horizontal and 19 vertical lines. Pebbles are placed at the intersection of lines. Initially the board is empty. Players alternate placing pebbles. Black goes first. If pebbles of one color completely enclose pebbles of the other color, the enclosed pebbles are forfeited. The winner is the player who finishes with the higher score, which is the number of pebbles that player has enclosed minus the number of his/her/their pebbles the other player has enclosed.

When AlphaGo, an AI system developed by DeepMind, now a Google subsidiary, defeated Lee Sedol, one of the world's top ranked Go players, in 2016, the Chinese leadership was reportedly shocked. Within a year President Xi announced plans for China to catch up with the United States in AI by 2025 and lead the world by 2030. The US national security establishment likewise embraced the potential of AI. The AlphaGo story demonstrates that AI can solve problems that are extremely hard for humans; it beat a Go master of the highest rank in a complex game with well-defined rules (see Figure 9.4).

A new version of AlphaGo, called AlphaGo Zero, was trained solely by self-play reinforced learning, that is, with no human help. It exhibits

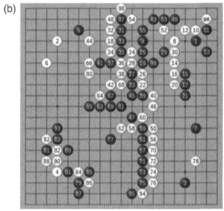

Figure 9.4 (a) Lee Sedol playing Go against AlphaGo licensed under Getty Images News/Handout/Handout (b) First 99 moves of the first game licensed under CC BY-SA 3.0

superhuman proficiency (Silver et al., 2017). Using similar technology, DeepMind researchers developed AlphaFold, an AI system that predicts the shape proteins will assume from their amino acid sequences. Since the biology of proteins is determined by their shape, this was a very important contribution. The protein-folding problem is extremely hard and has been considered an open grand challenge problem for the past 50 years (DeepMind, 2020).

Does that mean computers will soon be able to compete with humans in solving arbitrarily hard problems? As shown later, there are some important problems that are easy to state but have no computational solution. There are other problems that do have algorithmic solutions, but they are prohibitively expensive and attempts to solve them have been ongoing for more than 50 years (Definition of an NP-complete problem, n.d.).

9.3.3 Predictions for Artificial Intelligence

Thinking about AI possibilities for the future has always been a part of the AI community. While much progress has been made since Hero created his automata, many predictions for AI have been humbling.

- The attendees at the 1956 Dartmouth AI Workshop later would go on to become leaders of AI research. Enthusiastic pioneers Herb Simon, Allen Newell, and Marvin Minsky made some overly ambitious predictions. In 1958 Simon and Newell predicted that "a digital computer will be the world's chess champion," a prediction that was not realized until almost 40 years later when IBM's Deep Blue beat chess grandmaster Garry Kasparov (Levy, 2017).
- In 1960 Simon predicted that "machines will be capable, within twenty years of doing any work a man can do" (Simon, 1960). Fifty-seven years later this prediction has not been achieved.
- In 1967 Minsky predicted that "[w]ithin a generation … the problem of creating 'artificial intelligence' will substantially be solved" (Russell & Norvig, 2003, p. 17). Two generations later this goal has not been realized.
- In 1970 Minsky predicted that "[i]n from three to eight years we will have a machine with the general intelligence of an average human being" (Darrach, 1970). This prediction was also far too ambitious.

When it comes to the promises of AI and researchers' abilities to deliver, one thing has not changed since Hero of ancient Greece or Babbage of nineteenth-century England – human imagination is superior to human ability to replicate itself in machines. AI applications do well when there are defined rule sets in games such as chess or Go, but they have not yet done as well with autonomous driving where road conditions and human behavior are difficult to predict. That said, automated safety technologies, which are used in many new automobiles, are saving lives and offer the promise of fully automated driving when fully perfected. This is important because human error is the major factor in 94 percent of fatal automobile accidents.

There continue to be major public and private efforts to deliver the promises of AI. The information age in which we live has only accelerated interest and funding of AI research, but current efforts are built on a past of unrealized goals. To date, no machine has been able to pass the Turing test (Taulli, 2020).

Consequently, several other tests have been invented designed to capture the ability of AI systems. They are (a) the Marcus Test (Marcus, 2014), in which a system "watches" a television show and answers questions about it;

(b) the Total Turing Test (Harnad, 1991), where the interrogator tests the ability of the system to perceive and manipulate objects, and (c) the Lovelace Test (Pearson, 2014), in which a system "creates" art. As shown later, the Lovelace Test is close to being realized.

9.3.4 The Ups and Downs of Artificial Intelligence Research Funding

When the United States decided to make a massive investment in basic scientific research in response to the traumatizing Soviet launch of its Sputnik satellite in 1957, AI profited from government largesse. The United States created the Advanced Research Projects Agency (ARPA) and funded basic undirected research in many areas including AI.

By the early 1970s, however, it had become clear that the AI community had grossly underestimated the difficulty of realizing their claims for AI, an example of the planning fallacy. In 1973 the British Science Research Council asked James Lighthill to do a review of basic AI research. The "Lighthill Report" was very critical and led both the British and US governments to greatly curtail support for AI research, precipitating the "AI Winter" (Lighthill, 1973).

By 1982 the Japanese government announced a visionary AI initiative, the Fifth Generation Computer Systems project, that inspired other governments, including the United States, and industry to provide billions of dollars of support to AI. Unfortunately, by the late 1980s, disillusionment set in again, funding was again reduced, and the second AI Winter set in. By the early 2000s increased computing power, theoretical advancements, and improved access to large datasets precipitated a new AI boom, again fueled by corporate- and government-sponsored research and venture capital.

AI has been integrated into daily life through consumer products and industry-level tools. To support AI research, the US government issued a national strategy for AI in 2019. The strategy has five components: "increasing AI research investment, unleashing Federal AI computing and data resources, setting AI technical standards, building America's AI workforce, and engaging with international allies" (White House, 2019). The strategy was several years behind China's efforts; China's New Generation Artificial Intelligence Development Plan (AIDP) was issued in 2017 and President Xi said that China must "ensure that our country marches in the front ranks where it comes to theoretical research in this important area of AI, and occupies the high ground in critical and AI core technologies" (quoted in Kania & Creemers, 2018).

9.4 THE TECHNOLOGIES OF ARTIFICIAL INTELLIGENCE

Artificial intelligence technologies consist of (a) knowledge bases (KBs) to record knowledge useful to an AI system, such as the locations of objects in a room or the contents of a news article, (b) perceptual technologies to acquire knowledge of an environment through observation, (c) methods to reason from knowledge to make deductions, (d) problem-solving methods, such as algorithms to search a space of options or to learn from self-play, (e) techniques to control the motion of robots, and finally (f) sufficient knowledge of natural languages to support communication with humans.

Some of these technologies provide immediate results, such as neural nets that are reminiscent of human System 1 thinking that relies on mental shortcuts, as described in Chapter 4. ML and expert systems are in this category. They do pattern recognition and perform repeatable tasks with bounded solutions such as identifying people who are not wearing masks in a crowd, controlling traffic light switching based on automobile traffic, or identifying agricultural areas that need water. Others, such as symbol manipulation and state-based search, involve much more computation and are reminiscent of the human System 2 thinking that requires deep contemplation.

9.4.1 Symbolic Artificial Intelligence

Mathematical logic was one of the first areas that modern AI researchers investigated to see if they could use it to emulate human intelligence. Mathematical logic is symbol-based. It uses symbols to represent truth values, such as True and False, and combines them using operators, such as AND, OR, and NOT, as discussed in Chapter 2. It has a long history of being studied by anthropologists, mathematicians, philosophers, and social scientists. German philosopher Ernst Cassirer was deeply interested in understanding how modern thought developed from mythology to science and connected his theory of symbolism to Einstein's theory of relativity (Cassirer et al., 2021).

Symbolic computing emerged in the middle 1950s when researchers adopted Cassirer's idea and assumed that humans use symbols to process language, represent knowledge, reason, learn, and interact with the world. This idea was extended to political science when Murray Edelman (1985, p. 6) wrote in the *Symbolic Uses of Politics*, "every symbol stands for something other than itself, and it also evokes an attitude, set of impressions, or a pattern of events associated through time, through space, through logic, or through imagination with the symbol."

Reasoning is emulated by symbolic methods of computation where symbols denote objects with locations or values, such as pieces on a chess board or variables with truth values. Rules provide ways to manipulate symbols, such as the moves that can be executed by pawns, bishops, rooks, kings, and queens in chess or the evaluation of truth values of expressions formed using the operations AND, OR, and NOT in logic. Mathematical logic dominated AI research until the late 1980s when it was realized that it is difficult for a symbol-based AI system to acquire new knowledge from its environment.

9.4.1.1 The Logic Theory Machine

In 1956 Allen Newell, Herbert A. Simon, and Cliff Shaw produced a "complex information processing system" which they "call[ed] the logic theory machine that is capable of discovering proofs for theorems in symbolic logic" (Newell & Simon, 1956). The logic theory machine (LTM) did automated reasoning, one of the first contributions to symbolic AI. It proved theorems in propositional logic.

The LTM attempts to prove that a statement is correct by starting with a set of axioms and three rules of inference. One rule that is easy to understand is substitution, where if $A(p)$ is a true statement and p is a variable of the expression A, $A(B)$ is also true for any expression B.

Starting with the axioms, the LTM builds a search tree. From each axiom it constructs a set of expressions that result from one application of one rule of inference. It repeats this process on the results, and so on, and generates trees.

The LTM proved 38 of the first 52 theorems in chapter 2 of Alfred North Whitehead and Bertrand Russell's *Principia Mathematica*, the classic reference book on symbolic logic (Newell & Simon, 1956), which was a very impressive feat. However, when Newell and Simon presented the LTM to the computer science and symbolic logic communities, it was given a lukewarm reception, primarily, it appears, because neither side understood its implications, although today it is seen as the first serious contribution to machines that "think" (McCorduck, 2004).

From the LTM, the AI community learned the value of search and of heuristics to truncate searches. Also, because the LTM program was successfully written in LISP, a list processing language introduced in 1958, LISP became widely used in AI.

9.4.2 Problem-Solving and Search

Problem-solving involves attempts to efficiently reach a goal. For example, in chess this means for each intermediate board configuration, deciding which move by the current player is most likely to lead to checkmate for that player.

In logic, symbols are associated with statements, including axioms. The rules are methods to infer new true statements (theorems) from previous true statements. In both cases problem-solving involves search through a space of states.

Because many AI problems involve searches on graphs, the FSM introduced in Chapter 2 can be used to model such searches. It has multiple states and transitions occur between them when inputs are supplied.

The states of an FSM can be diagrammed as nodes of a graph. Edges between nodes are directed from a state to a successor state and labeled with the input that takes the FSM from the state to its successor. If the FSM can move back from a successor to a predecessor state, the edge is undirected.

When a state is reached, an output value may be assigned upon reaching it (the Moore model) or an output may be associated with the edge taken to reach it (the Mealy model). In an AI problem, the values generated are often summed as one moves through a graph. For example, in the traveling salesperson problem, the goal is to visit every state once and return home via the shortest route whose length is the sum of the weights of edges on the route.

A board game can be modeled by assigning one node in a graph to each board configuration. If there are 64 board positions, as in checkers, and 24 identical pieces, a game graph would have about 6×10^{17} configurations containing 24 or fewer pieces, an enormous number. This illustrates why problem-solving by search can be very challenging. For this reason, programmers make use of available information to reduce the size of the search space, that is, they apply *heuristics*.

If an AI agent is given a description of the nodes of a graph and possible moves between them, the search problem is much less time-consuming than if the agent must discover the states and possible moves between them. The latter situation is typical of a robot that must reach a location by moving from square to square in a room in which some squares contain obstacles whose locations are unknown to the robot a priori. This describes the task that the Roomba robot vacuum must solve while it makes its way around a room vacuuming and avoiding furniture (iRobot, n.d.).

9.4.3 Expert Systems

In the late 1950s AI researchers at Stanford began experimenting with expert systems. One of their objectives was to study how humans engage in inductive reasoning. That is, how they reason from data to formulate hypotheses, which they considered to be an aspect of human intelligence. They constructed expert systems in areas in which local experts were available.

Policy Matters 9.1 Algorithmic warfare

During the Obama administration, the Defense Department established the Algorithmic Warfare Cross-Functional Team to work on Project Maven to assist with analyzing drone videos (Pellerin, 2017). Through ML, the features of objects in images, such as vehicles, are learned. This data-labeling process is time-consuming. But once the ML system has learned, it can scan image databases for trucks, to be later confirmed by human operators. Then project manager Colonel Drew Cukor said: "People and computers will work symbiotically to increase the ability of weapon systems to detect objects".

Source: Pellerin (2017)

The team built DENDRAL, a system that produces a set of possible chemical structures for organic compounds from their mass spectrometry data, and MYCIN, a system designed to identify serious infectious diseases and recommend antibiotics from a series of Yes or No questions posed to doctors.

Work on DENDRAL began in 1965 and continued for decades. MYCIN was the result of a five- to six-year research effort in the early 1970s.

Both systems recorded their expert data in a set of *if-then-else* rules of the form *if* Pred *then* True_Clause *else* False_Clause. If the predicate Pred is true, the True_Clause applies, else the False_Clause applies. MYCIN employed about 600 *if-then-else* rules mirroring the diagnostic approach a physician would take.

As reported in 2018, several important lessons were learned from experiments in building expert systems (Brock, 2018). The first is summarized by the *Knowledge is Power* principle, which means knowledge is much more important than any other aspect of an expert system, such as formal system for drawing inferences. The second lesson is that an AI "program needs to be able to explain its reasoning in any decision-making situation with high stakes." Today such situations include autonomous vehicles with human occupants and lethal autonomous weapons now "[d]escribed as the third revolution in warfare after gunpowder and nuclear weapons" (LAWS, n.d.).

9.4.3.1 Applications of Expert Systems

Expert systems are now widely available. They provide advice on divorce law, consumer health, vacation planning, and filing income tax. For example, an expert system can offer vacation destinations by knowing when you want to travel, which type of destination you prefer, and your age. They also power the modern AI assistants Siri and Alexa, illustrating that expert systems work well when problems can be broken down into a set of questions. This also explains why AI systems are good at playing games since moves are governed by a set of rules and responses to other players.

9.4.4 Machine Learning

Machine learning has become one of the most important contributions of AI. ML began in the 1940s when Warren C. McCulloch and Walter Pitts created artificial models for neurons and showed they could be trained. Today most AI systems employ ML on neural nets, and most are trained using supervised learning, discussed later. Inputs to ML systems are typically bit vectors, such as the pixel values in an image.

An ML agent learns from experience. The three principal types of AI learning are supervised, unsupervised, and reinforcement learning. Each of them is designed to "learn" a mapping from input vectors $\{\mathbf{s}\}$ to output vectors $\{\mathbf{r}\}$, such as to associate a person with a face or to decide that an X-ray image of a skin lesion is benign or malignant.

In *supervised learning* (SL) an agent is trained on a set $T = \{(\mathbf{s}, \mathbf{r})\}$ of pairs of stimuli and responses. Given a stimulus $\mathbf{s}$, an n-tuple of real values, such as a facial image, the agent is expected to produce a response $\mathbf{r}$, an m-tuple of real values, for some values of n and m.

The response $\mathbf{r}$ could be a multidigit number or a string of text characters such as the name of an animal or a person. The agent being trained generates a response $\mathbf{z}$ that may differ from $\mathbf{r}$, producing an error. In supervised learning the agent's internal parameters are adjusted to minimize the error between $\mathbf{z}$ and $\mathbf{r}$, averaged over pairs in the training set T. A *loss function L* is used to measure the average error between stimulus and response, averaged over all inputs.

In *unsupervised learning* (UL) an agent trains on an n-dimensional data set $T = \{\mathbf{s}\}$ without active operator guidance by running an algorithm. Among the earliest UL agents were those that could separate points in the space of real n-tuples, such as $\mathbf{x} = (x_1, x_2, \ldots, x_n)$, into two sets by a *hyperplane*, an $(n-1)$-dimensional space defined by the n-tuple $\mathbf{y}$, where $\mathbf{y} = (y_1, y_2, \ldots, y_n)$ that satisfies $\mathbf{w} \cdot \mathbf{y} = w_1 y_1 + w_2 y_2 + \cdots + w_n y_n = b$ where $\mathbf{w} = (w_1, w_2, \ldots, w_n, b)$ is a set of $n + 1$ reals. In a 2-dimensional space a line is defined by the pairs (x_1, x_2) such that $w_1 x_1 + w_2 x_2 = b$ where w_1, w_2, and b are constant reals and x_1 and x_2 are variable reals. For example, $3x_1 + 2x_2 = 5$ defines a 1-dimensional line in a 2-dimensional space.

Figure 9.5 Synthetic images generated by StyleGAN 2 by permission of IEEE

Today one of the most exciting illustrations of UL is the *generative adversarial network* (GAN) invented by Ian Goodfellow (Giles, 2018). GANs have been used to translate photos of summer scenes to winter ones and produce "photorealistic photos of objects, scenes and people that humans cannot tell are fake" (Brownlee, 2019).

A GAN consists of two *deep neural nets* (DNNs), nets with many layers, as discussed later, one a *generator* designed to produce new examples of objects like those it has learned from a training set T and the other a *discriminator* designed to distinguish between good and bad representatives of T produced by the generator.

The two DNNs are then pitted against each other in zero-sum UL sessions; the generator produces a new output, and the discriminator decides if it is a good or bad representative of T. DNNs are modified after each session to improve their performance. Sessions continue until the discriminator says about half of the examples are good.

Shown in Figure 9.5 are remarkably realistic synthetic images generated by a GAN called StyleGAN 2 (Karras et al., 2020). Images such as these have been used in fake news releases.

In *reinforcement learning* (RL) an agent learns through trial-and-error interactions with a dynamic environment while trying to maximize rewards and minimize punishments. The environment can range from a board game, such as the game Go, to a room that a Roomba vacuum cleaner must map and navigate. An RL agent must both explore its environment to create a map and assess which moves are most likely to improve its performance, such as completing the cleaning quickly. Too little exploration may miss promising actions while too much exploration may waste time.

A new version of the AlphaGo system mentioned earlier is called AlphaGo Zero. It demonstrates the enormous power of RL (Silver et al., 2017). Its predecessor AlphaGo Lee, which beat grandmaster Lee Sedol, was trained using both SL and RL. The SL moves were provided by experts and RL consisted of self-play, that is, AlphaGo Lee played against itself. The system was trained over a two-month period. By contrast AlphaGo Zero was trained solely by self-play RL, starting from random play, without expert data. After 72 hours of training, AlphaGo Zero was evaluated against AlphaGo Lee. What is remarkable is that AlphaGo Zero beat AlphaGo Lee by 100 games to 0 under the same two-hour time controls and match conditions that applied when AlphaGo Lee defeated Lee Sedol!

AlphaZero is an improvement on AlphaGo Zero (Silver et al., 2018). It was designed by DeepMind, released in 2018, and has mastered the games of Go, chess, and shogi using an approach like that of AlphaGo Zero. In 24 hours of self-play and no human help, it achieved superhuman performance in all three games using a highly parallel computer containing specialized hardware. In 2019 DeepMind released MuZero, which improved upon AlphaZero on Go, chess, and shogi as well as mastered 57 Atari games without knowing their rules.

9.4.5 Artificial Neural Networks

Artificial neural networks (ANNs), that is, networks of artificial neurons, emerged in the early 1940s. It is one of the first AI research topics that is widely used today. In 1943, McCulloch and Pitts (1943) explored networks of artificial neurons (neural nets) inspired by human neural activity. This was one of the earliest computational models of human intelligence.

Shown in Figure 9.6 is a three-input McCulloch–Pitts artificial neuron. Its inputs are multiplied by adjustable real weights w_1, w_2, and w_3 and summed with a "bias" b, a positive or negative real, to form the sum z. We say that the sum z is a *linear combination of the inputs* x_1, x_2, and x_3 and b. The sum is passed through a *nonlinear activation function*, as suggested in the figure, to produce an output y that is typically in the range of -1 to $+1$ or 0 to $+1$.

In general, artificial neurons can have any number of inputs but operate in a similar manner; inputs are weighted and summed with a bias, which is passed through a nonlinear function to generate an output.

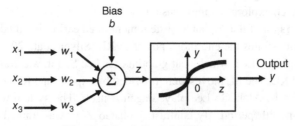

Figure 9.6 A three-input neuron

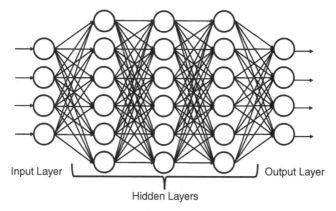

Figure 9.7   A five-level neural net with three hidden levels

An ANN consists of multiple layers of artificial neurons, as suggested in Figure 9.7. External data is supplied to neurons in the *input layer*. Outputs of a given layer serve as inputs to the next. Finally, the outputs of the ANN are the outputs of the *output layer*. The layers in between the input and output layers are called *hidden layers*. Each circle denotes an artificial neuron, and arrows denote groups of signals.

Note that an ANN is a feedforward network, like the logic circuits of Chapter 2. Inputs propagate only from one layer to the next until they reach the output. ANNs are also memoryless; outputs they produce depend only on the current inputs and are not influenced by previous inputs. That is not necessarily true of the recurrent neural nets discussed next.

9.4.6 Recurrent Neural Nets

If an ML system is needed to process a very long sequence of inputs, say to translate a book from one language to another, or to convert a long conversation (sound) into text, that is, take dictation, an ANN will typically not suffice primarily because it is difficult to train the ANN on long inputs. The alternative is to apply an ANN to nonoverlapping segments of the input. However, because an ANN is memoryless, the meaning of an output depends only on the current input, not previous inputs. To see why input segmentation will not be effective, consider the word "coach"; it can refer to a type of transport, a person, or the verb to coach. Thus, if its meaning is defined in one text segment, its meaning in a subsequent segment will be lost.

Recurrent neural nets (RNNs), ANNs with memory, were introduced so that neural nets can efficiently process long sequences of input, carrying knowledge acquired from the past to the present so that it can provide context for interpretation of current inputs.

A one-stage RNN has a *hidden state* $\underline{\mathbf{h}}$ before the t-th time step that is a tuple of n values, namely, $\underline{\mathbf{h}}^t = (h_1^t, h_2^t, \ldots, h_n^t)$ for some integer n. When the RNN is given an m-tuple $\underline{\mathbf{x}} = (x_1, x_2, \ldots, x_m)$ of m inputs, the RNN changes its hidden state to $\underline{\mathbf{h}}^{t+1} = (h_1^{t+1}, h_2^{t+1}, \ldots, h_n^{t+1})$, where h_j^{t+1} is the output n-tuple of an artificial neuron whose inputs are the weighted sum of components of $\underline{\mathbf{h}}^t$ and $\underline{\mathbf{x}}$. The RNN also produces an output tuple $\underline{\mathbf{y}} = (y_1, y_2, \ldots, y_p)$, where each y_i is also a linear weighted combination of components of $\underline{\mathbf{h}}^t$ and $\underline{\mathbf{x}}$. A one-stage RNN is quite powerful and can learn to perform many interesting tasks by adjusting its weights. However, typically RNNs consist of multiple layers of artificial neurons performing as indicated above.

ANNs are analogous to memoryless logic circuits and RNNs are analogous to FSMs, both introduced in Chapter 2.

9.4.7 Deep Neural Nets

Deep neural nets are neural nets with many layers, whether the network is recurrent or not. Today DNNs can consist of thousands of layers of neurons, involve hundreds of billions of weights and bias parameters, and cost millions of dollars to train.

DNNs have amazing capabilities. They can label pixelated images as human or animal, associate the image of a face with a person, and convert short strings of written or spoken text into characters, often with great accuracy. However, they are not without problems. The depth of DNNs introduces complexities, such as greater computing time and increased difficulty of ensuring the models learn correctly. As the size of DNNs grows, it becomes more difficult to explain how they make decisions.

After lots of refinement and improvement, DNNs are now one of the mainstays of ML. They recaptured the imagination of the AI community in 2012 when a team of students headed by AI pioneer and Turing Prize winner Geoffrey Hinton won the 2012 ImageNet competition with a computer vision DNN system within an unheard-of improvement of 10.8 percent (Hao, 2020).

Computer vision enables AI to derive meaningful information from images or full motion video.

9.4.8 How Neural Nets Are Trained

Artificial neural networks are generally trained using supervised learning. They classify their inputs into categories, such as dog, cat, horse, or person, or assign probabilities to each possible classification.

Training an ANN begins with the selection of a loss function L that measures how well or badly the model is doing. L measures the error between the response $\mathbf{z}$ of the network and the desired response $\mathbf{r}$ given a stimulus $\mathbf{s}$, averaged over all stimulus–response pairs pair $(\mathbf{s}, \mathbf{r})$ in a test set T. L is a function of the values of the parameters of the ANN. An optimization function then adjusts these parameters to minimize the loss. Many types of loss function are used in ML, depending on the problem and the judgment of the investigator.

The training goal is to adjust the parameters of the ANN to minimize the average loss $\bar{L}$. ANN parameters are typically initialized with random values that are then adjusted as the training progresses. If the loss function is convex, which means it has a single minimum, loss minimization can be done with a *gradient descent algorithm*, which adjusts the parameters so that each adjustment reduces the loss value, and the global minimum is eventually reached.

Unfortunately, typical ML loss functions are not convex. Consequently, the minimization operation often requires that AI experts resort to experimentation to find a way to reduce the loss to an acceptable level. It has been discovered empirically that minimization is best done using *backpropagation*, that is, the parameters on the output layer of an ANN are adjusted first followed by parameters of layers that are progressively closer to the input layer.

Frequently, ANNs require enormous numbers of days to reach an acceptable value for the loss function using extremely high-performance computers. Thus, if an investigator discovers a training set T set has been corrupted, by accident or by an attacker, it can take days to retrain the neural net. The good news is that on sequential inputs, such as speech or text, an RNN can require a considerably smaller neural net and can be trained more quickly.

9.4.8.1 Intuitive Understanding of Neural Nets

Experts have sought explanations for the exceptional performance of ML systems on classification and translation tasks. They have come to believe that neurons in early layers of neural nets identify basic components in the input, such as lines or edges in images, while neurons in later layers identify more complex structures, such as shapes like circles or rectangles, until finally neurons in the output layer identify a particular outcome, such as a person. However, ML experts do acknowledge that they don't fully understand how neural nets work. Fortunately, work has begun to address this gap in understanding.

9.4.9 Long Short-Term Memories

Many types of RNN have been designed and analyzed but few have been as successful as the *long short-term memory* (LSTM) invented by Sepp Hochreiter and Jürgen Schmidhuber (1997). An LSTM is an RNN that is capable of learning order dependence, which is important in sequence prediction as used in speech recognition and language translation. The interested reader is encouraged to consult the literature on LSTMs technology (Lindemann et al., 2021).

In 2009 at the International Conference on Document Analysis and Recognition (ICDAR) conference an LSTM system won an Arabic handwriting competition (Märgner & Abed, 2009). In 2015 Google announced that it was using LSTMs for speech recognition in Google Voice, reducing transcription errors by 4 percent, a remarkable achievement given the current state of research (Sak et al., 2015). And in 2016 Google used stacked LSTMs (the output of one is the input to the next) for its machine translation service, Google Translate. In some cases, it reduced errors by 60 percent and equaled or surpassed published results on standard benchmarks (Wu et al., 2016). The LSTM technology is so powerful that it readily adapts to new languages. As of early 2020 Google Translate was able to translate 108 languages (Statt, 2020). LSTMs were also used in the version of AlphaGo that beat Lee Sedol in 2016, discussed Section 9.3.2.

LSTMs are also used to generate sequences. After processing a story, they can generate a related story influenced by the input story. They can also propose a caption for an image after analyzing it. LSTMs are also used for speech and video generation, music composition, short-term traffic forecasting, drug design, and robot training. One of the more dramatic successes of LSTMs has been the completion of Beethoven's unfinished tenth symphony (Elgammal, 2021).

The success of LSTMs may reflect both the nature of problems that AI engineers want to solve and human nature. We humans have evolved to solve problems essential to our survival. They seem to require the use of both short-term and long-term memories. Thus, an LSTM that provides a crude approximation to human problem-solving ability may explain its success.

9.4.10 Why Neural Nets Are Trained Rather Than Programmed

Neural nets are trained and not programmed because it is very difficult for humans to identify the characteristics of important inputs, such as faces, speech, or video, that are sufficient to classify these inputs with high accuracy. Imagine, for example, trying to identify the features of a face that will distinguish one face from another. Thus, engineers have opted to train neural nets on patterns of representative inputs along with their expected responses with the expectation that the neural nets will *learn* instead of being programmed explicitly and be able to accurately classify inputs that it has not yet seen.

Training creates numerous problems. First, if the training data is biased, the ML systems will reflect that bias. Second, it is difficult to explain why an ML system made a particular decision; if the system were programmed, the explanation of a decision likely would be associated with a few lines of code, which would reflect human judgment as recorded by a programmer. Fortunately, research designed to make ML systems self-explanatory is underway. The jury is out on how successful it will be.

9.5 SURPRISES INTRODUCED BY MACHINE LEARNING SYSTEMS

Machine learning experimentalists were surprised by the uses that were made of ML systems, such as the creation of fake videos and speech that looked and sounded authentic when they are not, and by the ways in which these systems performed. That is, they did not expect that trained ML systems could change input classifications when small changes were made to an input, creating what are called *adversarial inputs*.

They were also surprised to find that data they collected could contain biases that would be carried over to the ML systems trained on that data. Finally, they were surprised to find that an ML system designed to learn through interaction with users, such as a chatbot, could be hijacked by malicious users who caused it to acquire offensive language. The latter two examples illustrate how important an ML training set is to the performance of an ML system.

Finally, great progress has been made in training ML systems with billions of variables that exhibit amazing performance. This is illustrated by large language models (LLMs) such as GPT-3 with 175 billion variables, GPT-4 with a reported trillion variables that were trained on enormously large corpuses of data, such as large portions of the text, images, books, and software accessible on the Internet.

9.5.1 Deepfakes

Deepfakes are AI-generated media, such as images, audio, or video, constructed using deep learning that has been used to alter real media to achieve an effect that might be malicious, such as attacking a person's credibility or attempting to influence the outcome of an election (Simonite, 2018).

The publication of deepfakes can be criminal if used for malicious purposes, such as the creation of pornographic videos using the faces of innocent individuals, thereby seriously damaging their reputations (Smith, 2020). Unfortunately, deepfakes can be produced with such high fidelity that it can be almost impossible to show they are fake and attribute their source. This illustrates one of the unintended consequences of AI research, the invention of tools that have serious malicious applications.

Training of ML systems can be costly and very time-consuming, requiring weeks or months to complete. However, once a system has been trained, it can be repurposed. The cybersecurity firm FireEye demonstrated this by using Style GAN 2 (see Figure 9.5), released by Nvidia researchers, to create synthetic images of the actor Tom Hanks from a few hundred of his images and other tools to synthesize his voice (Tully & Foster, 2021). There are now commercial firms that provide software to swap faces in videos (Robertson, 2018), as well as free open-source software to do the same (Faceswap, n.d.).

There are numerous videos that illustrate how realistic fake videos can be (Baker & Capestany, 2018). For example, words have been put in the mouth of a US president when his lips were synchronized with the false speech of an impersonator. It is reported that AI was used to mimic the voice of a CEO

Exploit 9.1 Deepfake face swaps

An autoencoder is a DNN in which the layers decrease in size up to its middle layer after which they increase that are trained to replicate their inputs. The network up to the middle layer is called the *encoder* and that from the middle layer to the output is called the *decoder*. The middle layer then captures essential features of the input.

To swap faces, autoencoders are trained on videos of persons A and B using the same encoder for both persons. When a new video of A is supplied to the encoder and its output connected to B's decoder, A's facial motions are mapped onto those of B in the video.

Source: Zucconi (2014)

of a UK energy firm that was sufficiently realistic to persuade his subordinate to transfer about $243,000 to a Hungarian supplier that eventually disappeared into a Mexican bank (Stupp, 2019). In 2021 a group of fraudsters using deepfake audio together with forged email messages persuaded an employee of a United Arab Emirates company to wire $35 million to their account (Brewster, 2021).

Researchers are now engaged in developing tools to detect anomalies in deepfake videos, such as unnatural eye blinking patterns, distortions when one face replaces another, inconsistencies in video features, such as lighting, and poor synchronism between speech and mouth movement. For example, Microsoft has released its Video Authenticator for this purpose (Burt & Horvitz, 2020). It should be noted, however, that the race between deepfake generators and deepfake discoverers is another neural net arms race like that associated with generative adversarial networks.

9.5.2 Adversarial Attacks

Designers had assumed that once ML systems were trained, the classifications they provide would be robust. This is not always the case. In 2013 researchers discovered that deep neural networks can be extremely fragile (Shamir et al., 2022). That is, after training an ML system on inputs, such as images, very small changes in an input can cause the ML to map the slightly altered input to a completely different output. For example, small changes to the image of a tumor known to be benign might change its classification to malignant. Altered inputs are called *adversarial inputs*. These are discussed later. In critical situations, such as when a vehicle is being driven by an ML system, changes in classification can be dangerous and even life threatening.

Adversarial attacks on ML systems have been exhibited for almost all ML algorithms and have been investigated since at least the early 2000s (Biggio & Roli, 2018).

In 2019 security researchers at Tencent's Keen Security Lab conducted an experiment with the neural net used by the Tesla autopilot for Model S. They demonstrated that placing three small stickers at strategic locations on the road caused the vehicle to be tricked into swerving into another lane without first obtaining driver authorization (Ackerman, 2019). This suggests that a malicious actor could exploit such a vulnerability to injure occupants in a vehicle.

Similarly, experiments show that a visual recognition system trained on street signs could be tricked by a few pieces of white and black tape on the Stop sign shown in Figure 9.8 to be interpreted as a Speed Limit 45 MPH sign. If

Figure 9.8 A stop sign with graffiti that was classified as a 45 MPH sign by permission of IEEE

this adversarial attack occurred at a busy intersection it could result in a serious incident (Eykholt et al., 2018).

Adversarial attacks are the bane of ML. Their existence warns us that we must be alert to the possibility that an ML system may be given inputs that can cause the system to make an important classification error that can cause a life-threatening scenario, such as suddenly applying the brakes on an autonomous vehicle while traveling at high speed on a busy highway.

A question that has confronted ML experts is whether adversarial attacks are rare or common. If rare, perhaps steps can be taken in critical systems to prevent their consequences. If common, that is, if they afflict every ML system, the problem must be treated as a systemic risk. Evidence has emerged that adversarial inputs exist in every ML system in which the number of inputs to the system is large relative to the number of categories into which the inputs are classified (Shamir et al., 2019).

9.5.3 Algorithmic Fairness

Despite the potential for bias, ML is now broadly used to assess risk and to make recommendations and predictions. It is consulted by loan officers when making risk assessments, online businesses to recommend products to customers, judges to predict whether a criminal defendant is likely to skip bail or commit another crime, and doctors when deciding whether a tumor is cancerous. In each case, ML systems are being deployed with the goal of improving decision-making. If the data on which ML systems are trained are biased, their recommendations will be biased. What ML systems do offer is consistency. Given the same set of inputs on different occasions, they will make the same recommendations. But consistency is not fairness.

As mentioned, ML systems are used throughout the American criminal justice system to perform risk assessments, set bail, determine sentences, and even provide information used to assess guilt or innocence (Kehl et al., 2017). Yet often the internal operation of these corporate AI systems is hidden from view to protect trade secrets. Neither judges who rely on them nor defendants who are sentenced or issued bail decisions via them are allowed to understand how they assign risk, which is often the basis for judicial decisions.

This is illustrated by a 2016 study by ProPublica of the widely used Correctional Offender Management Profiling for Alternative Sanctions (COMPAS) (Angwin et al., 2016).[2] Ellora Israni summarized the ProPublica study in an Op-Ed article in *The New York Times*, saying the study "found that COMPAS predicts black defendants will have higher risks of recidivism than they actually do, while white defendants are predicted to have lower rates than they actually do. ... The computer is worse than the human. It is not simply parroting back to us our own biases; it is exacerbating them" (Angwin et al., 2016; Israni, 2017). As Israni notes in her article, Northpointe Inc., the company that produces the COMPAS algorithm, disputes this analysis.

Pretrial Justice Institute (PJI, 2022), which had been an advocate for pretrial risk assessment tools, in February 2020 changed its position on them. It now states that "there is no pretrial justice without racial justice," concluding "[w]e now see that pretrial risk assessment tools, designed to predict an individual's appearance in court without a new arrest, can no longer be a part of our solution for building equitable pretrial justice systems."

Fairness in AI systems is a complex problem that has received a great deal of attention (Barocas et al., 2022).

Metrics for fairness between individuals and groups need to be defined. For example, one researcher has identified 21 definitions for this concept (Angwin et al., 2016). If possible, training data needs to be processed to remove bias before ML systems are trained, the resultant models must be assured to be both accurate and fair, and the system outputs may need to be transformed to reduce any remaining bias.

The good news is that the corporate world has come forward with interim solutions to some of these problems. IBM Research has developed open-source bias detection tools, which it calls the AI Fairness 360 toolkit, that it has contributed to GitHub so that others can contribute to it (Bellamy et al., 2019). And Microsoft has created a research group to study this issue (FATE, 2014).

---

[2] ProPublica, based in New York City, is a nonprofit newsroom that engages in investigative journalism for which it has won numerous awards. It publishes online.

9.5.4 Microsoft Surprised by the Behavior of Its "Tay" Chatbot

Many websites use chatbots to respond to standard user queries that address frequently asked questions. For example, when logging onto a website, the chatbot might ask "How can I help you?" and use your response as keywords searching a knowledge database to identify topics to assist you. To be effective, this requires extensive training. In March 2016 Microsoft conducted a public experiment by releasing a chatbot on Twitter called Tay, an acronym for Thinking about You (Schwarz, 2019). It was designed to use ML to acquire knowledge of language by engaging in conversation with users.

Unfortunately, within a few hours Tay was tweeting truly offensive messages, causing an outrage and resulting in its withdrawal within 16 hours of being released. Engineers did not anticipate that a troll on 4chan would encourage users to inundate Tay with racist, misogynistic, and anti-Semitic language, which the chatbot absorbed and played back on Twitter. A few months later Microsoft released Zo, a "politically correct" chatbot that was active from 2016 to 2022 without any serious incident (Stuart-Ulin, 2018). Tay and Zo are good reminders that developers must understand how their products will be used in the real world.

9.5.5 Monster Artificial Intelligence Language Models

Tremendous progress has been achieved in the creation of ML language models that, given a prompt, will compose text, poetry, music, or images and even write code in many programming languages.

OpenAI, a San Francisco-based AI research and deployment company founded in 2015 with the mission "to ensure that artificial general intelligence (AGI) … benefits all of humanity" (About OpenAI, 2015), introduced GPT-3 in 2020, a third-generation DNN that was "trained on the text of thousands of books and most of the internet." When introduced it shocked the AI community by "its ability to mimic human-written text with uncanny realism [which] seemed to many like a milestone on the road to true machine intelligence" (Heaven, 2021) or AGI, discussed later.

GPT-3 has 175 billion adjustable parameters and is estimated to have cost at least $10 million to train. GPT-3 is so good it sparked debates over whether AGI had been achieved. However, it is far from perfect and often requires multiple runs to produce a high-quality response.

Essential Principle 9.1 ChatGPT illustrations

Q: If 4 cars take 2 hours to drive from Providence to Boston, how long does it take for 8 cars to drive?

A: If 4 cars take 2 hours to drive from Providence to Boston, then the time it takes for one car to make the trip is 2 hours/4 cars = 0.5 hours.

If it takes 0.5 hours for one car to make the trip, then it would take 8 cars 0.5 hours * 8 cars = 4 hours to make the trip. So it would take 8 cars 4 hours to drive from Providence to Boston.

Q: What is neuro-symbolic AI?

A: Neuro-symbolic AI, also known as hybrid AI or hybrid artificial intelligence, is a type of artificial intelligence that combines symbolic artificial intelligence and connectionist artificial intelligence, also known as neural networks.

Symbolic AI refers to the use of symbolic representations and logical reasoning to solve problems, while connectionist AI refers to the use of artificial neural networks, which are inspired by the structure and function of the human brain, to learn and make decisions.

In neuro-symbolic AI, these two approaches are combined to take advantage of the strengths of both. Symbolic AI is good at handling complex logical reasoning and symbolic manipulation, while connectionist AI is good at handling large amounts of data and adapting to changing environments. By combining the two, neuro-symbolic AI can perform tasks that require both symbolic reasoning and data-driven learning. Examples of applications of neuro-symbolic AI include natural-language processing, computer vision, and decision-making.

It has been shown that the accuracy of responses to chatbot queries improves when the questions are made more explicit, such as asking that the bot "show its work."

Shortly after GPT-3 was announced, Facebook, Google, and other companies also announced their own impressive LLMs.

While it is agreed that none of these contributions constitute AGI, they are remarkable and will be incorporated in chatbots that will hold fluent conversations with customers, generate articles on a variety of topics, summarize customer responses, and create captions for images.

OpenAI has also released Codex (OpenAI Codex, 2021) trained on billions of lines of code, that is, software, found in code repositories. Codex translates natural language to code. OpenAI and GitHub, an open-source service for software development and version control, released Copilot, a descendant of GPT-3 that has been finetuned for programming tasks. Copilot is so good that instructors of college and university programming courses are advised to be aware of Copilot when evaluating student work.

In 2022 OpenAI released ChatGPT, also built on top of GPT-3, which engages users in remarkably natural text exchanges. It is so good that Google is said to be worried that it might constitute an existential threat to its business. Also, ChatGPT produces such high-quality text that instructors should be alert to its possible misuse by students.

To test the power of ChatGPT we asked it two questions: (a) What is neuro-symbolic AI? and (b) If 4 cars take 2 hours to drive from Providence to Boston, how long does it take for 8 cars to drive? The responses, shown in Essential Principle Box 9.1, show both how wrong and how sensible ChatGPT can be. Fortunately, progress has been made after its first release and the reasoning error seen here has been fixed.

In 2021 OpenAI also released DALL•E 2, a tool built on GPT-3 that creates realistic images from descriptions in natural language. Many other AI companies have announced their own text-to-image generation tools.

9.5.6 Training Machine Learning Systems

Training large ML systems, such as language models, raises several policy questions, including sustainability, outsourcing, and security.

9.5.6.1 Sustainability of Machine Learning Training

First, it has been said that training GPT-3 had the "same carbon footprint as driving a car the distance from the moon and back" (Heaven, 2021). Thus, the environmental impact associated with training large ML systems needs to be assessed.

9.5.6.2 Outsourcing of Machine Learning Training

Second, large ML systems require powerful computers and great expertise to train them effectively. This raises the question of whether organizations should outsource the training of their ML systems on their data to outside specialists, which is possible today via platforms such as Amazon Sagemaker or Microsoft Azure Machine Learning.

9.5.6.3 Security in Machine Learning Training

Third, should outsourcing be necessary, the issue of security of the training process becomes important, especially if ML systems are to be deployed in critical environments.

Security is especially problematic because cryptographers have recently shown that a *backdoor* can be inserted into *any* ML system during training such that it is computationally infeasible to determine if a backdoor has been inserted. In addition, if a malicious actor has a secret key, that actor can use the backdoor to alter the classification of any input data (Goldwasser et al., 2022). Not only does this mean that the ML system becomes completely unreliable but it also means that in such backdoored ML systems it is possible to find an adversarial input for each category of classified input, which speaks to the prevalence of adversarial inputs.

It follows that if ML systems are going to be used in highly secure environments, for highly sensitive tasks, or on mission critical platforms, such as ships or planes, and if their training is to be outsourced, the outsourcing process must be certifiably secure. Thus, outsourcing introduces another supply chain problem.

9.6 ARTIFICIAL GENERAL INTELLIGENCE

A question that has occupied philosophers for generations is whether computers can be constructed that will equal or exceed the intelligence of humans for most tasks. If so, they would say that we have achieved AGI and call the date upon which AGI is achieved "the singularity" (Goertzel, 2007). AI that does not meet this standard is called "weak AI."

It is unlikely that AGI will be achievable any time soon, especially if it requires at least as many neurons and computational operations as the human brain, which is estimated to "perform 38 thousand trillion operations a second" (Coombs, 2018), which is well beyond what our fastest supercomputer will perform for generations. However, ML has become so powerful and pervasive that AI will find many applications and have a profound effect on business, society, and government.

Professor and Turing Prize winner Geoffrey Hinton is particularly optimistic. He said:

I do believe deep learning is going to be able to do everything, but I do think there's going to have to be quite a few conceptual breakthroughs. For example, in 2017 Ashish Vaswani et al. [2017] introduced transformers, which derive good vectors representing word meanings. It was a conceptual breakthrough. It's now used in almost all the very best natural-language processing. We're going to need a bunch more breakthroughs like that. (quoted in Hao, 2020)

Hinton also believes that true intelligence requires techniques to acquire common sense and fine motor control. It remains to be seen how long it will take to reach these objectives.

9.7 ROBOTICS

The computer science and engineering equivalent to Mary Shelley re-creating life through Dr. Frankenstein's monster is a robot controlled by an AI system. A robot is "a machine that resembles a living creature in being capable of moving independently (as by walking or rolling on wheels) and performing complex actions (such as grasping and moving objects)" (Definition of ROBOT, n.d.). The word "robot" was introduced by the Czech writer Karel Čapek in his 1920 play *R.U.R.*, which is an acronym for Rossum's Universal Robots. Robotics is the design, construction, and study of robots.

Today, a wide variety of robots exist. Some emulate animals, such as a four-legged dog, while others take a human form. Some are designed simply to be utilitarian, such as a jointed arm that holds a welding gun employed in a car factory, a cart designed to deliver products in a large warehouse, or a flying drone. Many repetitious human tasks are performed by robots.

Shown in Figure 9.9 are two robots manufactured by Boston Dynamics, Spot, a dog-like robot, and Atlas, a humanoid robot. Spot is an amazingly agile

Figure 9.9 Spot and Atlas by permission of Boston Dynamics

quadruped. It weighs about 65 pounds, and walks at a speed of about 3.6 miles per hour. Modules can be added to its back to perform tasks, such as inspections in unsafe environments (Boston Dynamics, 2022b).

Atlas is an exceedingly nimble bipedal humanoid robot weighing 196 pounds and stands four foot eleven inches. It can do somersaults, walk across uneven terrain without falling, such as a wooded area, pick up and move a box to a shelf, and pick itself up when pushed to the ground (Boston Dynamics, 2022a).

The creation of robots has not obviated human roles but generated ways for humans and machines to interact together.

9.7.1 Human–Machine Interaction

Artificial intelligence systems can make refined decisions quickly and relieve workers from dangerous, heavy, and/or repetitive work. However, they also create a variety of problems. First, they remove humans from the decision-making process and, second, they remove the flexibility that humans can provide when the working conditions change in unpredictable ways (Heffernan, 2019).

When an automated system is designed, programmers cannot include responses to situations that they cannot imagine. If an unanticipated situation arises that could produce a serious negative consequence, having a human in the loop may be necessary since humans can be good at quick thinking in unanticipated situations. This is an issue to take into consideration when pondering the impact of automation on the nature of work.

An instance of this kind occurred with the flight-control system of the Boeing 737 MAX aircraft, leading to two deadly crashes. New software, the Maneuvering Characteristics Augmentation System (MCAS), was added to prevent stalling after the aircraft body was lengthened and heavier engines added. A new sensor was installed in the nose of the aircraft and MCAS added to the flight-control system, which used that sensor data to calculate the angle of the aircraft. When a failing sensor sent incorrect information, MCAS pushed the nose down. Pilots, not aware of the introduction of MCAS, were not told that they had four seconds to disable it. The result was two crashes and the suspension of 737 MAX flights until the problem was corrected (Gates, 2019).

Today we have automatic systems in our cars that are designed to protect humans. They apply the brakes when approaching a solid object, tell us when our vehicles are drifting out of a lane, and release air bags in a collision.

We also have military authorities planning to deploy lethal autonomous weapon systems designed to attack humans, such as AI-controlled drones equipped with rockets, the equivalent of flying robots. Armed autonomous systems underscore the ethical challenge of ensuring robots do not become the nightmare of science fiction. Yet, fiction can point the way to a code of conduct and institutionalize ethics to ensure technology benefits society.

9.7.2 Asimov's Rules of Robotics

In 1942, American writer Isaac Asimov introduced his Three Rules of Robotics in a science fiction story entitled "Runaround" set in 2015 in which he envisioned the existence of intelligent robots capable of reasoning. Two astronauts, who have been sent to Mercury, have a problem with their robot Speedy, which they solve by observing that it must adhere to the following three rules or what have become known as Asimov's "Three Laws of Robotics" (Asimov, 1942).

- First Law: A robot may not injure a human being or, through inaction, allow a human being to come to harm.
- Second Law: A robot must obey orders given it by human beings except where such orders would conflict with the First Law.
- Third Law: A robot must protect its own existence as long as such protection does not conflict with the First or Second Law.

Later Asimov added the Zeroth Law:

- Zeroth Law: A robot may not harm humanity, or, by inaction, allow humanity to come to harm.

Asimov's science fiction is said to have inspired Marvin Minsky, the famous AI expert from Massachusetts Institute of Technology, and many others. Minsky said, "I remember reading the first robot stories and deciding I was going to build them" (Teitelbaum, 1992).

The objective of Asimov's rules was to ensure robots (and AI) promote humanity rather than undermine it.

9.8 ETHICAL PRINCIPLES FOR ARTIFICIAL INTELLIGENCE

Given the ubiquity of and promise for AI, its impact on society has drawn a lot of attention, particularly with respect to mitigating or controlling its adverse impacts. Consequently, multiple parties have taken positions on the ethical issues in AI. The contemporary discussion is in the context of "drone warfare," where several countries employ remotely piloted vehicles to conduct targeted killings (Byman, 2006).

9.8.1 Lethal Autonomous Weapons Systems

Because nations have developed lethal autonomous weapons systems (LAWS), a vigorous debate has emerged concerning their legality and morality. In 2018 the International Committee of the Red Cross (ICRC, 2018) declared, "[H]uman control must be maintained over weapon systems and the use of force to ensure compliance with international law and to satisfy ethical concerns. ... States must work urgently to establish limits on autonomy in weapon systems."

The US Department of Defense has issued a directive on autonomous weapon systems that states, "Autonomous and semi-autonomous weapon systems shall be designed to allow commanders and operators to exercise appropriate levels of human judgment over the use of force" (DoD, 2017). There is an imperative to keep a human in the loop when life is at stake.

In 2016 the High Contracting Parties of the UN Conference on Convention on Certain Conventional Weapons (Wikiwand, 1983) "decided to establish an open-ended Government Group of Experts on emerging technologies in the area of LAWS" (Digital Watch, n.d.). The issues being discussed include whether the International Humanitarian Law (IHL) suffices to regulate LAWS or whether something more is needed. Given the ability of LAWS to remain active after launch, what responsibility does the launching party retain? Should LAWS be allowed to loiter? Should they self-disable after a reasonable length of time? What care should parties take to ensure that citizens are protected from indiscriminate use, not only initially but over their lifetime?

The private sector has also expressed its opinions about the desirability of deploying LAWS. One such organization is the Campaign to Stop Killer Robots, a coalition of more than 170 nongovernmental organizations (Campaign to Stop Killer Robots, n.d.).

9.8.2 Ethical Principles for Artificial Intelligence

The previous discussion highlights the pitfalls associated with AI and robots. Consequently, many different organizations have created ethical principles for AI (Jobin et al., 2019). We survey a few here.

The Organization for Economic Cooperation and Development has formulated the following principles for AI, reminiscent of Asimov's rules (OECD.AI, n.d.):

- AI should benefit people and the planet by driving inclusive growth, sustainable development, and well-being.
- AI systems should be designed in a way that respects the rule of law, human rights, democratic values, and diversity, and they should include appropriate safeguards – for example, enabling human intervention where necessary – to ensure a fair and just society.
- There should be transparency and responsible disclosure around AI systems to ensure that people understand AI-based outcomes and can challenge them.
- AI systems must function in a robust, secure, and safe way throughout their life cycles and potential risks should be continually assessed and managed.
- Organizations and individuals developing, deploying, or operating AI systems should be held accountable for their proper functioning in line with the above principles.

The US Department of Defense has endorsed the following five principles for AI, replicated here (DoD, 2020a):

- Responsible. DoD personnel will exercise appropriate levels of judgment and care while remaining responsible for the development, deployment, and use of AI capabilities.
- Equitable. The department will take deliberate steps to minimize unintended bias in AI capabilities.
- Traceable. The department's AI capabilities will be developed and deployed such that relevant personnel possess an appropriate understanding of the technology, development processes, and operational methods applicable to AI capabilities, including with transparent and auditable methodologies, data sources, and design procedures and documentation.
- Reliable. The department's AI capabilities will have explicit, well-defined uses, and the safety, security, and effectiveness of such capabilities will be subject to testing and assurance within those defined uses across their entire life cycles.
- Governable. The department will design and engineer AI capabilities to fulfill their intended functions while possessing the ability to detect and avoid unintended consequences and the ability to disengage or deactivate deployed systems that demonstrate unintended behavior.

IBM has developed what they call Everyday Ethics for Artificial Intelligence, which addresses the following five topics:

* Accountability: AI designers and developers are responsible for considering AI design, development, decision processes, and outcomes.
* Value alignment: AI should be designed to align with the norms and values of your user group in mind.
* Explainability: AI should be designed for humans to perceive, detect, and understand its decisions.
* Fairness: AI must be designed to minimize bias and promote inclusive representation.
* User data rights: AI must be designed to protect user data and preserve the user's power over access and uses.

Finally, in October 2019 the State of California passed a law concerning deepfakes, specifically criminalizing the "distribut[ion] with actual malice materially deceptive audio or visual media of the candidate [for public office] with the intent to injure the candidate's reputation or to deceive a voter into voting for or against the candidate" (Elections: Deceptive audio or visual media, 2019).

All these efforts illustrate that the technological advances that brought important uses for technology are fraught with deep concerns. These include deliberately creating AI systems that institutionalize discrimination and autonomous systems that can kill. As technology continues to develop, we cannot lose sight that the goal is to create tools to improve humanity. Ethics and morality have a place in a world governed by binary answers to if–then scenarios. This includes the applications of AI to cybersecurity.

9.9 APPLICATIONS OF ARTIFICIAL INTELLIGENCE TO CYBERSECURITY

Today many hope that deep learning will make possible large improvements in cybersecurity. In their excellent survey of the role of ML in cybersecurity, researchers Micah Musser and Ashton Garriott (2021) argue that absent breakthroughs in AI, that is not likely.

However, they observe that traditional ML, that is, the type in use before the advent of deep neural networks, has been used for decades to detect spam, identify malware, and help with intrusion detection. This section benefits from their report.

9.9.1 Spam Filters

The earliest spam filters attached a weight to each email based on the frequency of words known to be regularly used by spammers in an email as well as the reputation of the server that delivered the email. If the weight was large enough, the email was deposited in a spam folder. When too many false positives occurred, they switched to ML technologies. Musser and Garriott report that this basic approach to spam has not changed much over time.

9.9.2 Intrusion Detection Systems

Intrusion detection systems (IDSs) try to determine if an attacker has entered a computer network, typically by searching for anomalous network behavior or signs of malicious activity. IDSs are classified as "misuse-based" or "anomaly-based." The former identify attacks based on their "resemblance to previously seen attacks," such as attempting to contact a site that known malware tries to contact. Anomaly-based IDSs observe network traffic and try to classify it as normal or not. Both approaches make use of early ML technologies. Unfortunately, because much network traffic is anomalous by nature, anomaly-based detection systems generate too many false positives.

The Department of Homeland Security developed, maintains, and operates an IDS on federal civilian government networks. Originally referred to as Einstein I and II, the National Cybersecurity Protection System alerts cybersecurity analysts of malicious behavior on federal networks (Department of Homeland Security, 2019).

9.9.3 Malware Detection

Malware detection systems examine files. The standard approach, found in the earliest antivirus systems, is to search files for *signatures* or *indicators of compromise* (IoCs). These are strings found in known malware but are uncommon elsewhere. This approach requires a database of known IoCs. The good news is that this approach continues to be useful although the bad news is that a very large percentage of viruses are now polymorphic, as noted in Chapter 2. That is, they change their IoCs every time they replicate. Of course, if they replicate enough, they will be caught.

Many malware detection systems use "sandboxes," which are environments that generally look to the malware like a normal computer but is instrumented so that the defender can record what actions occur when an unidentified file is executed but which cannot corrupt the computer on which a sandbox is running. A sandbox is another name for a virtual machine. It has a copy of an operating system that it uses to simulate a real machine when running the file. Unfortunately, malware has become smart, and the more sophisticated malware can time the execution of commands and detect whether it is running on a real computer or a simulated one. The cat-and-mouse game goes on!

While many commercial anti-malware vendors advertise that they use AI in their products, they keep the details of their AI systems private. What we do know is that their antivirus algorithms focus on files because executable files can be compromised and the security of a computer lost. As noted earlier, attackers have learned to morph viruses and evade signature analysis. That is the reason that antivirus engineers have turned to using ML systems trained to find new malware as a supplement to traditional signature analysis.

9.9.4 Commercial Antivirus Software

Kaspersky, the Russian cybersecurity company, has given a sketch of the way its ML-based anti-malware software works (Kaspersky, n.d.). Kaspersky collects data on files in both pre-execution and post-execution phases. Pre-execution data consists of features such as file format, characterization of the code, and data collected from emulation. The anti-malware software trains its ML system by first creating lists of file features it will use. Then, it invokes a special type of hash function that distinguishes between files that are dissimilar, similar, and very similar and use it with supervised learning to distinguish between examples of infected and benign files.

Postexecution data reflects behavior of the code or events triggered by the code. As noted in Essential Principle Box 2.3, behavior can be determined from an operating system implant that reports actions that the operating system takes while executing code. Often a vendor collects such operating system reports on its cloud and uses them to train a second ML system to detect new malware.

Kaspersky notes that a trained ML system can cause a catastrophic error if it has been designed to remove infected software and falsely declares a benign file to be infected, creating a false positive and possibly removing software needed for continued operation. To minimize false positives, the training data needs to be representative of the threat. For example, if it classifies new files as infected, then the training set must have many samples of new benign files.

The American cybersecurity company CrowdStrike has also provided a high-level view of its anti-malware software (CrowdStrike, 2016). CrowdStrike's approach is like Kaspersky's. CrowdStrike begins by extracting a large set of features from a file, such as file size, number of sections, file entropy (a measurement of randomness), resources embedded in the file, such as images, icons, user interface templates, string tables, and many others. They also dissect the code and summarize it in numerical terms that can be fed to an ML classifier. This is followed by an analysis of actions taken while the code is running. To track execution, they embed a small "endpoint sensor" in the operating system that reports all executional activity inside the operating system. The management of the sensor is done in the cloud. They observe and record about one hundred types of events. They use this information to identify indicators of attacks. They also attack attribution and detect lateral movement from computer to computer and other functions. Threat intelligence is integrated to provide a real-time context.

CrowdStrike software will stop the execution of a file if static analysis of it reveals that it contains malware. If not, it begins execution and monitors the process. If it looks like the executing file behavior is malicious, it terminates it. It does the same if the interactions between processes on different machines are deemed malicious. It also correlates with the cloud. The software's goal is to "detect, prevent, and mitigate threats at every stage of execution."

9.10 CONCLUSIONS

Artificial intelligence has attracted a great deal of favorable attention from governments, businesses, and the media. It is easy to get excited about the potential of new technologies, especially those perceived to have positive disruptive potential. AI is one of these. It is seen as having the potential to revolutionize warfare, business, and government. However, as with all technologies, it surprises us with consequences that were not anticipated at their creation.

In the 1950s, the founders of AI were very optimistic about its potential to emulate human intelligence. Many of their predictions were not only too ambitious but some of them remain unrealized even today. This should both inspire researchers to continue the difficult work and temper their claims when explaining the capabilities of AI technologies. Nonetheless, AI has achieved some very impressive gains. Many problems that are very hard to solve, such as recognizing and classifying objects, translating from one language to another, and beating humans at very challenging structured games, such as Go, have been solved. Also, engaging in a conversation with a chatbot appears to be on the verge of being solved.

Many of the greatest achievements of AI were made through the development of algorithms to train neural networks. Introduced by McCulloch and Pitts in 1943, it was not until 2012, almost 70 years later, that the potential of neural nets and ML came to be fully appreciated.

Moreover, AI is powerful because computer scientists and mathematicians have found ways to train neural nets to recognize and classify the data presented to them rather than attempt to extract the features from the data needed to write software to perform tasks.

Now neural nets are used for many tasks, including the creation of deep-fake videos and the training of autonomous vehicles and robots, examples of potentially dangerous AI applications. Many other applications of AI are on the horizon.

While AI has put great power into the hands of those who deploy it, it is also true that we cannot fully explain how it arrives at decisions nor do we understand why it is possible to supply ML systems with adversarial inputs that cause it to misclassify inputs. These shortcomings of ML systems need to be addressed.

The potential negative consequences of AI have caused ethicists to debate such consequences of this technology, a debate that will not be resolved soon. The negative consequences should also be seen as a warning to all those who would deploy AI in those environments where unexpected results could have very negative consequences, such as in situations in which human life might be endangered. As noted earlier, this warning must be carried over to outsourced ML training.

9.11 DISCUSSION TOPICS

1. Symbolic AI was seen originally as a very promising approach to constructing intelligent computers. Explain why you think it was displaced by neural net-based technologies.
2. Do you think that facial recognition should be used to authenticate users in a very high security environment? Justify your answer.
3. Give some benign and threatening examples of autonomous robots and discuss the ethical issues that might arise from their use.
4. Reinforcement learning has been shown to be a powerful tool to train a computer to play rule-based games even when the rules must be deduced

from self-play. Do you see RL expressed in play by animals? Please explain why you think this statement is true or false.

5. Take and justify either the position that AGI is or is not possible. If possible, in what time frame might that be possible and provide a test to recognize AGI. If not, explain why such a test is not possible.

6. With new applications for AI being introduced, new ethical questions will undoubtedly be raised. How should we judge AI-generated artwork, artwork generators, or biographies generated from data on the Internet?

10

Conclusions and Future Directions of Cybersecurity Policy

The web has become a public square, a library, a doctor's office, a shop, a school, a design studio, an office, a cinema, a bank, and so much more. Of course, with every new feature, every new website, the divide between those who are online and those who are not increases, making it all the more imperative to make the web available for everyone.

Sir Tim Berners-Lee (2019),
pioneer of the World Wide Web

ENGINEERING AND SCIENTIFIC principles underlie the Internet, and we cannot overlook that humans write code, develop algorithms, and manufacture the hardware that make cyberspace with all its benefits and risks. Among the risks are coding flaws and bad user decision-making that get exploited, generating cyber insecurity. The growth of the cybersecurity industry and incorporation of cybersecurity training in people's daily lives hold promise for a more secure future. But, as the preceding chapters illustrate, cybersecurity is a cat-and-mouse game with one side focused on security and another side searching for new vulnerabilities to exploit for profit or political gain. Artificial intelligence (AI) offers both a promise for cybersecurity and also new hazards.

Technological solutions matter, but better cybersecurity lies within human behavior. Kenneth Geers (2010) reminds us that "[the] Internet today is merely a reflection of what came before – including crime, espionage, and warfare – and the international security environment is still closer to Pandemonium." Evidence of this pandemonium is regularly revealed when corporations publicize data breaches, rivals infringe intellectual property, and governments indict individuals for violating domestic hacking and privacy laws, expel suspected intelligence officers from embassies, or impose financial sanctions on governments that sponsored illicit cyber activities. To compensate for the insecurity, users seek new ways to improve cybersecurity through using virtual private networks, patching software, and following better security protocols. To be sure, there are concerted efforts to reduce the pandemonium in cyberspace.

Strategies, domestic regulation, international norms, law, international bodies, and ethics in technology attempt to ensure the web lives up to the potential Sir Tim Berners-Lee highlighted in this chapter's epigraph to keep the web available for everyone.

We must also remember that the Internet is simultaneously a commercial, social, national security, and sovereign space. Individuals are still citizens of countries with laws that govern behavior and companies locate data centers with telecommunication lines within recognized boundaries that governments control. Yet corporations scale products to cross borders and cut through culture and law with important impacts on individuals, organizations, and governments. States assert dominance within their borders through regulation and public safety institutions, but they also employ their military cyber commands and intelligence services to support their national objectives outside of their borders. The span of actors and their broad scope of interactions illustrate that attempts to improve cybersecurity must involve its users, its producers, and its regulators.

10.1 AN UNCERTAIN FUTURE

Without a doubt, convergence of traditional behavior with technology has already led to the disappearance of distinctions in our language: from e-commerce to commerce, cybercrime to crime, new media to media, and dot-coms to just companies. For all the talk about virtual learning, virtual dating, or virtual activities, these experiences are no less real than the same actions that take place in person simply because these activities occur with a screen, which will yield to wearables, implants, and augmented reality in the future. The Internet is essential to participate in life; those left out will fall further behind and those engaged will expand their reach beyond the digital domain. This underscores the important socio-economic consequences of poor cybersecurity.

At the same time, cybersecurity has become national security. Dozens of countries have been creating military cyber commands, and their intelligence services have been harnessing cyberspace operations beyond traditional political and military intelligence collection. The US Office of Director of National Intelligence forecast says that "States' increasing use of cyber operations as a tool of national power, including increasing use by militaries around the world, raises the prospect of more destructive and disruptive cyberactivity. As states attempt more aggressive cyber operations, they are more likely to affect civilian populations and to embolden other states that seek similar outcomes" (ODNI, 2021a). Consistent with this assessment, the Science and Security Board of the

Bulletin of the Atomic Scientists set its doomsday clock to just 100 seconds before midnight in part because "there are no serious efforts aimed at limiting risky developments in cyberweapons, space weapons, missile defenses, and hypersonic missiles" (John Mecklin, 2021). While remote, the prospect that cyberspace operations can lead to conflict is real, reinforced by the idea that international law applies to cyberspace operations, but there is no consensus on the precise application of international law (Schmitt, 2017b). Governments around the world interpret intellectual property theft, ransomware, and network disruptions through their own domestic laws, culture, and policies.

To structure thinking about the future directions of cybersecurity, we propose the following three questions.

First, whose Internet is it?

As we know it, scientists and engineers originally used federal and university funding to create networks that became the Internet; the Internet became global through private investment in commercial enterprises that linked the planet through hardware and software; it became ubiquitous with the widespread adoption by individuals and ease of access through affordable user-friendly interfaces; and it became a tool of power for governments that broadened intelligence activities and military operations into cyberspace. With a history characterized by a growing group of stakeholders, to answer the question of whose Internet is it, we must consider the extent to which the Internet is a fusion of individual, corporate, and governmental competing interests.

Next, how should we think about cybersecurity?

Collaborating on this book illustrates the value of thinkers from different disciplines and any attempt to answer this question will require diverse groups to fuse their perspectives. In isolation, it is easy to identify different lenses applied to the problem of cybersecurity that led to different outcomes. For example, the technology lens looks to developers of hardware, software, encryption, and AI to make cyberspace more secure; the cost imposition lens looks to governments both to raise the stakes for malicious behavior through swift and serious responses to shut down domestic actors who undermine cybersecurity and for international cooperation to limit unacceptable state and transnational behavior through technology, treaty, and norms; and the regulatory lens looks to ways governments impose restrictions on users and providers of information and communications technology (ICT).

The final question is, *What role governments should play in responding to significant cyber events?*

The question itself is difficult to answer since attempting to define an event as a "significant cyber event" is filled with its own set of biases and ambiguity. In the United States, there is currently a high standard to describe

Table 10.1 US cyber incident severity index

Severity level	Definition of severity level	Result of aggressor actions	Intended consequence
5: Emergency	Poses an imminent threat to the provision of wide-scale critical infrastructure (CI) services, national government stability, or to the lives of US persons	Visible effect	Jeopardizes CI services
4: Severe	Likely to result in a significant impact to public health or safety, national security, economic security, foreign relations, or civil liberties	Detectable presence	Damage computer and networking hardware
3: High	Likely to result in a demonstrable impact to public health or safety, national security, economic security, foreign relations, civil liberties, or public confidence	Theft of critical information or denial of service	Corrupt or destroy key data or deny availability to a key system or service
2: Medium	May impact public health or safety, national security, economic security, foreign relations, civil liberties, or public confidence	Engagement	Steal sensitive information
1: Low	Unlikely to impact public health or safety, national security, economic security, foreign relations, civil liberties, or public confidence	Engagement	Commit a financial crime
0: Baseline	Unsubstantiated or inconsequential event	Preparation of action	Nuisance denial of service or defacement

Source: Cyber Incident Severity Schema (Department of Homeland Security, 2016)

an event as significant that brings senior government leaders together to consider policy options. Individual instances of corporate espionage, ransomware attacks, or local outages caused by malicious actors tend to reside below the level of national government concern and are addressed at the individual or corporate level.

However, over the last decade, there has been an upswing of White House interest in cyberspace as the risk of existential events increases; Table 10.1 captures the Obama administration's attempt to bring rigor to cyber incident classification. Given that the impact of cyber incidents is often retrospective, where an effect is analyzed months or years after an intrusion, the value of a scale like this is still limited by interpretation. Further, there are larger policy considerations when classifying an incident as a use of force or an armed attack that could compel a government to respond with force in kind leading to military escalation in the physical world.

Outside the United States, some governments view privacy as an inherent human right that must be preserved and protected online, while others view privacy and freedom of association as a threat to their stability, necessitating content mitigation or censorship. While the different interpretations of significant cyber events through law, policy, and norms matter, how governments inject themselves in processes to improve cybersecurity will have lasting effects on the confidence, integrity, and availability of data, thereby shaping the nature of how users experience cyberspace.

10.2 WHOSE INTERNET?

The Internet is young and emerged from the modest ARPANET in 1969 to become the premiere internetworking system on the planet and in orbit. Driven by efforts to link scientists and researchers in an era marked by expensive computing and terrestrial correspondence such as a postal service, the Internet's commercial phase eclipsed its academic origins through several key innovations.

First, the shift from mainframe computing to personal computing broadened the base of participants in cyberspace. While it was not possible for an individual to own an IBM 1401, which accounted for half of the world's computers in the 1960s and rented for $2,500 per month (IBM, 2012), it was possible for an individual to own a Tandy Radio Shack TRS-80 for $600 in the 1980s (TRS-80, n.d.). Costs further declined, removing hardware as a barrier to access. By 2023, technology company Cisco estimates there will be 29 billion networked devices or 3.6 networked devices per person (Cisco, 2020).

History Matters 10.1 The first webpage

Written by Sir Tim Berners-Lee when he was at the European Organization for Nuclear Research, known as CERN, the first webpage went live on August 6, 1991. Berners-Lee used a simple programming language known as HyperText Markup Language or HTML. The page described the World Wide Web as an "informational retrieval initiative aiming to give universal access to a large number of documents" (Berners-Lee, 1991). It provided links to everything else that was online: software and technical details to provide users the source code for free. Vinton Cerf, who is recognized as being an internet pioneer, said, "no one paid much attention" at the time (Brooker, 2018), but the HTML improved accessibility of documents and paved the way for browsers and indexing algorithms that broadened users from those with coding knowledge to those who could click a mouse or tap a screen.

Second, domestic deregulation of phone companies and massive commercial investments in fiber-optic cabling gave rise to the modern telecommunications industry in the 1990s. It is hard to imagine this today, but the cost of a nonlocal phone call was several dollars per minute. Fiber-optic cabling replaced copper wire, which triggered significant upgrades to internet service. In 1995, for example, data rates were about 28 kilobytes per second. In 2023, data rates are about 100 megabytes or 104,857,600 kilobytes per second; 5G speeds will further accelerate data transfer and may reach 575 megabytes per second. Such speeds enable companies like Apple to provide over-the-air software upgrades measured in gigabytes, Netflix to stream a two-hour movie in seconds, and some level of autonomous driving with cars maintaining constant situational awareness while moving under certain environmental conditions.

Third, accessibility to the Internet grew with the introduction of a browser, a simple user interface, and a programming language that resulted in the first webpage to go live in 1991 at the European Organization for Nuclear Research (CERN) (Berners-Lee, 1991). The software CERN created was placed in the public domain, enabling programmers to support Berners-Lee's ambition to make the web truly worldwide. Since 1991, billions of webpages have been created. This enabled individuals to share information and form connections regardless of nationality and time zone. The proliferation of mobile apps further eased individual use of software and gave developers everywhere a simple means of distribution, which was accelerated when Apple launched its App Store in 2008 with just 500 apps and Android Market (later Google Play) launched the same year with just 50 apps. Both stores enabled developers to upload their own software and sell directly to consumers. In 2023, both stores have each made millions of apps available. While the emergence of so-called big tech appears certain, there were significant stumbling blocks along the way that threatened the development of cyberspace. While historical, we are reminded by Shakespeare's warning in the *Tempest*, what's past is prologue.

10.2.1 The Dot-Com Bubble

The dot-com boom began in 1993 with the introduction of the Mosaic browser. Unlike the text-based CERN browser, it displayed both text and images. It created a sensation. Suddenly entrepreneurs, venture capitalists, and the public saw the potential of the World Wide Web and the Internet, and startups proliferated. The dot-com boom had begun.

The United States enacted the Telecommunications Act of 1996 for the express purpose of providing a "national policy framework designed to accelerate rapidly private sector deployment of advanced information technologies and services to all Americans by opening all telecommunications markets to competition" (FCC, 1996). In the five years following the passage of the Act, US telecommunications companies invested more than $500 billion in laying down fiber-optic cable and supporting equipment and installing wireless networks. Between 1995 and 2000 the Nasdaq Composite Index, a measure of the price of stocks on the technology-heavy Nasdaq stock market, increased 400 percent and speculation blossomed. Cybersquatting mentioned in Chapter 1 became serious enough that the US government adopted the Anticybersquatting Consumer Protection Act (ACPA) in 1999.

By early 2000 it had become clear that the dot-com boom was in trouble. Dot-com companies were running out of money, Microsoft was found in violation of the Sherman Antitrust Act, and Japan had entered a recession, all of which depressed the technology-heavy Nasdaq stock index. In March the Nasdaq reached a peak but fell 9 percent in one day in April 2000; the heady investment atmosphere during this period led to several accounting scandals that eroded investor confidence and deprived technology companies of needed capital. Those developments as well as the September 2001 terrorist attacks led to a stock market loss of stock capitalization of $5 trillion in 2002. The dot-com bubble burst had occurred. By 2004, the markets had stabilized, but only 48 percent of the dot-com companies survived. Recovery was steady throughout the 2010s, with a few corporations dominating such as Apple and Samsung in the smartphone sector, Amazon and Microsoft in cloud computing, and Corning and Yangtze Optical FC in fiber-optic cabling.

In 2023 the market for cyberspace products and services matured and the market for AI products expanded with the introduction of ChatGPT. New companies continue to be created that promote accessibility through personal devices, enable secure financial and business transactions through commercially available encryption, and broaden interest in the Internet through entertainment content and shopping. The quarantines created by the COVID-19 pandemic further accelerated the shift to digital spaces. Telework and remote learning normalized and generated new rounds of investment in broadband access, while raising the importance of cybersecurity for individuals, corporations, and governments.

10.2.2 Stakeholders Expand

As discussed in Chapter 6, it was not until 30 years into the modern cyber age that countries started to create military cyber commands and use intelligence services for operations in cyberspace. Intergovernmental organizations also came late to cybersecurity: The United Nations first considered cyberspace in 1998 and then convened a series of experts to develop norms throughout the 2000s through today; The North Atlantic Treaty Organization recognized cyberattacks could result in invoking the collective defense clause in 2014 (seven years after its member Estonia suffered a catastrophic denial-of-service attack); the European Union started to protect individuals in cyberspace through implementation of the General Data Protection Regulation in 2018; and 60 countries joined together to prevent internet fragmentation in 2022.

These efforts accelerated, considering attacks on critical infrastructure, Russian influence operations during the 2016 and 2020 US elections, and Chinese data theft and manipulation in the wake of the 2019–22 health pandemic. Governments and international organizations recognize there continues to be much work to be done through multiple tracks. It remains to be seen how they will work with corporations that unwittingly provide the vulnerabilities exploited in cyberspace. These same corporations suffer the costs of intellectual property theft along with individuals who claim cybersecurity as an inherent human right that is violated when privacy is compromised through monetization of personal data or through bad actors who exploit software vulnerabilities. Vulnerability disclosures are public–private exchanges where Microsoft or other cybersecurity companies voluntarily work with the Cybersecurity and Infrastructure Security Agency, the Federal Bureau of Investigation (FBI), or similar organizations around the world. The Ukrainian government recognized the importance of public–private relationships when it awarded Microsoft, Amazon Web Services, and Google the Ukrainian Peace Prize for securing its networks and data when Russia invaded Ukraine in 2022.

10.3 INTERNET FOR INDIVIDUALS

Given how ubiquitous the Internet is, it is nearly impossible to envision life before it. As chips became smaller and cheaper, the personal computer expanded the user base from engineers and computer scientists to nearly everyone. The shift from the mainframe computer to the desktop, to the laptop, to the tablet, to the phone, to wearables further enmeshed individuals within cyberspace. This level of access meets Berners-Lee's expectations for the Internet as he saw it where "[t]he spirit there was very decentralized. The individual was incredibly empowered. It was all based on there being no central authority that you had to go to ask permission" (quoted in Brooker, 2018). This helps explain why early internet governance was dominated by technologists concerned with the technical functions of the Internet rather than security or malicious behavior.

Over the last several decades, however, internet governance has broadened to include multinational companies and intrusive governments that have created central authorities; individuals are largely commoditized through their data or subjected to corporate and government surveillance through their online behavior. These concerns have caused nongovernmental organizations to advocate for privacy and treat cybersecurity as fundamental to human security.

Cybersecurity implicitly addresses human security, since it is individuals who are vulnerable and exploited in cyberspace.[1] Defined as "a people-centered approach focused on individual human beings and their rights and needs," human security shifts focus from governments and countries to individuals and from tools of statecraft to conditions for social-economic development and civil liberties (Reveron & Mahoney-Norris, 2019). Human security is based in the Universal Declaration of Human Rights that exalts the individual, who "has the right to life, liberty and security of person" (UN, 1948). Despite the long history of human security, its role in cybersecurity has been limited.

Digital human security "prioritizes the individual, and views networks as part of the essential foundation for the modern exercise of human rights"

---

[1] We explored these ideas more in Reveron and Savage (2020).

(Deibert, 2018). In general, countries, including the United States, assert that international law is applicable to cyberspace and 180 governments reaffirmed the applicability of the Universal Declaration of Human Rights online (Rona & Aarons, 2016). As we explored in Chapter 7, the European Union went further and implemented the General Data Protection Regulation with an emphasis on an individual's privacy implicit in human security. By conceptualizing cybersecurity through a human security lens, considerations of its impact on populations are made more visible and seen as more important (Zojer, 2019). California followed suit in 2020 with its Consumer Privacy Act, "to provide consumers with a comprehensive description of a business's online and offline practices regarding the collection, use, disclosure, and sale of personal information and of the rights of consumers regarding their personal information" (California, 2018).

These legislative moves illustrate governments' new responsiveness to its citizens' concerns. With more than half the earth's population using the Internet regularly, individuals certainly matter for the future of cybersecurity. Within the United States, the FBI receives about 1,300 complaints every day and records billions of dollars in annual losses to individuals and businesses (FBI, 2020). Many losses are the result of scams; FBI chief of the Internet Crime Complaint Center Donna Gregory said, "criminals are getting so sophisticated. It is getting harder and harder for victims to spot the red flags and tell real from fake" (FBI, 2020). Generative AI tools will exacerbate this.

Poor password usage and careless clicking spur victimization. Being harassed through social media, fearing that one's identity can be stolen or finances compromised, and having electricity or telecommunications disrupted place cybersecurity as one of the top national security challenges (Smeltz et al., 2019). While cybersecurity is at the top of the federal government's agenda in 2023, the lack of cybersecurity is felt at the individual level; Berners-Lee recognizes "that feeling of individual control, that empowerment, is something we've lost" (quoted in Brooker, 2018). Apple CEO Tim Cook (2018) said, "Platforms and algorithms that promised to improve our lives can actually magnify our worst human tendencies. Rogue actors and even governments have taken advantage of user trust to deepen divisions, incite violence, and even undermine our shared sense of what is true and what is false. This crisis is real. It is not imagined, or exaggerated, or crazy."

Individuals' roles in cybersecurity do generate additional questions to consider for the future. First, how can efforts to universalize internet privacy and access be treated as human rights? Will efforts to strengthen user-level authentication support or undermine privacy online? Will the freedoms designed into the Internet be superseded by new protocols that place a government's ability to manage internet traffic over the privacy of individuals? Since crime through cyberspace is felt locally, but can be sourced internationally, whom do individuals turn to when they become victims? How can individuals gain control of their data and compel corporations to create mutually agreeable and understandable user agreements? As of this writing, answers are elusive. There is no cyberspace equivalent of calling 911 for the police in the United States, as one can when there is a physical emergency, corporations are not shielded from malicious actors, and law has been slowly applied to protect individuals in cyberspace as they are protected in real space.

10.4 INTERNET FOR CORPORATIONS

Corporations have always played a prominent role in cyberspace; after all, they design, manufacture, and distribute the hardware and software that make cyberspace possible. They also benefit from government research and development (R&D) expenditures, such as the Global Positioning System (still funded through the Defense Department budget), and lithium-ion batteries that propelled new industries. But corporations have displaced governments as the dominant source of R&D. In the 1960s, two-thirds of R&D funding was through the federal government compared to 2018 when three-quarters of funding was private (Scharre & Riikonen, 2020). Today, private capital markets can simply raise more money than legislative appropriations.

From its pioneering days in the computer field, IBM continues to evolve its business to remain an important information technology company while others such as Tandy, Apollo, Wang, and Commodore ceased to exist. Apple and Microsoft have been around since the 1970s and grew as their products scaled to a global level; this gives them tremendous influence on cybersecurity. If Apple and Microsoft were countries, in 2022 their combined market cap would make them the fourth largest economy in the world behind the United States, China and Japan. And like governments, ICT corporations are multinational, with offices in almost every capital around the world where they promote business and lobby governments.

Corporations do have a global focus, often see humanity as its customer-base, and often have a mission to change the world. Meta chairman Mark Zuckerberg (2019) testified before the US House of Representatives Committee on Financial Services: "Facebook is about putting power in people's hands. Our services give people voice to express what matters to them, and to build businesses that create opportunity. Giving people control of their money is important too." While Facebook has faced backlash around the world due to concerns about data privacy and hate speech content, there is no disputing that its programming choices on its platforms influence billions of users (WSJ, 2021). The depth of its networks gives it, and other major ICT companies, a unique role to play in cybersecurity. Some researchers have argued that retail distributors can pressure manufacturers to create higher security standards and provide individuals more secure products (Kim et al., 2020).

While their customer bases are global, corporations do have to operate within a particular country and therefore must balance their loyalty to customers against their compliance with national laws. Some governments are more open than others and that determines whether the government directs the corporation or the corporation assists the government in writing regulations. In the United States, technology companies engage in political advocacy. The largest companies want a role in establishing regulations not only to set the terms of the arrangement between them and government but also as a means of preserving their role by keeping out smaller companies that cannot comply with government regulations. In China, corporations aid and abet the Chinese Communist Party's efforts to control content and to suppress opposition to its monopoly of political power. These companies adapt their philosophies to local conditions to gain market access to a billion users; otherwise, they are shut out of China's market since the government often prioritizes domestic companies over foreign ones.

Corporations are not indifferent to domestic laws, however. With its roots in California, Apple has been promoting privacy on a global scale. As a part of its corporate charter, the company sees "privacy is a fundamental human right…[W]e design Apple products to protect your privacy and give you control over your information" (Apple, n.d.). While individuals likely embrace this philosophy, governments can object to this on grounds that privacy through strong encryption inhibits government's inherent public safety function. For example, Apple acknowledged the challenge of applying its philosophy while doing business in China. "Each country in which we do business has its own customs, culture, and legal process. While our values and beliefs don't change from country to country, we are subject to each country's laws" (quoted in Newton, 2018). But by designing products such that it cannot access an individual's data without their knowledge and participation, Apple has removed the company from having to choose between complying with a government's order that it thinks is inconsistent with its corporate philosophy and violating the privacy of a customer. Given that products are assembled in authoritarian countries, unless the hardware is compromised at the chip level, the odds increase that security can be maintained.

Exploit 10.1 Inauthentic behavior on Facebook

While technical exploitation often generates information security notices and patches to resolve, there is the nontechnical exploit of social media. For example, the Russia-based Internet Research Agency (IRA) created accounts and pages on Facebook and Instagram posting content on oppression, police brutality, and celebrity gossip. While the content was not grounds for removal, Facebook discovered that the accounts were operated by individuals in Ghana and Nigeria while claiming to be non-governmental organizations and personal blogs; additionally, Facebook linked the groups to the previously banned IRA. Once investigated and determined to be inauthentic behavior, the company removed 49 Facebook accounts, 69 pages, and 85 Instagram accounts that about 265,000 people followed.

Facebook considers inauthentic behavior a violation of its community standards; it occurs when groups mislead others about who they are and what they are doing. They can be identified by deceptive behavior such as stating that a group is in the United States but is in another country or claiming to be a person but actually is an agent of a foreign power. The company does not want to make judgments on speech content or the actors behind it, but rather it seeks to ensure that its users are who they say they are.

Source: Gleicher (2020)

Likewise, since social media platforms are vulnerable to manipulation, corporations are increasingly employing fact-checkers to help users identify deliberately false statements or to block access to those who violate their rules on content. This challenge has been a difficult one for US-based companies that just want to build networks and not judge or limit the content placed on its networks, but this is changing.

Following Russian intelligence operations in the 2016 US presidential election, Facebook created a team to address "the most sophisticated influence operations aimed to manipulate public debate as well as high volume inauthentic behaviors like spam and fake engagement" (Meta, 2020). Essentially, Facebook will remove inauthentic actors who deliberately misrepresent their identities to conduct nefarious activities to protect public debates on its network. In 2018, it removed pages and accounts controlled by the IRA since "[t]he IRA has repeatedly used complex networks of inauthentic accounts to deceive and manipulate people who use Facebook...We removed this latest set of Pages and accounts solely because they were controlled by the IRA — not based on the content" (Meta, 2018). Facebook attempts to distinguish between source misrepresentation and content of the message. Consistent with the US government objections to combatting racism and xenophobia on the Internet discussed in Chapter 7, Facebook chooses not to judge whether speech is acceptable or not. Rather, it looks to ensure Facebook users are aware of the source and bans fraudulent activities.

In thinking about the future role for corporations, several questions remain. How will governments' pressure on corporations to monitor and regulate speech impact business operations? Will judicial courts hold companies responsible for exploits based on flawed code? How will US-based corporations adapt to competition with China-based corporations as they continue to globalize? How will pressure to nationalize the ICT industry in China affect a globalized Internet? How do corporations wittingly or unwittingly facilitate intelligence operations? How will space-based internet service providers undercut governments' attempts to regulate?

10.5 INTERNET FOR GOVERNMENTS

The US-based ARPANET was largely fueled by government grants and contracts but was largely free from regulation except for technical decisions such as electromagnetic spectrum allocation. The US laissez-faire approach was mirrored internationally as the Internet expanded across North America, Europe, and East Asia, exporting a hands-off orientation for governments around the world. As discussed in Chapter 6, this was a product of the culture of the scientists and engineers who work in this field, which values transparency and collaboration regardless of national boundaries. Additionally, corporations and nongovernmental organizations effectively lobbied their governments to protect innovation in the technology field by ensuring ICT corporations were largely free of regulation.

The Soviet Union's collapse in 1991 vindicated this approach as it was viewed as the triumphalism of private enterprise and democracy over state-owned enterprises and communism (Fukuyama, 1992). With an emphasis on neoliberal economic policies and limited government, the end of the Cold War heralded massive deregulation of industries in the United States and Europe; governments were convinced that a hands-off approach was essential to the growth of the technology sector with all its social benefits obfuscating cybersecurity concerns.

When the Internet moved to noncapitalist and authoritarian countries in the 2000s, these governments used the Internet as a means of control. This may be

Table 10.2 Countries with the highest R&D expenditures

Rank	Country	Amount (in billions of current PPP[1] dollars)
1	United States	576
2	China	465
3	Japan	173
4	Germany	129
5	South Korea	95
6	France	63
7	United Kingdom	50
8	Taiwan	40
9	Russia	37
10	Italy	33

Source: R&D – Gross Domestic Spending on R&D (OECD, 2023)
PPP = Purchasing Power Parity compares currencies by the cost of a "basket of goods" in each currency.

as simple as blocking websites to censor information consumption or shutting down the Internet or as complex as conducting mass surveillance to preempt any individual or group opposing the incumbent's rule.

Authoritarian concern for an open Internet accelerated after the Arab Awakening in 2011. Protesters in Middle East countries, such as Tunisia and Egypt, used social media to organize protests that led to the downfall of long-standing authoritarian regimes (Burlacu & Tiganus, 2012; Howard & Hussain, 2013). When coupled with the individual-centric approach software developers take with US and European internet freedom policies, authoritarian countries view it as a vital interest to prevent social movements from challenging their authority and work hard to ensure regime survival through information control (Shahbaz et al., 2019). As social media emerged these countries moved to ban it: China banned Facebook, while India banned TikTok. The US government tried and failed to force TikTok to be shut down or spun off from its Chinese parent company.

Some governments also harnessed the Internet to promote development by connecting their economies through globalized industries such as call centers or engaging in intellectual property theft in support of their own domestic industries. While established multinational corporations saw the benefits of new markets and new consumers, developing countries saw the benefits of joint venture partnerships and corporate espionage to compete globally. Table 10.2 ranks countries by their research and development expenditures on which they rely to ensure economic growth.

Policy Matters 10.1 Banning technology

The proliferation of technology used by law enforcement and intelligence for surveillance has led to some backlash in democracies. In 2020, the city of Boston banned facial surveillance technology because it "has proven to be less accurate for African American and AAPI [Asian American and Pacific Islander] faces, and racial bias in facial surveillance has the potential to harm communities of color who are already facing increased levels of surveillance and harassment" (Guariglia, 2020). While Boston is not the first city to do this, it is in clear contrast to other cities around the world that rely on technology to increase surveillance and reduce the number of employees required for adequate security. While the benefits of technology clearly exist for public safety, Boston's ban recognizes that improperly trained AI systems incorporate the biases that humans have. A Massachusetts Institute of Technology study found that the error rate of commercial facial-analysis systems could be as bad as about one in three (Hardesty, 2008).

More recently, authoritarian governments have used cyberspace to conduct active measures internationally whereby they attempt to influence democratic processes in other countries (Rid, 2020). Laura Rosenberger and Lindsay Gorman (2020) argue that "authoritarian regimes like Russia and China see information and cyberwarfare as integrated domains of asymmetric conflict... [to] weaponize information to fight back against democracies' promotion of free information as a universal right."

A good example was Russia's 2016 release of material that was considered damaging to the Democratic Party's candidate Hilary Clinton. In the lead up to the 2020 presidential election, David Porter of the FBI's Foreign Influence Task Force, said, "We see Russia is willing to conduct more brazen and disruptive influence operations because of how it perceives its conflict with the West. To put it simply, in this space, Russia wants to watch us tear ourselves apart" (Barnes & Goldman, 2020). The National Intelligence Council later concluded that multiple countries, a foreign terrorist organization, and cybercriminals were engaged in efforts to disrupt the 2020 election. Russia was focused on creating mistrust in the electoral system, undermining the voting process, and accusing the Democratic Party of voter fraud (ODNI, 2021b). It is important to note that information operations and perception management work best if there are preexisting beliefs to manipulate (Callamari & Reveron, 2003).

Outside of the United States there are other examples that illustrate that open societies are particularly vulnerable to information manipulation (Rosenberger & Fly, 2017). "Truth" in democracy can be debatable. Consequently, competitive political parties seek to offer alternative interpretations of events and policy. Foreign governments exploit openness for their preferred candidates or policy outcomes.

There are also cultural reasons democracies are vulnerable: They lack state-run media to offer official accounts of events, reject censorship on the grounds of civil liberties, and detest propaganda as an affront to an open society. This is not new. Almost 250 years ago James Madison postulated that a democratic government's attempts to control a "faction" or group with a common passion should be through majority rule while protecting minorities' civil liberties rather than censorship (Hamilton et al., 1787). In other words, calls for violence would be matched with calls for peaceful resolution and political minorities would be protected from majority tyranny. In current times, however, social media platforms seem particularly vulnerable to passion by authoritarian-sponsored bots and troll farms that concentrate passions that undercut peaceful social norms. There are no Madisonian algorithms to bring the balance Madison envisioned.

As discussed in Chapter 5, dozens of countries have military cyber commands and seek to integrate cyber operations into their war plans. These efforts mirror conventional targeting against communications, energy infrastructure, and military bases. There are emerging policies for governments to conduct offensive operations to protect against external attacks. Consequently, there have been calls for no first use (NFU) rules to encourage restraint among states from creating violent strategic effects on civilian populations and threatening the control of nuclear forces (Schneider, 2020). To be effective, Stanford researcher Jacquelyn Schneider (2020, p. 172) argues, "a strategic cyber NFU policy needs to be incentivized through positive means—like information sharing, foreign aid, or transfers of cyber/military capabilities to other participating NFU nations—and deterred through credible cross-domain punishment."

For its part, the National Security Agency (NSA) and Cyber Command have taken steps to improve the general level of cybersecurity and has expanded its writ beyond an intelligence mission and supporting military plans and operations (Loleski, 2019). In January 2016 Rob Joyce, chief of NSA's Tailored Access Operations department, a group that does nation-state exploitation, gave a public talk at the Enigma conference in which he offered advice on how to defend against exploiters like his team, as discussed in Chapter 4 (Joyce, 2016). Additionally, in 2017 NSA published on GitHub, an open-source repository, some of its older technology such as Security Enhanced Linux (SELinux) (Chappellet-Lanier, 2017). In November 2018 the Cyber National Mission Force

(CNMF), a subordinate command of US Cyber Command, created an account on VirusTotal, an online virus scanning service, and announced that it would share malware samples through it that Cyber Command discovered on Department of Defense networks. It also created the Twitter account @CNMF_VirusAlert to announce its postings to VirusTotal (Goodin, 2020).

In 2019, again on GitHub, NSA released Ghidra, a powerful cybersecurity tool for software reverse engineering. Ghidra converts binary code, bit strings readable by computers but not humans, into human-readable instructions. It is used to analyze software looking for malware (Newman, 2019). These efforts, in addition to the creation by the Cybersecurity and Infrastructure Security Agency of the Joint Cyber Defense Collaborative in 2021, represent a larger shift in US strategy to bridge the government–private sector gap representing a whole-of-nation framing.

In 2021, the FBI, NSA, and CISA released a joint advisory on how to prevent a Russian intelligence organization from exploiting vulnerabilities in a Microsoft product (CISA, 2021b). These efforts signal a trend in the intelligence community to bridge the gap with the private sector. Similar efforts are underway in the United Kingdom, where the British equivalent of NSA, known as Government Communications Headquarters, also shares cybersecurity tools on GitHub. This type of outreach and information-sharing by intelligence agencies is a clear break from the past, where their existence was not even publicly acknowledged. With judicial and public oversight, these efforts bode well for the future of cybersecurity as governments look to partner with the private sector sharing information.

Additional questions remain. How can government promote public safety while not undercutting the value of encryption? As 5G enables more devices and meshes these devices in an Internet of Things construct, how will new policies affect technological advances? Given the national security concerns with a global supply chain, how will separate localization efforts in China, the United States, Russia, and Europe impact the global nature of cyberspace? Can government balance efforts to create a secure source of ICT without generating the negative effects observed when governments impose economic tariffs?

10.6 BRIDGING THE DIVIDES

As the preceding section suggests, considering the Internet from the personal, national, and international points of view brings into focus the different benefits and risks each level faces. Individuals derive benefits from information access and social connection. They also face the risk of identity theft, ransomware, and harassment. Corporations derive benefits from global supply chains, an earth-size market, and a global talent pool to create their products. Yet, globalized corporations face the risks of intellectual property theft, competition, and potential regulation by hundreds of countries where they operate. Governments have benefited from the economic boom related to the internet economy, enhanced global presence through soft power, and the ability to shape international institutions reflecting their domestic cultures. At the same time, governments face loss of sovereignty as national currencies are threatened by cryptocurrencies, loss of border control as data travels without customs inspections or passports, loss of cultural identity through exposure to other cultures, and geopolitical competitors who use the global medium to project power well beyond their borders and region.

While it is not possible or desirable to insulate one level from the other, considering cybersecurity with all three levels in mind is important and shaped by which lens someone adopts. If the Internet is for the individual, corporations can be held liable for vulnerabilities in their code, and governments are responsible for regulating for the benefit of the individual citizen, thereby protecting human security. If the Internet is for the corporation and the economy, then individuals are responsible for their own poor cyber hygiene and governments should refrain from attempts to regulate. If the Internet is for governments, then laws can govern individuals' behavior online and harness corporations' products for the benefit of the state. The Internet's pioneers would certainly argue for returning the focus back to individuals but given the wealth potential of a global audience and security implications for a society, it is unlikely that corporations and governments will moderate their efforts to exert control in cyberspace. The range of actors involved in internet governance illustrate this.

These limitations suggest a new model of shared responsibility for the cybersecurity triad discussed in Chapter 6, namely confidentiality, integrity, and accessibility. It requires individuals to become better users and more informed consumers. It requires corporations to produce fewer vulnerabilities and be held accountable through consumer demand for their products and through other markets such as insurance. And it requires governments to share intelligence on vulnerabilities with developers and regulate to ensure developers comply with the best technical practices. This is particularly important when it comes to cybersecurity as national security.

Essential Principle 10.1 Precautionary principle

Society has been concerned with the impact of technology on civilization at least since Alfred Nobel donated his fortune to annual prizes that recognize academic achievements to burnish the moniker of "merchant of death" he acquired after inventing dynamite and owning a major weapons company in the nineteenth century. In the twentieth century, Robert Oppenheimer while witnessing his invention of the first atomic weapon detonate recalled the Hindu spiritual text Bhagavad-Gita, "I am become death, the destroyer of worlds." Oppenheimer and his Manhattan Project colleagues recognized that their invention enabled mass killing, later witnessed in Nagasaki and Hiroshima, Japan. As the United States and Soviet Union armed themselves with the new technology, nuclear strategist Bernard Brodie (1978) wrote: "Thus far the chief purpose of our military establishment has been to win wars. From now on its chief purpose must be to avert them" (Brodie, 1978).

These concerns for inventions with social implications are encapsulated in the "Precautionary Principle" laid out by the United Nations Educational, Scientific and Cultural Organization (UNESCO) in 2005.

When human activities may lead to morally unacceptable harm that is scientifically plausible but uncertain, actions shall be taken to avoid or diminish that harm. Morally unacceptable harm refers to harm to humans or the environment that is threatening to human life or health, or serious and effectively irreversible, or inequitable to present or future generations, or imposed without adequate consideration of the human rights of those affected.

The principle is particularly important as governments and organizations employ AI without a clear sense of its effect on society.

Source: UNESCO (2005)

10.7 IMPORTANCE OF FRAMING CYBERSECURITY

The preceding chapters offer detailed explanations of various aspects of cybersecurity from technological solutions such as encryption to legal solutions through treaties. To be sure, the era of laissez-faire is being challenged and governments are using national organizations and processes in addition to international institutions and practices to increase regulation and improve cooperation with the goal of better cybersecurity. While there is no single solution to improve cybersecurity, during a significant cyberattack, it is important to consider the impact of framing the attacks and the lens one wears when interpreting it. The emerging strategic approach is one that views cyber as a larger piece of national power that includes diplomacy, foreign assistance, sanctions, intelligence, and conventional military power. This is true whether cyberspace operations are framed as an intelligence contest or a strategic competition, or through a coercion framework.

Since technology is at the heart of the benefits and risks of cyberspace, it is often viewed as a solution. Better encryption strengthens privacy, while better coding reduces vulnerabilities. AI has been identified as a means of improving cybersecurity, but it also poses serious ethical issues that need to be further explored. First, what domestic regulations will governments impose on AI? Should AI be restricted to noncritical tasks? What role will AI play in law enforcement and judicial matters? How can the benefits in medical diagnoses be balanced against the inherent flaws in the technology? Internationally, how will AI be incorporated into weapon systems? There is already a large body of knowledge on the problems associated with lethal autonomous weapon systems, and AI seems to make lethal strikes easier, which exempts policymakers from ethical considerations or efficacy. Finally, there are gaps between the promises of AI and social understanding of the risks and benefits of new technologies.

10.8 GOVERNMENT RESPONSES TO INTERNATIONAL CRISES

Increasingly, governments around the world have developed cyber commands and are attempting to integrate cyber tools into traditional operational military plans. When a government identifies significant cyber breaches, it is important to interpret cybersecurity in a wider international context. For example, Russian invasions of Georgia and Ukraine included cyber operations, with outright invasion making attribution of the cyber operations relatively straightforward.

Absent conventional military action that accompanies cyber actions, however, it is difficult to distinguish between intelligence operations for the sake of strategic analysis and intelligence operations as preparation for future military operations. Determining the underlying motivation for cyber actions by understanding intent is the key to informed decision-making.

The most dangerous scenario for cyber insecurity remains governments' uses of cyber operations that undermine critical infrastructure or sensitive sites such as nuclear facilities or military command and control nodes. They are prone to secondary infection if a malicious actor targets a nonsensitive site, exploiting a vulnerability common to civilian and military systems. The threat of blowback is real and may help explain why governments moderate their use of cyberspace operations (Smeets, 2018).

Cyberspace operations do enable a wide range of actors to retaliate against the most powerful countries in the world. To make sense of the actor's intentions, context can identify interstate rivals, understand how that rival uses cyber operations as a component of national power, and use existing international tools to prevent escalation. Important questions to ask are: What is the shape of the challenge? What are the key trends and drivers that led to the cyber intrusion in the first place? Why should a government care about the intrusion relative to other interests? How would action impact the larger relationship in bilateral and multilateral ways? Implicit in these questions is the ancient notion that diagnosis should precede prescription.[2]

10.8.1 Calibrating Responses to Crises

Once a malicious actor's behavior is understood, the next step is to develop strategic options to resolve the action. The priority in developing options for policymakers should be to provide viable alternative courses of action that can plausibly resolve the situation while advancing national interests or at least not undercutting national interests. National interests and the policymaking process should guide when governments respond, and the response should not make things worse.

As discussed in Chapter 5, the goal of action should be to link responses to cyber intrusions to a larger strategy of a government. The government's strategy and national interests should be used to consider pros and cons for each option. Recognizing that a crisis lacks a formal playbook, the recommended option should logically flow from an analysis of the situation through the lens of national interests to identify key trends and drivers that brought the issue to the fore. A good analyst should have a sense of what happens next, especially when talking about relations among countries that have nuclear weapons.

Recalling President John F. Kennedy, "While defending our vital interests, nuclear powers must avert those confrontations which bring an adversary to a choice of either a humiliating retreat or a nuclear war" (quoted in Allison

---

[2] Derek Reveron is grateful to Graham Allison for this formulation and working together with David Sanger at the Kennedy School of Government on a course using this formulation.

& Simes, 2016). This is sage advice, as the most prominent cyber forces are also nuclear weapon states, so governments must carefully weigh responses to cyberspace operations against the risk of escalation leading to conventional or nuclear wars.

To date, there has been a select list of options for governments to pursue: deterrence, entanglement, and cost imposition among them (Nye, Jr., 2017). As discussed in Chapter 5, deterrence suggests creating a situation where malicious behavior is prevented through fear of retaliation or through resilience. For deterrence to be effective, the potential attacker must believe the risk of retaliation by the attacked is greater than the reward. The signaling required for deterrence can be achieved through demarches by one government to tell another government it objects to its behavior or indicting cyber actors within the domestic court system. Further, negating the impact of cyberspace operations through network resilience can deny the adversary any benefit of the cyberspace operation.

Entanglement improves cybersecurity when international treaties and norms create security through interdependence (Keohane, 1977; Nye, Jr., 2017). Existing international institutions such as the United Nations can convene meetings to discuss diplomatic disputes while economic institutions such as the World Trade Organization and World Intellectual Property Organization can address copyright and patent infringement. The UN working groups explored in Chapter 8 illustrate how governments are taking their concerns about cybersecurity seriously and building norms to improve it. However, entanglement does not always create sufficient interdependence to preclude conflict.

Finally, the cost imposition option recognizes that the two previous options have not yet worked among large states such as the United States, Russia, and China or even with small states such as North Korea and Iran. Researcher Brandon Valeriano (2020) says, "Cost imposition is how you coerce the opposition. The goal is either to compel the enemy to change behaviors or to stop them dead in their tracks by deterring operations in the future. Cost imposition is a critical element of our national strategy and not simply an artifact of a process—it is the process." Through sanctions, public humiliation, and conventional military exercises or operations, governments can impose costs on one another.

While policy formulation is challenging, but straightforward, decisions do not implement themselves. After a government selects a course of action, implementation plans must be developed. Given the nature of bureaucracy that has competing actors and is governed by law and culture, it is important to consider how the government carries out actions (Lipsky, 2010). Not that uses of cyber operations are unique, but President Obama's secretary of defense Ash

Carter was frustrated with the challenges of conducting cyberspace operations with traditional military activities.[3]

Policymakers must work through the process of implementation both at the domestic and international levels. In all cases of implementation, government may also prepare the public through media announcements or authorized disclosures through background interviews with journalists. The latter can be a form of signaling to an adversary, but again it might be negated if the adversary patches the vulnerability that could be exploited. Domestically, the president, prime minister, or other head of government may need to notify the legislative branch or obtain a legal review if the proposed cyber actions can be interpreted as a use of force under international law. Further, given the dominance of the private sector in the development, deployment, and sustainment of technology, policymakers may have to engage technology companies since it is often proprietary technology that is exploited for malicious purposes.

Information-sharing mechanisms exist between government and industry to facilitate these interactions, but cooperation can be complicated when a corporation's global interests may not align with a country's national interests. If a government alerted a software company that it was exploiting a vulnerability in its software to attack an adversary, the government would want a guarantee that a patch did not reach the adversary before the exploitation occurred. Internationally, a government may also have to consult with key partners and allies, seek legitimacy through an international institution, or simply confront the government where the source of the attack originates either physically or politically.

Finally, some measure of effectiveness should be developed to provide oversight of the decision. It is important to know if the action taken resolves the issue, makes it worse, or has no effect at all. These can be as straightforward as the stopping of a denial-of-service attack, slowing of corporate espionage, or countries developing and adhering to new norms to improve cybersecurity. If the expected outcome did not occur, it would be important to

---

[3] "I was largely disappointed in Cyber Command's effectiveness against ISIS. It never really produced any effective cyber weapons or techniques. When CYBERCOM did produce something useful, the intelligence community tended to delay or try to prevent its use, claiming cyber operations would hinder intelligence collection. This would be understandable if we had been getting a steady stream of actionable intel, but we weren't. The State Department, for its part, was unable to cut through the thicket of diplomatic issues involved in working through the host of foreign services that constitute the Internet. In short, none of our agencies showed very well in the cyber fight. One exception was an international effort to combat ISIS's hateful online presence with counter-messaging, an effort that did achieve significant reach and had a real impact" (Carter, 2017).

restart the process and validate the assumptions made when the initial analysis was conducted. Additionally, the impact of the action should be considered with a deliberate effort to understand why the intended outcome did not occur.

10.9 CONCLUDING THOUGHTS

For people around the world, the question of who owns what, or who is responsible for what, is probably unimportant. An individual depending on the Internet to do banking just wants secure transactions in the .com domain; an individual trying to find information on charities just wants reliable information in the .org domain; someone trying to find information about driver's license requirements only wants access to timely, accurate data in the .gov domain; and a student trying to pursue education online wants an effective system in the .edu domain. In other words, most individuals want the cyber world to enhance their human security needs without having to contend with malicious actors exploiting vulnerabilities in the software they are using or manipulating the data they need to make decisions.

Yet myriad challenges are documented in this book. Cyberspace operations may originate from such varied bad actors as a domestic or foreign intelligence service, a terrorist group, a criminal group, hacktivists, individual hackers, or disgruntled insiders. As the online and physical worlds become closer over the next 20 years, new and unforeseen challenges will emerge. But one fact is certain: Cybersecurity will remain a key feature of the national security landscape, and all governments will struggle to keep pace, just as all citizens will feel compelled to protect their individual security online. Unfortunately, governments are not well-equipped to protect and promote cybersecurity for individuals either by capability or by policy.

Thus, cybersecurity increasingly demands citizens, companies, organizations, and governments to work together to make cyberspace safer and more secure. This involves understanding the technologies involved, identifying the policies and agencies responsible for cyber cybersecurity, and capturing the complexity of international cooperation to make cyberspace more secure.

10.10 DISCUSSION TOPICS

1. In what ways are problems observed in cyberspace merely a reflection of problems that existed before the Internet?

2. What obligations do the designers of cyberspace have to improve cybersecurity?
3. What obligations do governments have to protect individuals in cyberspace while ensuring it remains a relatively free and open space?
4. As the Internet matures, what are the implications for expanding the types of expertise of those involved in internet governance?
5. In what ways might a human security perspective impact thinking about cybersecurity?

11

Leading in the Cyber Age

Never tell people how to do things. Tell them what to do and they will
surprise you with their ingenuity.

General George S. Patton, Jr. (1947)

B OTH AUTHORS OF this book have spent substantial parts of our academic
careers teaching leaders through executive courses. Mid-career and senior
leaders often enroll in executive education to meet career milestones, to refresh
their knowledge base, and to network with leaders from different sectors. Since
they often work in a bubble, the courses give them ways to seek out diverse
perspectives and connect them individually to an institution's resources and
networks that might benefit their careers.

One common trait among executive-level students is that they approach
course work as practitioners. They look to build on their own experiences and
look to academics for ways to make sense of what they have encountered in
the world. Doing so broadens their aperture by learning from others who faced
similar situations but pursued different solutions. The classroom becomes a
venue to test ideas, learn from students and professors, and identify knowledge
to solve real problems they face in their day-to-day activities. Professors often
capture these encounters to understand real-world problems to address.

These professional experiences have undoubtedly influenced the structure
of our arguments in this book. While we offer a basic technical explanation of
cyberspace throughout, we continually highlight how human decision-making
and perception are key to improving cybersecurity. This is true in designing
internet protocols, developing hardware, and leading organizations in the cyber
age. The latter requires a basic technical understanding, good rapport with an
organization's information technology (IT) leaders, and an understanding of
the needs of employees and other users.

An important trait among leaders today is the need to identify problems to
solve in advance of a crisis. Hippocrates resonates throughout time—diagnosis
precedes prescription. Thus, the ability to forecast is an important leadership

characteristic in an uncertain marketplace and world. As discussed in Chapter 4, when humans make judgments, even when they have been rigorously trained, there is a tendency to rely on heuristics or System 1 shortcuts rather than the deep contemplation of System 2. This is especially true in stressful circumstances when we must rely on the intellectual capital that we have to apply during crises. Dr. Donald Redelmeier, who collaborated with both Daniel Kahneman and Amos Tversky, captured this concern for the limits on human judgment when he said, "wherever there is uncertainty there has got to be judgment, and wherever there is judgment there is an opportunity for human fallibility" (quoted in M. Lewis, 2017). Consequently, learning to be better thinkers and forecasters is important for leading in the cyber age.

11.1 SUPERFORECASTING

President Dwight D. Eisenhower (1957) was fond of recalling a statement he often heard when he was in the Army: "Plans are worthless, but planning is everything." Planning does identify options that may be needed, but more importantly, it allows relevant stakeholders to get to know each other before plan execution. Getting to know those who will be involved in crisis response before a crisis emerges builds trust and rapport, which are key to solving pressing problems.

Fundamentally, planning involves forecasting since it attempts to develop approaches to achieving goals or preparing for crises. As we discussed in Chapter 10, to develop strategic options, planners need confidence in identifying and analyzing trends that impact overall objectives while charting a path to a better future despite the negative forces working against the organization. While the future is unknown, good leaders need ways to think about the future and better ways to predict change to prepare their organizations.

Philip Tetlock has studied prediction for decades. In his book *Expert Political Judgment: How Good Is It? How Can We Know* (Tetlock, 2017), he found that the average expert was no better than a dart-throwing chimpanzee, yet experts continue to be popular because they tell interesting stories with conviction. At first blush, this should reassure everyone that anyone can be an expert but misses Tetlock's important point that judgments should be evaluated so that it is possible to separate the novice from the expert.

To discover ways to identify expertise, Tetlock and his colleagues conducted an experiment. In 2011 they recruited about 2,800 volunteers and started the Good Judgment Project to see if they could distill traits of those better at forecasting than others. Their research was summarized in his book

Superforecasting: The Art and Science of Prediction (Tetlock, 2016). In his *Wall Street Journal* column, Jason Zweig (2015) quotes Daniel Kahneman saying of Tetlock's book that it "shows that under the right conditions regular people are capable of improving their judgment enough to beat the professionals at their own game."

Tetlock found that some volunteers are genuinely good at forecasting the outcomes of high-stakes events that occur over periods ranging from months to a year and half. Examples of forecasts that volunteers were asked to make were: "Will Russia officially annex additional Ukrainian territory in the next three months?"; "In the next year, will any country withdraw from the Eurozone?"; "Will North Korea detonate a nuclear device before the end of the year?"; "How many additional countries will report cases of the Ebola virus in the next eight months?"; and "Will NATO invite new countries to join the Membership Action Plan (MAP)?" (Tetlock, 2016, p. 2). These questions have practical utility for policymakers and the answers would ensure governments are ready for breakthroughs or act to dissuade negative actions (e.g., nuclear detonation).

Working with researchers at the University of California, Berkeley, and the University of Pennsylvania they formulated a research program in which they varied the experimental conditions so that they could determine "which factors improved foresight, by how much, over which time frames, and how good the forecasts could become if best practices were layered on each other" (Tetlock, 2016, p. 16). Volunteers whose accuracy was in the top 2 percent were called superforecasters. Approximately 70 percent of those who were identified as superforecasters each year continued to deserve the rating in a subsequent year, which indicates that those individuals are truly special and can be identified.

The research discovered that superforecasters were not geniuses. Rather, their talent derives from the way they think, gather information, and update their beliefs to inform predictions. They have

habits of thought [that] can be learned and cultivated by any intelligent, thoughtful, determined person. ... [B]roadly speaking, superforecasting demands thinking that is open-minded, careful, curious, and – above all – self-critical. It also demands focus. The kind of thinking that produces superior judgment does not come effortlessly. Only the determined can deliver it reasonably consistently, which is why [Tetlock's] analyses have consistently found commitment to self-improvement to be the strongest predictor of performance. (Tetlock, 2016, p. 18)

Identifying these characteristics can help organizations select the right individuals to lead in the cyber age characterized by frequent technological market disruption and serious malicious activities. Harnessing human intelligence like this delivers the promises today that artificial intelligence evangelists promise in the future.

11.1.1 Testing the Forecasters

Tetlock's work gained the attention of the Intelligence Advanced Research Projects Agency (IARPA), which is an organization within the Office of the Director of National Intelligence that funds research to make the US intelligence community (IC) better. Tetlock and his colleagues observed that "[a]bsent accuracy metrics, there is no meaningful way to hold intelligence analysts accountable for accuracy" (Tetlock, 2016, p. 87). IARPA funded a tournament from September 2011 to June 2015 with five scientific research teams to see how it might improve intelligence forecasts. Prior to this tournament, analysts were provided a manual written by Richards Heuer (1999), a former CIA analyst, outlining cognitive biases that should be avoided. However, what was missing from the assessment was the judgment of the quality of IC predictions, so IARPA was looking for ways to see how to improve predictions.

IARPA provided the five teams with nearly 500 tough world affairs questions of the kind answered by intelligence analysts and asked them to make forecasts of possible outcomes from one month to one year in advance. They were allowed to predict using methods of their choosing and were expected to assign a likelihood to an outcome during a defined period, not assert whether it would occur. When the prediction tally was finalized, Tetlock's Good Judgment Project beat the control group by 60 percent in the first year and 78 percent in the second. It beat the other four teams by 30 percent to 70 percent and "outperformed professional intelligence analysts with access to classified information" (Tetlock, 2016). To explain why the techniques used by the Good Judgment Project were very effective, Tetlock summarized the approaches taken by superforecasters and the way teams were organized to increase their effectiveness in his ten commandments, as shown in Table 11.1.

11.1.2 Creating Superteams

Aware of the research literature and benefitting from personal experience with faculty committees, Tetlock observed that predictions can both profit and suffer from group contributions. Thus, team members were provided with a primer on teamwork. He warned that teams that are too friendly can slip into groupthink; members want to get along, so they gravitate too quickly to a position. Group work can also suffer from members who are either free riders or who attempt to dominate discussions and disrupt rather than enhance group effort.

Team members were advised to "be cooperative but not deferential." This was an issue because of the variety of volunteers' backgrounds; some might be intimidated by others. They were also warned to avoid rancor and dysfunction

Table 11.1 Ten commandments for aspiring superforecasters

1. Triage. Focus on questions that are likely to be amenable to prediction, avoiding those that are notoriously difficult to forecast.
2. Break down problems. Seemingly intractable problems can be managed if they are broken into tractable subproblems.
3. Balance inside and outside views. Strike the right balance between the two. Do not anchor your prediction on the specifics of a problem, the inside view. See the problem as an instance of a class, the outside view.
4. Update your beliefs. Strike the right balance between under- and overreacting to evidence. Be creative in finding new evidence, and wise on the weight you assign to it, so that you can continuously update the probabilities assigned to outcomes as your knowledge grows.
5. Everything is connected. Look for the clashing causal forces at work in each problem. Forecasts that reflect many different points of view, especially if they clash with personal worldviews, are more likely to identify the real forces that determine outcomes.
6. Remove uncertainty. Strive to distinguish as many degrees of doubt as the problem permits. Probabilities should be assigned to forecasts so that the work of forecasters can be assessed. This requires making refined estimations of probabilities, which can be learned.
7. Balance prudence and decisiveness. Do not rush to judgment nor delay a decision unnecessarily.
8. Learn from failure and success. Perform honest postmortems of prediction successes and failures.
9. Manage the team. Bring out the best in others and let others bring out the best in you. Understand the individual points of view, challenge them as necessary without being disagreeable, and be decisive without being autocratic.
10. Master the error-balancing bicycle. Just as we learn to ride a bicycle by trying (rather than studying physics), superforecasting requires practice.

Source: Tetlock (2016)

by practicing "constructive confrontation," a quotation attributed to Andy Grove, former Intel CEO, by formulating precise, pointed, but respectful questions. They were informed that some team members with strong views about an issue might be extra sensitive when their views were challenged. After the first year of the tournament "on average, teams were 23 percent more accurate than individuals" (Tetlock, 2016, p. 201). Thus, teams were incorporated into the tournament during the second year. With trepidation, some of the teams were composed of just individuals classified as superforecasters during the first year. Since these individuals had not worked together, they went through a testing period during which they got to know each other better before exercising the best practices they had been taught. The result of this experiment was spectacular. After one year on a superforecaster team, a superteam, on average a member was 50 percent more accurate! The same was true for their third year. Given that these individuals were initially strangers, this outcome was shocking. The key to the success of superteams is the right mix of ability and diversity of members. The role of ability is obvious, but diversity is not always obvious; it increases the likelihood that a member will have a key piece of information or point of view that influences a prediction. This conclusion reinforced our impulse for a computer scientist and a policy analyst to write this book. Diversity does matter for producing better outcomes.

11.1.3 Role of Expertise

An important question that emerged from the competition is, how did the non-experts beat the experts who are paid by the intelligence community to improve strategic warning? The answer is counterintuitive because one would think that expertise would be required to consider such problems as the probability that a highly computerized military system without adequate cybersecurity protection will fail during conflict or the vulnerabilities created if all military electronic systems are merged into one global network. Or how modern aircraft would perform in the face of an electronic warfare attack.

Tetlock observed that *his superforecasters are most effective in areas in which they are not experts*. Therefore, they have less ego involvement in the results of their forecasts. Superforecasters tend to be cautious, humble, and nondeterministic, that is, they do not believe that outcomes are foreordained. In abilities and thinking they are actively open-minded, intellectually curious – that is, they enjoy puzzles and mental challenges – introspective and self-critical, and comfortable with numbers and probabilities. Finally, their methods of forecasting are pragmatic, analytical, that is, capable of seeing an issue from a broad perspective, open to incorporating new ideas, and probabilistic, and they engage in careful updating, that is, they change their outcome probabilities when the facts change (Tetlock, 2016, p. 191).

To emulate superforecasters, leaders should practice intellectual humility through self-awareness of their knowledge limits and be ready to avail themselves of information from many sources. Whether they are in the technology sector, military, or other business, leaders require a deep understanding of their sector's underlying methodologies and the markets where they operate, an ability to forecast product or service demand, and a keen understanding of how to motivate employees. Finally, they must have the ability to monitor and evaluate changes in technologies that impact operations.

11.2 LEADING THROUGH UNCERTAINTY

There is increasing recognition that good leaders do more than articulate a vision and attract resources and talent to execute a vision. Instead, building the types of teams Tetlock identified has become salient as leaders increasingly value diversity in thought, experience, background, gender, and ethnicity. Margaret Heffernan (2019), the former CEO of five companies and author of five books, captured this: "[T]he unexpected is becoming the norm. ... [M]uch of the world has gone from being complicated to being complex ... [which] means that very small changes can [have] a disproportionate impact. And it means that expertise won't always suffice." Thomas Malone and other researchers at Massachusetts Institute of Technology discovered the best teams are not the ones composed of individuals with the most expertise or highest IQs. Rather, the best teams are composed of people who can make connections to combine different perspectives, skills, and knowledge; social perceptiveness of members increases a group's intelligence (Malone, 2018).

Further, diverse teams can challenge conventional wisdom. For example, during the COVID-19 pandemic, the focus on efficiency held by corporations and health care companies undercut society's resilience. Companies simply did not maintain stockpiles of ventilators or personal protection equipment because having a warehouse filled with unused (and expiring) resources was viewed as wasteful. In this case, however, just-in-time logistics in the name of corporate efficiency exacerbated the negative effects and is a good illustration of a collective action problem when everyone acting in one's best interests makes everyone worse off (Olson, 1971). *Wall Street Journal* columnist William Galston (2020) summarized the problem thusly:

Resilience in the face of unexpected shocks is a public good, and experience is confirming what economic theory predicts: In the relentless quest for increased efficiency, which remains a key source of competitive advantage, the decisions made by individual market actors will produce, in the aggregate, a less-than-optimal supply of resiliency, a public good. To solve this collective-action problem, government must act as a counterweight.

Heffernan (2019) agrees: "Efficiency [is effective] when you can predict exactly what you're going to need. But when the anomalous or unexpected comes along ... efficiency is no longer your friend." Increasingly, cybersecurity is a public good and the cyber age will be filled with anomalous and unexpected influences.

The experiences we have had with COVID-19 serve as a warning for leaders in other sectors such as technology. In many ways, cybersecurity is a collective action problem characterized by free riders and information asymmetries.

Corporations are incentivized to produce the best goods at the lowest prices to meet demand with minimal testing, not disclosing vulnerabilities and breaches. Individuals want to pay the least amount of currency to build their systems and make them secure. Governments largely see cyberspace as part of the economy that should largely be left alone to innovate and have not embraced cybersecurity as a public good. But major cases of cyber insecurity caused by nation-state uses of malware, such as BlackEnergy and NotPetya, or corporate breaches that began with a simple phishing email illustrate that cybersecurity is indeed a collective action problem where individual action and inaction challenge security in cyberspace.

When strong teams are missing, complex problems are hard to identify and harder to address. Yet the brief history of the Internet is replete with leaders who built teams that changed the world, such as Steve Jobs, Bill Gates, Reed Hastings, Mark Zuckerberg, Sergey Brin, Larry Page, and Elon Musk. They offered important models to lead in the cyber age. Their main contribution may be the teams they assembled that improved the automata of Hero of Alexandria of the first century, built the machines Charles Babbage envisioned, and developed the code Ada Lovelace wrote in the nineteenth century. Successful leaders create new corporate cultures, demand excellence from their employees, and empower subordinates.

11.3 DISCUSSION TOPICS

1. What are ways that senior leaders can ensure cybersecurity professionals have opportunities to communicate about the state of cybersecurity in their organizations?
2. What are ways that cybersecurity professionals can communicate to senior leaders the risks to their enterprises?
3. What are ways to create a culture of cybersecurity in any organization?

Glossary

5G: the fifth-generation technology standard for broadband cellular networks.

Abacus: a mechanical aid to computation that makes use of beads on rods to represent decimal numbers as well as add and subtract them.

Access privilege: the right "to perform security-related functions on a computer system" – Wikipedia.

Accumulator: a special register that is the target for many results computed by a central processing unit (CPU).

Additive bias: the tendency to improve something by addition rather reassembly or rewrite.

Advanced persistent threat: a threat created by a highly capable and persistent threat actor.

Advanced Research Projects Agency (ARPA): was an agency in the US Department of Defense authorized by President Eisenhower in 1958 to execute research and development projects. It was permanently renamed the Defense Advanced Research Projects Agency (DARPA) in 1996. DARPA's current mission is "to make pivotal investments in breakthrough technologies for national security."

Air gap: a gap between a computer and a computing device that consists of free space.

Algorithm: a procedure to perform a calculation. It is not unlike a cookbook recipe. As with the latter, steps are normally executed in sequence until a test is given, such as determining the appearance of a loaf of bread in an oven, in which case the test may dictate a change in cooking steps. This is called *branching*. The algorithm can then branch back to a previous step, thereby implementing a *loop*.

Algorithm, straight-line: an algorithm that performs instructions in sequence without returning to an earlier instruction.

ALU: the acronym for arithmetic-logical unit.

American Standard Code for Information Exchange: or *ASCII*. It provides a 7-bit encoding for the Latin alphabet. It encodes 26 upper-case and 26 lower-case letters, 10 digits, punctuation symbols, and special characters.

Analytical Engine: a design of a general-purpose mechanical computer by Charles Babbage, which he could not implement given the primitive state of mechanical engineering at the time. Ava Lovelace wrote programs for this machine.

Anchoring bias: the tendency to fixate on the first piece of evidence that has been seen.

AND: a logic gate whose inputs and output have value 1 (True) or 0 (False) and whose output is 1 (True) only if both of its inputs are 1 (True).

AND, vector: the bitwise AND of two n-tuples sets of bits for some integer n.

Antivirus software: software designed to identify malware using either signature or behavioral analysis.

Arithmetic-logical unit (ALU): logic circuit whose outputs are the results of arithmetical and logical operations on its inputs.

Armed attack: a use of force that causes physical damage or violence against people.

ARPANET: experimental packet-based network funded by ARPA and developed largely by American engineers over a period of more than a decade beginning in 1969 using ideas originating in the United States and Britain.

Artificial general intelligence (AGI): artificial intelligence that is indistinguishable from human intelligence.

Artificial intelligence (AI): the capability given to computers so that they perform functions similar to those performed by humans.

Artificial neuron: a unit that forms a weighted sum of its inputs to which is added a bias and the result passed through a nonlinear one-input and one-output activation function.

Assembler: software to translate an assembly language program into machine language.

Assembly language: a programming language using mnemonics for instructions.

Attack: an aggressive action designed to provide something of value or disrupt an operation.

Attack, acoustic: an attack that extracts data from a computer using audible or inaudible (ultrasonic) sound

Attack, computer: an attack on a computer that violates security to access valuable data or to disrupt the operation of the computer.

Attack, dictionary: a table containing words that are likely to be used as passwords and their hashes so that a valid password can be retrieved quickly from the table.

Attack, electromagnetic radiation: an attack that exploits electromagnetic radiation, such as Bluetooth.

Attack, memory cache: an attack that exploits a hardware vulnerability to extract information from a protected memory space by abusing CPU functions designed to increase performance.

Attack, power consumption: an attack that extracts information by observing power consumed by a computer, typically knowing which algorithm is being executed.

Attack, rainbow: synonymous with dictionary attack.

Attack, timing: an attack that measures the time used for computations to extract information.

Authentication: "The process or action of verifying the identity of a user or process" – Lexico, Oxford.

Authentication, multifactor: authentication using multiple secrets.

Authentication, single-factor: authentication using a single secret or password.

Authentication, two-factor: authentication based on two secrets, such as a password and a private smartphone.

Authority bias: the tendency to comply with a request from an authority figure.

Autoencoder: a neural network in which the layers decrease in size up to a middle layer and then increase in size. The layers up to and including the middle layer constitute the *encoder*. The remaining layers constitute the *decoder*.

Automata: a word derived from Greek that means "acting of one's own will." Today automata are computational models. Historically, they were machines that emulated some aspect of human behavior.

Autonomous system (AS): an independently managed internet subnetwork. Each AS has a unique binary string identifier and advertises announcements of blocks of Internet Protocol (IP) addresses that it has assigned to nodes on its subnetwork.

Autonomous system number (ASN): the number assigned by the Internet Corporation of Assigned Names and Numbers (ICANN) to an AS.

Availability bias: a mental shortcut that invokes a recently encountered word or idea when making a judgment.

Backdoor: a type of access that allows a third party to gain entry without the owner's knowledge.

Behavioral analysis: observation of the behavior of software, such as a suspicious sequence of requests to an operating system or attempts to communicate with a website run by attackers.

Bit: a value of 1 or 0 denoting True or False, respectively.

BlackEnergy: malware used to shut down the electric grid in Estonia in December 2015.

Blockade: a denial of access.

Bluetooth: a short-range form of electromagnetic radiation with a nominal 30-meter range.

Bluetooth, rifle: a Bluetooth receiver, such as a computer, combined with a directional antenna. Combined they can extend the range of Bluetooth to nearly 2 kilometers.

Boolean operation: named for the logician George Boole, an operation on binary inputs that produces a binary output.

Boot program: the program that is run when the computer is first turned on.

Border Gateway Protocol (BGP): a protocol that defines standards for transmitting announcements of paths that can be followed by packets to reach blocks of internet addresses.

Border Gateway Protocol hijacking: it occurs when an anonymous system announces an IP prefix that has not been assigned to it by ICANN.

Breach: a violation of security that occurs when secrets are revealed to unauthorized users.

Breach detection system: a combination of detection tools.

BRICS: Brazil, Russia, India, China, and South Africa.

Budapest Convention: the first international treaty addressing cybercrime.

Buffer overflow: a security vulnerability in which a programming error allows an attacker to supply more inputs than the storage space reserved for it, resulting in the replacement of a return address on a stack, thereby allowing an attacker to choose the code to execute.

Business email compromise (BEC): use of social engineering in email to cause harm to a business, government, or organization.

Byte: a unit of 8 bits.

Cache: a fast auxiliary memory, usually one component of a memory hierarchy.

Canadian Security Intelligence Service (CSIS): investigates activities suspected of constituting threats to the security of Canada, reports on these to the government of Canada, and takes measures to reduce threats to the security of Canada in accordance with well-defined legal requirements and ministerial direction.

Carrier Sense Multiple Access with Collision Detection Protocol (CSMA/CD): a protocol that transmits blocks of bits, called frames. To prevent multiple devices from sending bits at the same time and garbling the communications, a node waits to transmit data until no data is detected on the wire. If while sending a frame, data from another computer is detected (a collision), the node halts its transmission, waits for a random amount of time, and repeats the attempt to transmit the frame, repeating this multistep process if collisions occur.

Cell: a memory device holding either a 1 or a 0.

Central Intelligence Agency (CIA): a civilian foreign intelligence agency of the US government.

Central processing unit (CPU): a finite-state machine (FSM) containing registers, an arithmetic-logical unit, an instruction decoder, and a program counter; an ALU, a component that performs elementary operations such as additions, subtractions, comparisons of binary strings, and operations on strings such as shifting them and performing Boolean operations on strings, such as bitwise AND, OR, and NOT.

Certificate: a cryptographically signed message.

Certificate authority (CA): a trusted entity that issues certificates confirming that the CA has verified the ownership of a particular piece of data, such as a public key.

Checksum: the sum of bits using the Exclusive OR operator.

Chip, computer: electronic components on a small, flat piece of semiconductor.

CIA triad: confidentiality(C), integrity(I), and availability(A), which are the core foundations for information security.

Cipher: a system of secret writing.

Circuit-switched network: a method to move data directly between two connected pairs of hosts. For example, when a customer dials a number, the network connects the caller to a remote party by creating a dedicated communication path, or *circuit*, between them.

Clock: a value that alternates between 1 and 0 at a steady rate.

Code: computer code, a synonym for software.

Code, legacy: code that was written many years earlier when software engineers were not paying sufficient attention to security vulnerabilities.

Code of ethics: a set of values, principles, and standards by which professionals are judged.

Code signing: a cryptographic signature of code, that is, software.

Cognitive bias: humans generally attempt to make judgments quickly, which often lead to judgmental errors, which are called cognitive biases.

Collective defense: exemplified by the North Atlantic Treaty Organization (NATO).

Committee on Foreign Investment in the United States (CFIUS): an interagency committee authorized to review certain transactions involving foreign investment in the United States.

Common vulnerabilities and exposures (CVEs): cybersecurity vulnerabilities that are discovered and published.

Compilers: software to translate programs in a high-level language into a machine-level program.

Computer: a device that receives inputs and produces outputs that result from the application of algorithms.

Computer architecture: the art or practice of designing computers.

Computer Emergency Response Team (CERT): a group of IT professionals that responds to computer incidents.

Computer Security Incident Response Team (CSIRT): a group of IT professionals that responds to computer security-related incidents.

Confidence-building measures (CBMs): measures designed to prevent conflicts, misperception, and misunderstandings.

Confidentiality: the state of being or keeping a secret.

Configuration error: an error in assigning access privileges that grants unauthorized access to a computer system.

Confirmation bias: the tendency to find evidence that confirms one's preconceptions.

Convention on Cybercrime: another name for the Budapest Convention.

Core: one of several CPUs on a processor chip.

Credential: information that authorizes the credential holder to access a specific computer, such as an identity ID and a password PSSWD (ID, PSSWD).

Cryptographic system: an encryption (cipher) and its decryption algorithm.

Cryptographic signature: a signature created using a cryptographic system.

Cryptography: the science of creating secret codes (ciphertexts) from messages (plaintext).

Cryptography, public-key: a cryptographic scheme in which each party has both a private and a public key. One party sends an encrypted message to another party using that party's public key and the recipient decrypts it using their private key.

Cryptosystem: a synonym for the cryptographic system.

Cryptosystem, symmetric: A cryptosystem in which both the sender and the receiver use the same key to encrypt and decrypt messages.

Customary International Law: general principles of law recognized by civilized nations and established customs practiced by states over time.

Cyber economics: the application of economics principles to cyberspace.

Cybergeddon: a cataclysm resulting from large-scale attacks on computers and networks.

Cyber Mission Force (CMF): CMF is US Cyber Command's action arm. Its teams execute the command's mission to direct, synchronize, and coordinate cyberspace operations in defense of US national interests. It consists of 133 Cyber Mission Teams, 4 Joint Force Headquarters-Cyber, 1 for each service, and 1 Cyber National Mission Force.

Cybersecurity: protection of data from theft (loss of confidentiality), manipulation (loss of integrity), while remaining available, summarized by the acronym CIA.

Cybersecurity and Infrastructure Security Agency (CISA): a United States federal agency within the Department of Homeland Security responsible for improving cybersecurity across all levels of government, coordinating cybersecurity programs with US states, and improving the government's cybersecurity protections against private and nation-state hackers.

Cybersecurity framework: standards, guidelines, and practices developed by the National Institute for Standards and Technology (NIST) to promote the protection of critical infrastructure.

Cyberspace: the vast network of interconnected computers that span the globe, equipment attached to the network, and the information that traverses and is stored in it.

Dark web: the part of the web that is not indexed by search engines and not accessible without specialized software and encryption keys. It has become the Internet's black market.

Decoder: a computational device that maps an input string to an output string. If the input string is the output of an encoder, the decoder output string is either the input to the encoder or a string close to it.

Decoder, instruction: a decoder that maps a binary string denoting an instruction to a set of steps that implement the instruction.

Deepfakes: real images, audio, or video modified using technology, such as machine learning, to mislead observers by creating media that appears to be authentic.

Defend forward: a defensive measure practiced by US Cyber Command to help other nations to hunt for malware on their networks.

Denial of service (DoS): denial of access for legitimate users, often accomplished by flooding a targeted host or network with so much traffic that the target cannot respond.

Denial-of-service attack: an attack that makes a resource on the Internet unavailable.

Department of Defense (DoD): an executive branch department of the US federal government charged with coordinating and supervising all agencies and functions of the government directly related to national security and the United States Armed Forces.

Department of Defense Information Network (DODIN): DoD's globally interconnected, end-to-end set of electronic information capabilities and associated processes for collecting, processing, storing, disseminating, and managing digital information on-demand to warfighters, policy makers, and support personnel, including owned and leased communications and computing systems and services, software (including applications), data, security services, and other associated services, and national security systems.

Deterrence: the effort to dissuade an adversary from taking an action.

Difference Engine: a mechanical aid to computation invented in 1822 by Charles Babbage to compute polynomial functions.

Digital Geneva Convention: a Microsoft-proposed treaty designed to protect civilians from nation-state attacks.

Digital Markets Act (DMA): DMA is a proposed act that will ban certain practices used by large platforms acting as "gatekeepers" and enable the European Commission to carry out market investigations and sanction noncompliant behavior.

Digital Services Act (DSA): DSA is a proposed act that will give better protection to users and to fundamental rights online, establish a powerful transparency and accountability framework for online platforms, and provide a single, uniform framework across the European Union.

Direction de la Surveillance du Territoire (DST): a directorate of the French National Police operating as a domestic intelligence agency.

Distributed denial of service (DDoS): a denial of service obtained when multiple computers bombard a single computer with high volumes of traffic.

Domain names: text strings punctuated with periods, such as *www.papers.bostonpos.net*

Domain name system (DNS): the "telephone book" for the Internet. It maps from domain names to IP addresses.

Doxing: a form of cyberbullying that reveals sensitive or secret information about individuals to intimidate them, encourage harassment, and potentially cause them financial and/or physical harm.

DRAM: a bit is stored in a cell consisting of a transistor (a switch) and a capacitor (a charge storage device). The value of a bit is denoted by the level of the charge on the transistor. A very low charge (a small number of electrons) denotes a 0 and a charge above a certain threshold denotes the value 1. Because electrons will leak from a capacitor, all the data stored in a DRAM must be refreshed every few milliseconds.

Dunning–Kruger Effect: the tendency of individuals with low ability at a task to overrate their ability and that of individuals with high ability to underrate their ability.

Economic espionage: copying, theft, receipt, or possession of trade secrets.

Electromagnetic pulse (EMP): a brief burst of electromagnetic energy such as is associated with a solar flare, a lightning strike, a nuclear explosion, or a man-made electrostatic discharge.

Encoder: a computational device that maps an input string to an output string.

Encryption: a process of encoding information using secret(s) that make deciphering of encrypted information difficult.

Endowment effect: the tendency to overvalue a person or thing that they manage or control.

End-to-end encryption: encryption of information at the source that cannot be decrypted without great effort until it reaches the destination.

Ethernet: a local area network (LAN) that uses the Ethernet protocol.

Ethernet protocol: a protocol to transmit bits over wired LANs using CSMA/CD.

Ethics: the principles of conduct governing an individual or a profession.

Exceptional access: access to encrypted communications authorized by a court.

Externality: in economics a side effect that affects others other than the producer of a product.

Externality, negative: an externality that has a negative effect, such as penalizing a market for releasing software with vulnerabilities.

Externality, positive: an externality that has a positive effect.

Facebook: an online social networking website.

Facebook Messenger: a mobile product to instantly send chat messages to others.

Fetch–execute cycle: a cycle of instruction executions by a CPU.

File: an electronic document.

File system: a program within an operating system to manage a collection of files.

Fingerprint: the hash of a public key.

Finite-state machine (FSM): a state-based computer with a bounded number of states that has an internal state recorded in a binary memory. Its logic circuit maps the current input and the current state of the FSM to the output and the successor state.

Firewall: software that monitors and filters incoming and outgoing internet traffic based on criteria set by an organization.

Firewall, application-layer: software that protects applications or services by looking deeply within packet streams for inconsistencies, invalid or malicious inputs, or executable programs.

Firmware: a boot program that is recorded in *read-only memory (ROM) chips* that are programmed before installation.

Foreign Intelligence Surveillance Act (FISA): US federal law establishing procedures for the physical and electronic collection of foreign intelligence information.

Foreign Intelligence Surveillance Court (FISC): a US court authorized to oversee requests for surveillance warrants by federal law enforcement agencies.

Framing effect: the tendency for a decision to be influenced by the way it is presented or "framed."

Free riding: a negative externality in which a party enjoys a benefit due to expenditures of other parties in the same market.

Gate: the embodiment of a logic function, such as AND, OR, and NOT.

General Data Protection Regulation (GDPR): a regulation in European Union law on data protection and privacy. One of its provisions is the "right to be forgotten," that is, to have personal data be erased when it is no longer needed for the purpose for which it was collected.

Ghost user: a third party added surreptitiously to a two-party conversation.

Gigabyte: 2^{30} or $(1024)^3$ or 1,072,741,824 bytes.

Global Positioning System (GPS): a satellite-based radionavigation system owned by the United States.

Group of Governmental Experts (GGE): a UN group operating in the field of information and telecommunications in the context of international security with a small number of participating nations and a mandate to further develop the rules, norms, and principles of responsible behavior of states.

Group of Seven (G7): an intergovernmental forum comprising Canada, France, Germany, Italy, Japan, the United Kingdom, and the United States, and the European Union as a nonenumerated member.

Group of Twenty (G20): an intergovernmental forum comprising the 19 richest countries based on gross domestic products and the European Union. It works to address major issues related to the global economy.

Hacking: the gaining of unauthorized access to data in a system or computer.

Hard disk drive (HDD): uses electromagnetic technologies to read and record data using one of two patterns of magnetization in a region on the surface of a spinning disk for each stored bit.

Hash function: a function that is applied to a string of characters and produces a fixed-length string, called a "hash" or "hash value."

Hash function, cryptographic: a hash function that is cryptographically secure. That is, given a hash value, it is very difficult to find any string that will produce the same hash value using the hash function.

Hindsight bias: the tendency to fool oneself into thinking that an outcome was the result that one had predicted.

Host: a computer that is connected via a network.

HyperText Markup Language: a language in which to create hypertext documents.

Hypertext: documents of the kind viewed with browsers that contain links to related other documents or images.

ICT: acronym for information and communications technology.

iMessage: Apple's instant messaging services for its products.

Information environment: the combination of cyberspace and the decisions humans make within it.

Information technology (IT): computer and communications technology.

In-order instruction execution (IOE): the execution of instruction by a CPU in the order in which they appear in a program, also known as *program order*.

Instruction, computer: one of a set of operations that a computer can perform.

Instruction decoder: an FSM typically used inside a CPU to decompose a computer instruction into small sets (microcode) and execute them.

Instruction, machine-level: instruction that is understood by a CPU.

Integrated circuit: chip technology in which transistors and wires are implanted in the surface of a semiconductor crystal.

Integrity: an unimpaired or unaltered condition.

International law: a body of rules established by custom or treaty and recognized by nations as binding in their relations with one another. *Jus ad bellum* sets the criteria for going to war, while *jus in bello* serves to regulate conduct within war.

International Telecommunication Union (ITU): a specialized agency of the United Nations responsible for global communications.

Internet: (a portmanteau of interconnected networks) a packet-based switching network designed to interconnect networks, regardless of what technologies are used to realize each network. A network connects to neighboring networks via a *router* that decides to which neighbor a packet is to be sent.

Internet Assigned Numbers Authority (IANA): a not-for-profit public-benefit company with participants from all over the world that is dedicated to keeping the Internet secure, stable, and interoperable. It maintains databases of the Internet's unique identifiers such as autonomous system numbers (ASNs), protocol numbers, and IP addresses for top-level domains that are used by domain name resolvers.

Internet Corporation of Assigned Names and Numbers (ICANN): an American corporation responsible for coordinating the maintenance and procedures of databases related to the namespaces and numerical spaces of the Internet.

Internet Engineering Task Force (IETF): a loosely organized group of people who contribute to the design and evolution of internet technologies.

Internet four-layer protocol model: the four layers are Application, Transport, Internet, and Link layers.

Internet governance: the rules, policies, standards, and practices that coordinate and shape the global cyberspace.

Internet of Things (IoT): the system of objects with computing capabilities that are interconnected via the Internet.

Internet Protocol: a set of rules for addressing and routing packets of data so that they travel across networks from the designated source to the designated destination.

Internet Protocol (IP) address: the unique address or number that identifies a device on the Internet.

Internet service provider (ISP): a company providing access to the Internet.

Interrupt: a signal to a computer that requests the attention of the processor.

Intrusion detection system (IDS): a system designed to detect the presence of an intruder, an unauthorized person or software, in a computer system.

Intrusion detection system, host (HIDS): a host IDS.

Intrusion detection system, network (NIDS): a network IDS.

Intrusion prevention system (IPS): an IDS system with a response capability such as to reject a packet stream from a suspicious IP address.

Joint Chiefs of Staff (JCS): the most senior uniformed leaders of the US Department of Defense, consisting of a chairman (CJCS), a vice chairman (VJCS), the service chiefs of the Army, Marine Corps, Navy, Air Force, and Space Force, and the chief of the National Guard Bureau.

Joint Cyber Defense Collaborative (JCDC): established by CISA, it is a private–public partnership of organizations worldwide that proactively gathers, analyzes, and shares actionable cyber risk information to enable synchronized, holistic cybersecurity planning, cyber defense, and response.

Joint Force Headquarters: provides a cyber combat mission team for each service and support teams to combatant commands.

Joint Force Headquarters-Cyber: protects DODIN and local DoD networks.

Kerckhoffs' Principle: asserts that a cryptographic system should be designed to be secure, even if all its details, except for a key or keys, are publicly known.

Kilobyte: 2^{10} or 1024 bytes.

Language: a method of communication.

Language, programming: a language that can be interpreted as instructions for a computer.

Law of armed conflict (LOAC): the component of international law that regulates state behavior during wartime. LOAC encapsulates the Hague and Geneva Conventions and its Protocols, and customary international law. The use of force is constrained by three principles, that of necessity, distinction, and proportionality.

Lethal autonomous weapons (LAWS): autonomous weapons with the capability to kill.

Local area network (LAN): a network that links computers within a local area such as a building or adjacent buildings.

Logarithm: A number $log_b(n)$ that is the power to which a base b is raised to produce a given real number n. It is a function that can simplify *multiplication or division*. For example, if two numbers are multiples of 4, such as $16 = 4^2$ and $64 = 4^3$, we can multiply them ($16 \times 64 = 4^2 \times 4^3 = 4^5$) by adding the exponents of 4 and then raising 4 to that exponent, which is 5 in this case. That is, $16 \times 64 = 4^5 = 1024$. In the representation of 1024 as a power of 4, its exponent, namely, 5, is *the logarithm of 1024 to the base 4*.

Logic bomb: instructions inserted in software so that if a condition occurs, the instructions will be activated.

Logic circuit: a wiring diagram showing connections between devices that perform logical operations.

Logic gate: a device that performs a logical operation on its inputs, such as AND, OR, or NOT.

Loss aversion: the tendency to be more upset by a loss of some value than to be pleased by a gain of the same value.

Malware: malicious software designed to gain unauthorized access to a computer or computer network for the purpose of stealing, modifying, or denying access to data, thereby violating the confidentiality (C), integrity (I), or availability (A) of data on the computer or network.

Man-in-the-middle (MITM) attack: a security threat that may arise when two parties communicate via a third party who can eavesdrop on the communication.

Media Access Control (MAC) address: globally unique, permanent, 48-bit number assigned by manufacturers to networkable devices.

Megabyte: 2^{20} or 1,048,576 bytes or 1024 kilobytes.

Memory: a storage device that holds one or more bits.

Memory, random-access: see random-access memory.

Memory hierarchy: a collection of memories of increasing size and increasing access time that is designed to function as a single, large, reasonably fast memory.

Memory safety violation: such a violation occurs if one program can read the memory of another program without authorization including, possibility, the memory of the operating system.

Microarchitectural design: design of the microcode of computer instructions.

Microcode (μ-code): small steps into which a machine-level instruction is decomposed so that μ-code steps can be executed, potentially out-of-order, while waiting for data to be available.

MicroOps (μ-OPs): the small steps into which μ-code is subdivided.

Moore's Law: the observation, first noted in 1965 by Gordon Moore, that the number of transistors embedded into a chip of fixed area approximately doubled every two years.

Multicore processors: a chip that contains multiple cores.

Multifactor authentication: is based on multiple secrets being deployed. A typical *two-factor authentication system* uses not only login credentials but also the user's phone number.

Multistakeholder governance: a form of governance, often informal, in which nominally all stakeholders are invited to participate.

Multitasking: shared use of a computer by multiple users or tasks that gives the impression to each user or task that, except for the speed of execution, each is running alone on the computer.

National Cyber Investigative Joint Task Force (NCIJTF): a partnership between 30 US government agencies from law enforcement, the intelligence community, and the Department of Defense whose purpose is to address crimes, such as terrorism, espionage, financial fraud, and identity theft, being perpetrated using technology and the Internet.

National Institute for Standards and Technology (NIST): a federal agency whose mission is to promote US innovation and industrial competitiveness by advancing measurement science, standards, and technology in ways that enhance economic security and improve our quality of life.

National Security Agency (NSA): a national-level intelligence agency of the US Department of Defense under the authority of the Director of National Intelligence.

NATO Cyber Defence Pledge: a pledge to enhance cyber defenses of national infrastructures and networks.

Nongovernmental organization (NGO): an organization that is independent of governments.

Norm: established expectations for actors with respect to actions. It has an actor, an action, and an "oughtness," that is, an expectation.

Norm, GGE: norms endorsed by the GGE.

North Atlantic Treaty Organization (NATO): an intergovernmental military alliance with 30 members. The North Atlantic Council is the principal political decision-making body within NATO, overseeing the political and military processes.

NOT: a logic gate whose input and output have value 1 (True) or 0 (False) and whose output is 1 (True) if its input is 0 (False) and 0 (False) if its input is 1 (True).

NotPetya: a worm that was embedded in the update procedure of M.E.Doc, a Ukrainian tax preparation program. It spread rapidly across the globe and is estimated to have caused at least $10 billion in damages.

Office of the Director of National Intelligence (ODNI): a senior-level US agency with the mission of coordinating the entire US intelligence community.

One-time pad: a substitution cipher in which two identical copies of a code book of randomly generated numbers is used, one for the sender and one for the receiver. For an alphabet containing A numbers, the numbers range from 0 to $A-1$. The letters in the alphabet are associated with the numbers 0 to $A-1$. To encode a message of n characters, the next n numbers from the code book are retrieved. To encrypt the message, the n integers from the code book are added to the corresponding integers in the message modulo $A-1$. The integers are converted back into letters and the letters are transmitted. While this encryption scheme has been shown to provide perfect secrecy (the letters in the encrypted message are random), if sender and receiver are out of synchronism, the decrypted messages will be garbled.

Opcode: a contraction of *operation code*.

Open-Ended Working Group (OEWG): a UN group operating in the field of information and telecommunications in the context of international security with no limit to the number of participating nations and a mandate to further develop the rules, norms, and principles of responsible behavior of states. Unlike GGE, OEWG is open to all countries.

Open-source code: software made public so that it can be modified and used by others.

Operating system: software that runs on a computer and manages its hardware and software resources.

Operation code: a collection of bits in a computer-level instruction that identifies the instruction.

Operational technology (OT): a technology that controls a manufacturing process such as supervisory control and data acquisition technology (SCADA).

Opportunity cost: a benefit that is foregone by choosing one investment over another.

OR: a logic gate whose inputs and output have value 1 (True) or 0 (False) and whose output is 1 (True) if either or both of its inputs are 1 (True).

Organization for Security and Co-operation in Europe (OSCE): the world's largest regional security-oriented intergovernmental organization. It has 57 member states, most of which are European.

Out-of-order execution (O-o-OE): a model that increases CPU efficiency by allowing instructions to execute when their data arrives, even if that violates the program order.

Packet-based switching: a method of sending bundled data or *packets* from the source to the destination. Packets can be sent to their destinations by potentially different paths.

Packets: fixed-size blocks of data containing the addresses of the source and destination and control information that are sent to their destinations via potentially different paths.

Parallel computing: computation performed on a computer that contains multiple processors capable of simultaneous execution.

Password: a secret string used in authenticating a computer user.

Penetration testing (pen testing): testing of a computer network to determine if an unauthorized access is feasible. Red teams are engaged in such activities.

Persistent engagement: persistently contesting with adversaries in cyberspace.

Phishing: a type of social engineering attack designed to steal user information.

Phishing, spear: phishing in which a specific person or group is the target.

Pipelined computation: a computation in which microcode instructions are overlapped.

Planning fallacy: the tendency on the part of an individual to be optimistic and underestimate the time it will take to complete a task.

Prefix: a set of IP addresses identified by an IP address followed by / and, for IPv4, an integer n between 1 and 31 to denote the IP addresses that have the same common first n bits as this address. For IPv6, n is between 1 and 127.

Prefix, hijacking: the announcement by an autonomous system of a prefix that belongs to another autonomous system, thereby making it possible to steal packets destined for it.

Presidential Decision Directive: a written, or oral instruction or declaration issued by the president of the United States.

PRISM: An NSA surveillance program revealed by Edward Snowden designed to collect metadata for the purpose of identifying terrorist networks.

Process: a program running on a computer characterized by its activity.

Program: a set of instructions and data designed to provide functionality on a computer system.

Program, assembly language: a program in which instructions and data involve opcode and address mnemonics.

Program, machine language: a program in which each word is a bit string. One block of bits denotes an Opcode.

Programmer: a person who writes computer programs.

Program order: the order in which instructions appear in a program.

Protocols: rules that specify accepted ways to package data and send and receive it over media.

Punched cards: cards with holes punched in them. In early computers the open and closed holes represented values of bits.

Quantum computer: a computer that depends on the quantum entanglement of its qubits.

Quantum entanglement: a physical phenomenon in which groups of particles interact in such a way that their state depends on the state of the others, even when separated by large distances.

Qubit: a quantum bit whose state of 1 or 0 may be entangled with that of other qubits.

Rainbow table: a table containing words that are likely to be used as passwords and their hashes so that a valid password can be retrieved knowing the hash of a user password.

Random access computer: a model of a computer consisting of a CPU and a random-access memory (RAM).

Random-access memory (RAM): a very simple storage device or memory that acts like a file cabinet but is implemented as a *finite-state machine*. It contains fixed-length words, each of which has an address, and for which any word can be selected for reading or writing (i.e., replacement). A device connected to it, such as a CPU, can issue one of three commands, Read, Write or NOP, the latter instrucing the RAM to do nothing.

Ransomware: malware that blocks access to a computer until a ransom is paid.

Read-only memory (ROM): Memory whose contents are permanent.

Red team: a team of computer experts who think like adversaries and are charged with discovering computer and network vulnerabilities.

Register: a storage device consisting of a small number of binary memory cells. A CPU has many registers of potentially different numbers of bits.

Relational database: a database in which data is stored in tables consisting of rows and columns. Each row in a table has a unique ID called a key. Columns other than the ID column are labeled with data attributes. Three operations can be performed on the tables – (a) Two tables containing the same column of Ids can be "joined" to create a new table. Each row of this table is obtained by appending the row of the second table to the row of the first table with the same ID after deleting the ID. (b) A new table can be "projected" from an existing table by removing specified columns. (c) Finally, a new table can be "selected" from an existing table by removing all rows from an existing table except those that meet specified conditions on columns.

Representativeness error: the tendency to make a judgment based on evidence that best represents a particular condition but which is insufficient to justify the judgment.

Risk: the possibility of losing something of value, such as confidential information, integrity, availability, or funds.

Robot: a machine that resembles a living creature capable of moving independently and performing complex tasks.

Route flapping: alternation between the announcement and the withdrawal of an internet announcement.

Routers: specialized computers designed to make packet-routing decisions.

Routing table: a table that shows for each internet prefix the neighbor network to send a packet with an IP address that falls within the prefix.

RuNet: the Russian internet in which domains have the top-level domain .ru.

Salt: a secret string that is concatenated with passwords before hashing them for entry into a password table.

Sampling Theorem: states that a signal or *waveform* $x(t)$ that contains no frequencies higher than W hertz (W cycles per second) is completely determined by samples taken every $1/(2W)$ seconds. That is, these samples can be passed through a low-pass filter, one that passes only frequencies of at most W hertz, and the filter output will replicate exactly the original waveform $x(t)$. The filter reconstructs the input by smoothing the samples.

Sandbox: a simulated computer in which suspicious applications can be run to determine whether they are malicious or not without damaging the computer on which the sandbox runs.

Security information and event management (SIEM) system: a system for the collection and analysis of security information from all components of a computer network.

Security operations center (SOC): a team of skilled professionals responsible for supervising the security of a network and investigating and remediating potential intrusions.

Security vulnerability: a vulnerability in hardware or software that when exploited provides unauthorized access to a computer system.

Side-channel attack: an attack that exfiltrates information via a channel that was not designed to reveal such information.

Signal: an instant messaging service that offers end-to-end encrypted communication.

Signature: a hash of a digital document. Because it is computationally difficult to find a string that will produce the hash value computed from a known document, a hash value is a "good" signature for that document.

Signature, cryptographic: a signature created using a cryptographic system. Crytographic signatures, computed with computational secure hash functions, provide very high confidence that the signed document is authentic.

Signature analysis: categorization of software as malware by the strings it contains.

Single-factor authentication: based on *one shared secret*, a user *password*, which when combined with a *user ID* authenticates the user. Together a *user ID* and *password* constitute a *credential*.

Slide rule: "A ruler with a sliding central strip, marked with logarithmic scales and used for making rapid calculations, especially multiplication and division" – Lexico, Oxford.

Smishing: phishing via SMS messaging.

Social engineering: "The use of deception to manipulate individuals into divulging confidential or personal information that may be used for fraudulent purposes" – Lexico, Oxford.

Software: consists of instructions and data, that is, programs, used to operate computers for specific tasks.

Software engineering: the application of engineering principles to software development.

Solid-state disk drive (SSD): emulates an HDD but has no moving parts and is faster.

SORM: Russian System of Operational-Investigatory Measures.

Sovereignty: a fundamental concept in international relations whose purpose is to protect governments from foreign interference.

Speculative execution: a technique that exploits parallelism to make programs run more quickly on average by predicting the demand for instructions or data and executing the instructions or fetching the data.

Splinternet: a pejorative name for the Internet after it has been disaggregated into separate networks, also referred to as the fragmentation or *Balkanization* of the Internet.

SQL: a programming language in which instructions to a relational database can be specified.

SQL injection attack: an error on the part of a database manager to fail to properly "sanitize" user responses to database queries, that otherwise would allow a user to submit a response that provides access to prohibited information or to execute prohibited commands.

SRAM: a memory cell consisting of multiple transistors. Consequently, an SRAM cell occupies more space than a DRAM cell, which explains its higher cost per bit. Data stored in an SRAM persists as long as power is supplied to the memory and disappears when the power is cut.

Stakeholder: a person, group, or organization with an interest in a project.

State: the value of binary cells of a memory.

Stateless computer: one without memory, is given a set of input bits each of value 1 or 0, denoting the truth values *True* and *False*, respectively, and produces a set of output bits.

Storage cell: synonymous with cell.

Storage device: a device containing a collection of storage cells and for which there is a mechanism to select cells for reading or writing (i.e., replacement).

Strategy: the art of planning.

Strategy, grand: the plans and policies that guide the full use of national power to secure a nation.

Stuxnet: a worm designed to destroy centrifuges in a nuclear refinement facility in Natanz, Iran. The worm was programmed to make the operators believe that the centrifuges were poorly constructed. It was discovered in 2010 when it escaped the Natanz facility.

Substitution cipher: a cipher that maps the letters of an alphabet to permuted letters.

Sunk cost fallacy: the tendency to persist with a failing investment because of the large costs that have been incurred. This is a manifestation of loss aversion.

Supervisory control and data acquisition technology (SCADA): technology that involves control system technology, as is found in petrochemical refinement and water purification.

Supply chain: the network of individuals, organizations, resources, activities, and technologies involved in the creation of a product.

Supply chain attack: corruption of a supply chain through insertion, deletion, or modification of elements of the chain.

Targeted lawful access: A synonym for exceptional access.

TCP three-way handshake: a protocol used to synchronize a sender and receiver of IP packets.

Top-level domain: the rightmost label in a domain name such as .com, .org, or .net.

Transmission Control Protocol (TCP): an Internet Protocol in which each packet is sent to a destination and is expected to be acknowledged through the TCP three-way handshake. If a packet is not acknowledged within a time limit set by the source, it is repeated. If too many packets fail to be acknowledged within the time limit, the limit is increased up to a point set by the source.

Trapdoor function: functions that are easy to compute but hard to invert.

Treaty of Westphalia: it established the fundamental concept of sovereignty in international relations where a state has the ultimate authority to rule within its borders, free from external interference.

Trojan: malware that, once implanted in a computer, provides remote access to an attacker.

Unicode: an industry standard for encoding text in most of the world's writing systems. *UTF-8* is an instance of Unicode that can encode up to 1,112,064 characters using between one and four bytes for each character. Since 2009 UTF-8 has been the dominant digital encoding standard for the World Wide Web and plays an important role in the internationalization and localization of software.

Universal Declaration of Human Rights (UDHR): a document that articulates 30 rights and freedoms to which every individual everywhere is entitled. UDHR was adopted by the United Nations on December 10, 1948, in response to the atrocities of World War II. The drafting of UDHR began in 1946 by representatives from a wide variety of countries. These rights, which include to be free from torture and have *freedom of expression, life, liberty*, and *privacy*, form the basis for international human rights law. UDHR also includes economic, social, and cultural rights, such as *social security, health* and *adequate housing*.

URL: uniform resource locater is a website address.

US Cyber Command (USCYBERCOM): one of the eleven unified combatant commands of the US Department of Defense (DoD). It unifies the direction of cyberspace operations, strengthens DoD cyberspace capabilities, and integrates and bolsters DoD's cyber expertise.

User Datagram Protocol (UDP): a send-and-forget Internet Protocol in which each packet is sent to the destination address without any expectation of a response from the destination.

Vector: a means through which a computer can be attacked.

Virtual memory: an operating system feature that hides the individual memories of a memory hierarchy and presents to a programmer a single flat memory space in which storage locations are indexed in increasing numeric order.

Virtual private network (VPN): an encrypted connection over the public Internet from a device to a private network.

Virus: malware that can replicate itself and infect other computers.

Virus, polymorphic: a virus that changes the way it is embeds itself in a program, thereby changing its signature.

Vishing: phishing via a phone call.

Wales Summit Declaration: 2014 declaration by NATO that a cyberattack could trigger the invocation of Article 5 of the NATO treaty and require a collective response to the attack.

WannaCry: ransomware that exploits a vulnerability in the Microsoft Windows XP OS.

War Powers Act of 1973: an attempt to provide Congress a greater check on the president's authority as commander-in-chief to deploy military forces.

Warsaw Summit Declaration: a declaration in which NATO agreed that cyberspace is a domain like land, air, and sea.

Watering hole: a site frequented by a targeted group, industry, or region.

Webpage: a document written in the HyperText Markup Language that may contain text, images, sound, or video as well as links to other webpages.

WeChat: a Chinese instant messaging, social media, and mobile payment app developed by Tencent.

Whale: a very important target of a phishing exploit, such as a CEO.

Whaling: phishing a high-value person or group.

WhatsApp: cross-platform instant messaging and voice over IP software provided free of charge by Meta, Inc., the company formerly known as Facebook.

Whitelisting: making a list of applications that are allowed to run on a computer network.

Wi-Fi: a form of radio communication used to connect computers to the Internet.

Wiper: malware designed to corrupt or erase a significant portion of memory, usually to make a computer inoperable.

Wireless LAN: a LAN in which transmission is via a communication technology other than a wire or cable, such as Bluetooth, light, or sound.

Word: a collection of bits.

Work factor: the amount of effort required for a task.

World Summit on the Information Society (WSIS): a summit first held at Geneva in 2003 and then in Tunis in 2005 to discuss the information society opportunities and challenges. Frequent meetings are held.

Worm: self-propagating virus. It activates when it lands on a computer, infecting that computer, and attempts to infect computers to which it is attached. It does not need to infect an application to be activated. However, it does need to exploit a vulnerability in an operating system.

ZTE: a Chinese telecommunications company.

References

47 U.S. Code § 230 – Protection for private blocking and screening of offensive material. (n.d.). LII/Legal Information Institute. Retrieved July 5, 2022, from www.law.cornell.edu/uscode/text/47/230

Abbate, J. (1999). *Inventing the Internet*. MIT Press.

Abbott, K. W., & Snidal, D. (1998). Why states act through formal international organizations. *Journal of Conflict Resolution*, *42*(1), 3–32.

Abelson, H., Anderson, R., Bellovin, S. M. et al. (2015). Keys under doormats: Mandating insecurity by requiring government access to all data and communications. *Journal of Cybersecurity*, *1*(1), 69–79. https://doi.org/10.1093/cybsec/tyv009

About OpenAI. (n.d.). Retrieved December 11, 2015, from https://openai.com/about/

Ackerman, E. (2019, April 1). Three Small Stickers in Intersection Can Cause Tesla Autopilot to Swerve into Wrong Lane. *IEEE Spectrum*. https://spectrum.ieee.org/three-small-stickers-on-road-can-steer-tesla-autopilot-into-oncoming-lane

ACPA Anticybersquatting Consumer Protection Act, 15 U.S.C. No. 1125(d) (1999). www.govinfo.gov/content/pkg/CRPT-106srpt140/html/CRPT-106srpt140.htm

Adams, G. S., Converse, B. A., Hales, A. H., & Klotz, L. E. (2021). People systematically overlook subtractive changes. *Nature*, *592*(7853), Article 7853. https://doi.org/10.1038/s41586-021-03380-y

AI at Google (n.d.). *Our Principles*. Retrieved July 31, 2022, from https://ai.google/principles/

Akerlof, G. A. (1970). The market for "Lemons": Quality uncertainty and the market mechanism. *The Quarterly Journal of Economics*, *84*(3), 488–500. https://doi.org/10.2307/1879431

Alagic, G., Alperin-Sheriff, J., Apon, D. et al. (2020). Status report on the Second Round of the NIST Post-Quantum Cryptography Standardization Process (NIST Internal or Interagency Report (NISTIR) 8309). National Institute of Standards and Technology. https://doi.org/10.6028/NIST.IR.8309

Alexander, K. B. (2007). Warfighting in cyberspace. *Joint Force Quarterly*, *46*, 58–61.

Allen-Ebrahimian, B. (2021, February 16). Growing number of countries issue warnings on China's espionage. *Axios*. www.axios.com/2021/02/16/china-espionage-europe

Allied Powers. (1941). *The Declaration of St. James Palace*, History of the United Nations, June 12, 1941. See https://avalon.law.yale.edu/imt/imtjames.asp

347

Allison, G., & Simes, D. K. (2016, December 18). A Blueprint for Donald Trump to Fix Relations with Russia [Text]. The National Interest; The Center for the National Interest. https://nationalinterest.org/feature/blueprint-donald-trump-fix-relations-russia-18776

Alphabet Inc. (2020). Form 10-K: Annual Report Pursuant to Section 13 or 15(d) of the Securities Exchange Act of 1934. https://abc.xyz/investor/static/pdf/20200204_alphabet_10K.pdf?cache=cdd6dbf

American Civil Liberties Union. (2003, December 18). Seven Reasons the US Should Reject the International Cybercrime Treaty. www.aclu.org/other/seven-reasons-us-should-reject-international-cybercrime-treaty

Angwin, J., Larson, J., Mattu, S., & Kirchner, L. (2016, May 23). Machine bias: There's software used across the country to predict future criminals. And it's biased against blacks. ProPublica. www.propublica.org/article/machine-bias-risk-assessments-in-criminal-sentencing?token=Tu5C70R2pCBv8Yj33AkMh2E-mHz3d6iu

Apple. (n.d.). Privacy. Apple. Retrieved September 5, 2022, from www.apple.com/privacy/

Aristotle. (2012). *Aristotle's Nicomachean Ethics* (R. C. Bartlett & S. D. Collins, Trans.; Reprint edition). University of Chicago Press.

Army cyber fact sheet: Army Cyber Command. (2019, October 4). U.S. Army Cyber Command. www.arcyber.army.mil/Info/Fact-Sheets/Fact-Sheet-View-Page/Article/1435502/army-cyber-fact-sheet-army-cyber-command/https%3A%2F%2Fwww.arcyber.army.mil%2FInfo%2FFact-Sheets%2FFact-Sheet-View-Page%2FArticle%2F1435502%2Farmy-cyber-fact-sheet-army-cyber-command%2F

Arquilla, J., & Ronfeldt, D. (1993). *Cyberwar is Coming!* (RP-223; p. 38). RAND Corporation. www.rand.org/pubs/reprints/RP223.html

Asimov, I. (1942). Runaround. In *Astounding Science Fiction* (Vol. 29). Street & Smith Publications, Inc.

Bain, B. (2010, July 26). Military wrestles with cyber war battle planning. Defense One. www.defenseone.com/defense-systems/2010/07/military-wrestles-with-cyber-war-battle-planning/188817/

Baker, H., & Capestany, C. (Directors). (2018). It's Getting Harder to Spot a Deep Fake Video. www.youtube.com/watch?v=gLoI9hAX9dw

Balzano, J. (2012). Crimes and the foreign sovereign immunities act: New perspectives on an old debate. *NCJ International Law & Commercial Regulation, 38*, 43.

Baran, P. (1964). *On Distributed Communications: I. Introduction to Distributed Communications Networks*. The Rand Corporation. www.rand.org/content/dam/rand/pubs/research_memoranda/2006/RM3420.pdf

Barlow, J. P. (1996, February 8). *A Declaration of the Independence of Cyberspace*. Electronic Frontier Foundation. www.eff.org/cyberspace-independence

Barnes, J. E., & Goldman, A. (2020, May 30). Russia trying to stoke U.S. racial tensions before election, officials say. *New York Times (Online)*.

Barocas, S., Hardt, M., & Narayanan, A. (2022). Fairness and machine learning. 253.

Beck, K. et al. (2001). Manifesto for Agile Software Development. https://agilemanifesto.org/

Beckstrom, R. (2014, December 16). CyberVaR: Quantifying the risk of loss from cyber attacks. Premiere Speakers Bureau. https://premierespeakers.com//rod_beckstrom/blog/2014/12/16/cybervar_quantifying_the_risk_of_loss_from_cyber_attacks

Bellamy, R. K. E., Dey, K., Hind, M. et al. (2019). AI Fairness 360: An extensible toolkit for detecting and mitigating algorithmic bias. *IBM Journal of Research and Development*, *63*(4/5), 4:1–4:15. https://doi.org/10.1147/JRD.2019.2942287

Bensoussan, A. (2018). *General Data Protection Regulation: Texts, Commentaries and Practical Guidelines (GDPR)*. Wolters Kluwer Belgium NV.

Berners-Lee, T. (1991). World Wide Web. CERN. http://info.cern.ch/hypertext/WWW/TheProject.html

Berners-Lee, T. (2019, March 12). 30 years on, what's next #ForTheWeb? World Wide Web Foundation. https://webfoundation.org/2019/03/web-birthday-30/

Bertuzzi, L. (2022, March 2). *China, Russia prepare new push for state-controlled internet.* www.euractiv.com/section/digital/news/china-russia-prepare-new-push-for-state-controlled-internet/

Biggio, B., & Roli, F. (2018). Wild patterns: Ten years after the rise of adversarial machine learning. *Proceedings of the 2018 ACM SIGSAC Conference on Computer and Communications Security*, 2154–2156. https://doi.org/10.1145/3243734.3264418

Blinken, A. J. (2022, November 3). Remarks at a U.S.-German Futures Forum Moderated Discussion with German Foreign Minister Annalena Baerbock. United States Department of State. www.state.gov/remarks-at-a-u-s-german-futures-forum-moderated-discussion-with-german-foreign-minister-annalena-baerbock/

Borelli, S. (2017). *State Responsibility in International Law: International Law-Oxford Bibliographies*. Oxford Press. 10.9780199796953–0031.

Borghard, E. D., & Lonergan, S. W. (2017). The logic of coercion in cyberspace. *Security Studies*, *26*(3), 452–481. https://doi.org/10.1080/09636412.2017.1306396

Bossert, T. P. (2017, December 18). It's official: North Korea Is behind WannaCry. Wall Street Journal. www.wsj.com/articles/its-official-north-korea-is-behind-wannacry-1513642537

Boston Dynamics (Director). (2022a). Atlas, the Biped Robot. www.bostondynamics.com/products/spot

Boston Dynamics (Director). (2022b). Spot, the Quadruped Robot. www.bostondynamics.com/products/spot

Boutros-Ghali, B. (1992, December 30). Empowering the United Nations. Foreign Affairs. www.foreignaffairs.com/articles/san-marino/1992-12-01/empowering-united-nations

Brandeis, L. D. (1914). *Other People's Money, and How the Bankers Use It*. Frederick A. Stokes. www.gutenberg.org/ebooks/57819

Bremmer, I., & Keat, P. (2009). *The Fat Tail: The Power of Political Knowledge for Strategic Investing*. Oxford University Press.

Brent, L. (2019, February 12). NATO's role in cyberspace. NATO Review. www.nato.int/docu/review/articles/2019/02/12/natos-role-in-cyberspace/index.html

Brewster, T. (2021, October 14). Fraudsters cloned company director's voice in $35 million bank heist, police find. *Forbes*. www.forbes.com/sites/thomasbrewster/2021/10/14/huge-bank-fraud-uses-deep-fake-voice-tech-to-steal-millions/

Brock, D. C. (2018). Learning from artificial intelligence's previous awakenings: The history of expert systems. *AI Magazine*, *39*(3), 3–15.

Brodie, B. (1978). The development of nuclear strategy. *International Security 2*(4), 65–83. www.muse.jhu.edu/article/446210.

Brooker, K. (2018, July 1). *"I Was Devastated": The Man Who Created the World Wide Web Has Some Regrets. Vanity Fair.* www.vanityfair.com/news/2018/07/the-man-who-created-the-world-wide-web-has-some-regrets

Brownlee, J. (2019, June 16). A Gentle Introduction to Generative Adversarial Networks (GANs). Machine Learning Mastery. https://machinelearningmastery.com/what-are-generative-adversarial-networks-gans/

Brunner, I. (2020). 1998 – UNGA Resolution 53/70 "Developments in the field of information and telecommunications in the context of international security" and its influence on the international rule of law in cyberspace (SSRN Scholarly Paper No. 3856900). https://doi.org/10.2139/ssrn.3856900

Buchanan, B., & Cunningham, F. S. (2020). Preparing the cyber battlefield: Assessing a novel escalation risk in a Sino-American crisis. *Texas National Security Review, 3*(4), 54–81.

Buntz, B. (2019, July 24). Charter of Trust: Siemens, NXP, Partners' Growing Alliance. IoT World Today. www.iotworldtoday.com/2019/07/24/charter-of-trust-siemens-nxp-partners-growing-alliance/

Burlacu, M., & Tiganus, D. (2012). The role of the internet in the Arab spring. *Annals – Series on Military Sciences, 4*(1), 38–50.

Burt, T., & Horvitz, E. (2020, September 1). New Steps to Combat Disinformation. Microsoft on the Issues. https://blogs.microsoft.com/on-the-issues/2020/09/01/disinformation-deepfakes-newsguard-video-authenticator/

Byman, D. (2006). Do targeted killings work? *Foreign Affairs, 85*(2), 95–111. https://doi.org/10.2307/20031914

California. (2018, June 29). Privacy Law. California Legislative Information. https://leginfo.legislature.ca.gov/faces/billNavClient.xhtml?bill_id=201720180AB375

Callamari, P., & Reveron, D. S. (2003). China's use of perception management. *International Journal of Intelligence and Counter Intelligence, 16*(1), 1–15. https://doi.org/10.1080/713830380

Campaign to Stop Killer Robots. (n.d.). www.stopkillerrobots.org/about-us/#about

Campbell-Kelly, M. (1987). Data communications at the national physical laboratory (1965-1975). *Annals of the History of Computing, 9*(3/4), 221–247. https://doi.org/10.1109/MAHC.1987.10023

CARICOM-Caribbean Community. (2023, August 7). CARICOM. https://caricom.org/

Carnegie. (n.d.). Cybernorms. Carnegie Endowment for International Peace. Retrieved November 7, 2022, from https://carnegieendowment.org/specialprojects/cybernorms/

Caroline Case. (1837). The Avalon Project, Yale Law School. https://avalon.law.yale.edu/19th_century/br-1842d.asp

Carter, A. (2017, October 1). *A Lasting Defeat: The Campaign to Destroy ISIS.* Belfer Center for Science and International Affairs. www.belfercenter.org/publication/lasting-defeat-campaign-destroy-isis

Cassirer, E., Lofts, S. G., & Gordon, P. E. (2021). *The Philosophy of Symbolic Forms: Three Volume Set.* Routledge. https://doi.org/10.4324/9780429284922

Castro, D., & Atkinson, R. D. (2014). Beyond Internet Universalism: A Framework for Addressing Cross-Border Internet Policy. ITIF, 22. https://doi.org/10.2139/ssrn.3079821

Cate, F. H. (2015). China and information security threats: Policy responses in the United States. In *China and Cybersecurity: Espionage, Strategy, and Politics in the Digital Domain* (pp. 297–332). Oxford University Press. https://academic.oup .com/book/25744

CCDCOE. (2015). *2015 UN GGE Report: Major Players Recommending Norms of Behaviour, Highlighting Aspects of International Law*. NATO Cooperative Cyber Defence Centre of Excellence. https://ccdcoe.org/incyder-articles/2015-un-gge-report-major-players-recommending-norms-of-behaviour-highlighting-aspects-of-international-law/

Cellan-Jones, R. (2014, December 2). Stephen Hawking warns artificial intelligence could end mankind. BBC News. www.bbc.com/news/technology-30290540

Center for Strategic and International Studies (CSIS) (2010, June 3). CSIS Cybersecurity Policy Debate Series: U.S Cybersecurity Policy and the Role of U.S. CYBERCOM. https://csis-website-prod.s3.amazonaws.com/s3fs-public/ event/100603csis-alexander.pdf

Cerf, V. (1999, April). *The Internet is for everyone*. Annual Computers, Freedom, and Privacy Conference, Washington, DC. www.internetsociety.org/news/ speeches/2011/the-internet-is-for-everyone/

Chappellet-Lanier, T. (2017, June 22). The NSA is now sharing a bunch of code on GitHub. FedScoop. www.fedscoop.com/nsa-now-sharing-bunch-code-github/

Charter of the United Nations. (n.d.). Chapter vii – Action with respect to threats to the peace, breaches of the peace, and acts of aggression. Repertory of Practice of United Nations Organs. Retrieved August 6, 2022, from https://legal.un.org/ repertory/art51.shtml

Charter of Trust Principles. (n.d.). Cybersecurity Is critical for everyone. www .charteroftrust.com/wp-content/uploads/2021/03/Charter-of-Trust_Principles_ EN_2021-02-25.pdf#page=4

Chen, J. (2022). Normal distribution definition. In *Investopedia*. www.investopedia .com/terms/n/normaldistribution.asp

Chesney, R., & Smeets, M. (2020). Policy roundtable: Cyber conflict as an intelligence contest. Texas National Security Review. https://tnsr.org/roundtable/policy-roundtable-cyber-conflict-as-an-intelligence-contest/

China Focus: China adopts law on cryptography. (2019, October 26). The National People's Congress of the People's Republic of China. www.npc.gov.cn/englishnpc/ c2763/201910/bba90400f72b454e86c96d3964ca5bbe.shtml

CISA. (2021a, August 1). Joint Cyber Defense Collaborative. www.cisa.gov/jcdc

CISA. (2021b, September 28). NSA-CISA-FBI Joint Advisory on Russian SVR Targeting U.S. and Allied Networks. www.cisa.gov/uscert/ncas/current-activity/ 2021/04/15/nsa-cisa-fbi-joint-advisory-russian-svr-targeting-us-and-allied

Cisco. (2020, March 9). Cisco Annual Internet Report. *Cisco*. www.cisco.com/c/en/ us/solutions/collateral/executive-perspectives/annual-internet-report/white-paper-c11-741490.html

Clapper, J. (2013, June 8). DNI Statement on the collection of intelligence pursuant to Section 702 of the Foreign Intelligence Surveillance Act. www.intelligence .gov/ic-on-the-record-database/results/50-dni-statement-on-the-collection-of-intelligence-pursuant-to-section-702-of-the-foreign-intelligence-surveillance-act

Clark, W. K., & Levin, P. L. (2009). Securing the information highway. Foreign Affairs. www.foreignaffairs.com/articles/united-states/2009-11-01/securing-information-highway

Clarke, R. A., & Knake, R. K. (2011). *Cyber War: The Next Threat to National Security and What to Do about It.* HarperCollins. www.harpercollins.com/products/cyber-war-richard-a-clarkerobert-knake

Clausewitz, C. von. (1976). *On War* (M. Howard & P. Paret, Eds.). Princeton University Press.

CoE. (2001). Convention on Cybercrime (European Treaty Series No. 185; p. 22). Council of Europe. https://rm.coe.int/1680081561

Comey, J. B. (2014). *Going Dark: Are Technology, Privacy, and Public Safety on a Collision Course?* Brookings Institution. www.fbi.gov/news/speeches/going-dark-are-technology-privacy-and-public-safety-on-a-collision-course

The Commission on America's National Interests. (2000). *America's national interests.* www.belfercenter.org/sites/default/files/legacy/files/amernatinter.pdf

Confirmation bias. (n.d.). Oxford Reference. https://doi.org/10.1093/oi/authority .20110810104644335

Conger, K. (2020, August 20). Former Uber security chief charged with concealing hack. The New York Times. www.nytimes.com/2020/08/20/technology/joe-sullivan-uber-charged-hack.html

Congressional Document. (1928). *General pact for renunciation of war* [text *of Pact of Paris]* [Text]. https://avalon.law.yale.edu/20th_century/kbhear.asp

Constantin, L. (2012, April 12). *New Ransomware Prevents Windows from Starting.* InfoWorld. www.infoworld.com/article/2616774/new-ransomware-prevents-windows-from-starting.html

Cook, T. (2016, February 16). A message to our customers. Apple. www.apple.com/customer-letter/

Cook, T. (2018, October 24). *Debating ethics: Dignity and respect in data driven life.* 40th International Conference of Data Protection and Privacy Commissioners (ICDPPC), Brussels. www.youtube.com/watch?v=kVhOLkIs20A

Coombs, T. (2018). Artificial Intelligence & Cybersecurity for Dummies®, IBM Limited Edition. 51.

Cooper, D. A. (2021). *Arms Control for the Third Nuclear Age: Between Disarmament and Armageddon.* Georgetown University Press. http://press.georgetown.edu/book/georgetown/arms-control-third-nuclear-age

Council of Europe. (2003). Additional protocol to the convention on cybercrime, concerning the criminalisation of acts of a racist and xenophobic nature committed through computer systems (European Treaty Series-No. 189; p. 6). https://rm.coe .int/168008160f

Court of Justice of the EU (July 16, 2020). Data Protection Commissioner v Facebook Ireland and Maximillian Schrems, Case C-311/18. https://curia.europa.eu/jcms/upload/docs/application/pdf/2020-07/cp200091en.pdf

Crane, C. (2020, February 28). 20 ransomware statistics you're powerless to resist reading. Security Boulevard. https://securityboulevard.com/2020/02/20-ransomware-statistics-youre-powerless-to-resist-reading/

Crichton, D., Miller, C., & Schneider, J. (2021). *Labs over Fabs: How the U.S. Should Invest in the Future of Semiconductors.* Foreign Policy Research Institute. https://issuu.com/foreignpolicyresearchinstitute/docs/semiconductors_report_issuu

CrowdStrike. (2016, August 25). *CrowdStrike Machine Learning and VirusTotal.* Crowdstrike.Com. www.crowdstrike.com/blog/crowdstrike-machine-learning-virustotal/

CVE List Home. (n.d.). Retrieved July 23, 2022, from https://cve.mitre.org/cve/

Cyber Incident Reporting for Critical Infrastructure Act of 2022 (CIRCIA), Pub. L. No. 117-103., 1068 (2022). www.cisa.gov/circia

Cyberspace operations (Joint Publication 3-12). (2018). Joint Chiefs of Staff. www.jcs.mil/Portals/36/Documents/Doctrine/pubs/jp3_12.pdf?ver=2018-06-19-092120-930

Damrosch, L. F. (2019). *International Law: Cases and Materials* (Seventh edition.). West Academic Publishing.

Darrach, B. (1970, November 20). Meet Shaky, the first electronic person: The fascinating and fearsome reality of a machine with a mind of its own. LIFE.

Darwin, C. (1981). *The Descent of Man, and Selection in Relation to Sex.* Princeton University Press. www.biblio.com/book/descent-selection-relation-sex-darwin-charles/d/1240259683

Davis, J. H., & Sanger, D. E. (2015, September 25). Obama and Xi Jinping of China agree to steps on cybertheft. The New York Times. www.nytimes.com/2015/09/26/world/asia/xi-jinping-white-house.html

DC3I (2015). *Cybersecurity Culture and Compliance Initiative.* US Department of Defense. https://dod.defense.gov/Portals/1/Documents/pubs/OSD011517-15-RES-Final.pdf

DeepMind. (2020, November 30). AlphaFold: A solution to a 50-year-old grand challenge in biology. www.deepmind.com/blog/alphafold-a-solution-to-a-50-year-old-grand-challenge-in-biology

Definition of an NP-complete problem. (n.d.). Retrieved September 6, 2022, from www.britannica.com/science/NP-complete-problem

Definition of ROBOT. (n.d.). In *Merriam Webster.* Retrieved November 8, 2022, from www.merriam-webster.com/dictionary/robot

Definition of social engineering. (n.d.). Lexico Dictionaries. Retrieved July 17, 2022, from www.lexico.com/en/definition/social_engineering

Deibert, R. J. (2018). Toward a human-centric approach to cybersecurity. *Ethics & International Affairs,* 32(4), 411–424. https://doi.org/10.1017/S0892679418000618

Demchak, C., & Dombrowski, P. (2013). Cyber Westphalia: Asserting state prerogatives in cyberspace. *Georgetown Journal of International Affairs,* 29–38.

Department of Homeland Security (2016). National Cyber Incident Response Plan. www.cisa.gov/sites/default/files/ncirp/National_Cyber_Incident_Response_Plan.pdf

Department of Homeland Security. (2019). National Cybersecurity Protection System. www.dhs.gov/sites/default/files/publications/privacy-pia-dhscisa033-ncpsintrusiondetection-sept2019.pdf

Dickinson, S. (2019, November 7). *China's New Cryptography Law: Still No Place to Hide.* Harris Bricken Sliwoski LLP. https://harrisbricken.com/chinalawblog/chinas-new-cryptography-law-still-no-place-to-hide/

Digital Watch. (n.d.). GGE on lethal autonomous weapons systems. *Geneva Internet Platform.* Retrieved September 5, 2022, from https://dig.watch/processes/gge-laws

DoD. (2016). *Department of Defense Law of War Manual.* Office of General Counsel, Department of Defense. https://dod.defense.gov/Portals/1/Documents/pubs/DoD%20Law%20of%20War%20Manual%20-%20June%202015%20Updated%20Dec%202016.pdf?ver=2016-12-13-172036-190

DoD. (2017). *Autonomy in Weapon Systems*. Department of Defense. https://irp.fas.org/doddir/dod/d3000_09.pdf

DoD. (2019). *Annual Report to Congress: Military and Security Developments Involving the People's Republic of China* (p. 124). https://media.defense.gov/2019/May/02/2002127082/-1/-1/1/2019_CHINA_MILITARY_POWER_REPORT.pdf

DoD. (2020a, February 24). *DoD Adopts Ethical Principles for Artificial Intelligence*. U.S. Department of Defense. www.defense.gov/News/Releases/Release/Article/2091996/dod-adopts-ethical-principles-for-artificial-intelligence/

DoD. (2020b, May 21). DOD statement on Open Skies Treaty Withdrawal. U.S. Department of Defense. www.defense.gov/News/Releases/Release/Article/2195239/dod-statement-on-open-skies-treaty-withdrawal/

Dorsey, J. (2021). *Written testimony of Twitter CEO Jack Dorsey (@Jack)*. U.S. House Committee on Energy & Commerce. https://energycommerce.house.gov/sites/democrats.energycommerce.house.gov/files/documents/Witness_Testimony_Dorsey_CAT_CPC_2021.03.25.pdf

Dwight, D. Eisenhower. (1957, November 14). Remarks at the National Defense Executive Reserve Conference. www.presidency.ucsb.edu/documents/remarks-the-national-defense-executive-reserve-conference

Edelman, M. J. (1985). *The Symbolic Uses of Politics*. University of Illinois Press.

Edwards, E. (2017, February 16). Research into artificial intelligence should not be left to military, says Google exec. The Irish Times. www.irishtimes.com/business/technology/research-into-artificial-intelligence-should-not-be-left-to-military-says-google-exec-1.2977720

Eitan, O. (2018). The missing link in assessing cyberrisk factors through supply chains. *ISACA Journal*, 2. www.isaca.org/resources/isaca-journal/issues/2018/volume-2/the-missing-link-in-assessing-cyberrisk-factors-through-supply-chains

Elections: Deceptive audio or visual media., AB-730. (2019). https://leginfo.legislature.ca.gov/faces/billTextClient.xhtml?bill_id=201920200AB730

Elgammal, A. (2021, September 21). How Artificial Intelligence Completed Beethoven's Unfinished Tenth Symphony. Smithsonian Magazine. www.smithsonianmag.com/innovation/how-artificial-intelligence-completed-beethovens-unfinished-10th-symphony-180978753/

Engel, J. M. (2018). Why does culture "eat strategy for breakfast"? Forbes. www.forbes.com/sites/forbescoachescouncil/2018/11/20/why-does-culture-eat-strategy-for-breakfast/

ENISA. (2018). Information sharing and analysis centers (ISACs) – Cooperative models (p. 51) [Report/Study]. ENISA. www.enisa.europa.eu/publications/information-sharing-and-analysis-center-isacs-cooperative-models

Epley, N., & Kumar, A. (2019, May 1). How to design an ethical organization. Harvard Business Review. https://hbr.org/2019/05/how-to-design-an-ethical-organization

ETNO position paper on the New IP proposal. (2020). European Telecommunications Network Operators' Association. https://etno.eu/downloads/positionpapers/etno%20position%20on%20new%20ip_short.pdf

EU. (n.d.). European Union, principles and values. https://european-union.europa.eu/
principles-countries-history/principles-and-values_en

European Union. (2018). Regulation (EU) 2018/1807 of the European Parliament and
of the Council of 14 November 2018 on a framework for the free flow of non-
personal data in the European Union. https://eur-lex.europa.eu/legal-content/EN/
TXT/?uri=celex:32018R1807

EUROPOL. (2019). SIRIUS EU digital evidence situation report 2019: Cross-border
access to electronic evidence. Europol. www.europol.europa.eu/cms/sites/default/
files/documents/sirius_eu_digital_evidence_report.pdf

Evans, D. (2020, February 22). *Why the US government is questioning WhatsApp's
encryption.* CNBC. www.cnbc.com/2020/02/21/whatsapp-encryption-under-
scrutiny-by-us-government.html

EXTERNALITY English Definition and Meaning | Lexico.com. (n.d.). Lexico
Dictionaries | English. Retrieved July 23, 2022, from www.lexico.com/en/
definition/externality

Eykholt, K., Evtimov, I., Fernandes, E., Li, B., Rahmati, A., Xiao, C., Prakash, A.,
Kohno, T., & Song, D. (2018). Robust physical-world attacks on deep learning
visual classification. *2018 IEEE/CVF Conference on Computer Vision and Pattern
Recognition*, 1625–1634. https://doi.org/10.1109/CVPR.2018.00175

Faceswap. (n.d.). Faceswap. Retrieved November 8, 2022, from https://faceswap
.dev/

FATE: Fairness, Accountability, Transparency & Ethics in AI. (2014). *Microsoft
Research Blog.* www.microsoft.com/en-us/research/theme/fate/

FBI. (2016, March 24). Iranians charged with hacking U.S. financial sector [Story].
FBI Most Wanted. www.fbi.gov/news/stories/iranians-charged-with-hacking-us-
financial-sector

FBI. (2020, February 11). *2019 Internet Crime Report Released [Story].* Federal
Bureau of Investigation. www.fbi.gov/news/stories/2019-internet-crime-report-
released-021120

FCC. (1996). Telecommunications Act of 1996. *Federal Communications Commission*,
1–128. www.fcc.gov/general/telecommunications-act-1996

Fearon, J. D. (1995). Rationalist explanations for war. *International Organization*,
49(3), 379–414. https://doi.org/10.1017/S0020818300033324

Federal Register. (2016, December 20). Announcing request for nominations for
public-key post-quantum cryptographic algorithms. *Federal Register.* www
.federalregister.gov/documents/2016/12/20/2016-30615/announcing-request-for-
nominations-for-public-key-post-quantum-cryptographic-algorithms

Federal Register. (2019). *NIST reveals 26 algorithms advancing to the post-quantum
crypto 'semifinals.'* www.nist.gov/news-events/news/2019/01/nist-reveals-26-
algorithms-advancing-post-quantum-crypto-semifinals

Feynman, R. P. (1997). *"Surely you're joking, Mr. Feynman!" Adventures of a Curious
Character* (R. Leighton, Ed.) (p. 350). W. W. Norton. https://wwnorton.co.uk/
books/9780393316049-surely-you-re-joking-mr-feynman

Fick, N. C. (n.d.). *Bureau of Cyberspace and Digital Policy.* U.S. Department of State.
www.state.gov/bureaus-offices/deputy-secretary-of-state/bureau-of-cyberspace-
and-digital-policy/

Fidler, D. P. (2012). Inter arms silent leges Redux? The Law of Armed Conflict and Cyber Conflict. In *Cyberspace and National Security: Threats, Opportunities, and Power in a Virtual World*. Georgetown University Press.

Fidler, M. (2018, March 7). African union bugged by China: Cyber espionage as evidence of strategic shifts. Council on Foreign Relations. www.cfr.org/blog/african-union-bugged-china-cyber-espionage-evidence-strategic-shifts

Finnemore, M. (2017). Cybersecurity and the concept of norms. https://policycommons.net/artifacts/431552/cybersecurity-and-the-concept-of-norms/1402610/

Finnemore, M., & Sikkink, K. (1998). International norm dynamics and political change. *International Organization*, 52(4), 887–917. www.cambridge.org/core/journals/international-organization/article/abs/international-norm-dynamics-and-political-change/0A55ECBCC9E87EA49586E776EED8DB57

Fishman, C. (1996, December 31). They Write the Right Stuff. *Fast Company*. www.fastcompany.com/28121/they-write-right-stuff

Fiske, S. T., & Taylor, S. D. (1991). *Social Cognition*. McGraw-Hill.

Foltz, A. C. (2012). Stuxnet, Schmitt Analysis, and the cyber "Use-of-Force" debate. *Joint Force Quarterly*, 67, 40–48.

Ford, Dr. C. A. (2019, September 11). Huawei and its siblings, the Chinese tech giants: National security and foreign policy implications. United States Department of State. https://2017-2021.state.gov/huawei-and-its-siblings-the-chinese-tech-giants-national-security-and-foreign-policy-implications/

France. (2019). *International Law Applied to Operations in Cyberspace* (UN Open Ended Working Group (OEWG), p. 19). France. https://documents.unoda.org/wp-content/uploads/2021/12/French-position-on-international-law-applied-to-cyberspace.pdf

Freedman, L. (2013). *Strategy: A History*. Oxford University Press.

Freedom on the Net 2020, Countries. (n.d.). Freedom House. Retrieved October 25, 2022, from https://freedomhouse.org/countries/freedom-net/scores

Freymann, E. (2020). *One Belt One Road*. Harvard University Press. www.hup.harvard.edu/catalog.php?isbn=9780674247956

Fukuyama, F. (1992). *The End of History and the Last Man*. Free Press; Maxwell Macmillan Canada; Maxwell Macmillan International.

G7. (2016, May 27). G7 Ise-Shima Leaders' Declaration. European Council. https://obamawhitehouse.archives.gov/the-press-office/2016/05/27/g7-ise-shima-leaders-declaration

G20. (2015). *Leaders' communiqué*. G20 Information Centre. www.g20.utoronto.ca/2015/151116-communique.html

G20. (2017). *Hamburg G20 leaders' statement on countering terrorism*. G20 Information Centre. www.g20.utoronto.ca/2017/170707-counterterrorism.html

Galston, W. A. (2020, March 10). *Efficiency Isn't the Only Economic Virtue*. WSJ. www.wsj.com/articles/efficiency-isnt-the-only-economic-virtue-11583873155

Garamone, J. (2009, October 1). Lynn calls for collaboration in establishing cyber security. American Forces Press Service.

Gardam, J. G. (1993). Proportionality and force in international law. *American Journal of International Law*, 87(3), 391–413. https://doi.org/10.2307/2203645

Gartzke, E. (2013). The myth of cyberwar: Bringing war in cyberspace back down to earth. *International Security, 38*(2), 41–73.

Gartzke, E., & Lindsay, J. R. (2017). Thermonuclear cyberwar. *Journal of Cybersecurity, 3*(1), 37–48. https://doi.org/10.1093/cybsec/tyw017

Gates, D. (2019, March 17). Flawed analysis, failed oversight: How Boeing, FAA certified the suspect 737 MAX flight control system. The Seattle Times. www .seattletimes.com/business/boeing-aerospace/failed-certification-faa-missed-safety-issues-in-the-737-max-system-implicated-in-the-lion-air-crash/

Gates, R. M. (2008). *National Defense Strategy* (p. 29). Department of Defense. https:// history.defense.gov/Portals/70/Documents/nds/2008_NDS.pdf

GCSC. (2017). Global Commission on Stability of Cyberspace. https://hcss.nl/global-commission-on-the-stability-of-cyberspace-homepage/

GCSC. (2019). Advancing Cyberstability – Final Report. The Hague Centre for Strategic Studies. https://hcss.nl/wp-content/uploads/2019/11/GCSC-Final-Report-November-2019.pdf

Geers, K. (2010). Cyber weapons convention. *The Computer Law and Security Report, 26*(5), 547–551. https://doi.org/10.1016/j.clsr.2010.07.005

Geers, K. (2014). Pandemonium: Nation states, national security, and the internet. *The Tallinn Papers, 1*(1), 17.

Gerstell, G. (2019, September 10). I Work for N.S.A. We cannot afford to lose the Digital Revolution. www.nytimes.com/2019/09/10/opinion/nsa-privacy.html

GGE. (1999). Developments in the Field of Information and Telecommunications in the Context of International Security (No. 53/70). https://documents-dds-ny .un.org/doc/UNDOC/GEN/N99/760/03/PDF/N9976003.pdf?OpenElement

GGE. (2000). Developments in the field of information and telecommunications in the context of international security (A/55/140). https://ccdcoe.org/uploads/2018/10/ UN-000710-ITISreply.pdf

GGE. (2018). Developments in the field of information and telecommunications in the context of international security (A/73/27). United Nations. https://digitallibrary .un.org/record/1655670

GGE. (2019). Group of governmental experts, United Nations Office for Disarmament Affairs. www.un.org/disarmament/group-of-governmental-experts/

Gidney, C., & Ekerå, M. (2021). How to factor 2048 bit RSA integers in 8 hours using 20 million noisy qubits. *Quantum, 5*, 433. https://doi.org/10.2233 1/q-2021-04-15-433

Gilad, Y. (2019). Metadata-private communication for the 99%. *Communications of the ACM, 62*(9), 86–93. https://doi.org/10.1145/3338537

Giles, M. (2018, February 21). The GANfather: The man who's given machines the gift of imagination. www.technologyreview.com/2018/02/21/145289/the-ganfather-the-man-whos-given-machines-the-gift-of-imagination/

Gleicher, N. (2020, July 8). Removing coordinated inauthentic behavior. https://about .fb.com/news/2020/07/removing-political-coordinated-inauthentic-behavior/

Goertzel, B. (2007). Human-level artificial general intelligence and the possibility of a technological singularity A reaction to Ray Kurzweil's The Singularity Is Near, and McDermott's critique of Kurzweil. *Artificial Intelligence, 171*(18), 1161–1173.

Goldman, E. O. (2021). Cyber diplomacy for strategic competition. The Foreign Service Journal. https://afsa.org/cyber-diplomacy-strategic-competition

Goldsmith, J. (2011). Cybersecurity treaties: A Skeptical View. In *Future Challenges in National Security and Law*, Perer Berkowitz, Ed. (p. 16). Hoover Institution, Stanford University. www.hoover.org/sites/default/files/research/docs/futurechallenges_goldsmith.pdf

Goldsmith, J. L., & Posner, E. A. (1998). *A theory of customary international law* (SSRN Scholarly Paper No. 145972). https://doi.org/10.2139/ssrn.145972

Goldwasser, S., Kim, M. P., Vaikuntanathan, V., & Zamir, O. (2022). *Planting undetectable backdoors in machine learning models* (arXiv:2204.06974). IEEE 63rd Annual Symposium on Foundations of Computer Science (FOCS), pp. 931–942, doi: 10.1109/FOCS54457.2022.00092

Goodin, D. (2020, February 14). US government goes all in to expose new malware used by North Korean hackers. Ars Technica. https://arstechnica.com/tech-policy/2020/02/us-government-exposes-malware-used-in-north-korean-sponsored-hacking-ops/

Google. (2010, January 12). A new approach to China. Google Official Blog. https://googleblog.blogspot.com/2010/01/new-approach-to-china.html

Gotterbarn, D., Miller, K., & Rogerson, S. (1997). Software engineering code of ethics. *Communications of the ACM*, *40*(11), 110–118. https://doi.org/10.1145/265684.265699

Gouzien, É., & Sangouard, N. (2021). Factoring 2048-bit RSA integers in 177 days with 13,436 qubits and a multimode memory. *Physical Review Letters*, *127*(14), 140503. https://doi.org/10.1103/PhysRevLett.127.140503

GPS.gov: Other Global Navigation Satellite Systems (GNSS). (n.d.). Retrieved July 23, 2022, from www.gps.gov/systems/gnss/

Greenberg, A. (2018, August 22). The Untold Story of NotPetya, the Most Devastating Cyberattack in History. *Wired*. www.wired.com/story/notpetya-cyberattack-ukraine-russia-code-crashed-the-world/

Greenberg, A. (2019a). A Boeing Code Leak Exposes Security Flaws Deep in a 787's Guts. *Wired*. www.wired.com/story/boeing-787-code-leak-security-flaws/

Greenberg, A. (2019b). A Brief History of Russian Hackers' Evolving False Flags. *Wired*. www.wired.com/story/russian-hackers-false-flags-iran-fancy-bear/

Greenberg, A. (2020, October 23). How 30 Lines of Code Blew Up a 27-Ton Generator. *Wired*. www.wired.com/story/how-30-lines-of-code-blew-up-27-ton-generator/

Greenemeier, L. (2009, December 4). Vint Cerf: Connecting with an Internet Pioneer, 40 Years Later. Scientific American. www.scientificamerican.com/article/internet-pioneer-cerf/

Grones, G. (2019, December 20). Top 10 cyber insurance companies in the US. Insurance Business America. www.insurancebusinessmag.com/us/news/cyber/top-10-cyber-insurance-companies-in-the-us-195463.aspx

Groopman, J. (2007, January 29). What's the Trouble? – How Doctors Think. The New Yorker. www.newyorker.com/magazine/2007/01/29/whats-the-trouble

Grotius, H. (1916). *The Freedom of the Seas, or, the Right Which belongs to the Dutch to Take Part in the East Indian Trade: A Dissertion* (J. B. Scott, Ed.; R. V. D. Magoffin, Trans.). Oxford University Press. https://hdl.handle.net/2027/aeu.ark:/13960/t6k08bs06

Guariglia, M. (2020, June 24). Victory! Boston Bans Government Use of Face Surveillance. Electronic Frontier Foundation. www.eff.org/de/deeplinks/2020/06/victory-boston-bans-government-use-face-surveillance

Guinness. (n.d.). *Murtogh D. Guinness Collection of Mechanical and Musical Automata.* Morris Museum.

Guri, M. (2021). Gairoscope: Injecting data from air-gapped computers to nearby gyroscopes. 18th International Conference on Privacy, Security and Trust (PST), 1–10. https://doi.org/10.1109/PST52912.2021.9647842

Guterres, A. (2017). *Foreword to "Fast Forward Progress: Leveraging Tech to Achieve the Global Goals."* www.itu.int/en/sustainable-world/Documents/Fast-forward_progress_report_414709%20FINAL.pdf

Guterres, A. (2019, March 25). Autonomous weapons that kill must be banned, insists UN chief. UN News. https://news.un.org/en/story/2019/03/1035381

Gvosdev, N. K., Blankshain, J. D., & Cooper, D. A. (2019). *Decision-Making in American Foreign Policy: Translating Theory into Practice.* Cambridge University Press. https://doi.org/10.1017/9781108566742

Hafner, K. (2019, July 12). Fernando Corbató, a father of your computer (and your password), dies at 93. The New York Times. www.nytimes.com/2019/07/12/science/fernando-corbato-dead.html

Hamilton, A., Madison, J., & Jay, J. (1787, November 23). *The Federalist Papers No. 10* [Text]. https://avalon.law.yale.edu/18th_century/fed10.asp

Hammond. (2017). *National Cyber Security Strategy 2016 to 2021* (p. 80). United Kingdom Cabinet Office. https://assets.publishing.service.gov.uk/government/uploads/system/uploads/attachment_data/file/567242/national_cyber_security_strategy_2016.pdf

Hao, K. (2020, November 3). *AI pioneer Geoff Hinton: "Deep learning is going to be able to do everything."* MIT Technology Review. www.technologyreview.com/2020/11/03/1011616/ai-godfather-geoffrey-hinton-deep-learning-will-do-everything/

Hardesty, L. (2018, February 11). Study finds gender and skin-type bias in commercial artificial-intelligence systems. http://news.mit.edu/2018/study-finds-gender-skin-type-bias-artificial-intelligence-systems-0212

Harknett, R. J., & Smeets, M. (2020). Cyber campaigns and strategic outcomes. *Journal of Strategic Studies, 45*(4), 534–567. https://doi.org/10.1080/01402390.2020.1732354

Harknett, R. J., & Stever, J. A. (2009). The cybersecurity triad: Government, private sector partners, and the engaged cybersecurity citizen. *Journal of Homeland Security and Emergency Management, 6*(1). https://doi.org/10.2202/1547-7355.1649

Harnad, S. (1991). Other bodies, other minds: A machine incarnation of an old philosophical problem. *Minds and Machines, 1*(1), 43–54. https://doi.org/10.1007/BF00360578

Hash Functions. (2020, June 22). Computer Security Resource Center, NIST. https://csrc.nist.gov/projects/hash-functions

Hatch, B. B. (2018). Defining a class of cyber weapons as WMD: An examination of the merits. *Journal of Strategic Security, 11*(1), 43–61.

Hayden, Gen. M. (2017, July 17). Cutting Cyber Command's umbilical cord to the NSA. *The Cipher Brief.* www.thecipherbrief.com/cutting-cyber-commands-umbilical-cord-to-the-nsa

Hayden, M. V. (2011). The future of things "cyber." *Strategic Studies Quarterly, 5*(1), 3–7.

Hayden, M. V. (2017, May 11). Cyber Strategy and Policy. Hearing to Receive Testimony on Cyber Policy, Strategy, and Organization. www.govinfo.gov/content/pkg/CHRG-115shrg28907/html/CHRG-115shrg28907.htm

Hayes, A. (2020). Interwoven 'Destinies': The Significance of Xinjiang to the China Dream, the Belt and Road Initiative, and the Xi Jinping Legacy. *Journal of Contemporary China, 29*(121), 31–45. https://doi.org/10.1080/10670564.2019.1621528

Hayes, A. (2022). Financial risk: The art of assessing if a company is a good buy. In *Investopedia.* www.investopedia.com/terms/f/financialrisk.asp

Healey, J. (2011). *The five futures of cyber conflict and cooperation* (Cyber Statecraft Initiative) [IssueBrief]. *Atlantic Council.* www.atlanticcouncil.org/wp-content/uploads/2011/12/121311_ACUS_FiveCyberFutures.pdf

Healey, J., & Jordan, K. T. (2014, August 29). Nato's cyber capabilities: Yesterday, today, and tomorrow. Atlantic Council. www.atlanticcouncil.org/in-depth-research-reports/issue-brief/natos-cyber-capabilities/

Heaven, W. D. (2021, February 24). Why GPT-3 is the best and worst of AI right now. *MIT Technology Review, 124*(2), 24–35.

Heffernan, M. (2019). The human skills we need in an unpredictable world. TED: Ideas Worth Spreading. www.ted.com/talks/margaret_heffernan_the_human_skills_we_need_in_an_unpredictable_world

Heuer, R. J. (1999). *Psychology of Intelligence Analysis.* Center for the Study of Intelligence, Central Intelligence Agency. www.cia.gov/library/center-for-the-study-of-intelligence/csi-publications/books-and-monographs/psychology-of-intelligence-analysis/PsychofIntelNew.pdf

Hildebrandt, M. (2013). Extraterritorial jurisdiction to enforce in cyberspace? Bodin, Schmitt, Grotius in cyberspace. *University of Toronto Law Journal, 63*(2), 196–224.

History of the Internet. (2022). In *Wikipedia.* https://en.wikipedia.org/w/index.php?title=History_of_the_Internet&oldid=1098114815

Hochreiter, S., & Schmidhuber, J. (1997). Long short-term memory. *Neural Computation, 9*(8), 1735–1780. https://doi.org/10.1162/neco.1997.9.8.1735

Hoffman, W., & Levite, A. (2017). *Private Sector Cyber Defense: Can Active Measures Help Stabilize Cyberspace?* Carnegie Endowment for International Peace.

Hoffmann, S., Lazanski, D., & Taylor, E. (2020). Standardising the splinternet: How China's technical standards could fragment the internet. *Journal of Cyber Policy, 5*(2), 239–264. https://doi.org/10.1080/23738871.2020.1805482

Holl Lute, J., & McConnell, B. (2011, February 14). Op-ed: A civil perspective on cybersecurity. Wired. www.wired.com/2011/02/dhs-op-ed/

Horn, J. (2017). Project Zero: Reading privileged memory with a side-channel. Google. https://googleprojectzero.blogspot.com/2018/01/reading-privileged-memory-with-side.html

Hörnle, J. (2021). *Internet Jurisdiction Law and Practice.* Oxford University Press, Incorporated.

Howard, P. N., & Hussain, M. M. (2013). *Democracy's Fourth Wave?: Digital Media and the Arab Spring.* Oxford University Press. https://deepblue.lib.umich.edu/bitstream/handle/2027.42/117564/Democracy's+Fourth+Wave.pdf?sequence=1

Hsu, J. (2019). How the United States Is developing post-quantum cryptography. IEEE Spectrum. https://spectrum.ieee.org/how-the-us-is-preparing-for-quantum-computings-threat-to-end-secrecy

Hui, M. N. (2009, October 6). Threat of next world war may be in cyberspace: UN, Agence France-Presse, Available through Communications of the ACM, October

6, 2009. https://cacm.acm.org/news/45269-threat-of-next-world-war-may-be-in cyberspace-n/fulltext

Hughes, R. (2010). A treaty for cyberspace. *International Affairs*, *86*(2), 523–541. https://doi.org/10.1111/j.1468-2346.2010.00894.x

Hutchins, E. M., Cloppert, M. J., & Amin, R. M. (2011). Intelligence-driven computer network defense informed by analysis of adversary campaigns and intrusion kill chains. *Leading Issues in Information Warfare & Security Research*, *1*(1), 14.

IBM. (2012, March 7). *IBM 1401: The Mainframe [CTB14]*. IBM Corporation. www-03.ibm.com/ibm/history/ibm100/us/en/icons/mainframe/

ICANN History Project—ICANN. (n.d.). Retrieved August 9, 2023, from www.icann .org/history

ICANN (1999, January 17). IANA Functions Agreement Negotiations. https://features .icann.org/1999-01-17-iana-functions-agreement-negotiations

ICANN (2013, October 3). Montevideo statement on the future of Internet cooperation. ICANN Announcements. www.icann.org/en/announcements/details/montevideo-statement-on-the-future-of-internet-cooperation-7-10-2013-en

ICANN. (2019, November 28). Bylaws for Internet Corporation for Assigned Names and Numbers. www.icann.org/resources/pages/governance/bylaws-en/#article1

ICRC. (1950). Treaties, States parties, and Commentaries – Geneva Convention (I) on Wounded and Sick in Armed Forces in the Field, 1949. https://ihl-databases.icrc .org/ihl/full/GCI-commentary

ICRC. (2018). Ethics and autonomous weapon systems: An ethical basis for human control? *International Committee of the Red Cross*. www.icrc.org/en/document/ ethics-and-autonomous-weapon-systems-ethical-basis-human-control

Incidents at Sea Agreement. (1972). https://2009-2017.state.gov/t/isn/4791.htm

Internet Engineering Task Force (IETF) (n.d.). IETF Overview. www.ietf.org/proceedings/ 35/ietf-overview.html

Internet World Stats (2022). World Internet Usage and Population Statistics. www .internetworldstats.com/stats.htm

Inkster, N. (2018). *China's Cyber Power* (First edition). Routledge. https://doi .org/10.4324/9780429031625

International Committee of the Red Cross. (2002). Introduction to the law of armed conflict-basic knowledge. 29.

International Committee of the Red Cross. (2016). The Geneva Conventions of 1949 and their Additional Protocols. www.icrc.org/en/document/geneva-conventions-1949-additional-protocols

Investigation: WannaCry cyber-attack and the NHS (p. 33). (2018). National Audit Office, UK.

iRobot. (n.d.). *Roomba Vacuum*. IRobot. www.irobot.com/en_US/us-roomba.html

Israni, E. T. (2017, October 26). When an Algorithm Helps Send You to Prison. The New York Times. www.nytimes.com/2017/10/26/opinion/algorithm-compas-sentencing-bias.html

ITU. (2019). Collection of the basic texts of the International Telecommunication Union adopted by the Plenipotentiary Conference. ITU Publications. www.itu.int/ opb/ecommercedownload/0015021470-42330-EN.pdf

Jagoda, P. (2012). Speculative security. In *Cyberspace and National Security: Threats, Opportunities, and Power in a Virtual World*, Derek S. Reveron, Ed. (Washington D.C.: Georgetown UP, 2012), pp. 21–36. (pp. 21–26). Georgetown University Press.

James Madison's proposed amendments to the Constitution. (1789). Annals of Congress, House of Representatives, 1st Congress, 1st Session, 451–453.

Janis, M. W. (1984). Jeremy Bentham and the fashioning of "international law." *American Journal of International Law, 78*(2), 405–418.

Jobin, A., Ienca, M., & Vayena, E. (2019). Artificial Intelligence: The global landscape of ethics guidelines. *Nature Machine Intelligence, 1*(9), 389–399. https://doi.org/10.1038/s42256-019-0088-2

Johnson, D. B. (2019, February 1). *Moving the needle on cyber norms. FCW.* https://fcw.com/security/2019/02/moving-the-needle-on-cyber-norms/211140/

Johnson, L. (2008, April 24). Thru the Looking Glass: Why virtual worlds matter, where they are heading, and why we are all here. Federal Consortium on Virtual Worlds Expo.

Joint Chiefs of Staff. (2016). Joint Operating Environment 2035: The Joint Force in a Contested and Disordered World. www.jcs.mil/Portals/36/Documents/Doctrine/concepts/joe_2035_july16.pdf?ver=2017-12-28-162059-917

Joyce, R. (2016, January 28). *USENIX Enigma 2016 – NSA TAO Chief on Disrupting Nation State Hackers* (Video). YouTube. www.youtube.com/watch?v=bDJb8WOJYdA

Joyner, A. (2012). Competing Transatlantic Vision of Cybersecurity. In *Cyberspace and National Security: Threats, Opportunities, and Power in a Virtual World* (p. 23). Georgetown University Press. www.amazon.com/Cyberspace-National-Security-Threats-Opportunities/dp/1589019180

Judiciary Committee. (2020, June 23). Graham, Cotton, Blackburn Introduce Balanced Solution to Bolster National Security, End Use of Warrant-Proof Encryption that Shields Criminal Activity. United States Senate Committee on the Judiciary. www.judiciary.senate.gov/press/rep/releases/graham-cotton-blackburn-introduce-balanced-solution-to-bolster-national-security-end-use-of-warrant-proof-encryption-that-shields-criminal-activity

Jurkovich, M. (2020). What isn't a norm? Redefining the conceptual boundaries of "norms" in the human rights literature. *International Studies Review, 22*(3), 693–711.

Kahn, R., Leiner, B. M., Cerf, V. G., Clark, D. D., Kleinrock, L., Lynch, D. C., Postel, J., Roberts, L. E., & Wolff, S. (1997). The evolution of the Internet as a global information system. *The International Information & Library Review, 29*(2), 129–151. https://doi.org/10.1006/iilr.1997.0042

Kahneman, D. (2013). *Thinking, Fast and Slow.* Farrar, Straus and Giroux. https://us.macmillan.com/books/9780374533557/thinkingfastandslow

Kahneman, D., & Tversky, A. (1979). Prospect theory: An analysis of decision under risk. *Econometrica, 47*(2), 263–291. https://doi.org/10.2307/1914185

Kania, E., & Creemers, R. (2018, November 5). Xi Jinping Calls for 'Healthy Development' of AI (Translation). New America. http://newamerica.org/cybersecurity-initiative/digichina/blog/xi-jinping-calls-for-healthy-development-of-ai-translation/

Kapur, A. & United Nations Development Programme. (2005). *Internet Governance: A Primer.* Elsevier.

Karras, T., Laine, S., Aittala, M., Hellsten, J., Lehtinen, J., & Aila, T. (2020). Analyzing and improving the image quality of StyleGAN. 8110–8119. https://openaccess.thecvf.com/content_CVPR_2020/html/Karras_Analyzing_and_Improving_the_Image_Quality_of_StyleGAN_CVPR_2020_paper.html

Kaspersky. (n.d.). Machine learning for malware detection. https://media.kaspersky .com/en/enterprise-security/Kaspersky-Lab-Whitepaper-Machine-Learning.pdf

Kaspersky. (2016, November 22). Cybercriminals use DDoS as smokescreen for other attacks on business. www.Kaspersky.Com. www.kaspersky.com/about/ press-releases/2016_research-reveals-hacker-tactics-cybercriminals-use-ddos-as-smokescreen-for-other-attacks-on-business

Katzenstein, M. F. (1996). *The Culture of National Security: Norms and Identity in World Politics.* Columbia University Press.

Kehl, D., Guo, P., & Kessler, S. (2017). *Algorithms in the Criminal Justice System: Assessing the Use of Risk Assessments in Sentencing. Responsive Communities Initiative.* Berkman Klein Center for Internet & Society, Harvard Law School.

Kennedy, J. F. (1961). *Address to Joint Session of Congress, May 25, 1961.* JFK Presidential Library. www.jfklibrary.org/learn/about-jfk/historic-speeches/ address-to-joint-session-of-congress-may-25-1961

Keohane, R. O. (1977). *Power and Interdependence: World Politics in Transition.* Little, Brown.

Khalip, A. (2018, February 19). U.N. chief urges global rules for cyber warfare. *Reuters.* www.reuters.com/article/us-un-guterres-cyber-idUSKCN1G31Q4

Kilovaty, I. (2015). Rethinking the prohibition on the use of force in the light of economic cyber warfare: Towards a broader scope of article 2(4) of the UN Charter. *Journal of Law & Cyber Warfare, 4*(3), 210–244.

Kim, N., Herr, T., & Schneier, B. (2020, June 15). The reverse cascade: Enforcing security on the global IoT supply chain. Atlantic Council. www.atlanticcouncil .org/in-depth-research-reports/report/the-reverse-cascade-enforcing-security-on-the-global-iot-supply-chain/

King, S. A., & Gallagher, R. M. (2020). U.S. Cyberspace Solarium Commission Report (p. 182). www.solarium.gov/

Kissinger, H. (1957). *Nuclear Weapons and Foreign Policy.* Harper (for the Council on Foreign Relations). www.hoover.org/research/nuclear-weapons-and-foreign-policy-henry-kissinger-council-foreign-relations-1957

Koch, C. (2016, March 19). *How the Computer Beat the Go Master.* Scientific American. www.scientificamerican.com/article/how-the-computer-beat-the-go-master/

Kocher, P. C. (1996). *Timing attacks on implementations of Diffie-Hellman, RSA, DSS, and other systems* (pp. 104–113). Advances in Cryptology – CRYPTO '96. https:// link.springer.com/chapter/10.1007/3-540-68697-5_9

Koh, Y. (2018). Silicon Valley rivals take shots at Facebook. www.wsj.com/articles/ silicon-valley-rivals-take-shots-at-facebook-1522595763

Kollars, N. (2020). Cyber conflict as an intelligence competition in an era of open innovation. *Texas National Security Review, 3*(4). http://dx.doi.org/10.26153/ tsw/10964

Korolov, M. (2019, May 7). What is GPS spoofing? And how you can defend against it. CSO Online. www.csoonline.com/article/3393462/what-is-gps-spoofing-and-how-you-can-defend-against-it.html

Kruger, J., & Dunning, D. (1999). Unskilled and unaware of it: How difficulties in recognizing one's own incompetence lead to inflated self-assessments.

Journal of Personality and Social Psychology, 77(6), 1121–1134. https://doi.org/10.1037/0022-3514.77.6.1121

Kurtz, G. (2010, January 14). Operation "Aurora" Hit Google, Others. https://web.archive.org/web/20120911141122/http:/blogs.mcafee.com/corporate/cto/operation-aurora-hit-google-others

Landau, S. (2015a). Control use of data to protect privacy. *Science (New York, N.Y.)*, 347(6221), 504–506. https://doi.org/10.1126/science.aaa4961

Landau, S. (2015b, July 7). Keys under doormats: Mandating insecurity. Lawfare. www.lawfareblog.com/keys-under-doormats-mandating-insecurity

Landau, S. (2016a). Choices: Privacy & surveillance in a once & future Internet. *Daedalus*, 145(1), 54–64. https://doi.org/10.1162/DAED_a_00365

Landau, S. (2016b). The real security issues of the iPhone case. *Science*, 352(6292), 1398–1399. https://doi.org/10.1126/science.aaf7708

Langevin, J. (2022). *Opening Statement*. Subcommittee on Cyber, Innovative Technologies, and Information Systems, US House of Representatives. https://armedservices.house.gov/_cache/files/d/3/d3a8eb33-2b90-4a02-8454-70795ab992ec/C049B7C355EE7BFFEA179AE1FD5A62EB.20220405-citi-opening-statement-langevin.pdf

LAWS. (n.d.). *Lethal Autonomous Weapons Systems*. Future of Life Institute. Retrieved September 6, 2022, from https://futureoflife.org/lethal-autonomous-weapons-systems/

Leiner, B. M., Cerf, V. G., Clark, D. D., Kahn, R. E., Kleinrock, L., Lynch, D. C., Postel, J., Roberts, L. G., & Wolff, S. (2009). A Brief History of the Internet. *ACM SIGCOMM Computer Communication Review*, 39(5), 22–31. https://doi.org/10.1145/1629607.1629613

Leonhardt, D. (2008, September 26). Washington's invisible hand. The New York Times. www.nytimes.com/2008/09/28/magazine/28wwln-reconsider.html

Lessig, L. (1998). The Laws of Cyberspace. Taiwan Net '98, 16.

Levy, I., & Robinson, C. (2018, November 29). Principles for a More Informed Exceptional Access Debate. Lawfare. www.lawfareblog.com/principles-more-informed-exceptional-access-debate

Levy, S. (1999, April 1). The Open Secret. Wired. www.wired.com/1999/04/crypto/

Levy, S. (2017, May 23). What Deep Blue tells us about AI in 2017. Wired. www.wired.com/2017/05/what-deep-blue-tells-us-about-ai-in-2017/

Lewis, D. (2019, February 4). What Is NATO Really Doing in Cyberspace? *War on the Rocks*. https://warontherocks.com/2019/02/what-is-nato-really-doing-in-cyberspace/

Lewis, J. A. (2009). *The "Korean" Cyber Attacks and Their Implications for Cyber Conflict* (p. 10). Center for Strategic & International Studies.

Lewis, J. A. (2013). *Internet Governance: Inevitable Transitions* (Paper No. 4; Internet Governance). Centre for International Governance Innovation. www.cigionline.org/publications/internet-governance-inevitable-transitions/

Lewis, J. A. (2021, March 4). Toward a More Coercive Cyber Strategy. www.csis.org/analysis/toward-more-coercive-cyber-strategy

Lewis, J. A., Nye, J. S., Scowcroft, B. (2012). Harnessing Leviathan: Internet Governance, and Cybersecurity. In Nicholas Burns and Jonathon Price (Eds.), *Securing Cyberspace: A New Domain for National Security*. Aspen Institute (pp. 113–126). www.jstor.org/stable/j.ctt19x3h93.9

Lewis, M. (2017). *The Undoing Project*. W. W. Norton. https://wwnorton.com/books/9780393354775

Li, S. (2020, March 6). Made-in-China Censorship for Sale. The Wall Street Journal. www.wsj.com/articles/made-in-china-censorship-for-sale-11583448433

Lighthill. (1973). *Artificial Intelligence: A General Survey*. Science Research Council (SRC). www.chilton-computing.org.uk/inf/literature/reports/lighthill_report/contents.htm

Lin, H. (2010). Offensive cyber operations and the use of force. *Journal of National Security Law & Policy*, 4(1), 61–86.

Lin, H. (2012). Operational considerations in cyber-attack and cyber exploitation. In *Cyberspace and National Security*, D. S. Reveron (Ed.). Georgetown University Press.

Lin, H. (2019). The existential threat from cyber-enabled information warfare. *Bulletin of the Atomic Scientists*, 75(4), 187–196. https://doi.org/10.1080/00963402.2019.1629574

Lindemann, B., Müller, T., Vietz, H., Jazdi, N., & Weyrich, M. (2021). A survey on long short-term memory networks for time series prediction. *Procedia CIRP*, 99, 650–655. https://doi.org/10.1016/j.procir.2021.03.088

Lindsay, J. R. (2013). Stuxnet and the limits of cyber warfare. *Security Studies*, 22(3), 365–404. https://doi.org/10.1080/09636412.2013.816122

Lindsay, J. R. (2020, March 12). Digital Strangelove: The Cyber Dangers of Nuclear Weapons. Lawfare. www.lawfareblog.com/digital-strangelove-cyber-dangers-nuclear-weapons

Lindsay, J. R., Cheung, T. M., & Reveron, D. S. (Eds.). (2015). *China and Cybersecurity: Espionage, Strategy, and Politics in the Digital Domain*. Oxford University Press. https://academic.oup.com/book/25744

Lipsky, M. (2010). Street-Level Bureaucracy, 30th Ann. Ed. Dilemmas of the Individual in Public Service (30th anniversary expanded ed.). Russell Sage Foundation, Project MUSE.

Litt, R. (2016). *Financial Times Op-ed by ODNI General Counsel Robert Litt: "The ECJ has its facts wrong about Prism."* www.dni.gov/index.php/newsroom/news-articles/news-articles-2015/item/1258-financial-times-op-ed-by-odni-general-counsel-robert-litt-the-ecj-has-its-facts-wrong-about-prism

Loleski, S. (2019). From cold to cyber warriors: The origins and expansion of NSA's Tailored Access Operations (TAO) to Shadow Brokers. *Intelligence and National Security*, 34(1), 112–128. https://doi.org/10.1080/02684527.2018.1532627

Lonergan, E. D. (2020, March 12). Operationalizing Defend Forward: How the Concept Works to Change Adversary Behavior. Lawfare. www.lawfareblog.com/operationalizing-defend-forward-how-concept-works-change-adversary-behavior

Lou, X., Zhang, T., Jiang, J., & Zhang, Y. (2021). A survey of microarchitectural side-channel vulnerabilities, attacks, and defenses in cryptography. *ACM Computing Surveys*, 54(6), 1221–12237. https://doi.org/10.1145/3456629

Lovelace, A. A. (1844). Quoted in 1977: Donald E. Knuth: The Art of Computer Programming: Volume 1: Fundamental Algorithms (Third edition). Addison-Wesley.

Malone, T. W. (2018). *Superminds: The Surprising Power of People and Computers Thinking Together* (First edition.). Little, Brown and Company.

Manebrea, L. F. (1842). *Sketch of The Analytical Engine* (A. Lovelace, Trans.). Bibliothèque de Genève. www.fourmilab.ch/babbage/sketch.html

Maness, R. C., & Valeriano, B. (2016). The impact of cyber conflict on international interactions. *Armed Forces & Society, 42*(2), 301–323. https://doi.org/10.1177/0095327X15572997

Mann, A. (2022, March 4). What is quantum mechanics? *LIVESCIENCE*. www.livescience.com/33816-quantum-mechanics-explanation.html

Mann, A., Pultarova, T., & Howell, E. (2022, April 14). SpaceX Starlink internet: Costs, collision risks and how it works. Space.Com. www.space.com/spacex-starlink-satellites.html

Marcus, G. (2014, June 9). What comes after the turing test? | The New Yorker. The New Yorker. www.newyorker.com/tech/annals-of-technology/what-comes-after-the-turing-test

Marczak, B., Weaver, N., Dalek, J., Ensafi, R., Fifield, D., McKune, S., Rey, A., Scott-Railton, J., Deibert, R., & Paxson, V. (2015). China's Great Cannon (No. 52). Citizen Lab Research, University of Toronto. https://citizenlab.ca/2015/04/chinas-great-cannon/

Märgner, V., & Abed, H. E. (2009). ICDAR 2009 Arabic Handwriting Recognition Competition. *2009 10th International Conference on Document Analysis and Recognition*, 1383–1387. https://doi.org/10.1109/ICDAR.2009.256

Mari, A. (2022, February 22). Data protection becomes a fundamental right in Brazil. ZDNET. www.zdnet.com/article/data-protection-becomes-a-fundamental-right-in-brazil/

Maurer, T., & Healey, J. (2017). What it'll take to forge peace in cyberspace. Christian Science Monitor.

Mazarr, M. J., Cevallos, A. S., Priebe, M., Radin, A., Reedy, K., Rothenberg, A. D., Thompson, J. A., & Willcox, J. (2017). *Measuring the Health of the Liberal International Order* (p. 229) [RR-1994-OSD]. RAND Corporation. www.rand.org/pubs/research_reports/RR1994.html

McCarthy, J., Minsky, M. L., Rochester, N., & Shannon, C. E. (2006). A proposal for the Dartmouth summer research project on artificial intelligence, August 31, 1955. *AI Magazine, 27*(4), Article 4. https://doi.org/10.1609/aimag.v27i4.1904

Mcclain, C., Vogels, E. A., Perrin, A., Sechopoulos, S., & Rainie, L. (2021, September 1). The Internet and the Pandemic. *Pew Research Center: Internet, Science & Tech*. www.pewresearch.org/internet/2021/09/01/the-internet-and-the-pandemic/

McClintock, B., Hornung, J. W., & Costello, K. (2021). *Russia's Global Interests and Actions: Growing Reach to Match Rejuvenated Capabilities*. RAND Corporation. https://doi.org/10.7249/PE327

McConnell, M., Chertoff, M., & Lynn, W. (2015, July 28). Why the fear over ubiquitous data encryption is overblown. Washington Post. www.washingtonpost.com/opinions/the-need-for-ubiquitous-data-encryption/2015/07/28/3d145952-324e-11e5-8353-1215475949f4_story.html

McCorduck, P. (2004). *Machines Who Think: A Personal Inquiry into the History and Prospects of Artificial Intelligence* (25th anniversary update). A.K. Peters.

McCullagh, D. (2008, February 25). *How Pakistan knocked YouTube offline (and how to make sure it never happens again)*. CNET. www.cnet.com/

culture/how-pakistan-knocked-youtube-offline-and-how-to-make-sure-it-never-happens-again/

McCulloch, W. S., & Pitts, W. (1943). A logical calculus of the ideas immanent in nervous activity. *The Bulletin of Mathematical Biophysics*, 5(4), 115–133. https://doi.org/10.1007/BF02478259

McKay, A., Neutze, J., Nicholas, P., & Sullivan, K. (2014). *International Cybersecurity Norms: Reducing Conflict in an Internet-dependent World* (p. 24). Microsoft.

McKune, S. (2015). "Foreign Hostile Forces": The Human Rights Dimension of China's Cyber Campaigns. In J. R. Lindsay, T. M. Cheung, & D. S. Reveron (Eds.), *China and Cybersecurity: Espionage, Strategy, and Politics in the Digital Domain* (pp. 260–294). Oxford University Press. https://doi.org/10.1093/acprof:oso/9780190201265.003.0011

McLeod, S. (2017). The Milgram Shock Experiment. Simply Psychology. www.simplypsychology.org/milgram.html

McMillan, R., & Seetharaman, D. (2018, July 31). Facebook pulls fake accounts that mimic Russian tactics ahead of election. Wall Street Journal. www.wsj.com/articles/facebook-removes-fake-accounts-that-displayed-activity-consistent-with-russian-efforts-during-2016-election-1533055712

Mechanical Art & Design Museum. (n.d.). History of Automata. *The Mechanical Art & Design Museum*. Retrieved September 6, 2022, from https://themadmuseum.co.uk/history-of-automata/

Mecklin, J. (Ed.). (2020). Closer than ever: It is 100 seconds to midnight – 2020 Doomsday Clock Statement. https://thebulletin.org/doomsday-clock/2020-doomsday-clock-statement/

Mecklin, J. (Ed.). (2021). This is your COVID Wake-Up Call: It is 100 Seconds to Midnight: 2021 Doomsday Clock Statement. https://thebulletin.org/2020/01/press-release-it-is-now-100-seconds-to-midnight/

Medberry. (2019, September 3). Cisco Ranked #1 in Market Share for Industrial Networking. Cisco Blogs. https://blogs.cisco.com/internet-of-things/cisco-ranked-1-in-market-share-for-industrial-networking

Merton, R. (1936). The unanticipated consequences of purposive social action. *American Sociological Review*, 1(6), 894–904.

Meta. (2018, April 3). Authenticity matters: The IRA has no place on Facebook. *Meta*. https://about.fb.com/news/2018/04/authenticity-matters/

Meta. (2020, May 5). April 2020 Coordinated Inauthentic Behavior Report. https://about.fb.com/news/2020/05/april-cib-report/

Metz, C. (2015, September 16). Google Is 2 Billion Lines of Code – And It's All in One Place. *Wired*. www.wired.com/2015/09/google-2-billion-lines-codeand-one-place/

Meyer, F. (2019, December 11). *A new network design for the "Internet from space."* TechXplore. https://techxplore.com/news/2019-12-network-internet-space.html

Microsoft. (2022). Special Report: Ukraine, An overview of Russia's cyberattack activity in Ukraine. https://query.prod.cms.rt.microsoft.com/cms/api/am/binary/RE4Vwwd

Miles, D. (2009). Gates Establishes New Cyber Subcommand. Armed Forces Press Service. www.dvidshub.net/news/35575/gates-establishes-new-cyber-subcommand

Miles, R. E. (1978). The origin and meaning of Miles' Law. *Public Administration Review*, 38(5), 399–403.

Miller, C. C. (2014, January 24). Google pushes back against data localization. The New York Times. https://archive.nytimes.com/bits.blogs.nytimes.com/2014/01/24/google-pushes-back-against-data-localization/

MIT TR. (2018, February 21). The GANfather: The man who's given machines the gift of imagination. www.technologyreview.com/2018/02/21/145289/the-ganfather-the-man-whos-given-machines-the-gift-of-imagination/

MITRE ATT&CK®. (2015). The MITRE Corporation. https://attack.mitre.org/

Moore, T. (2010). The economics of cybersecurity: Principles and policy options. *International Journal of Critical Infrastructure Protection, 3*(3–4), 103–117. https://doi.org/10.1016/j.ijcip.2010.10.002

Morgan, P. M. (2003). *Deterrence Now.* Cambridge University Press. https://doi.org/10.1017/CBO9780511491573

MSFT. (2017). A Digital Geneva Convention to protect cyberspace, Microsoft Cybersecurity. www.microsoft.com/en-us/cybersecurity/content-hub/a-digital-geneva-convention-to-protect-cyberspace

MSFT. (2020, January 17). Microsoft appoints senior government affairs leaders in Brussels and New York, establishes New York office to work with the United Nations. EU Policy Blog. https://blogs.microsoft.com/eupolicy/2020/01/17/senior-gov-affairs-leaders-appointed-brussels-new-york/

M-Trends 2022, Special Report (p. 95). (2022). FireEye-Mandiant Services. www.mandiant.com/media/15671

Murgia, M., & Gross, A. (2020, March 17). Inside China's Controversial Mission to Reinvent the Internet. Financial Times Magazine. www.ft.com/content/ba94c2bc-6e27-11ea-9bca-bf503995cd6f

Murphy, S. D. (2002). Hate-Speech Protocol to Cybercrime Convention. *American Journal of International Law, 96*(4), 973–975. https://doi.org/10.2307/3070700

Musser, M., & Garriott, A. (2021). *Machine Learning and Cybersecurity: Hype and Reality.* Center for Security and Emerging Technology, School of Foreign Service, Georgetown University. https://cset.georgetown.edu/publication/machine-learning-and-cybersecurity/

Nakashima, E. (2021, April 21). Biden administration plans to name former senior NSA officials to White House cyber position and head of CISA. Washington Post. www.washingtonpost.com/national-security/former-senior-nsa-officials-named-to-white-house-cyber-position-and-head-of-dhs-cyber-agency/2021/04/11/b9d408cc-9b2d-11eb-8005-bffc3a39f6d3_story.html

Nakashima, E., & Pomfret, J. (2009, November 11). China proves to be an aggressive foe in cyberspace. Washington Post. www.washingtonpost.com/wp-dyn/content/article/2009/11/10/AR2009111017588.html

Nakasone, G. P. M. (2019). Statement of General Paul M. Nakasone, Commander, United States Cyber Command Before the Senate Committee on Armed Services. February 14, 2019. Unclassified|National Security Archive. https://nsarchive.gwu.edu/document/20133-national-security-archive-167-statement

Nakasone, P. M. (2019). A Cyber Force for Persistent Operations. Joint Force Quarterly, *92*.

Nakasone, P. M., & Sulmeyer, M. (2021, August 25). How to Compete in Cyberspace: Cyber Command's New Approach. Foreign Affairs. www.foreignaffairs.com/articles/united-states/2020-08-25/cybersecurity

National Institute of Standards and Technology. (2012). Information Security. https://nvlpubs.nist.gov/nistpubs/Legacy/SP/nistspecialpublication800-30r1.pdf

National Institute of Standards and Technology (2013). Digital Signature Standard (DSS) (FIPS PUB 186-4; Federal Information Processing Standards (FIPS) Publication). Information Technology Laboratory, U.S. Department of Commerce. https://nvlpubs.nist.gov/nistpubs/fips/nist.fips.186-4.pdf

National Security Agency/Central Security Service. (n.d.a). *About NSA/CSS*. Retrieved July 19, 2022, from www.nsa.gov/about/mission-values/

National Security Agency/Central Security Service. (n.d.b). "Authorities." www.nsa.gov/Culture/Operating-Authorities/Authorities/

NATO. (1949). The North Atlantic Treaty. North Altlantic Treaty Organization. www.nato.int/cps/en/natohq/official_texts_17120.htm

NATO. (2014, September 5). *Wales Summit Declaration* www.nato.int/cps/en/natohq/official_texts_112964.htm#cyber

NATO. (2016, July 8). *Cyber Defence Pledge.* www.nato.int/cps/en/natohq/official_texts_133177.htm

NATO. (2021). Brussels Summit Communiqué issued by NATO Heads of State and Government. www.nato.int/cps/en/natohq/news_185000.htm

NATO. (2022, July 11). *Collective Defence—Article 5*. North Atlantic Treaty Organization. www.nato.int/cps/en/natohq/topics_110496.htm

NATO Secretary General Jens Stoltenberg. (2015, March 25). Keynote Speech. www.nato.int/cps/en/natohq/opinions_118435.htm?selectedLocale=en

NCIJT. (n.d.). FBI, National Cyber Investigative Joint Task Force. Federal Bureau of Investigation. Retrieved August 4, 2022, from www.fbi.gov/investigate/cyber/national-cyber-investigative-joint-task-force

NCSC. (2020). National Counterintelligence Strategy of the United States of America, 2020–2022. www.dni.gov/files/NCSC/documents/features/20200205-National_CI_Strategy_2020_2022.pdf

Nelson, T. H. (1974). *Computer Lib: You Can and Must Understand Computers NOW* (First edition). Nelson.

New Scientist (Director). (2007, July 5). New Scientist recreates a robot made by the ancient Greeks. www.youtube.com/watch?v=xyQIo9iS_z0

Newell, A., & Simon, H. (1956). The logic theory machine: A complex information processing system. *IRE Transactions on Information Theory*, 2(3), 61–79. https://doi.org/10.1109/TIT.1956.1056797

Newman, L. H. (2018, May 6). What Israel's Strike on Hamas Hackers Means for Cyberwar. *Wired.* www.wired.com/story/israel-hamas-cyberattack-air-strike-cyberwar/

Newman, L. H. (2019, March 5). The NSA Makes Ghidra, a Powerful Cybersecurity Tool, Open Source. www.wired.com/story/nsa-ghidra-open-source-tool/

Newton, C. (2018, October 25). *How China Complicates Apple's Chest-thumping about Privacy*. The Verge. www.theverge.com/2018/10/25/18020508/how-china-complicates-apples-chest-thumping-about-privacy

Nichols, T. M. (2017). *The Death of Expertise: The Campaign against Established Knowledge and Why it Matters*. Oxford University Press.

Nikolas K Gvosdev. (2012). The Bear Goes Digital: Russia and Its Cyber Capabilities. In Derek S. Reveron (Ed.), *Cyberspace and National Security*. Georgetown University Press, pp. 173–190.

NIST. (2018, February 5). Framework Documents: Cybersecurity Framework Version 1.1. *NIST*. www.nist.gov/cyberframework/framework

NIST (Computer Security Resource Center). (2023, June 11). Hash Functions. Retrieved July 16, 2023, from https://csrc.nist.gov/projects/hash-functions

Nusca, A. (2020, February 17). The Conversation: Microsoft CEO Satya Nadella on How the Tech Industry Can Win Back Public Trust. Fortune. https://fortune.com/longform/microsoft-ceo-satya-nadella-interview-conversation-tech-society/

NYC Cyber Command. (n.d.). Retrieved October 24, 2022, from www1.nyc.gov/content/oti/pages/meet-the-team/cyber-command

Nye Jr., J. S. (2010). *Cyber Power*. Belfer Center, Harvard University

Nye, Jr., J. S. (2011). Nuclear Lessons for Cyber Security? *Strategic Studies Quarterly*, 5(4), 18–38.

Nye, Jr., J. S. (2014). *The Regime Complex for Managing Global Cyber Activities* (p. 20). Global Commission on Internet Governance. www.cigionline.org/sites/default/files/gcig_paper_no1.pdf

Nye Jr., J. S. (2015, October 1). The world needs new norms on cyberwarfare. Washington Post. www.washingtonpost.com/opinions/the-world-needs-an-arms-control-treaty-for-cybersecurity/2015/10/01/20c3e970-66dd-11e5-9223-70cb36460919_story.html

Nye, Jr., J. S. (2017). Deterrence and Dissuasion in Cyberspace. *International Security*, 41(3), 44–71. https://doi.org/10.1162/ISEC_a_00266

Obama, P. B. (2013, May 23). Remarks by the President at the National Defense University. https://obamawhitehouse.archives.gov/the-press-office/2013/05/23/remarks-president-national-defense-university

ODNI. (2021a). *Annual Threat Assessment of the U.S. Intelligence Community*. Office of Director of National Intelligence. www.dni.gov/files/ODNI/documents/assessments/ATA-2021-Unclassified-Report.pdf

ODNI. (2021b). *Foreign Threats to the 2020 US Federal Elections*. Office of Director of National Intelligence. www.odni.gov/files/ODNI/documents/assessments/ICA-declass-16MAR21.pdf

OECD. (2023). *Gross Domestic Spending on R&D (Indicator)*. https://doi.org/10.1787/d8b068b4-en

OECD.AI. (n.d.). *OECD AI Principles*. Retrieved September 5, 2022, from www.oecd.org/digital/artificial-intelligence/

OEWG. (2021a). Chair's Summary: Open-ended working group on developments in the field of information and telecommunications in the context of international security (A/AC.290/2021/CRP.3; p. 20). UN General Assembly. https://front.un-arm.org/wp-content/uploads/2021/03/Chairs-Summary-A-AC.290-2021-CRP.3-technical-reissue.pdf

OEWG. (2021b). *Open-ended working group* (A/AC.290/2021/CRP.2; p. 11). UN General Assembly.

OEWG. (2021c). Open-ended Working Group, UN Office for Disarmament Affairs, Final Substantive Report. https://front.un-arm.org/wp-content/uploads/2021/03/Final-report-A-AC.290-2021-CRP.2.pdf

OEWG. (2021d). Revised Consensus-aimed Draft Report of the OEWG Tabled by the Russian Federation.

Office of the Coordinator for Cyber Issues (S/CCI). (2015). *Cybercrime Fact Sheet*. Department of State.

Office of the Historian, US Department of State. (n.d.). *Sputnik, 1957*. Retrieved July 17, 2022, from https://history.state.gov/milestones/1953-1960/sputnik

Olmstead, K., & Smith, Aa. (2017). American Views about Cybersecurity Policy. www.pewresearch.org/internet/2017/01/26/3-attitudes-about-cybersecurity-policy/

Olson, M. (1971). *The Logic of Collective Action: Public Goods and the Theory of Groups, Second Printing with a New Preface and Appendix*. Harvard University Press. https://doi.org/10.2307/j.ctvjsf3ts

On confidence- and security-building measures. (2011). Organization for Security and Co-operation in Europe (OSCE). www.osce.org/files/f/documents/a/4/86597.pdf

OpenAI Codex. (2021, August 10). OpenAI. https://openai.com/blog/openai-codex/

Organization for Security and Co-operation in Europe. (1992). Treaty on Open Skies. www.osce.org/files/f/documents/1/5/14127.pdf

Orszag, P. (2007). Report by Director of CBO on Climate Change. www.cbo.gov/sites/default/files/presentation/11-16-climatechangeconf0.pdf

OSCE. (2016, March 10). Permanent Council Decision No. 1202. www.osce.org/pc/227281

OSI Model. (2022). In *Wikipedia*. https://en.wikipedia.org/wiki/OSI_model

O'Sullivan, K. (2021, March 29). UN Makes Critical Progress on Cybersecurity. Microsoft On the Issues. https://blogs.microsoft.com/on-the-issues/2021/03/29/un-working-group-cybersecurity-report/

O'Toole, G. (n.d.). *It's Difficult to Make Predictions, Especially About the Future*. Quote Investigator. Retrieved July 19, 2022, from https://quoteinvestigator.com/2013/10/20/no-predict/

Ottis, R. (2008). *Analysis of the 2007 Cyber Attacks against Estonia from the Information Warfare Perspective* (p. 6). Cooperative Cyber Defence Centre of Excellence. https://ccdcoe.org/uploads/2018/10/Ottis2008_AnalysisOf2007From TheInformationWarfarePerspective.pdf

Owen, M. (2021, March 16). Apple capitulates to Russia laws requiring preinstalled software on iPhone, Mac. AppleInsider. https://appleinsider.com/articles/21/03/16/apple-agrees-to-russia-laws-requiring-preinstalled-software-on-iphone-mac

Pagden, A. (2002). *The Idea of Europe From Antiquity to the European Union* (L. H. Hamilton, Ed.; 1st ed.). Cambridge University Press

Pan American Union. (1933). *The Seventh Pan-American Conference, "Convention on Rights and Duties of States"* (pp. 19–44) [Treaty Series]. League of Nations. https://treaties.un.org/doc/Publication/UNTS/LON/Volume%20165/v165.pdf

Patton, G. S. (1947). *War as I Knew It*. Houghton Mifflin Co., Boston.

Pearson, H. (n.d.). *Mechanical miracles: The rise of the automaton | Christie's*. Retrieved September 6, 2022, from www.christies.com/features/The-History-of-the-Automaton-Mechanical-miracles-6382-1.aspx

Pearson, J. (2014, July 8). Forget Turing, the Lovelace Test Has a Better Shot at Spotting AI. Vice. www.vice.com/en/article/pgaany/forget-turing-the-lovelace-test-has-a-better-shot-at-spotting-ai

Peking University School of Law. (2018). National Intelligence Law of the People's Republic of China (2018 Amendment). https://en.pkulaw.cn/display.aspx?cgid=313975&lib=law

Pellerin, C. (2014, November 21). *Cybercom Chief Details U.S. Cyber Threats, Trends*. U.S. Department of Defense. www.defense.gov/News/News-Stories/Article/Article/603696/

Pellerin, C. (2017, July 21). Project Maven to Deploy Computer Algorithms to War Zone by Year's End. *DOD News*. Retrieved from www.defense.gov/News/News-Stories/Article/Article/1254719/project-maven-to-deploy-computer-algorithms-to-war-zone-by-years-end/

PJI. (2022). *Pretrial Justice Institute*. Pretrial Justice Institute. www.pretrial.org/mission

Posture statement of General Paul M. Nakasone, Commander, United States Cyber Command before the 117th Congress. (2022). www.armed-services.senate.gov/imo/media/doc/5%20Apr%20SASC%20CYBERCOM%20Posture%20Statement%20(GEN%20Nakasone)%20-%20FINAL.pdf

Poznansky, M. (2021, March 23). Covert Action, Espionage, and the Intelligence Contest in Cyberspace. War on the Rocks. http://warontherocks.com/2021/03/covert-action-espionage-and-the-intelligence-contest-in-cyberspace/

President Obama. (2013). The National Security Agency: Missions, Authorities, Oversight and Partnerships. https://irp.fas.org/nsa/nsa-story.pdf

Presidential directive. (n.d.). In *Wikipedia*. https://en.wikipedia.org/wiki/Presidential_directive

PPD-41 (2016) Presidential Policy Directive on United States Cyber Incident Coordination. (2016, July 26). Whitehouse.Gov. https://obamawhitehouse.archives.gov/the-press-office/2016/07/26/fact-sheet-presidential-policy-directive-united-states-cyber-incident-1e

Preskill, J. (2018). Quantum Computing in the NISQ era and beyond. *Quantum*, 2, 79. https://doi.org/10.22331/q-2018-08-06-79

Protocol Additional to the Geneva Conventions of 12 August 1949, and Relating to the Protection of Victims of International Armed Conflicts, art. 49, 1. (1977).

Pry, P. V. (2017). Nuclear EMP Attack Scenarios and Combined-Arms Warfare: Report to the Commission to Assess the Threat to the United States from Electromagnetic Pulse (EMP) Attack. https://apps.dtic.mil/sti/pdfs/AD1097009.pdf

Qiu, Q. (2019, December 17). India's internet shutdown shows normal practice for sovereign countries. People's Daily Online, 1.

Quattrociocchi, W., Scala, A., & Sunstein, C. R. (2016). *Echo Chambers on Facebook* (SSRN Scholarly Paper No. 2795110). https://doi.org/10.2139/ssrn.2795110

Raman, K. (2008). Ask and you will receive: The psychology of social engineering: Why does it work? *McAfee Security Journal*, Fall. www.wired.com/images_blogs/threatlevel/files/mcafee_security_journal_fall_2008.pdf

Reagan, R. (1986). *News Conference*. www.reaganfoundation.org/ronald-reagan/reagan-quotes-speeches/news-conference-1/

Reich, S., & Dombrowski, P. (2017). *The End of Grand Strategy: US Maritime Operations in the Twenty-First Century*. Cornell University Press. www.cornellpress.cornell.edu/book/9781501714627/the-end-of-grand-strategy/

Reno, Attorney General of the United States, et al. V. American Civil Liberties Union et al., No. 96-11 (US District Court for the Eastern District of Pennsylvania June 26, 1997). www.aclu.org/legal-document/reno-v-aclu-supreme-court-decision

Return-oriented programming. (2022). In *Wikipedia*. https://en.wikipedia.org/w/index.php?title=Return-oriented_programming&oldid=1092917481

Reuters. (2018, November 8). U.S. accuses China of violating bilateral anti-hacking deal. *Reuters*. www.reuters.com/article/us-usa-china-cyber-idUSKCN1NE02E

Reuters Staff. (2021, February 15). SolarWinds hack was "largest and most sophisticated attack" ever: Microsoft president. *Reuters*. www.reuters.com/article/us-cyber-solarwinds-microsoft-idUSKBN2AF03R

Reveron, D. S., & Cook, J. L. (2013). From National to Theater: Developing Strategy. *Joint Force Quarterly, 70*, 8.

Reveron, D. S., & Gvosdev, N. K. (2015). (Re)Discovering the National Interest: The Future of U.S. Foreign Policy and Defense Strategy. *Orbis, 59*(3), 299–316. https://doi.org/10.1016/j.orbis.2015.04.001

Reveron, D. S., & Mahoney-Norris, K. A. (2019). *Human and National Security: Understanding Transnational Challenges*. Routledge. https://doi .org/10.4324/9780429503726

Reveron, D. S., & Mahoney-Norris, K. A. (2011). *Human Security in a Borderless World: Understanding Transnational Challenges*. Routledge. https://doi .org/10.4324/9780429499951

Reveron, D. S., & Murer, J. S. (2006). *Flashpoints in the War on Terrorism* (First edition). Routledge, Taylor & Francis Group. www.routledge.com/Flashpoints-in-the-War-on-Terrorism/Reveron-Murer/p/book/9780415954914

Reveron, D. S. & Savage, J. E. (2020). Digital Human Security, *Orbis*, 64 (4): 555–570.

Revised consensus-aimed draft report of the OEWG tabled by the Russian Federation. (2021d). Open Ended Working Group (OEWG).

Reveron, D. S., Gvosdev, N. K., & Owens, M. T. (2014). *US Foreign Policy and Defense Strategy: The Evolution of an Incidental Superpower*. Georgetown University Press. http://press.georgetown.edu/book/georgetown/us-foreign-policy-and-defense-strategy

Rid, T. (2013). *Cyber War Will Not Take Place*. Oxford University Press.

Rid, T. (2020). *Active Measures: The Secret History of Disinformation and Political Warfare* (First edition.). Farrar, Straus and Giroux.

Riley, T. (2021, January 14). The Cybersecurity 202: NSA cyber chief Anne Neuberger is heading to the Biden White House. Washington Post. www.washingtonpost .com/politics/2021/01/14/cybersecurity-202-nsa-cyber-chief-anne-neuberger-is-heading-biden-white-house/

Roberts, L. G. (1978). The Evolution of Packet Switching. *Proceedings of the IEEE, 66*(11), 7.

Robertson, A. (2018, February 11). *I'm using AI to face-swap Elon Musk and Jeff Bezos, and I'm really bad at it*. The Verge. www.theverge.com/2018/2/11/16992986/ fakeapp-deepfakes-ai-face-swapping

Robertson, J., & Riley, M. (2018, October 4). The Big Hack: How China Used a Tiny Chip to Infiltrate U.S. Companies. *Bloomberg Businessweek*. www.bloomberg .com/news/features/2018-10-04/the-big-hack-how-china-used-a-tiny-chip-to-infiltrate-america-s-top-companies

Robertson, J., & Riley, M. (2021, February 12). The Long Hack: How China Exploited a U.S. Tech Supplier. *Bloomberg.Com*. www.bloomberg.com/features/2021-supermicro/

Robertson, J., Mehrotra, K., & Gallagher, R. (2021, March 9). China's Microsoft Hack, Russia's SolarWinds Hacks Could Overwhelm U.S. – Bloomberg. *Bloomberg*

News. www.bloomberg.com/news/articles/2021-03-09/microsoft-solarwinds-breaches-spark-two-front-war-on-hackers#xj4y7vzkg

Rodríguez, M. (2017). *Declaration by Miguel Rodríguez, representative of Cuba, at the final session of Group of Governmental Experts on Developments in the Field of Information and Telecommunicatioins in the Context of International Security.* UNODA.

Roman Zakharov v. Russia, No. 47143/06 (European Court of Human Rights December 1, 2015). https://hudoc.echr.coe.int/fre#{%22itemid%22:[%22002-10793%22]}

Rona, G., & Aarons, L. (2016). State responsibility to respect, protect and fulfill human rights obligations in cyberspace. *Journal of National Security Law & Policy, 8*(3), 503.

Rosenbach, E., Kayyem, J., & Mitra, L. (2021, August 19). The Limits of Cyberoffense. www.foreignaffairs.com/articles/united-states/2021-08-11/limits-cyberoffense

Rosenberger, L., & Fly, J. (2017). Lessons from France for fighting Russian interference in democracy. https://securingdemocracy.gmfus.org/lessons-from-france-for-fighting-russian-interference-in-democracy/

Rosenberger, L., & Gorman, L. (2020). How Democracies Can Win the Information Contest. *The Washington Quarterly, 43*(2), 75–96. https://doi.org/10.1080/01636 60X.2020.1771045

Rowland, T. (n.d.). *Church-Turing Thesis.* Wolfram MathWorld, Created by Eric. W. Weisstein; Wolfram Research, Inc. Retrieved September 6, 2022, from https://mathworld.wolfram.com/Church-TuringThesis.html

Royce, W. W. (1987). Managing the development of large software systems: Concepts and techniques. *Proceedings of the 9th International Conference on Software Engineering, 328–338.* https://doi.org/978-0-89791-216-7

Ruan, L., Knockel, J., & Crete-Nishihata, M. (2020). *Censored Contagion: How Information on the Coronavirus is Managed on Chinese Social Media* (Citizen Lab Research Report No. 125). University of Toronto. https://citizenlab.ca/2020/03/censored-contagion-how-information-on-the-coronavirus-is-managed-on-chinese-social-media/

Ruhl, C., Hollis, D., Hoffman, W., & Maurer, T. (2020). Cyberspace and Geopolitics: Assessing Global Cybersecurity Norm Processes at a Crossroads. Carnegie Endowment for International Peace, 32.

Rumsfeld, D. H. (2005). *The National Defense Strategy of the United States of America.* https://nssarchive.us/wp-content/uploads/2020/04/2005_NDS.pdf

Rundle, J., & Stupp, C. (2022, April 12). Ukraine Thwarts Cyberattack on Electric Grid, Officials Say. Wall Street Journal.

Russell, A. L. (2014). *Cyber Blockades.* Georgetown University Press. http://press.georgetown.edu/book/georgetown/cyber-blockades

Russell, S. J., & Norvig, P. (2003). *Artificial Intelligence: A Modern Approach.* Pearson Education.

Sak, H., Senior, A., Rao, K., Beaufays, F., & Schalkwyk, J. (2015, September 24). Google voice search: Faster and more accurate. Google AI Blog. https://ai.googleblog.com/2015/09/google-voice-search-faster-and-more.html

Sanger, D. E. (2010, September 25). Iran Fights Malware Attacking Computers. The New York Times. www.nytimes.com/2010/09/26/world/middleeast/26iran.html

Sanger, D. E. (2018). *The Perfect Weapon: War, Sabotage, and Fear in the Cyber Age*. Penguin Random House. www.penguinrandomhouse.com/books/547683/the-perfect-weapon-by-david-e-sanger/

Sanger, D. E., & Perlroth, N. (2021, May 14). Pipeline Attack Yields Urgent Lessons About U.S. Cybersecurity. The New York Times. www.nytimes.com/2021/05/14/us/politics/pipeline-hack.html

Sanger, D. E., Barnes, J. E., & Perlroth, N. (2021, October 25). Preparing for Retaliation Against Russia, U.S. Confronts Hacking by China. The New York Times. www.nytimes.com/2021/03/07/us/politics/microsoft-solarwinds-hack-russia-china.html

Savage, J. E., & McConnell, B. W. (2015). Exploring Multi-Stakeholder Internet Governance | EastWest Institute (p. 16) [Discussion Paper]. EastWestInstitute. www.eastwest.ngo/idea/exploring-multi-stakeholder-internet-governance

Scharre, P., & Riikonen, A. (2020). *Defense Technology Strategy*. Center for New American Security. www.cnas.org/publications/reports/defense-technology-strategy

Schlegel, A. (2017, July 27). Divided Differences Method of Polynomial Interpolation. R-Bloggers. www.r-bloggers.com/2017/07/divided-differences-method-of-polynomial-interpolation/

Schleifer, T. (2018, January 19). *Google CEO Sundar Pichai says AI is more profound than electricity and fire—Vox*. Vox. www.vox.com/2018/1/19/16911180/sundar-pichai-google-fire-electricity-ai

Schmid, J. (2018, February 16). *Siemens and partners sign joint charter on cybersecurity*. Munich Security Conference, Munich, Germany. www.charteroftrust.com/wp-content/uploads/2020/02/180216-Siemens-and-partners-sign-joint-charter-on-cybersecurity.pdf

Schmitt, M. (2020, February 28). Norm-Skepticism in Cyberspace? Counter-factual and Counterproductive. Just Security. www.justsecurity.org/68892/norm-skepticism-in-cyberspace-counter-factual-and-counterproductive/

Schmitt, M. (2021, June 10). *The Sixth United Nations GGE and International Law in Cyberspace*. Just Security. www.justsecurity.org/76864/the-sixth-united-nations-gge-and-international-law-in-cyberspace/, www.justsecurity.org/76864/the-sixth-united-nations-gge-and-international-law-in-cyberspace/

Schmitt, M. N. (2002). Preemptive strategies in international law. *Michigan Journal of International Law*, *24*, 513.

Schmitt, M. N. (2012). "Attack" as a Term of Art in International Law: The Cyber Operations Context. 4th International Conference on Cyber Conflict, 11.

Schmitt, M. N. (2017a). *Tallinn Manual 2.0 on the International Law Applicable to Cyber Operations* (Second edition). Cambridge University Press. https://doi.org/10.1017/9781316822524

Schmitt, M. N. (2017b). *Peacetime Cyber Responses and Wartime Cyber Operations Under International Law: An Analytical* Vade Mecum (SSRN Scholarly Paper No. 3180699). https://papers.ssrn.com/abstract=3180699

Schmitt, M., & Vihul, L. (2017, June 30). International Cyber Law Politicized: The UN GGE's Failure to Advance Cyber Norms. Just Security. www.justsecurity.org/42768/international-cyber-law-politicized-gges-failure-advance-cyber-norms/

Schneider, J. (2020). A Strategic Cyber No-First-Use Policy? Addressing the US Cyber Strategy Problem. *The Washington Quarterly*, *43*(2), 159–175. https://doi.org/10.1080/0163660X.2020.1770970

Schneier, B. (2015, March 25). NSA Doesn't Need to Spy on Your Calls to Learn Your Secrets. Wired. www.wired.com/2015/03/data-and-goliath-nsa-metadata-spying-your-secrets/

Schneier, B. (2017, January 27). Click Here to Kill Everyone. New York Magazine. www.schneier.com/essays/archives/2017/01/click_here_to_kill_e.html

Schulman, R. (2019, July 18). Why the Ghost Keys "Solution" to Encryption is No Solution. Just Security. www.justsecurity.org/64968/why-the-ghost-keys-solution-to-encryption-is-no-solution/

Schultz, T. (2017, April 26). A Decade After "Web War 1," Former Estonian President Blasts EU Cyber Inertia. *Atlantic Council.* www.atlanticcouncil.org/blogs/new-atlanticist/a-decade-after-web-war-1-former-estonian-president-blasts-eu-cyber-inertia/

Schwarz, O. (2019). In 2016, Microsoft's Racist Chatbot Revealed the Dangers of Online Conversation. IEEE Spectrum. https://spectrum.ieee.org/in-2016-microsofts-racist-chatbot-revealed-the-dangers-of-online-conversation

Schwarzenbach, A., Voo, J., Hemani, I., Jones, S., DeSombre, W., & Cassidy, D. (2021). Harvard Belfer National Cyber Power Index 2020 [Data set]. Harvard Dataverse. https://doi.org/10.7910/DVN/LT55JY

Scott, K. D. (2018). *Joint Publication 3-0* (p. 224). Joint Chiefs of Staff. https://irp.fas.org/doddir/dod/jp3_0.pdf

Section 230 as First Amendment rule. (2018). Harvard Law Review. https://harvardlawreview.org/2018/05/section-230-as-first-amendment-rule/

Section 230 of the Communications Decency Act. (n.d.-a). Electronic Frontier Foundation. Retrieved August 5, 2022, from www.eff.org/issues/cda230

Section 230 of the Communications Decency Act. (n.d.-b). Electronic Frontier Foundation. Retrieved October 25, 2022, from www.eff.org/issues/cda230

Segal, A. (2017). The Hacked World Order: How Nations Fight, Trade, Maneuver, and Manipulate in the Digital Age. www.publicaffairsbooks.com/titles/adam-segal/the-hacked-world-order/9781610394161/

Segal, A. (2020). China's Alternative Cyber Governance Regime. Council on Foreign Relations, for the U.S. China Economic Security Review Commission, 8.

Sermpezis, P. et al. (2018). ARTEMIS: Neutralizing BGP Hijacking Within a Minute, *IEEE/ACM Transactions on Networking*, 26 (6), 2471–2486.

Shackelford, S., Russell, S., & Kuehn, A. (2016). Unpacking the International Law on Cybersecurity Due Diligence: Lessons from the Public and Private Sectors. *Chicago Journal of International Law*, *17*(1), 1–50. https://chicagounbound.uchicago.edu/cjil/vol17/iss1/1

Shahbaz, A., Funk, A., & Vesteinsson, K. (2022). Freedom on the Net 2022: Countering an Authoritarian Overhaul of the Internet. *Freedom House.* https://freedomhouse.org/sites/default/files/2022-10/FOTN2022Digital.pdf

Shamir, A., Melamed, O., & BenShmuel, O. (2022). *The Dimpled Manifold Model of Adversarial Examples in Machine Learning* (arXiv:2106.10151). arXiv. https://doi.org/10.48550/arXiv.2106.10151

Shamir, A., Safran, I., Ronen, E., & Dunkelman, O. (2019). *A Simple Explanation for the Existence of Adversarial Examples with Small Hamming Distance* (arXiv:1901.10861). arXiv. https://doi.org/10.48550/arXiv.1901.10861

Shane, S., & Wakabayashi, D. (2018, April 4). 'The Business of War': Google Employees Protest Work for the Pentagon. The New York Times. www.nytimes.com/2018/04/04/technology/google-letter-ceo-pentagon-project.html

Shannon, C. E. (1949), Communication Theory of Secrecy Systems. *Bell System Technical Journal*, 28, 65–715. https://doi.org/10.1002/j.1538-7305.1949.tb00928.x

Shelley, M. (1922). *Frankenstein or, The Modern Prometheus.* The Cornhill Publishing Company. www.gutenberg.org/files/84/84-h/84-h.htm

Sherman, J. (2020, May 1). The Russian Doll of Putin's Internet Clampdown. Wired. www.wired.com/story/opinion-the-russian-doll-of-putins-internet-clampdown/

Sherman, W. R. (2022, September 16). Global Emerging Technology Summit, Remarks. www.state.gov/global-emerging-technology-summit/

Shor, P. W. (1997). Polynomial-time algorithms for prime factorization and discrete logarithms on a quantum computer. *SIAM Journal on Computing*, 26(5), 1484–1509. https://doi.org/10.1137/S0097539795293172

Shuttleworth, M. (n.d.). Heron's Inventions includes Holy Water Dispenser and the Aeolipile. Explorable. Retrieved September 6, 2022, from https://explorable.com/heron-inventions

Silver, D., Hubert, T., Schrittwieser, J. et al. (2018). A general reinforcement learning algorithm that masters chess, shogi, and Go through self-play. *Science*, 362(6419), 1140–1144. https://doi.org/10.1126/science.aar6404

Silver, D., Schrittwieser, J., Simonyan, K. et al. (2017). Mastering the game of Go without human knowledge. *Nature*, 550(7676), Article 7676. https://doi.org/10.1038/nature24270

Simon, H. A. (1960). *The New Science of Management Decision.* Harber & Brothers.

Simon, H. A., & Newell, A. (1958). Heuristic problem solving: The next advance in operations research. *Operations Research*, 6(1), 1–10. https://doi.org/10.1287/opre.6.1.1

Simonite, T. (2018, November 1). Will "Deepfakes" Disrupt the Midterm Election? *Wired.* www.wired.com/story/will-deepfakes-disrupt-the-midterm-election/

Slayton, R. (2021). What is a cyber warrior? The Emergence of U.S. Military Cyber Expertise, 1967–2018. *Texas National Security Review*, 4(1), 61–96.

Smart, W. (2018). *Lessons Learned Review of the WannaCry Ransomware Cyber Attack* (p. 42). Department of Health & Social Care, NHS.

Smeets, M. (2018). A matter of time: On the transitory nature of cyberweapons. *Journal of Strategic Studies*, 41(1–2), 6–32. https://doi.org/10.1080/01402390.2017.1288107

Smeltz, D., Daalder, I., Friedhoff, K., Kafura, C., & Helm, B. (2019). Rejecting Retreat: Americans Support US Engagement in Global Affairs. *Chicago Journal on Global Affairs*, 1–40.

Smith, A. (2020, August 5). Deepfakes are the most dangerous crime of the future, researchers say. *The Independent.* www.independent.co.uk/tech/deepfakes-dangerous-crime-artificial-intelligence-a9655821.html

Smith, A. (2021, January 1). H.R.6395 – 116th Congress (2019–2020): William M. (Mac) Thornberry National Defense Authorization Act for Fiscal Year 2021 (2019/2020) [Legislation]. www.congress.gov/

Smith, B. (2017, February 14). The need for a Digital Geneva Convention. Microsoft on the Issues. https://blogs.microsoft.com/on-the-issues/2017/02/14/need-digital-geneva-convention/

Smith, B., & Browne, C. A. (2019). *Tools and Weapons: The Promise and the Peril of the Digital Age*. Penguin Press.

Smith, D. (2002, December 1). Psychologist wins Nobel Prize. www.apa.org, *33*(11), 22.

Smith, D. (2008, May 31). Stream Cipher Reuse: A Graphic Example. Cryptosmith. https://cryptosmith.com/2008/05/31/stream-reuse/

Smith, R. (2014, March 12). U.S. Risks National Blackout from Small-Scale Attack. *WSJ*. http://online.wsj.com/article/SB10001424052702304020104579433670284061220.html

Solove, D. J. (2006). A brief history of information privacy law. *Proskauer on Privacy, PLI*, 47, 1–46. https://scholarship.law.gwu.edu/cgi/viewcontent.cgi?article=2076&context=faculty_publications

South Africa. (2021). Statement by South Africa at the Informal OEWG. OEWG.

Sparkes, M. (2021, November 15). IBM creates largest ever superconducting quantum computer. New Scientist. www.newscientist.com/article/2297583-ibm-creates-largest-ever-superconducting-quantum-computer/

Spector, M., & Ma, W. (2018, June 3). If You Want to Do Business in China, Mind Your T's: Taiwan and Tibet. The Wall Street Journal. www.wsj.com/articles/if-you-want-to-do-business-in-china-mind-your-ts-taiwan-and-tibet-1527937201

Spinazze (2020). *Disciplinary Counsel v. Spinazze*, 159 Ohio St.3d 187, 2020-Ohio-957. www.supremecourt.ohio.gov/rod/docs/pdf/0/2020/2020-Ohio-957.pdf

Stahl, R. (2017, December 12). Justice Department Announces Charges And Guilty Pleas In Three Computer Crime Cases Involving Significant Cyber Attacks, USAO-NJ, Department of Justice. https://web.archive.org/web/20171213203120/www.justice.gov/usao-nj/pr/justice-department-announces-charges-and-guilty-pleas-three-computer-crime-cases

Statement for the Record, Nominee for the National Cyber Director. (2021). www.hsgac.senate.gov/imo/media/doc/Prepared%20Statement-Inglis-2021-06-10.pdf

Statista. (n.d.). Global Market Share Held by Operating Systems for Desktop PCs. *Statista*. Retrieved October 25, 2022, from www.statista.com/statistics/218089/global-market-share-of-windows-7/

Statt, N. (2020, February 26). Google Translate supports new languages for the first time in four years, including Uyghur. *The Verge*. www.theverge.com/2020/2/26/21154417/google-translate-new-languages-support-odia-tatar-turkmen-uyghur-kinyarwanda

Statute of the International Court of Justice. (1945). *Statute of the International Court of Justice*. Great Neck Publishing. www.icj-cij.org/en/statute

Stoltenberg, N. S. G. J. (2020, June 8). Stoltenberg Urges NATO Unity Amid Challenges from China, Russia. Radio Free Europe/Radio Liberty. www.rferl.org/a/stoltenberg-urges-nato-unity-amid-challenges-from-china-russia/30659609.html

Stone, G. R., & Bollinger, L. C. (2018). *The Free Speech Century*. Oxford University Press.

Strayer, R. L. (2019, July 25). Remarks at the 2019 Internet Governance Forum USA Conference. *United States Department of State*. https://2017-2021.state.gov/remarks-at-the-2019-internet-governance-forum-usa-conference/

Strickling, L. E. (2013, March 2). Moving Together Beyond Dubai|National Telecommunications and Information Administration. National Telecommunications and Information Administration, United States Department of Commerce. www.ntia.doc.gov/blog/2013/moving-together-beyond-dubai

Struckman, D. (2022, July 20). America Cannot Afford to Leave The Open Skies Treaty [Text]. The National Interest. https://nationalinterest.org/feature/america-cannot-afford-leave-open-skies-treaty-106986

Stuart-Ulin, C. R. (2018, July 31). Microsoft's politically correct chatbot is even worse than its racist one. *Quartz*. https://qz.com/1340990/microsofts-politically-correct-chat-bot-is-even-worse-than-its-racist-one/

Stupp, C. (2019, August 30). Fraudsters Used AI to Mimic CEO's Voice in Unusual Cybercrime Case. Wall Street Journal. www.wsj.com/articles/fraudsters-use-ai-to-mimic-ceos-voice-in-unusual-cybercrime-case-11567157402

Suarez, F. F., & Lanzolla, G. (2005, April 1). The Half-Truth of First-Mover Advantage. Harvard Business Review. https://hbr.org/2005/04/the-half-truth-of-first-mover-advantage

Sullivan, J. J. (2019, September 23). Remarks at the Second Ministerial Meeting on Advancing Responsible State Behavior in Cyberspace. United States Department of State. https://2017-2021.state.gov/remarks-at-the-second-ministerial-meeting-on-advancing-responsible-state-behavior-in-cyberspace/index.html

Sunstein, C. R., & Thaler, R. (2016, December 7). The Two Friends Who Changed How We Think About How We Think. The New Yorker. www.newyorker.com/books/page-turner/the-two-friends-who-changed-how-we-think-about-how-we-think

Swaine, M. R., & Freiberger, P. A. (2020). Analytical Engine | Description & Facts | Britannica. In *Britannica*. Encyclopedia Britannica. www.britannica.com/technology/Analytical-Engine

Taleb, N. N. (2010). *The Black Swan* (Second edition). Penguin Random House. www.penguinrandomhouse.com/books/176226/the-black-swan-second-edition-by

Tarabay, J. (2018, December 6). Australian Government Passes Contentious Encryption Law. The New York Times. www.nytimes.com/2018/12/06/world/australia/encryption-bill-nauru.html

Taulli, T. (2020, November 27). Turing Test At 70: Still Relevant for AI (Artificial Intelligence)? *Forbes*. www.forbes.com/sites/tomtaulli/2020/11/27/turing-test-at-70-still-relevant-for-ai-artificial-intelligence/

Tavakoli, O. (2021, April 30). A Tale of Two Hacks: From SolarWinds to Microsoft Exchange. Threatpost. https://threatpost.com/solarwinds-hack-seismic-shift/165758/

Team, T. (2019, September 24). AMD vs Intel: A Detailed Comparison of Revenue and Key Operating Metrics. *Forbes*. www.forbes.com/sites/greatspeculations/2019/09/24/amd-vs-intel-a-detailed-comparison-of-revenue-and-key-operating-metrics/

Teitelbaum, S. (1992). Scientists Say Asimov Put the Stars in Their Eyes. The Los Angeles Times. www.latimes.com/archives/la-xpm-1992-04-08-vw-636-story.html

Temple-Raston, D. (2021, April 16). A "Worst Nightmare" Cyberattack: The Untold Story Of The SolarWinds Hack. *NPR*. www.npr.org/2021/04/16/985439655/a-worst-nightmare-cyberattack-the-untold-story-of-the-solarwinds-hack

Tetlock, P. E. (2016). *Superforecasting: The Art and Science of Prediction*. Random House Books.

Tetlock, P. E. (2017). *Expert Political Judgment: How Good Is It? How Can We Know.* Princeton University Press. https://press.princeton.edu/books/hardcover/9780691178288/expert-political-judgment

The Internet Society. (n.d.). Internet Society. Retrieved August 6, 2022, from www.internetsociety.org/

The National Academies. (2018). *Decrypting the Encryption Debate: A Framework for Decision Makers.* National Academies Press. https://doi.org/10.17226/25010

The Tao of IETF: A Novice's Guide to the Internet Engineering Task Force. (n.d.). IETF. Retrieved August 6, 2022, from www.ietf.org/about/participate/tao/

Thompson, N. (2020, January 15). UN Secretary-General: US-China Tech Split Worse Than Cold War. Wired. www.wired.com/story/un-secretary-general-antonio-guterres-internet-risks/

Thumfart, J. (2020). Public and private just wars: Distributed cyber deterrence based on Vitoria and Grotius. *Internet Policy Review, 9*(3). https://doi.org/10.14763/2020.3.1500

Title 10 USC 394: Authorities concerning military cyber operations. (n.d.). Retrieved August 4, 2022, from https://uscode.house.gov/view.xhtml?req=granuleid:USC-prelim-title10-section394&num=0&edition=prelim

Tombs, N., & Fournier-Tombs, E. (2020, August). Ambiguity in authenticity of top-level coronavirus-related domains. *The Harvard Kennedy School Misinformation Review, 1*(Covid-19 and Misinformation). misinforeview.hks.harvard.edu

TRS-80. (n.d.). *Radio Shack TRS-80 Model 1 Personal Computer.* National Museum of American History. Retrieved November 9, 2022, from https://americanhistory.si.edu/collections/search/object/nmah_334337

Tully, P., & Foster, L. (2021, October 31). Repurposing Neural Networks to Generate Synthetic Media for Information Operations. Mandiant. www.mandiant.com/resources/blog/repurposing-neural-networks-to-generate-synthetic-media-for-information-operations

Turing, A. M. (1996). Computing Machinery and Intelligence. In *Readings in Language and Mind*, Geirsson, Heimir, & Losonsky, Michael [Eds], Blackwell Publishers Inc, pp. 245–264.

Tversky, A., & Kahneman, D. (1973). Availability: A heuristic for judging frequency and probability. *Cognitive Psychology, 5*(2), 207–232. https://doi.org/10.1016/0010-0285(73)90033-9

Tversky, A., & Kahneman, D. (1986). Rational choice and the framing of decisions. *The Journal of Business, 59*(4), 251–278.

Twitter. (2020, July 18). An Update on Our Security Incident. Retrieved from https://blog.twitter.com/en_us/topics/company/2020/an-update-on-our-security-incident.html

UN. (1948, December 10). *Universal Declaration of Human Rights.* United Nations; United Nations. www.un.org/en/about-us/universal-declaration-of-human-rights

UN. (2004). *UN Security Council Resolution 1540.* United Nations. www.un.org/disarmament/wmd/sc1540/

UN Office on Drugs and Crime. (2018). Comments Received in Accordance with the Chair's Proposal for the Work Plan for the Period 2018-2021.

UN Press Bureau. (2014). Cyber warfare, unchecked, could topple entire edifice of international security, says speaker in First Committee at conclusion of thematic debate segment. United Nations. https://press.un.org/en/2014/gadis3512.doc.htm

UN Press Bureau. (2018, October 30). First Committee delegates exchange views on best tools for shielding cyberspace from global security threats triggered by dual-use technologies, innovations. UN Press Blog. https://press.un.org/en/2018/gadis3613.doc.htm

UNESCO. (2005). *Precautionary Principle.* www.precautionaryprinciple.eu/

UNGA. (2018). UN General Assembly, Resolution 73/266, Advancing Responsible State Behaviour in Cyberspace in the Context of International Security. UN General Assembly. https://undocs.org/A/RES/73/266

United Nations. (n.d.-a). Charter. United Nations; United Nations. Retrieved September 7, 2022, from www.un.org/en/about-us/un-charter/preamble

United Nations. (n.d.-b). Full Text, Charter of the United Nations.

United Nations. (n.d.-c). Growth in United Nations membership. United Nations; United Nations. Retrieved September 7, 2022, from www.un.org/en/about-us/growth-in-un-membership

United Nations. (1994). *United Nations Convention on the Law of the Sea (UNCLOS).* United Nations. www.un.org/depts/los/convention_agreements/texts/unclos/unclos_e.pdf

United Nations. (2018). Developments in the Field of Information and Telecommunications in the Context of International Security: Report to the Secretary General (A/RES/73/27; p. 5). https://documents-dds-ny.un.org/doc/UNDOC/GEN/N18/418/04/PDF/N1841804.pdf?OpenElement

United Nations Office on Genocide Prevention and the Responsibility to Protect. (n.d.). Retrieved September 7, 2022, from www.un.org/en/genocideprevention/about-responsibility-to-protect.shtml

UNODA. (2019). Fact Sheet: Developments in the field of information and telecommunications in the context of international security. United Nations Office for Disarmaments Affairs.

UNODA. (2022). Index to UNODA Reports on Developments in the field of information and telecommunications in the context of international security.

U.S. (1978). U.S. Foreign Intelligence Surveillance Court. www.fisc.uscourts.gov/

U.S. Attorney's Office, Eastern District of New York. (2018, November 27). Two International Cybercriminal Rings Dismantled and Eight Defendants Indicted for Causing Tens of Millions of Dollars in Losses in Digital Advertising Fraud. www.justice.gov/usao-edny/pr/two-international-cybercriminal-rings-dismantled-and-eight-defendants-indicted-causing

US Fleet Cyber Command/US Tenth Fleet. (2020). *Strategic Plan 2020–2025.* US Navy.

U.S. Government Publishing Office. (2011). *U.S. Code Title 18 – Crimes and Criminal Procedure. Govinfo.* www.govinfo.gov/content/pkg/USCODE-2011-title18/html/USCODE-2011-title18-partI-chap90.htm

U.S. House Committee on Energy & Commerce. (2021). *Hearing on "Disinformation Nation: Social Media's Role in Promoting Extremism and Misinformation."*

https://energycommerce.house.gov/committee-activity/hearings/hearing-on-disinformation-nation-social-medias-role-in-promoting

U.S. Senate Armed Services Committee (2017). Hearing to Receive Testimony on Cyber Policy, Strategy, and Organization. www.armed-services.senate.gov/imo/media/doc/17-45_05-11-17.pdf

US Supreme Court ____ (2023, May 18). *Gonzales v. Google LLC*, 598 U. S., No. 21-1333. www.supremecourt.gov/opinions/22pdf/21-1333_6j7a.pdf

USA v. Basaaly Faeed Moalin, USA v. Mohamed Mohamed Mohamud, USA v. Issa Doreh, USA v. Ahmed Nasir Taalil Mohamud, US Court of Appeals, Ninth Circuit (p. 59). (2020). https://cdn.ca9.uscourts.gov/datastore/opinions/2020/09/02/13-50572.pdf

USA v. Viktor Borisovich Netyksho [and 11 others], defendants: Case 1:18-cr-00215-ABJ, (US District Court for the District of Columbia (Washington, D.D.) 2018). https://permanent.fdlp.gov/gpo115873/file1080281download.pdf

Utsumi, Y. (2002). *Information Society-The Strategy for Development in the 21st Century*. International Telecommunications Union. www.itu.int/osg/sg/speeches/2003/0401kiev-wsis.html

Valeriano, B. (2020, March 27). Cost Imposition Is the Point: Understanding U.S. Cyber Operations and the Strategy Behind Achieving Effects. *Lawfare*. www.lawfareblog.com/cost-imposition-point-understanding-us-cyber-operations-and-strategy-behind-achieving-effects

Valeriano, B., & Maness, R. C. (2015). *Cyber War versus Cyber Realities: Cyber Conflict in the International System*. Oxford University Press. https://doi.org/10.1093/acprof:oso/9780190204792.001.0001

Valeriano, B., Jensen, B., & Maness, R. C. (2018). *Cyber Strategy: The Evolving Character of Power and Coercion*. Oxford University Press. https://doi.org/10.1093/oso/9780190618094.001.0001

Vaswani, A., Shazeer, N., Parmar, N., Uszkoreit, J., Jones, L., Gomez, A. N., Kaiser, L., & Polosukhin, I. (2017). *Attention Is All You Need* (arXiv:1706.03762). arXiv. http://arxiv.org/abs/1706.03762

Vavra, S. (2021, February 17). White House warns SolarWinds breach cleanup will take time. CyberScoop. www.cyberscoop.com/solarwinds-cyber-espionage-russia-neuberger/

Vestergaard, C., & Roul, A. (2011). A (F)utile Intersessional Process?: Strengthening the BWC by Defining Its Scope. *The Nonproliferation Review*, *18*(3), 489–497. https://doi.org/10.1080/10736700.2011.618616

Vietnamese Law 24 on Cybersecurity. (2018). Allens Law. https://data.allens.com.au/pubs/pdf/priv/cupriv22jun18.pdf

W3C (2022). The World Wide Web Consortium. www.w3.org/Consortium/

Wallace, D., & Visger, M. (2017). Responding to the Call for a Digital Geneva Convention: An Open Letter to Brad Smith and the Technology Community. *JL & Cyber Warfare*, *6*, 3.

Warner, M. (2020). The Character of Cyber Conflict. *Texas National Security Review*, *3*(4). https://tnsr.org/roundtable/policy-roundtable-cyber-conflict-as-an-intelligence-contest/#essay2, 26-42.

Warner, U. S. Mark. R. (2020, January 14). *National Security Senators Introduce Bipartisan Legislation to Develop 5G Alternatives to Huawei*. Mark R. Warner.

www.warner.senate.gov/public/index.cfm/2020/1/national-security-senators-introduce-bipartisan-legislation-to-develop-5g-alternatives-to-huawei

Weinstein, D. (2021, February 26). Hackers May Be Coming for Your City's Water Supply: More digitized and connected than ever, the nation's infrastructure is vulnerable to cyberattack. The Wall Street Journal. www.wsj.com/articles/hackers-may-be-coming-for-your-citys-water-supply-11614379990?page=1

Weiss, T. G., Forsythe, D. P., Coate, R. A., & Pease, K.-K. (2019). *The United Nations and Changing World Politics* (Seventh edition). Routledge. https://doi.org/10.4324/b22600

White House. (1998, May 22). The Clinton Administration's Policy on Critical Infrastructure Protection: Presidential Decision Directive 63. https://clintonwhitehouse4.archives.gov/WH/EOP/NSC/html/documents/NSCDoc3.html

White House. (2001, November 23). Message from the President of the United States transmitting the Council of Europe Convention on Cybercrime ("The "Cybercrime Convention" or the "Convention") which was signed by the United States on November 23, 2001 (11/17/2003–08/03/2006) [Legislation]. www.congress.gov/

White House. (2003). The National Strategy to Secure Cyberspace. https://georgewbush-whitehouse.archives.gov/pcipb/

White House. (2005). Dr. Vinton Cerf and Dr. Robert Kahn, Medal of Freedom Recipients. The White House. https://georgewbush-whitehouse.archives.gov/government/cerf-kahn-bio.html

White House. (2010). The National Security Strategy of The United States of America. https://obamawhitehouse.archives.gov/sites/default/files/rss_viewer/national_security_strategy.pdf

White House. (2015, February 13). Executive Order – Promoting Private Sector Cybersecurity Information Sharing. Whitehouse.Gov. https://obamawhitehouse.archives.gov/the-press-office/2015/02/13/executive-order-promoting-private-sector-cybersecurity-information-shari

White House. (2017). *National Security Strategy of the United States of America.* United States. White House Office. www.hsdl.org/?abstract&did=806478

White House. (2018). *National Cyber Strategy.* US White House, President Donald J. Trump. https://trumpwhitehouse.archives.gov/wp-content/uploads/2018/09/National-Cyber-Strategy.pdf

White House. (2019). *Artificial Intelligence for the American People* (Executive Order 13859,). https://trumpwhitehouse.archives.gov/ai/2019-02-01

White House. (2021a, March 3). Interim National Security Strategic Guidance. *The White House.* www.whitehouse.gov/briefing-room/statements-releases/2021/03/03/interim-national-security-strategic-guidance/

White House. (2021b, July 27). Remarks by President Biden at the Office of the Director of National Intelligence. *White House.* www.whitehouse.gov/briefing-room/speeches-remarks/2021/07/27/remarks-by-president-biden-at-the-office-of-the-director-of-national-intelligence/

White House. (2022). Declaration for the Future of the Internet. www.whitehouse.gov/wp-content/uploads/2022/04/Declaration-for-the-Future-for-the-Internet_Launch-Event-Signing-Version_FINAL.pdf

White, S. P. (2019). Subcultural Influence on Military Innovation: The Development of U.S. Military Cyber Doctrine [Doctoral, Harvard University]. https://dash.harvard.edu/handle/1/42013038

Wikiwand. (1983). *Convention on Certain Conventional Weapons, Arms Control Treaty.* Wikiwand. https://wikiwand.com/en/Convention_on_Certain_Conventional_Weapons

Wikiwand—SORM. (n.d.). Wikiwand. Retrieved August 9, 2023, from www.wikiwand.com/en/SORM

Williams, B. D. (2021, July 22). US Playing Long Game to Pressure China on Cyber Ops: Experts. Breaking Defense. https://breakingdefense.com/2021/07/us-playing-long-game-to-pressure-china-on-cyber-ops-experts/

Williams-King, D., Gobieski, G., Williams-King, K. et al. (2016). Shuffler: Fast and deployable continuous code re-randomization. Proceedings of the 12th USENIX Conference on Operating Systems Design and Implementation, 367–382.

Wilshusen, G. C. (2018). *Supply Chain Risks Affecting Federal Agencies* (GAO-18-667T; Information Security). US Government Accountability Office (GAO). www.gao.gov/assets/gao-18-667t.pdf

Winnefeld Jr., J. A. (Sandy), Kirchhoff, C., & Upton, D. M. (2015, September 1). Cybersecurity's Human Factor: Lessons from the Pentagon. *Harvard Business Review.* https://hbr.org/2015/09/cybersecuritys-human-factor-lessons-from-the-pentagon

WIPO Arbitration and Mediation Center. (2001, January 25). WIPO Domain Name Decision: D2000-1532. Administrative Panel Decision: Bruce Springstein v. Jeff Burgar and Bruce Springsteen Club, Case No. D2000-1532. www.wipo.int/amc/en/domains/decisions/html/2000/d2000-1532.html

Wong, C. Y. (2013, April). *Bubble Value at Risk: A Countercyclical Risk Management Approach,* revised edition. Wiley. www.wiley.com/en-us/Bubble+Value+at+Risk%3A+A+Countercyclical+Risk+Management+Approach%2C+Revised+Edition-p-9781118550342

Wray, C. A. (2017). Statement of Christopher A. Wray, Director Federal Bureau of Investigation, before the Committee on Homeland Security, U.S. House of Representatives. https://docs.house.gov/meetings/HM/HM00/20171130/106651/HHRG-115-HM00-Wstate-WrayC-20171130.pdf

Wray, C. A. (2019). Statement of Christopher Wray Director Federal Bureau of Investigation Before the Committee on the Judiciary of the United States Senate. www.judiciary.senate.gov/imo/media/doc/Wray%20Testimony1.pdf

WSIS (2005, November 18) Tunis agenda for the Information Society.). World Summit on the Information Society, Geneva 2001 – Tunis 2005. www.itu.int/net/wsis/docs2/tunis/off/6rev1.html

WSJ. (2021, September 1). The Facebook Files: A Wall Street Journal investigation. Wall Street Journal. www.wsj.com/articles/the-facebook-files-11631713039

Wu, Y., Bao, W.-S., Cao, S. et al. (2021). Strong Quantum Computational Advantage Using a Superconducting Quantum Processor. *Physical Review Letters, 127*(18), 180501. https://doi.org/10.1103/PhysRevLett.127.180501

Wu, Y., Schuster, M., Chen, Z. et al. (2016). *Google's Neural Machine Translation System: Bridging the Gap between Human and Machine Translation* (arXiv:1609.08144). arXiv. https://doi.org/10.48550/arXiv.1609.08144

Xi, J. (2017). Secure a Decisive Victory in Building a Moderately Prosperous Society in All Respects and Strive for the Great Success of Socialism with Chinese Characteristics for a New Era. 19th National Congress of the Communist Party of China. www.xinhuanet.com/english/download/Xi_Jinping's_report_at_19th_CPC_National_Congress.pdf

Yang, Y., & Liu, N. (2019, December 8). Beijing orders state offices to replace foreign PCs and software. Financial Times. www.ft.com/content/b55fc6ee-1787-11ea-8d73-6303645ac406

Zelikow, P. (1997). George C. Marshall and the Moscow CFM meeting of 1947. *Diplomacy & Statecraft*, *8*(2), 97–124. https://doi.org/10.1080/09592299708406045

Zelikow, P. (2019, September 10). To Regain Policy Competence: The Software of American Public Problem-Solving. Texas National Security Review. https://tnsr.org/2019/09/to-regain-policy-competence-the-software-of-american-public-problem-solving/

Zetter, K. (2013). Legal Experts: Stuxnet Attack on Iran Was Illegal "Act of Force." *Wired*. www.wired.com/2013/03/stuxnet-act-of-force/

Zetter, K. (2016, March 3). Inside the Cunning, Unprecedented Hack of Ukraine's Power Grid. Wired. www.wired.com/2016/03/inside-cunning-unprecedented-hack-ukraines-power-grid/

Zitun, Y. (2017, April 16). Head of IDF's new Cyber Division: It's a world with no rules. Ynetnews. www.ynetnews.com/articles/0,7340,L-4949752,00.html

Zojer, G. (2019). The interconnectedness of digitalisation and human security in the European High North: Cybersecurity conceptualised through the human security lens. *The Yearbook of Polar Law*, *10*(1), 297–320. https://doi.org/10.1163/22116427_010010014

Zucconi, A. (2014, March 14). Understanding the Technology Behind Deepfakes. Retrieved from www.alanzucconi.com/2018/03/14/understanding-the-technology-behind-deepfakes/

Zuckerberg, M. (2018, July 31). Facebook Blog Post [Blog]. SEC Wire. www.facebook.com/zuck/posts/10105140110214721

Zuckerberg, M. (2019). An Examination of Facebook and Its Impact on the Financial Services and Housing Sectors before the US House Committee on Financial Services. https://financialservices.house.gov/uploadedfiles/hhrg-116-ba00-wstate-zuckerbergm-20191023-u1.pdf

Zweig, J. (2015, September 26). The trick to making better forecasts. *Wall Street Journal* (Online), n/a.

Index

Bold page numbers indicate a main section on a particular subject in the text. Page numbers in italics indicate tables or figures